2

I was REINCARNATED as the
_____
Villainess
in an OTOME GAME *but the boys love me anyway!*

CONTENTS

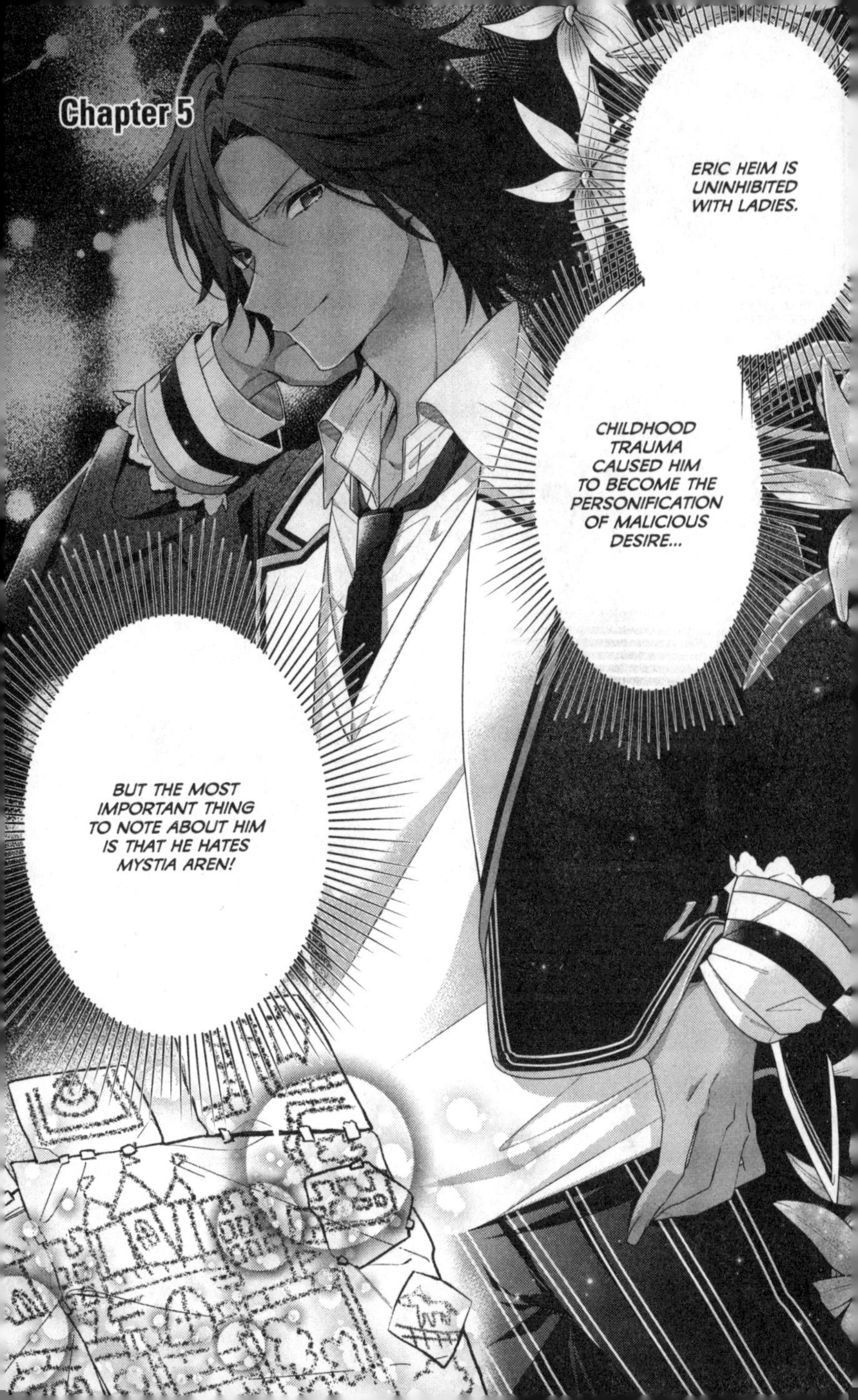
Chapter 5
ERIC HEIM IS UNINHIBITED WITH LADIES.
CHILDHOOD TRAUMA CAUSED HIM TO BECOME THE PERSONIFICATION OF MALICIOUS DESIRE...
BUT THE MOST IMPORTANT THING TO NOTE ABOUT HIM IS THAT HE HATES MYSTIA AREN!

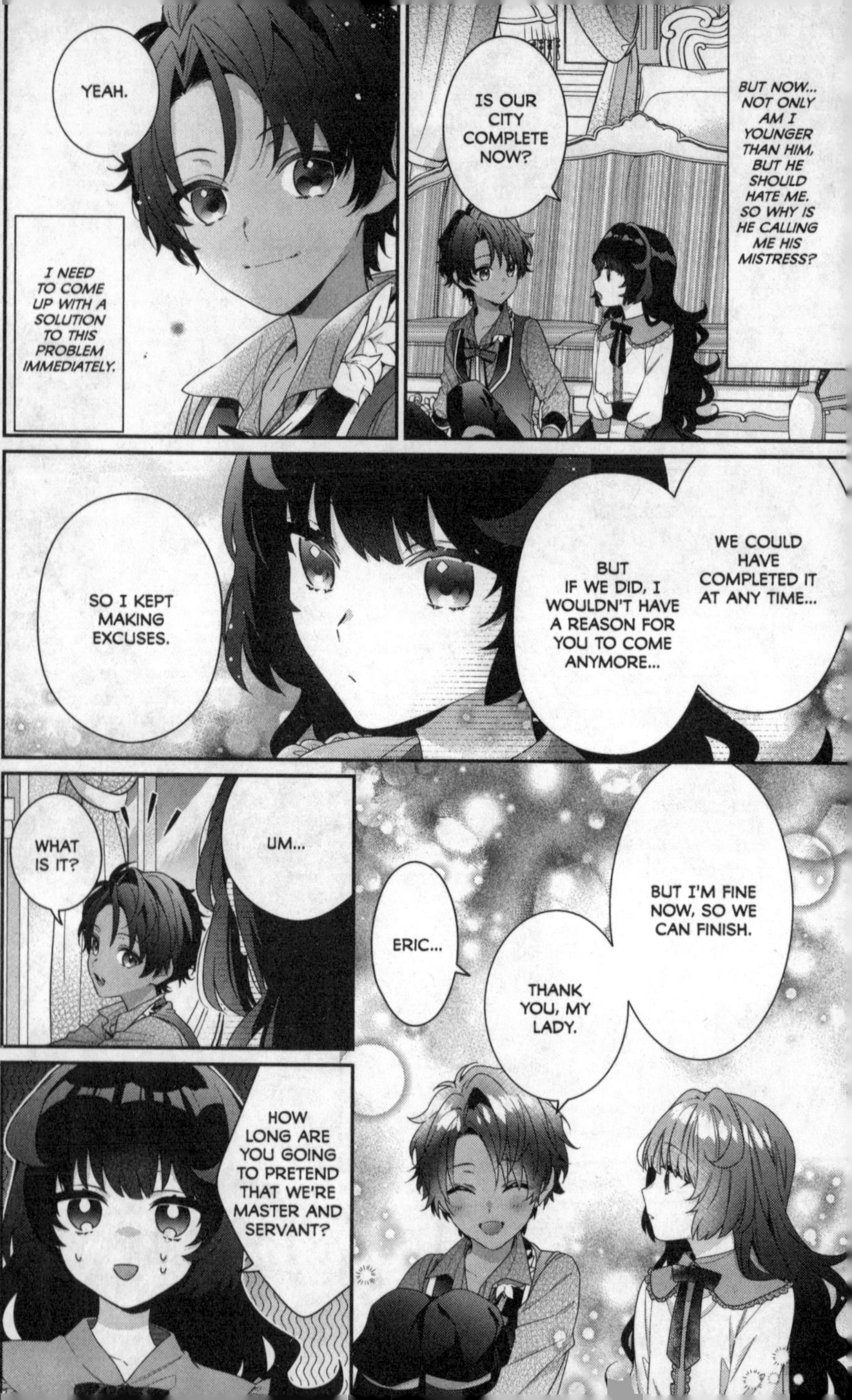
BUT NOW... NOT ONLY AM I YOUNGER THAN HIM, BUT HE SHOULD HATE ME. SO WHY IS HE CALLING ME HIS MISTRESS?
IS OUR CITY COMPLETE NOW?
YEAH.
I NEED TO COME UP WITH A SOLUTION TO THIS PROBLEM IMMEDIATELY.
WE COULD HAVE COMPLETED IT AT ANY TIME...
BUT IF WE DID, I WOULDN'T HAVE A REASON FOR YOU TO COME ANYMORE...
SO I KEPT MAKING EXCUSES.
BUT I'M FINE NOW, SO WE CAN FINISH.
THANK YOU, MY LADY.
ERIC...
UM...
WHAT IS IT?
HOW LONG ARE YOU GOING TO PRETEND THAT WE'RE MASTER AND SERVANT?

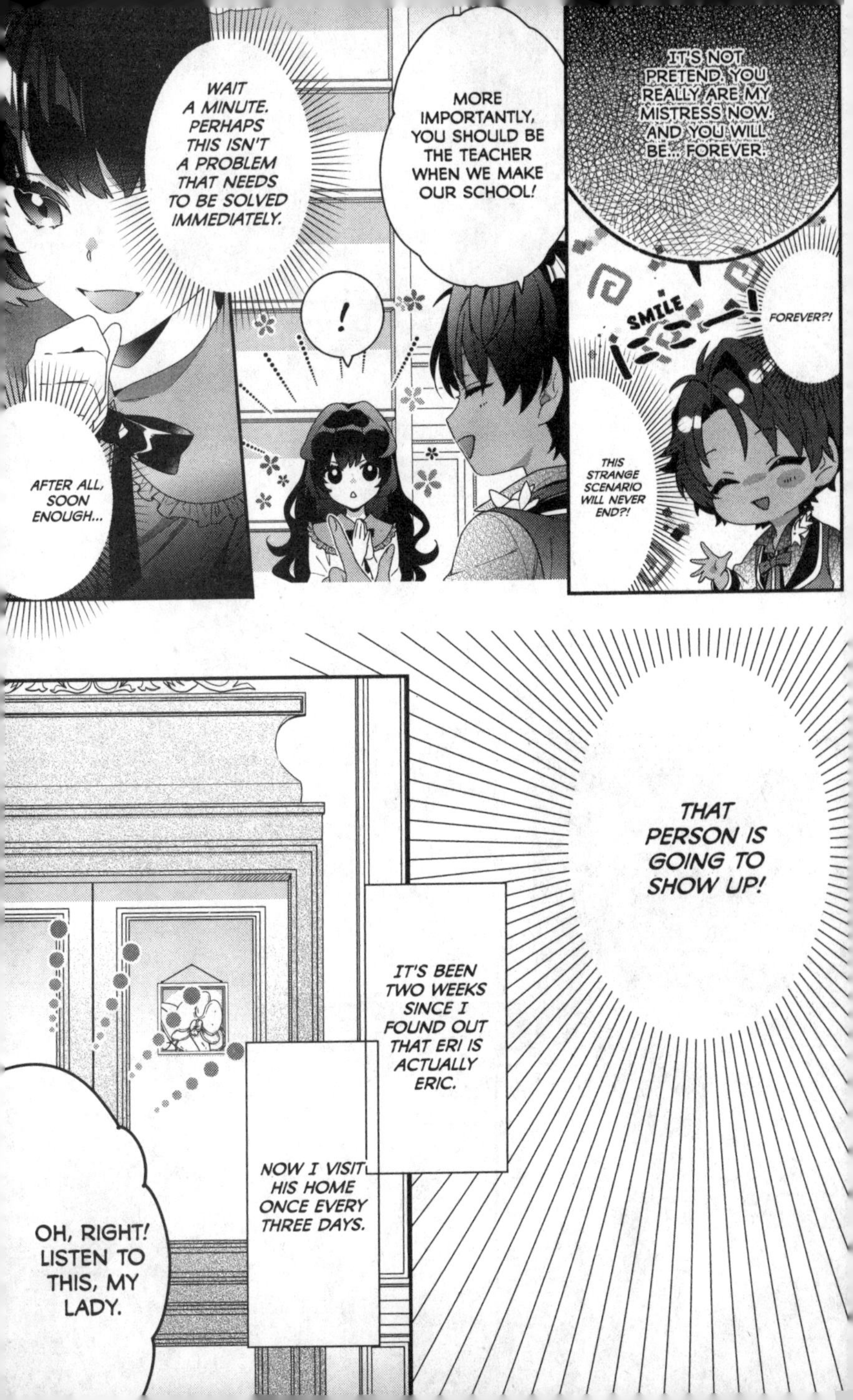
IT'S NOT PRETEND. YOU REALLY ARE MY MISTRESS NOW. AND YOU WILL BE... FOREVER.
SMILE
FOREVER?!
THIS STRANGE SCENARIO WILL NEVER END?!
MORE IMPORTANTLY, YOU SHOULD BE THE TEACHER WHEN WE MAKE OUR SCHOOL!
!
WAIT A MINUTE. PERHAPS THIS ISN'T A PROBLEM THAT NEEDS TO BE SOLVED IMMEDIATELY.
AFTER ALL, SOON ENOUGH...
THAT PERSON IS GOING TO SHOW UP!
IT'S BEEN TWO WEEKS SINCE I FOUND OUT THAT ERI IS ACTUALLY ERIC.
NOW I VISIT HIS HOME ONCE EVERY THREE DAYS.
OH, RIGHT! LISTEN TO THIS, MY LADY.

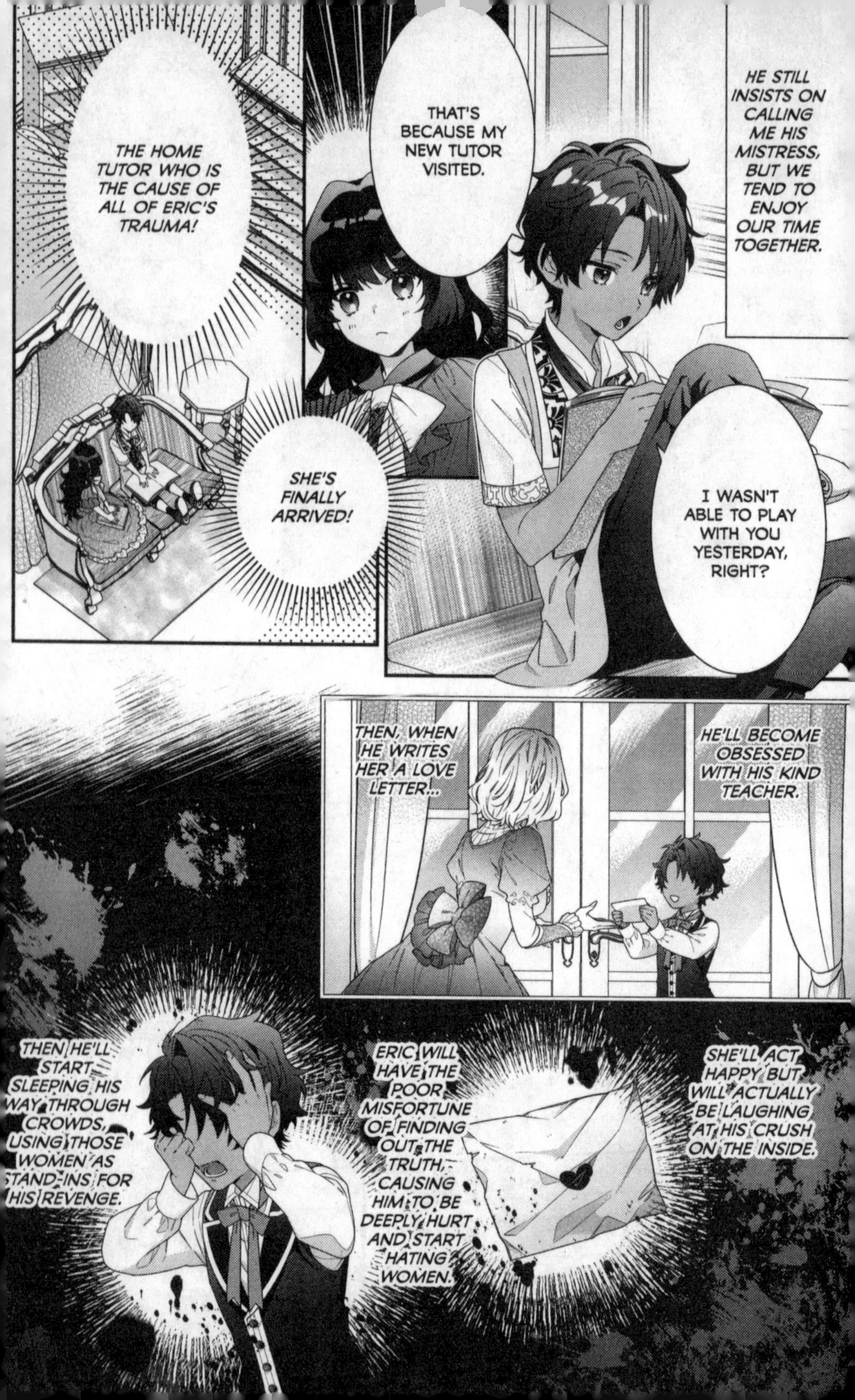
HE STILL INSISTS ON CALLING ME HIS MISTRESS, BUT WE TEND TO ENJOY OUR TIME TOGETHER.
I WASN'T ABLE TO PLAY WITH YOU YESTERDAY, RIGHT?
THAT'S BECAUSE MY NEW TUTOR VISITED.
THE HOME TUTOR WHO IS THE CAUSE OF ALL OF ERIC'S TRAUMA!
SHE'S FINALLY ARRIVED!
HE'LL BECOME OBSESSED WITH HIS KIND TEACHER.
THEN, WHEN HE WRITES HER A LOVE LETTER...
SHE'LL ACT HAPPY BUT WILL ACTUALLY BE LAUGHING AT HIS CRUSH ON THE INSIDE.
ERIC WILL HAVE THE POOR MISFORTUNE OF FINDING OUT THE TRUTH, CAUSING HIM TO BE DEEPLY HURT AND START HATING WOMEN.
THEN HE'LL START SLEEPING HIS WAY THROUGH CROWDS, USING THOSE WOMEN AS STAND-INS FOR HIS REVENGE.

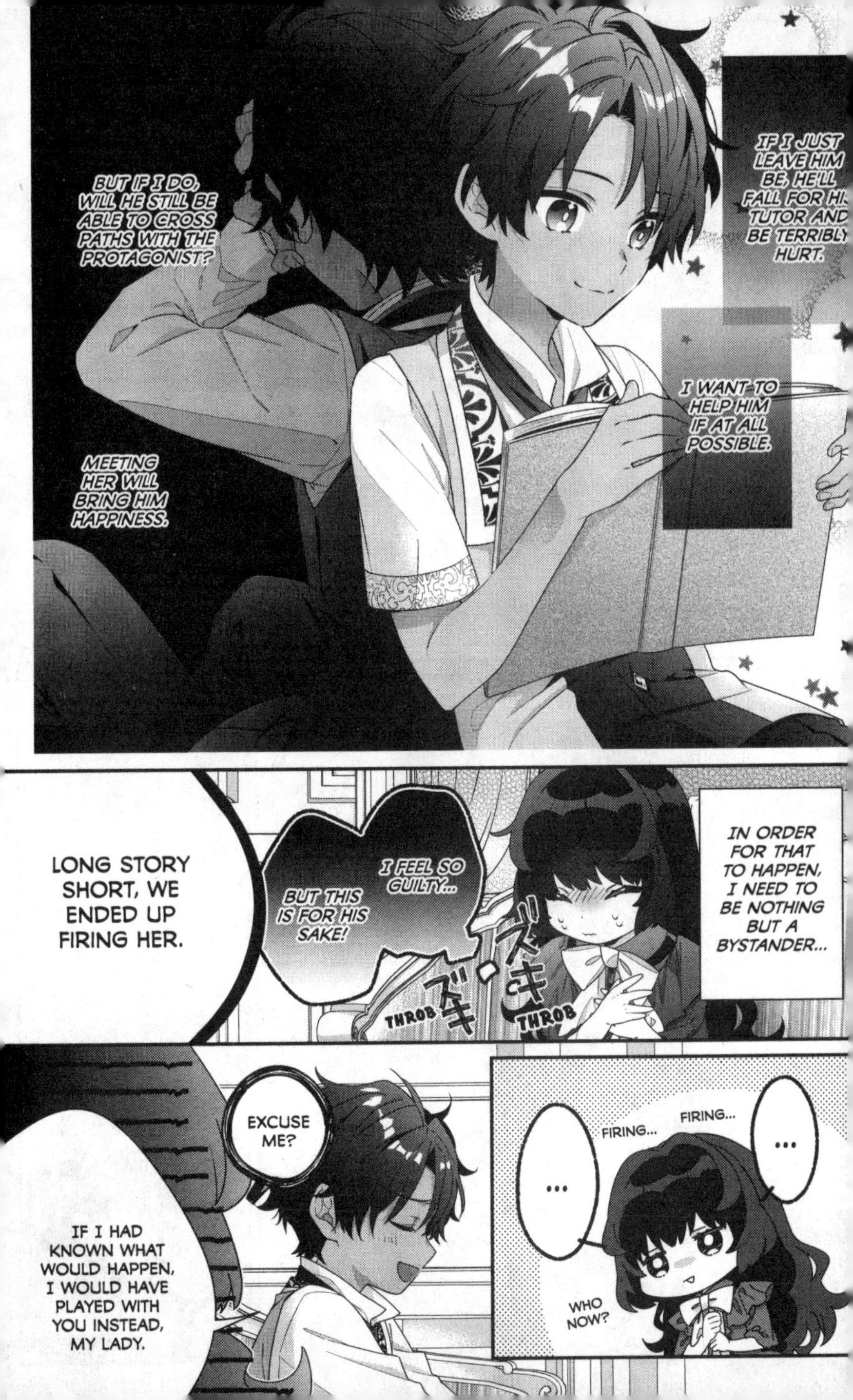
IF I JUST LEAVE HIM BE, HE'LL FALL FOR HIS TUTOR AND BE TERRIBLY HURT.
I WANT TO HELP HIM IF AT ALL POSSIBLE.
BUT IF I DO, WILL HE STILL BE ABLE TO CROSS PATHS WITH THE PROTAGONIST?
MEETING HER WILL BRING HIM HAPPINESS.
IN ORDER FOR THAT TO HAPPEN, I NEED TO BE NOTHING BUT A BYSTANDER...
ズキ THROB
ズキ THROB
I FEEL SO GUILTY...
BUT THIS IS FOR HIS SAKE!
LONG STORY SHORT, WE ENDED UP FIRING HER.
...
FIRING...
FIRING...
...
WHO NOW?
EXCUSE ME?
IF I HAD KNOWN WHAT WOULD HAPPEN, I WOULD HAVE PLAYED WITH YOU INSTEAD, MY LADY.

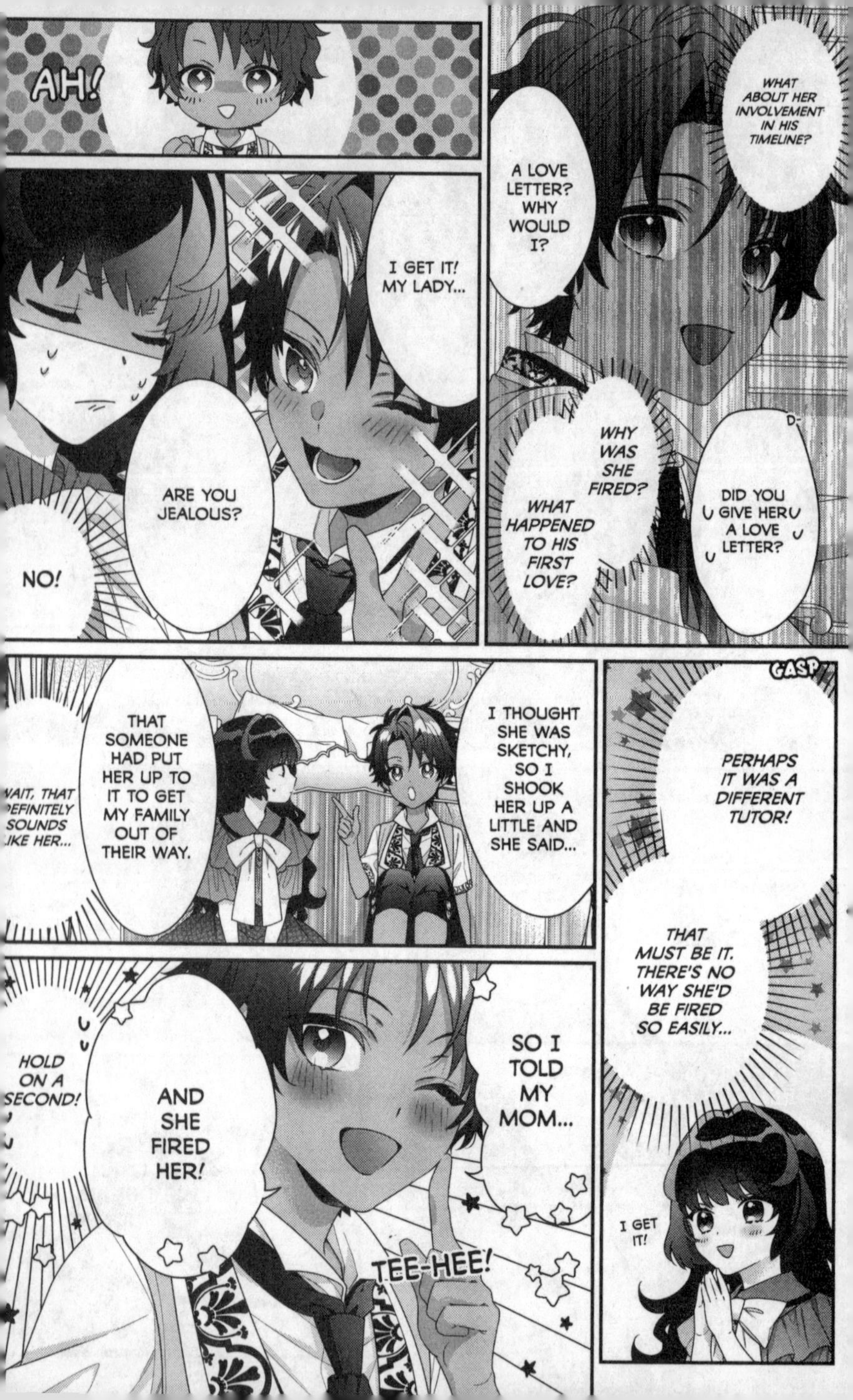
WHAT ABOUT HER INVOLVEMENT IN HIS TIMELINE?
A LOVE LETTER? WHY WOULD I?
D-
DID YOU GIVE HER A LOVE LETTER?
WHY WAS SHE FIRED? WHAT HAPPENED TO HIS FIRST LOVE?
AH!
I GET IT! MY LADY...
ARE YOU JEALOUS?
NO!
GASP
PERHAPS IT WAS A DIFFERENT TUTOR!
THAT MUST BE IT. THERE'S NO WAY SHE'D BE FIRED SO EASILY...
I GET IT!
I THOUGHT SHE WAS SKETCHY, SO I SHOOK HER UP A LITTLE AND SHE SAID...
THAT SOMEONE HAD PUT HER UP TO IT TO GET MY FAMILY OUT OF THEIR WAY.
WAIT, THAT DEFINITELY SOUNDS LIKE HER...
SO I TOLD MY MOM...
AND SHE FIRED HER!
TEE-HEE!
HOLD ON A SECOND!

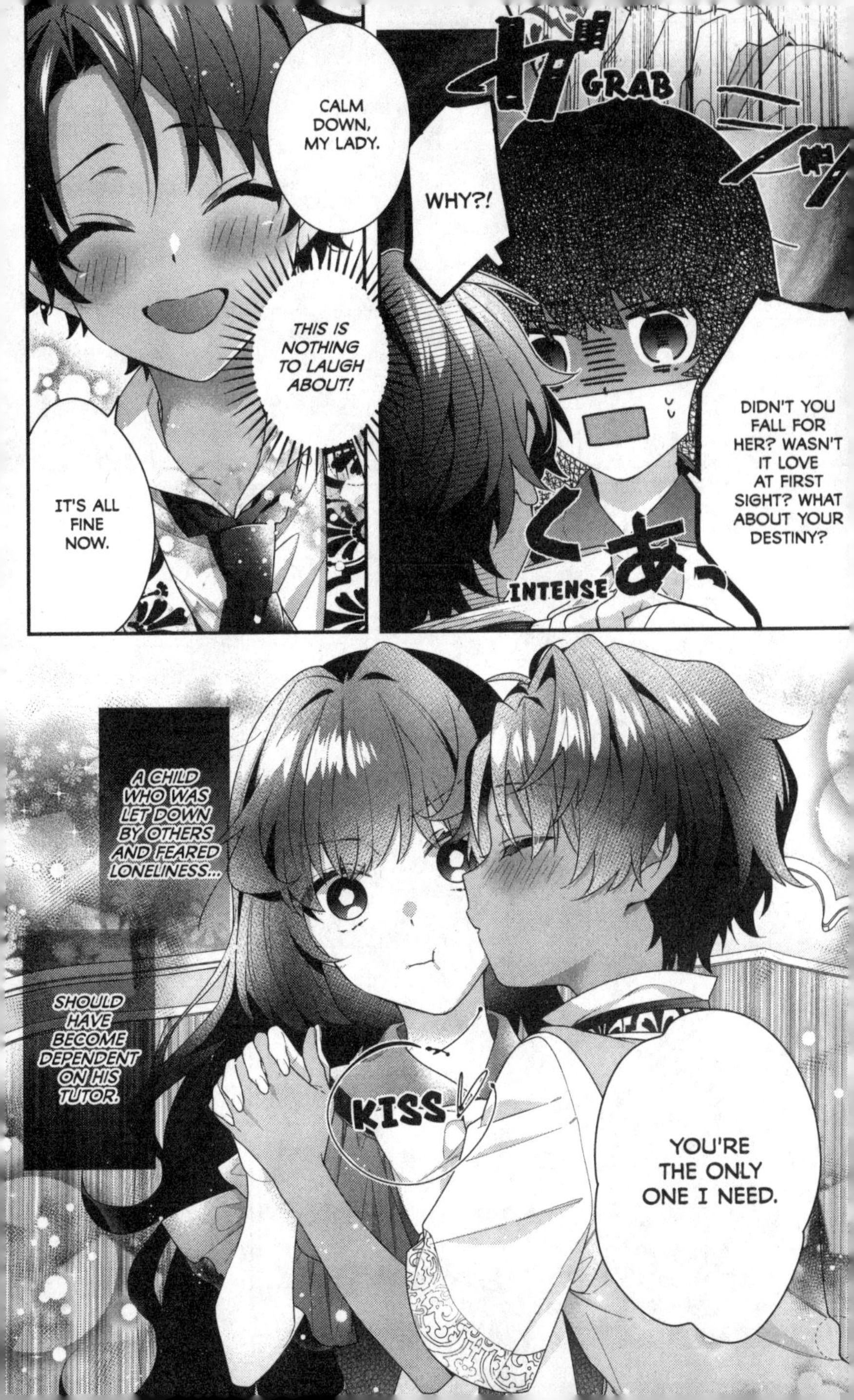
GRAB
WHY?!
DIDN'T YOU FALL FOR HER? WASN'T IT LOVE AT FIRST SIGHT? WHAT ABOUT YOUR DESTINY?
INTENSE
CALM DOWN, MY LADY.
THIS IS NOTHING TO LAUGH ABOUT!
IT'S ALL FINE NOW.
YOU'RE THE ONLY ONE I NEED.
KISS
A CHILD WHO WAS LET DOWN BY OTHERS AND FEARED LONELINESS...
SHOULD HAVE BECOME DEPENDENT ON HIS TUTOR.

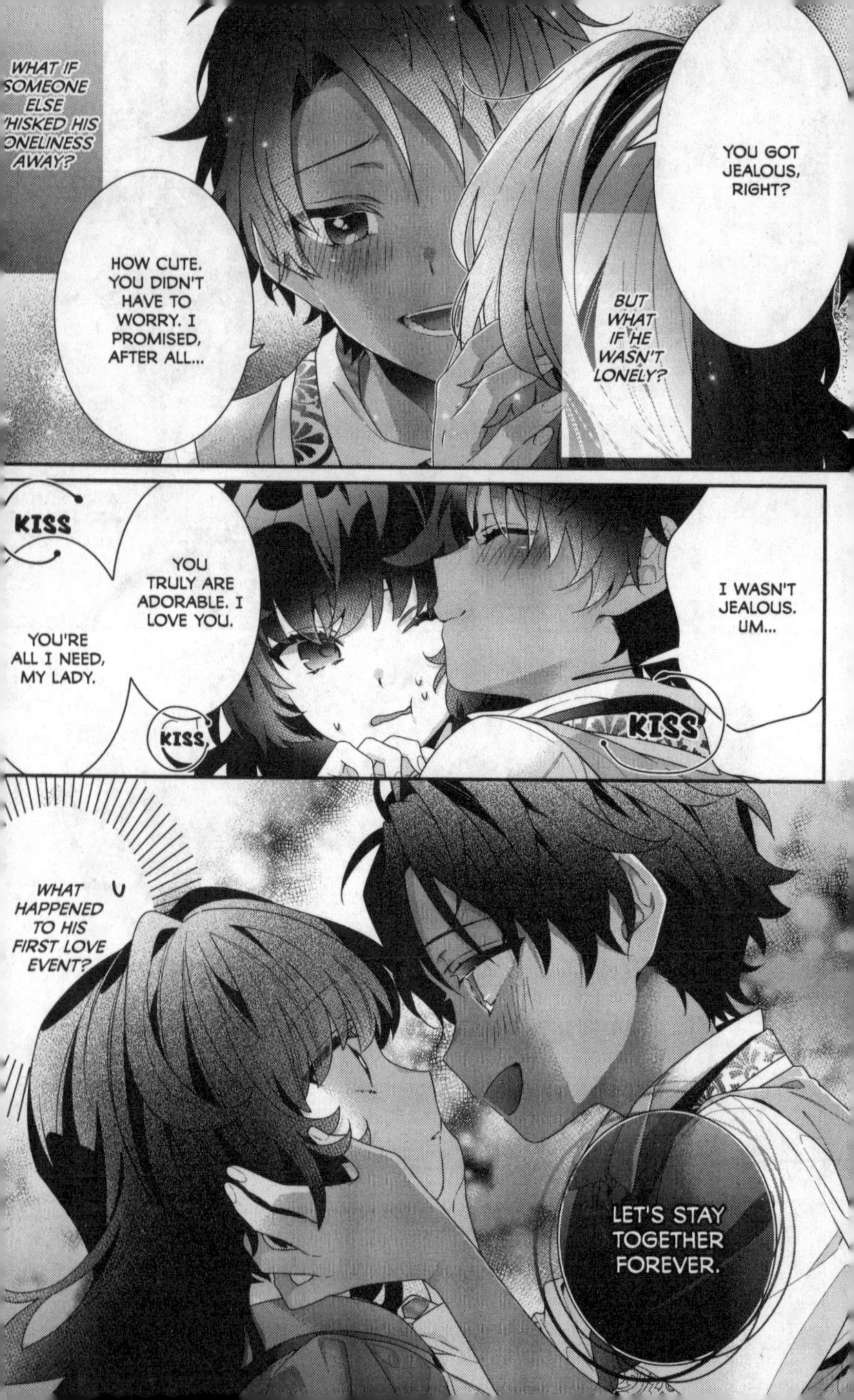
YOU GOT JEALOUS, RIGHT?
BUT WHAT IF HE WASN'T LONELY?
HOW CUTE. YOU DIDN'T HAVE TO WORRY. I PROMISED, AFTER ALL...
WHAT IF SOMEONE ELSE WHISKED HIS LONELINESS AWAY?
I WASN'T JEALOUS. UM...
KISS
YOU TRULY ARE ADORABLE. I LOVE YOU.
KISS
YOU'RE ALL I NEED, MY LADY.
KISS
LET'S STAY TOGETHER FOREVER.
WHAT HAPPENED TO HIS FIRST LOVE EVENT?

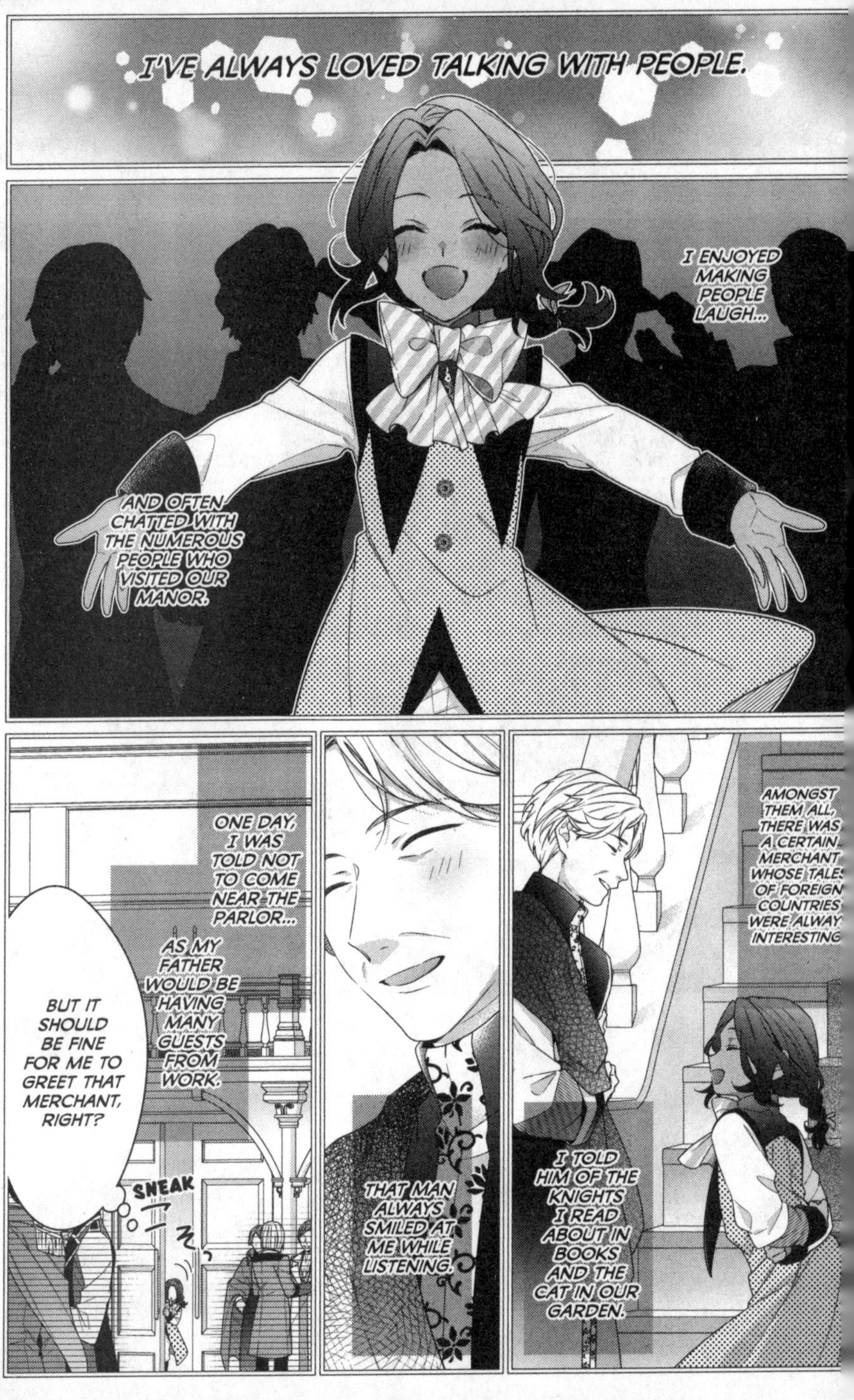
I'VE ALWAYS LOVED TALKING WITH PEOPLE.
I ENJOYED MAKING PEOPLE LAUGH...
AND OFTEN CHATTED WITH THE NUMEROUS PEOPLE WHO VISITED OUR MANOR.
AMONGST THEM ALL, THERE WAS A CERTAIN MERCHANT WHOSE TALE OF FOREIGN COUNTRIES WERE ALWAY INTERESTING
I TOLD HIM OF THE KNIGHTS I READ ABOUT IN BOOKS AND THE CAT IN OUR GARDEN.
THAT MAN ALWAYS SMILED AT ME WHILE LISTENING.
ONE DAY, I WAS TOLD NOT TO COME NEAR THE PARLOR...
AS MY FATHER WOULD BE HAVING MANY GUESTS FROM WORK.
BUT IT SHOULD BE FINE FOR ME TO GREET THAT MERCHANT, RIGHT?
SNEAK

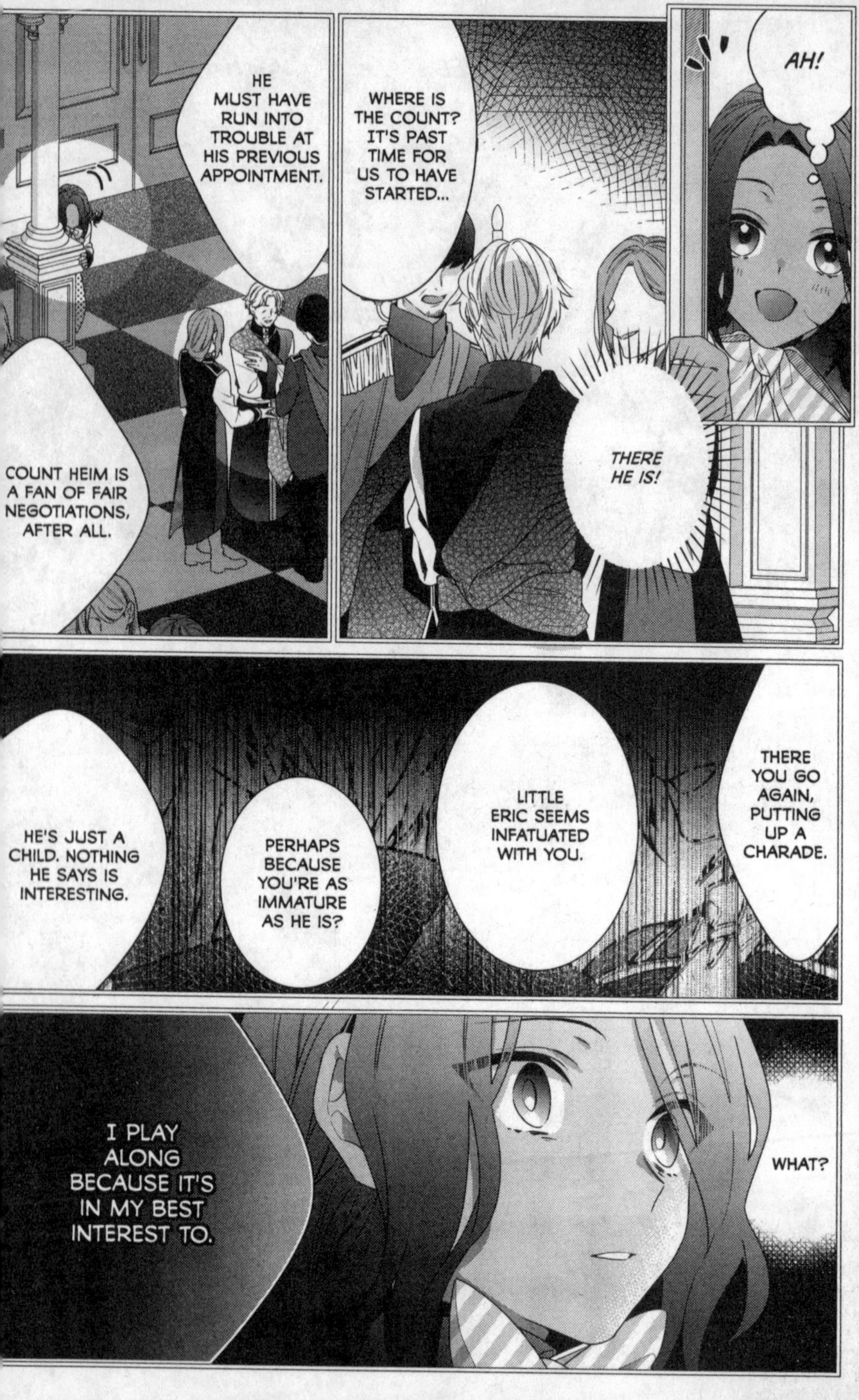
AH!
WHERE IS THE COUNT? IT'S PAST TIME FOR US TO HAVE STARTED...
THERE HE IS!
HE MUST HAVE RUN INTO TROUBLE AT HIS PREVIOUS APPOINTMENT.
COUNT HEIM IS A FAN OF FAIR NEGOTIATIONS, AFTER ALL.
THERE YOU GO AGAIN, PUTTING UP A CHARADE.
LITTLE ERIC SEEMS INFATUATED WITH YOU.
PERHAPS BECAUSE YOU'RE AS IMMATURE AS HE IS?
HE'S JUST A CHILD. NOTHING HE SAYS IS INTERESTING.
WHAT?
I PLAY ALONG BECAUSE IT'S IN MY BEST INTEREST TO.

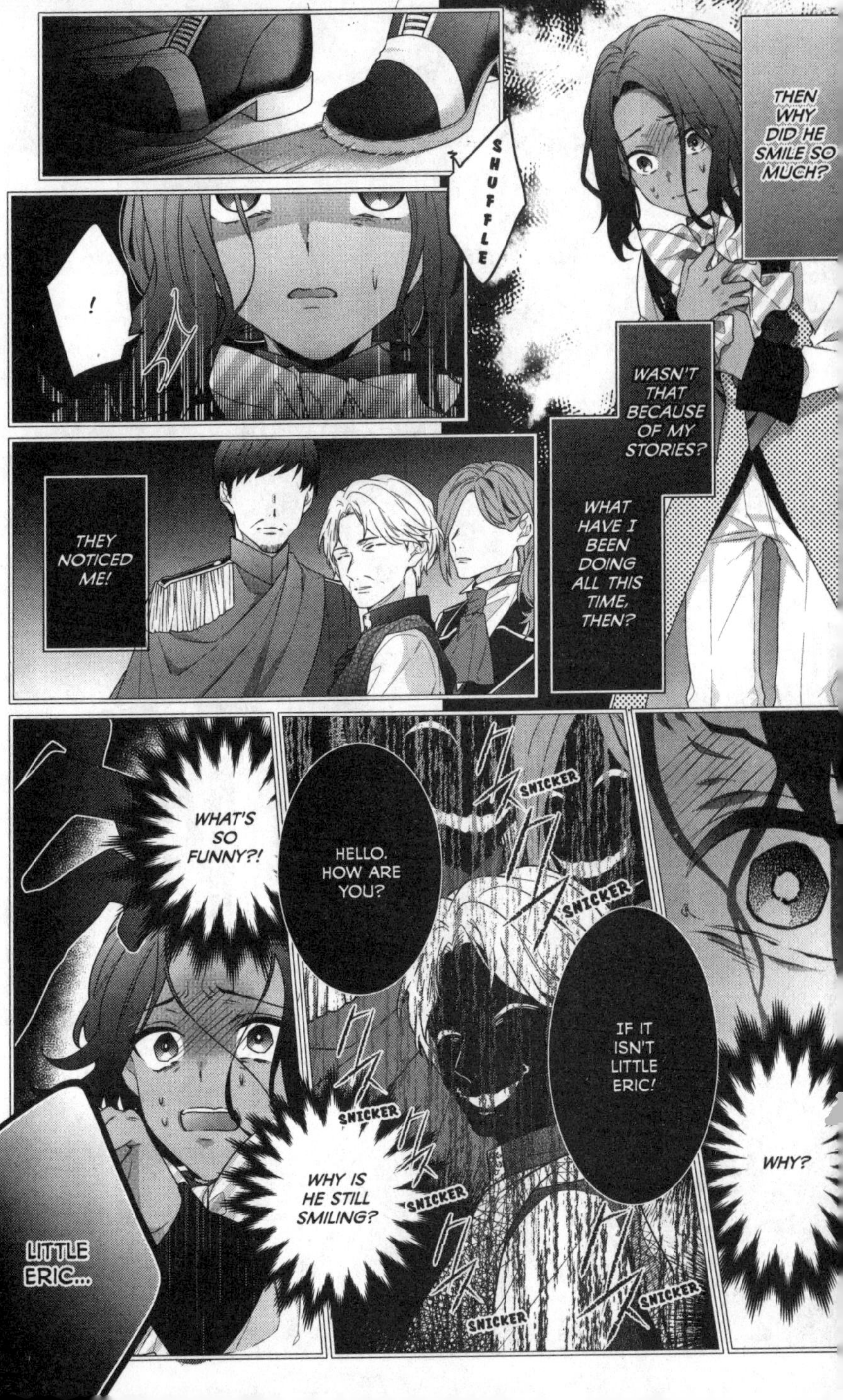
THEN WHY DID HE SMILE SO MUCH?
WASN'T THAT BECAUSE OF MY STORIES?
WHAT HAVE I BEEN DOING ALL THIS TIME, THEN?
SHUFFLE
!
THEY NOTICED ME!
WHY?
IF IT ISN'T LITTLE ERIC!
HELLO. HOW ARE YOU?
SNICKER
SNICKER
SNICKER
SNICKER
SNICKER
SNICKER
WHAT'S SO FUNNY?!
WHY IS HE STILL SMILING?
LITTLE ERIC...

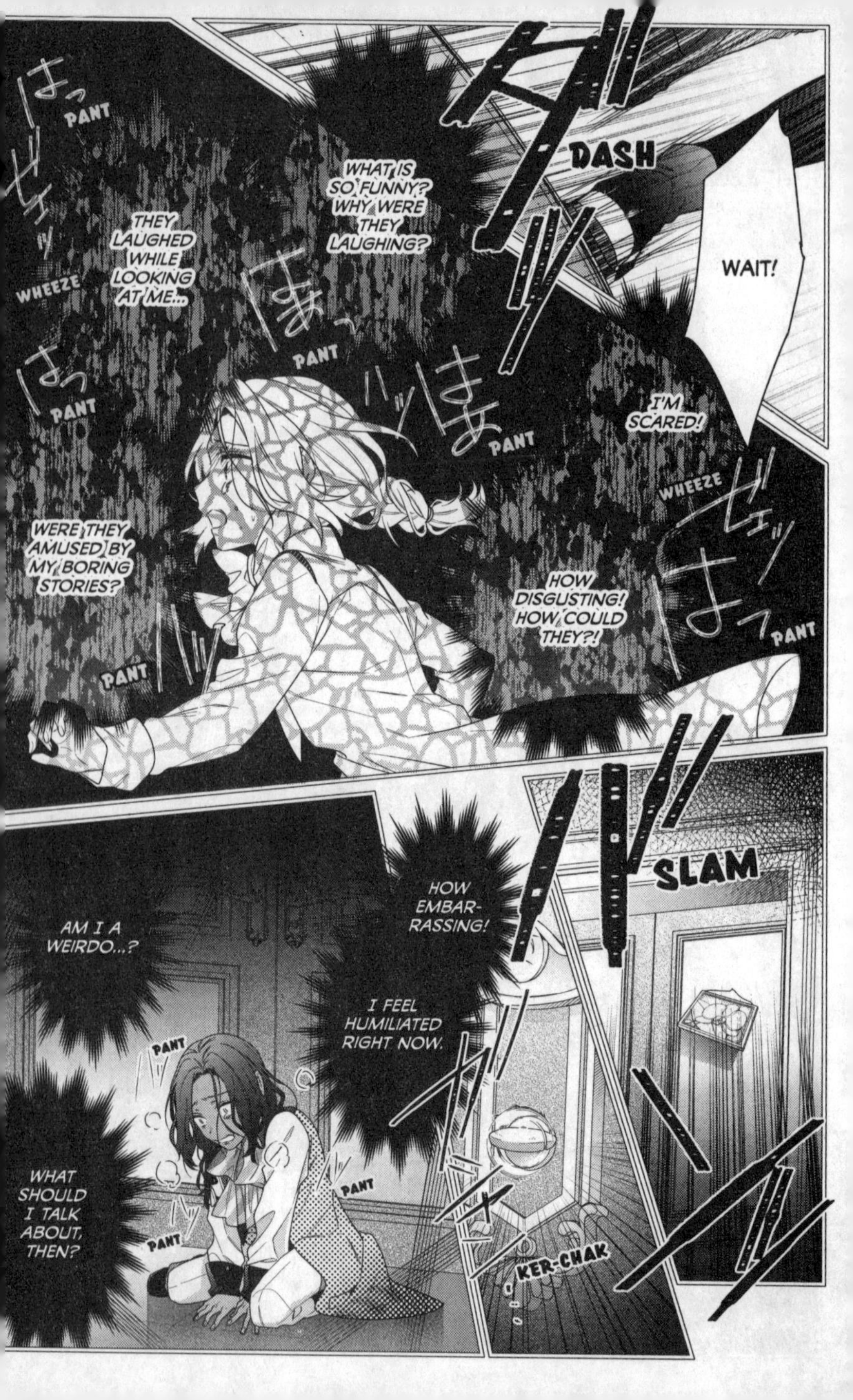
WAIT!
DASH
WHAT IS SO FUNNY? WHY WERE THEY LAUGHING?
THEY LAUGHED WHILE LOOKING AT ME...
PANT
PANT
WHEEZE
PANT
PANT
I'M SCARED!
WHEEZE
PANT
HOW DISGUSTING! HOW COULD THEY?!
WERE THEY AMUSED BY MY BORING STORIES?
PANT
SLAM
KER-CHAK
HOW EMBARRASSING!
I FEEL HUMILIATED RIGHT NOW.
AM I A WEIRDO...?
PANT
PANT
PANT
WHAT SHOULD I TALK ABOUT, THEN?

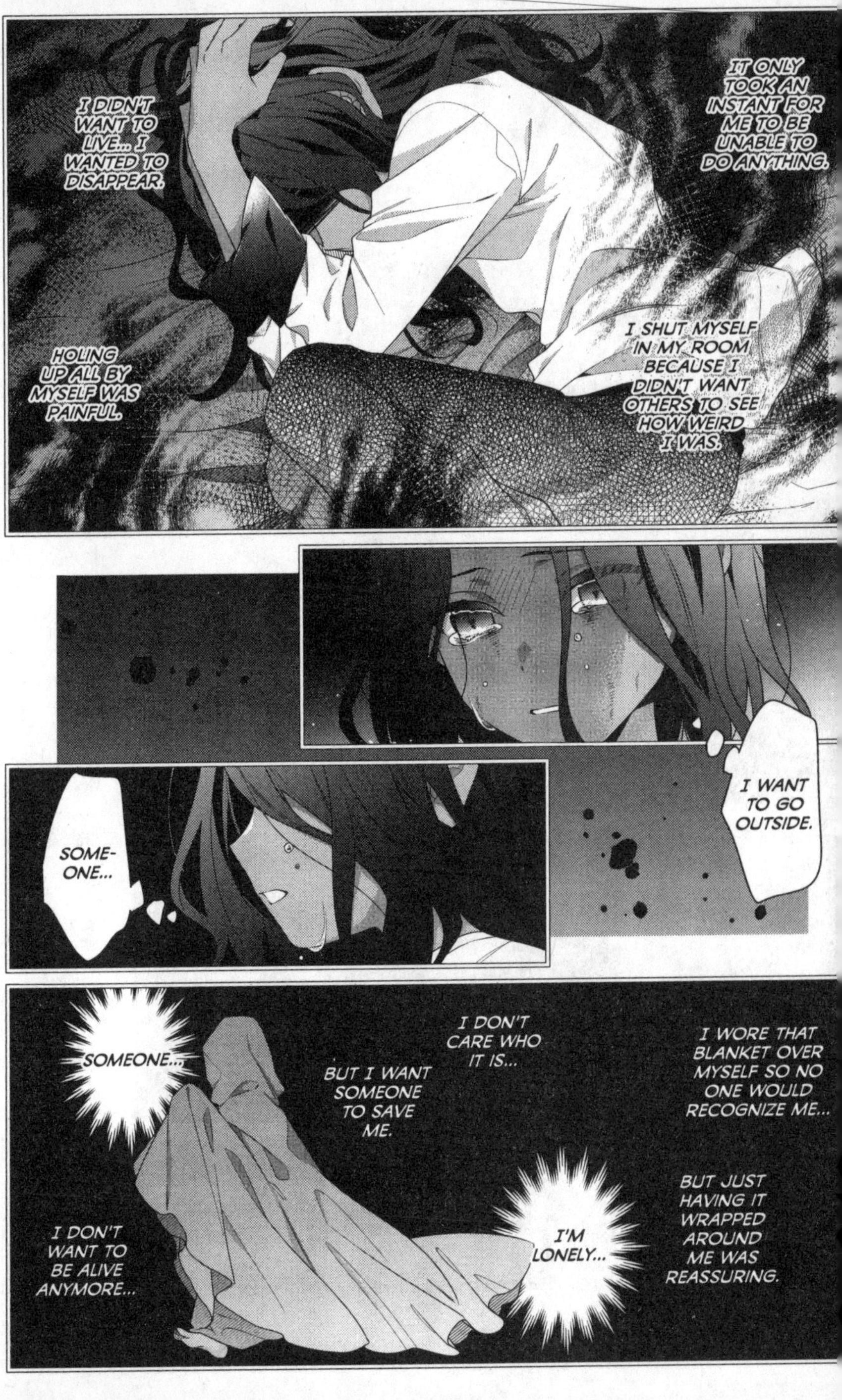
IT ONLY TOOK AN INSTANT FOR ME TO BE UNABLE TO DO ANYTHING.
I DIDN'T WANT TO LIVE... I WANTED TO DISAPPEAR.
I SHUT MYSELF IN MY ROOM BECAUSE I DIDN'T WANT OTHERS TO SEE HOW WEIRD I WAS.
HOLING UP ALL BY MYSELF WAS PAINFUL.
I WANT TO GO OUTSIDE.
SOME-ONE...
I WORE THAT BLANKET OVER MYSELF SO NO ONE WOULD RECOGNIZE ME...
I DON'T CARE WHO IT IS...
BUT I WANT SOMEONE TO SAVE ME.
SOMEONE...
BUT JUST HAVING IT WRAPPED AROUND ME WAS REASSURING.
I'M LONELY...
I DON'T WANT TO BE ALIVE ANYMORE...

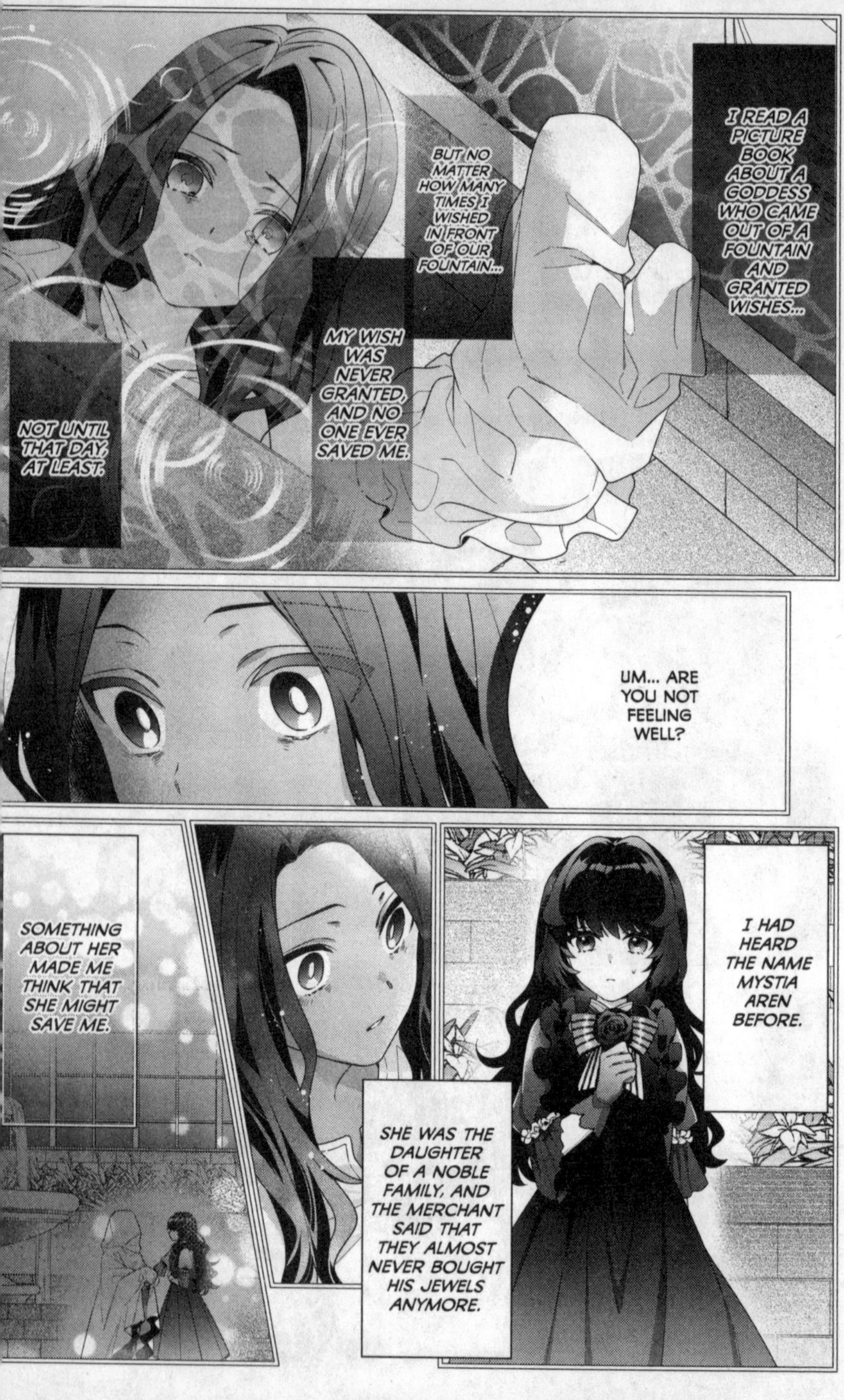
I READ A PICTURE BOOK ABOUT A GODDESS WHO CAME OUT OF A FOUNTAIN AND GRANTED WISHES...
BUT NO MATTER HOW MANY TIMES I WISHED IN FRONT OF OUR FOUNTAIN...
MY WISH WAS NEVER GRANTED, AND NO ONE EVER SAVED ME.
NOT UNTIL THAT DAY, AT LEAST.
UM... ARE YOU NOT FEELING WELL?
I HAD HEARD THE NAME MYSTIA AREN BEFORE.
SHE WAS THE DAUGHTER OF A NOBLE FAMILY, AND THE MERCHANT SAID THAT THEY ALMOST NEVER BOUGHT HIS JEWELS ANYMORE.
SOMETHING ABOUT HER MADE ME THINK THAT SHE MIGHT SAVE ME.

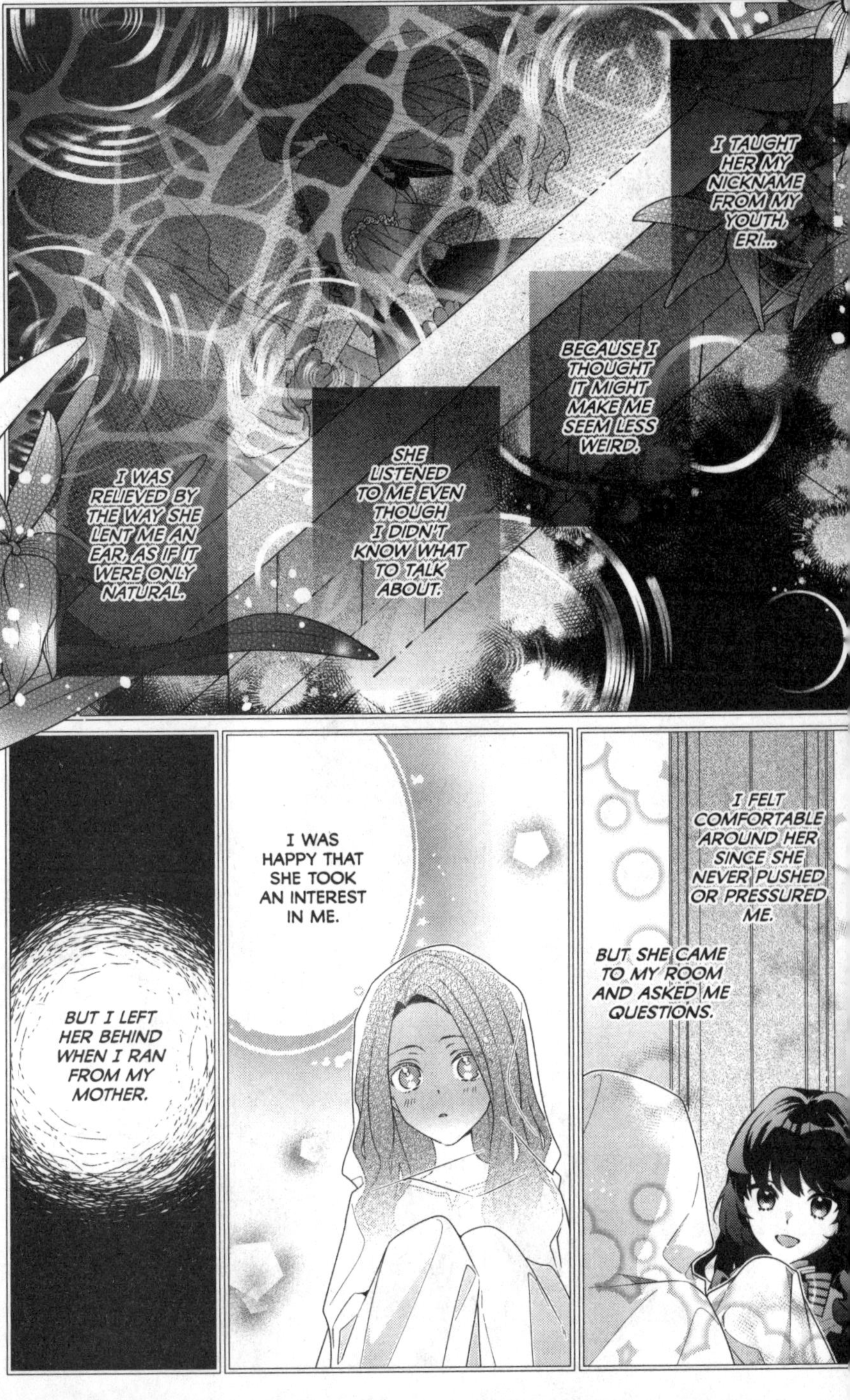
I TAUGHT HER MY NICKNAME FROM MY YOUTH, ERI...
BECAUSE I THOUGHT IT MIGHT MAKE ME SEEM LESS WEIRD.
SHE LISTENED TO ME EVEN THOUGH I DIDN'T KNOW WHAT TO TALK ABOUT.
I WAS RELIEVED BY THE WAY SHE LENT ME AN EAR, AS IF IT WERE ONLY NATURAL.
I FELT COMFORTABLE AROUND HER SINCE SHE NEVER PUSHED OR PRESSURED ME.
BUT SHE CAME TO MY ROOM AND ASKED ME QUESTIONS.
I WAS HAPPY THAT SHE TOOK AN INTEREST IN ME.
BUT I LEFT HER BEHIND WHEN I RAN FROM MY MOTHER.

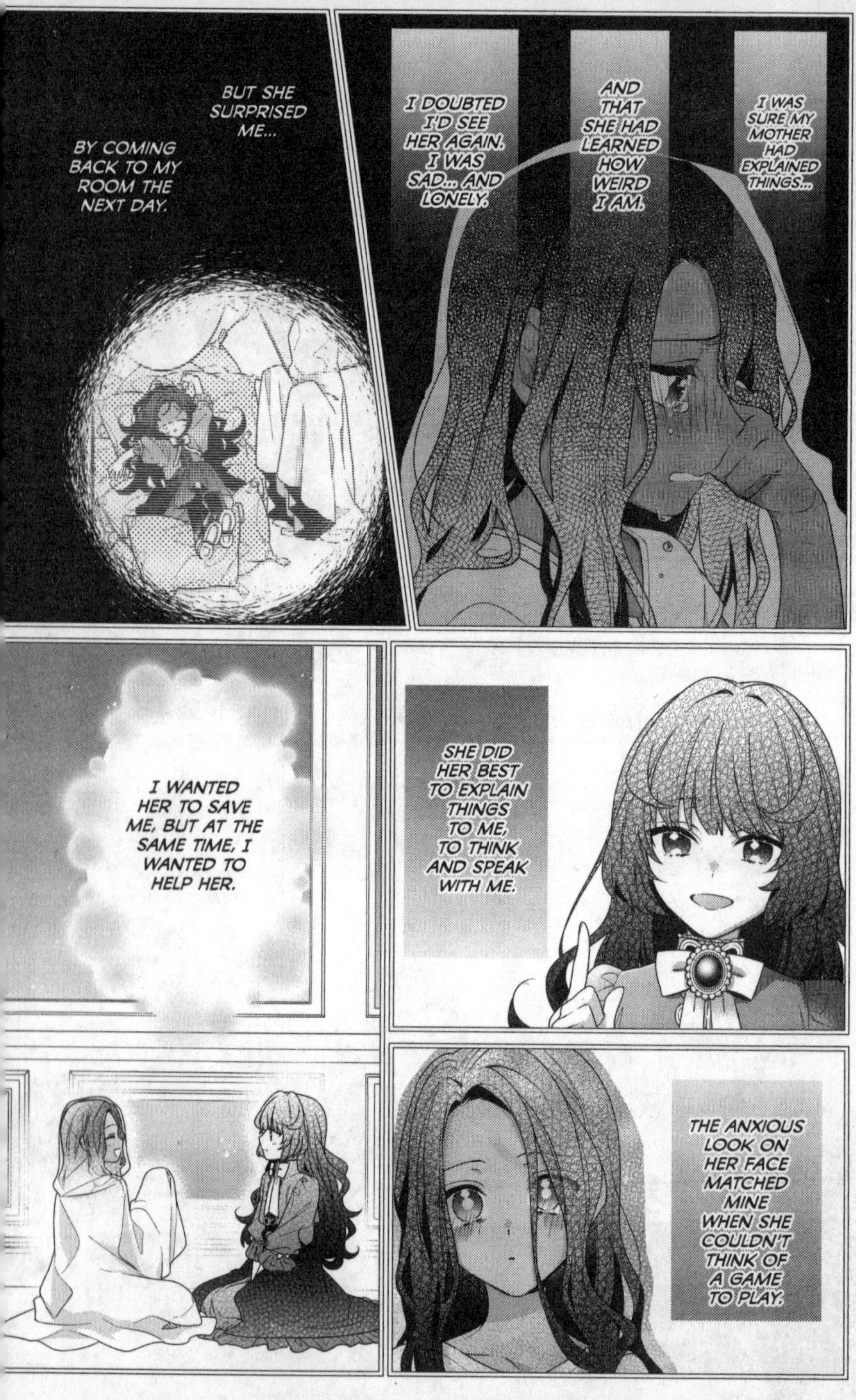
I WAS SURE MY MOTHER HAD EXPLAINED THINGS...
AND THAT SHE HAD LEARNED HOW WEIRD I AM.
I DOUBTED I'D SEE HER AGAIN. I WAS SAD... AND LONELY.
BUT SHE SURPRISED ME...
BY COMING BACK TO MY ROOM THE NEXT DAY.
SHE DID HER BEST TO EXPLAIN THINGS TO ME, TO THINK AND SPEAK WITH ME.
I WANTED HER TO SAVE ME, BUT AT THE SAME TIME, I WANTED TO HELP HER.
THE ANXIOUS LOOK ON HER FACE MATCHED MINE WHEN SHE COULDN'T THINK OF A GAME TO PLAY.

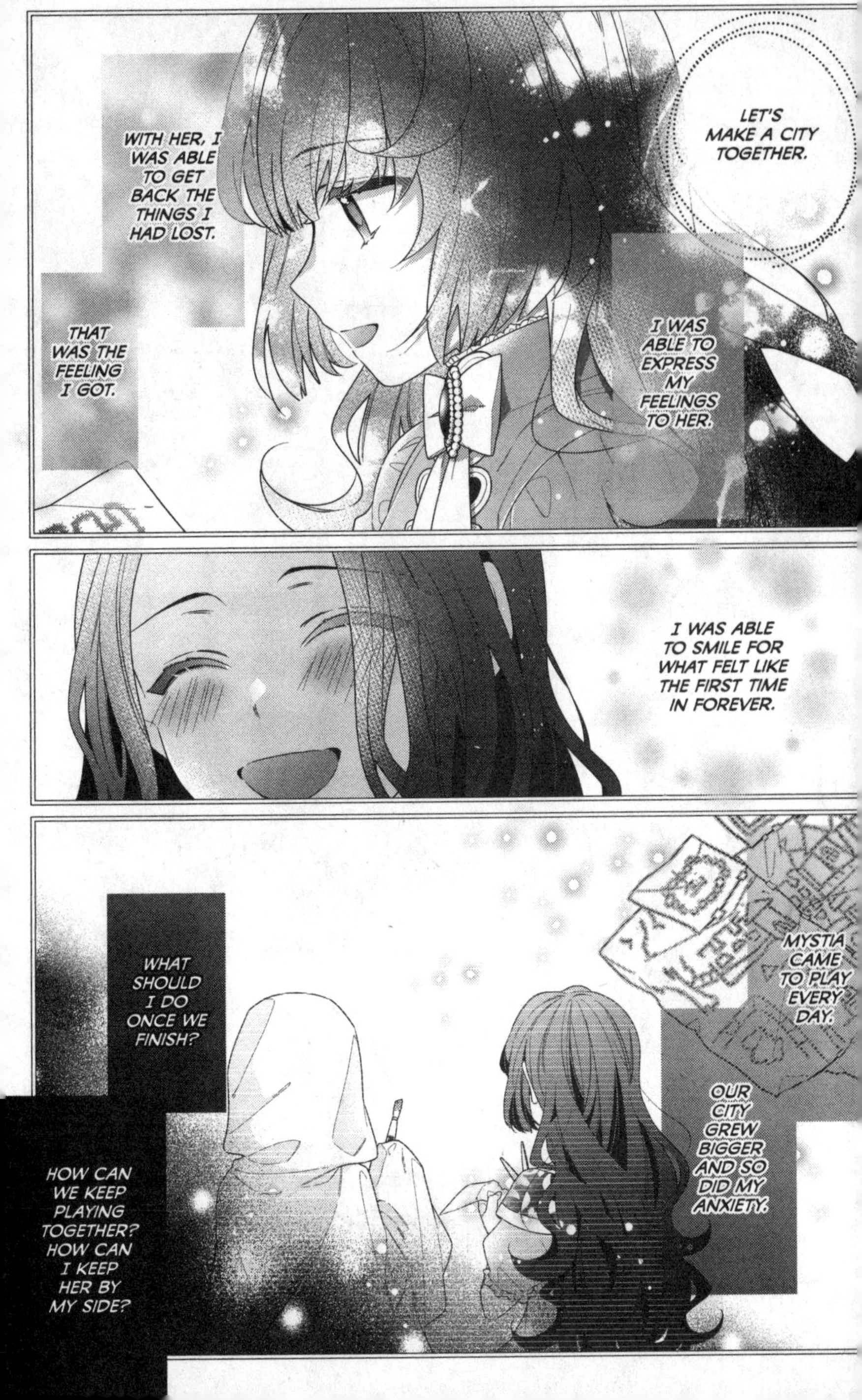
LET'S MAKE A CITY TOGETHER.
I WAS ABLE TO EXPRESS MY FEELINGS TO HER.
WITH HER, I WAS ABLE TO GET BACK THE THINGS I HAD LOST.
THAT WAS THE FEELING I GOT.
I WAS ABLE TO SMILE FOR WHAT FELT LIKE THE FIRST TIME IN FOREVER.
MYSTIA CAME TO PLAY EVERY DAY.
OUR CITY GREW BIGGER AND SO DID MY ANXIETY.
WHAT SHOULD I DO ONCE WE FINISH?
HOW CAN WE KEEP PLAYING TOGETHER? HOW CAN I KEEP HER BY MY SIDE?

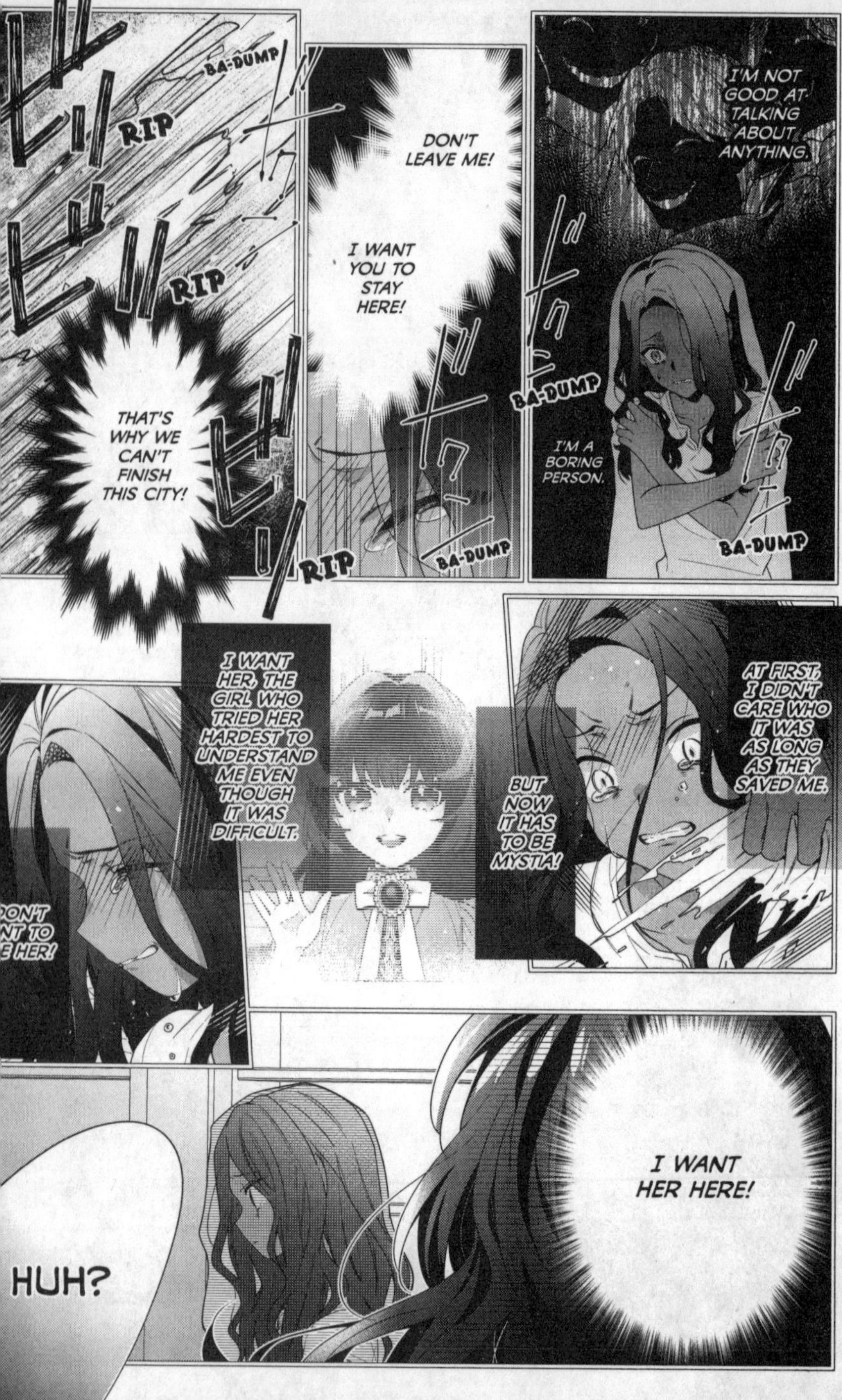
I'M NOT GOOD AT TALKING ABOUT ANYTHING.
BA-DUMP
I'M A BORING PERSON.
BA-DUMP
DON'T LEAVE ME!
I WANT YOU TO STAY HERE!
BA-DUMP
BA-DUMP
RIP
RIP
THAT'S WHY WE CAN'T FINISH THIS CITY!
RIP
AT FIRST, I DIDN'T CARE WHO IT WAS AS LONG AS THEY SAVED ME.
BUT NOW IT HAS TO BE MYSTIA!
I WANT HER, THE GIRL WHO TRIED HER HARDEST TO UNDERSTAND ME EVEN THOUGH IT WAS DIFFICULT.
DON'T
NT TO
E HER!
I WANT HER HERE!
HUH?

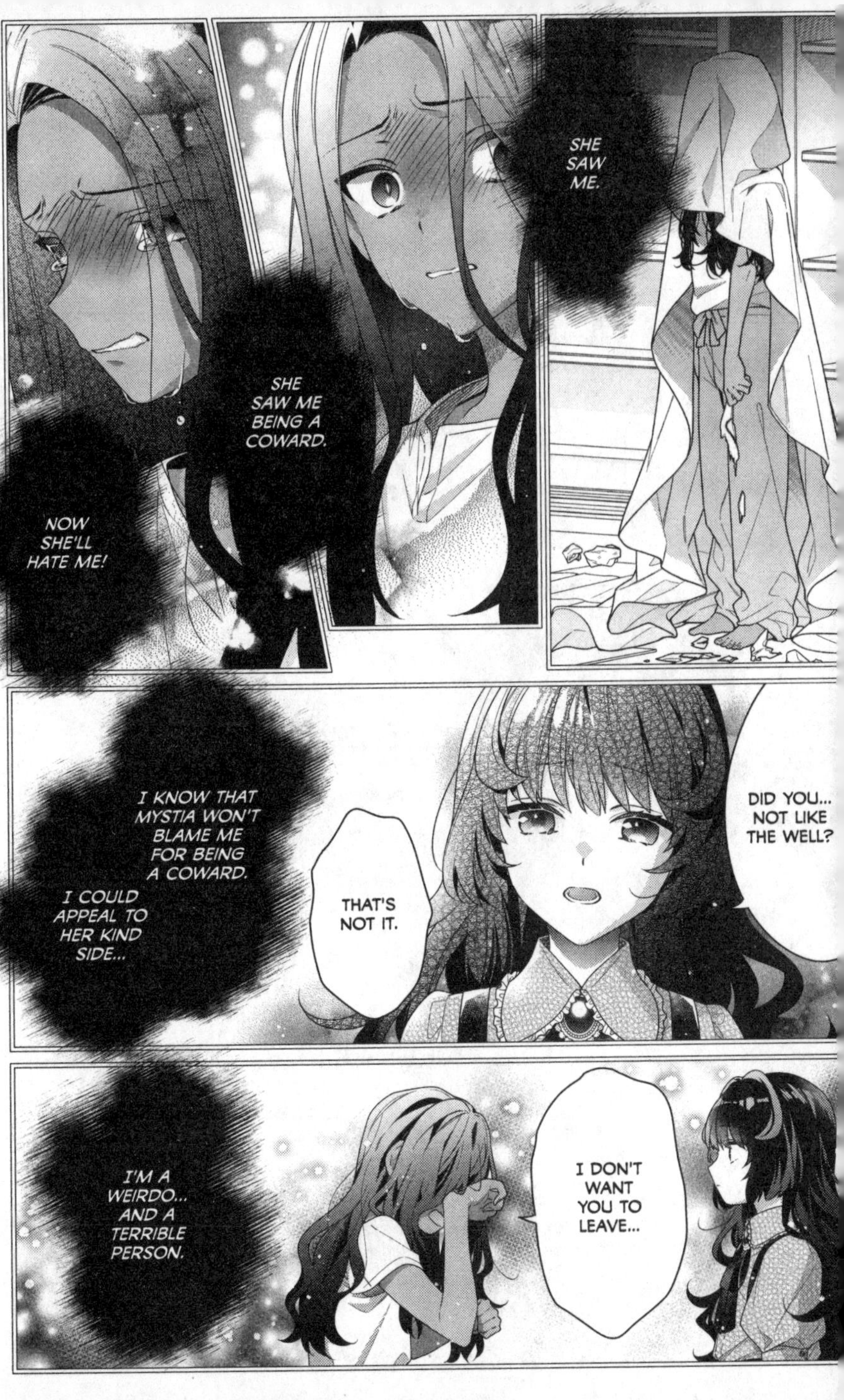
SHE SAW ME.
SHE SAW ME BEING A COWARD.
NOW SHE'LL HATE ME!
DID YOU... NOT LIKE THE WELL?
THAT'S NOT IT.
I KNOW THAT MYSTIA WON'T BLAME ME FOR BEING A COWARD.
I COULD APPEAL TO HER KIND SIDE...
I DON'T WANT YOU TO LEAVE...
I'M A WEIRDO... AND A TERRIBLE PERSON.

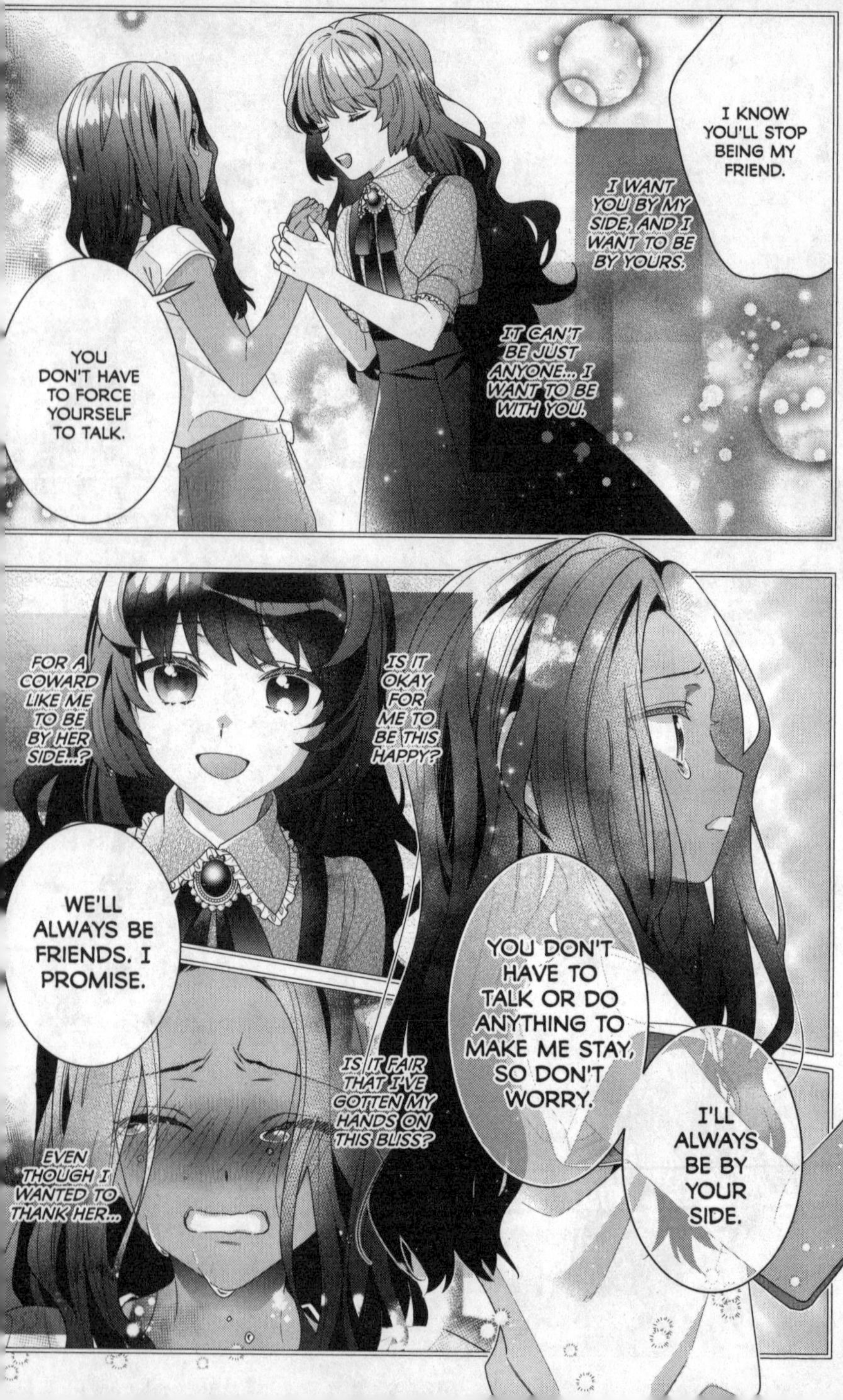
I KNOW YOU'LL STOP BEING MY FRIEND.
I WANT YOU BY MY SIDE, AND I WANT TO BE BY YOURS.
IT CAN'T BE JUST ANYONE... I WANT TO BE WITH YOU.
YOU DON'T HAVE TO FORCE YOURSELF TO TALK.
YOU DON'T HAVE TO TALK OR DO ANYTHING TO MAKE ME STAY, SO DON'T WORRY.
I'LL ALWAYS BE BY YOUR SIDE.
IS IT OKAY FOR ME TO BE THIS HAPPY?
FOR A COWARD LIKE ME TO BE BY HER SIDE...?
WE'LL ALWAYS BE FRIENDS. I PROMISE.
IS IT FAIR THAT I'VE GOTTEN MY HANDS ON THIS BLISS?
EVEN THOUGH I WANTED TO THANK HER...

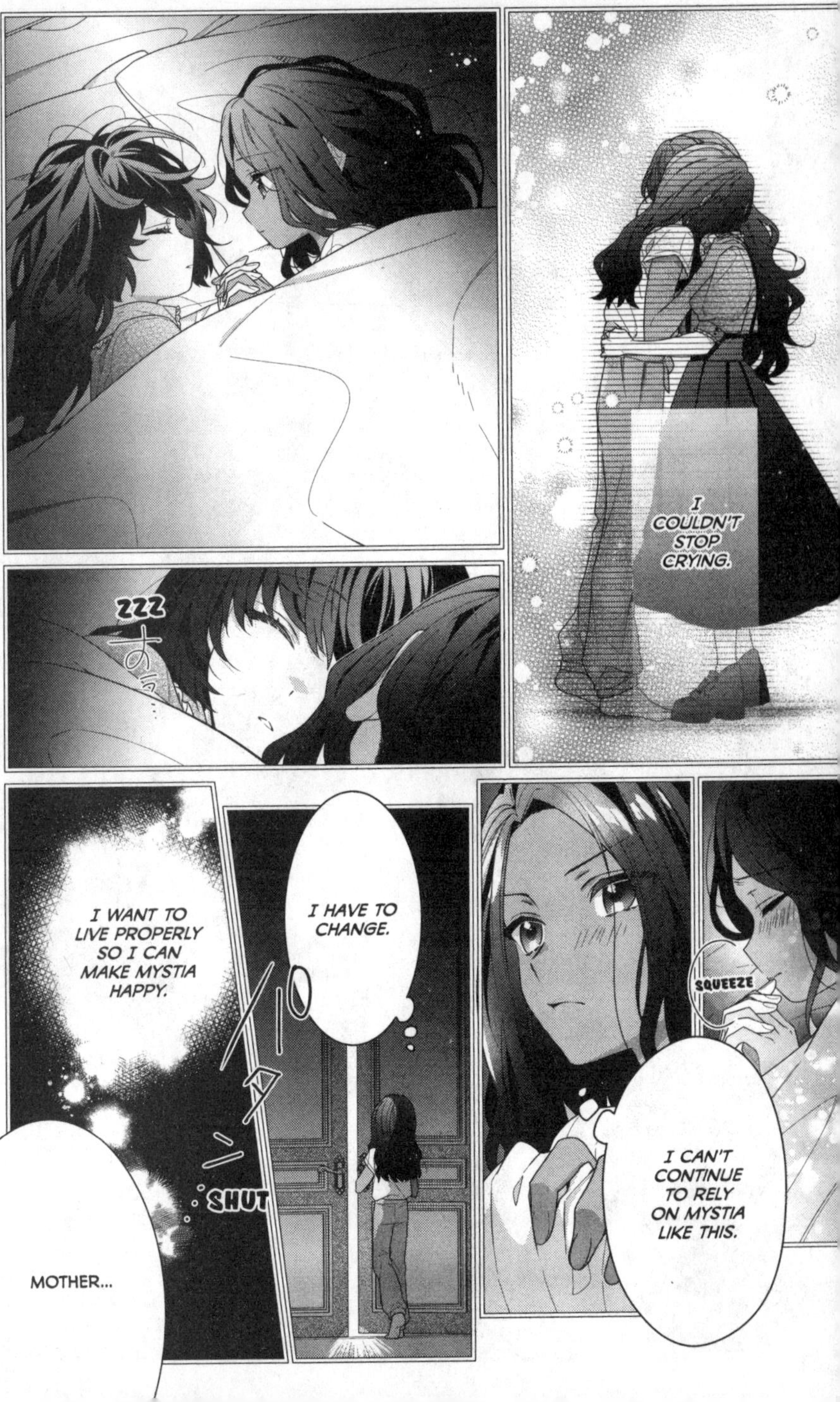
I COULDN'T STOP CRYING.
ZZZ
SQUEEZE
I CAN'T CONTINUE TO RELY ON MYSTIA LIKE THIS.
I HAVE TO CHANGE.
SHUT
I WANT TO LIVE PROPERLY SO I CAN MAKE MYSTIA HAPPY.
MOTHER...

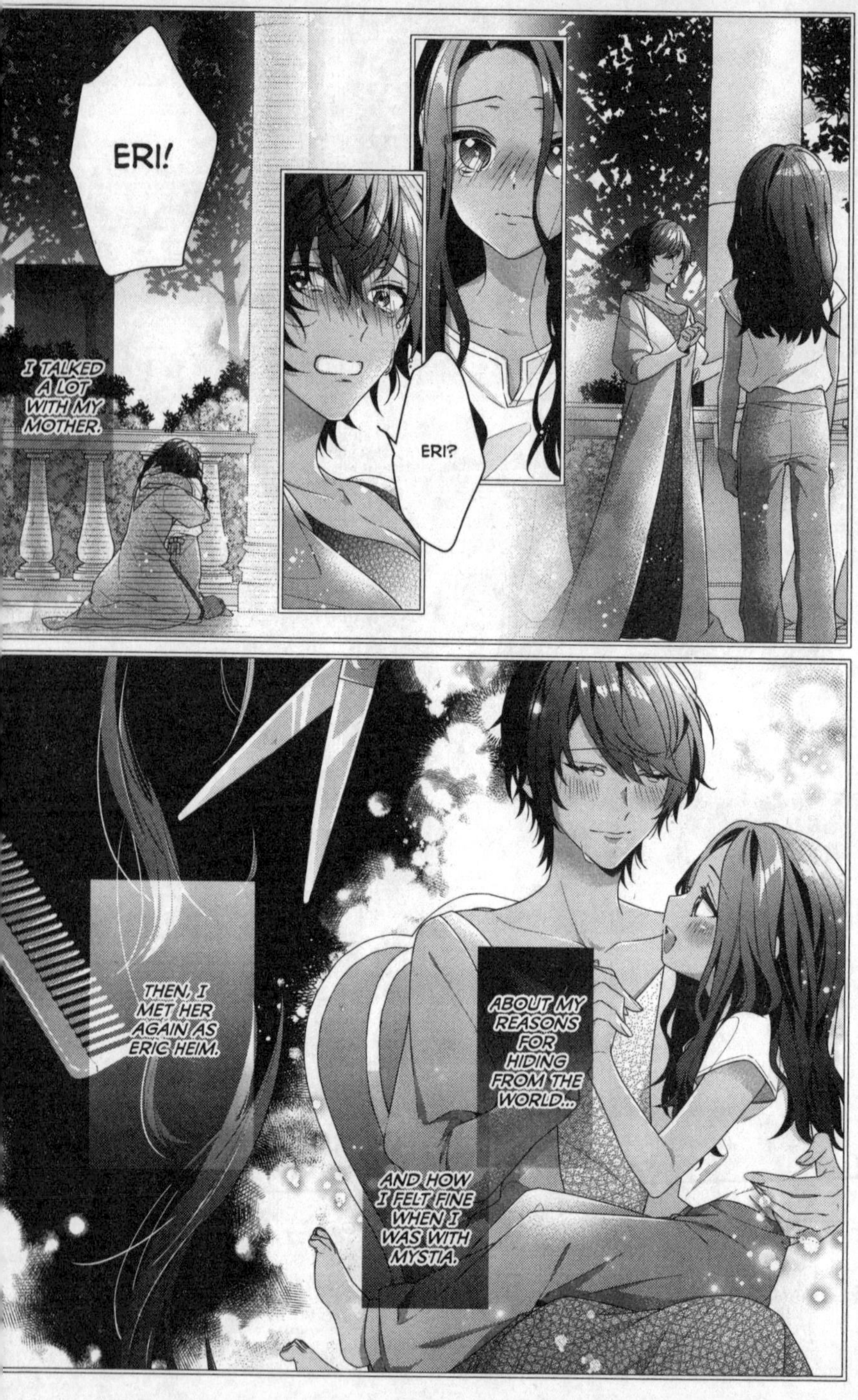
ERI!
ERI?
I TALKED A LOT WITH MY MOTHER.
ABOUT MY REASONS FOR HIDING FROM THE WORLD...
AND HOW I FELT FINE WHEN I WAS WITH MYSTIA.
THEN, I MET HER AGAIN AS ERIC HEIM.

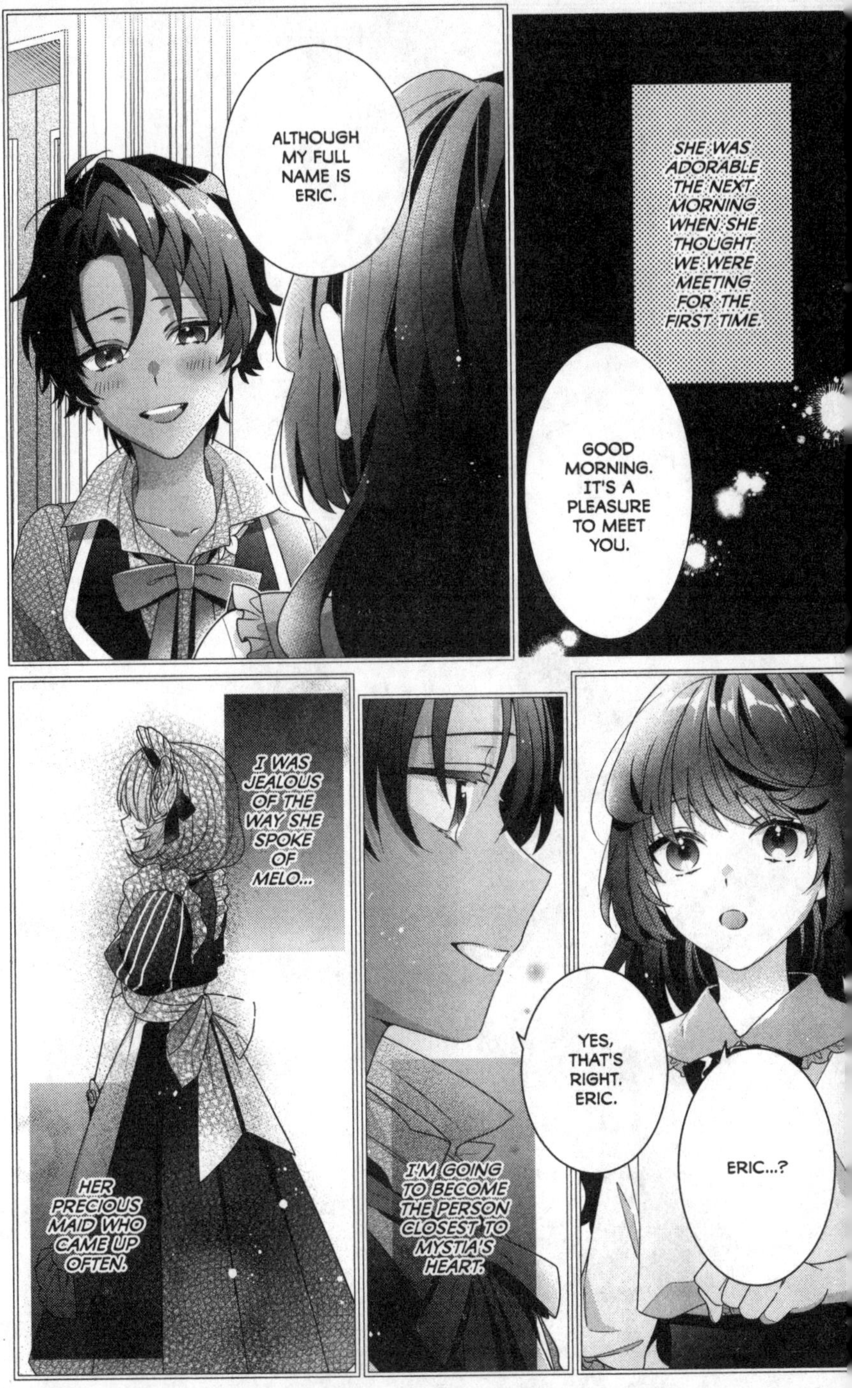
SHE WAS ADORABLE THE NEXT MORNING WHEN SHE THOUGHT WE WERE MEETING FOR THE FIRST TIME.
GOOD MORNING. IT'S A PLEASURE TO MEET YOU.
ALTHOUGH MY FULL NAME IS ERIC.
ERIC...?
YES, THAT'S RIGHT. ERIC.
I'M GOING TO BECOME THE PERSON CLOSEST TO MYSTIA'S HEART.
I WAS JEALOUS OF THE WAY SHE SPOKE OF MELO...
HER PRECIOUS MAID WHO CAME UP OFTEN.

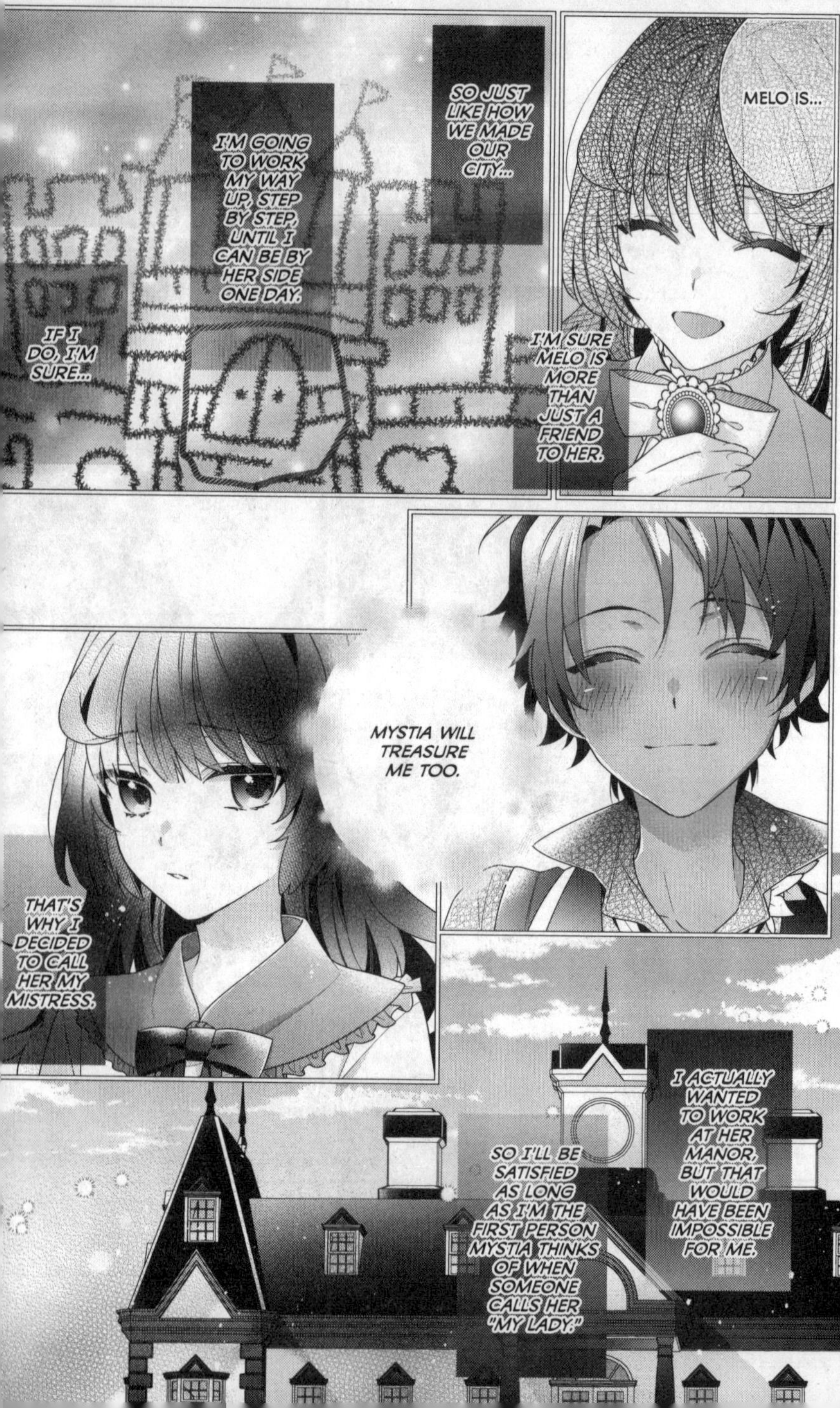
MELO IS...
I'M SURE MELO IS MORE THAN JUST A FRIEND TO HER.
SO JUST LIKE HOW WE MADE OUR CITY...
I'M GOING TO WORK MY WAY UP, STEP BY STEP, UNTIL I CAN BE BY HER SIDE ONE DAY.
IF I DO, I'M SURE...
MYSTIA WILL TREASURE ME TOO.
THAT'S WHY I DECIDED TO CALL HER MY MISTRESS.
I ACTUALLY WANTED TO WORK AT HER MANOR, BUT THAT WOULD HAVE BEEN IMPOSSIBLE FOR ME.
SO I'LL BE SATISFIED AS LONG AS I'M THE FIRST PERSON MYSTIA THINKS OF WHEN SOMEONE CALLS HER "MY LADY."

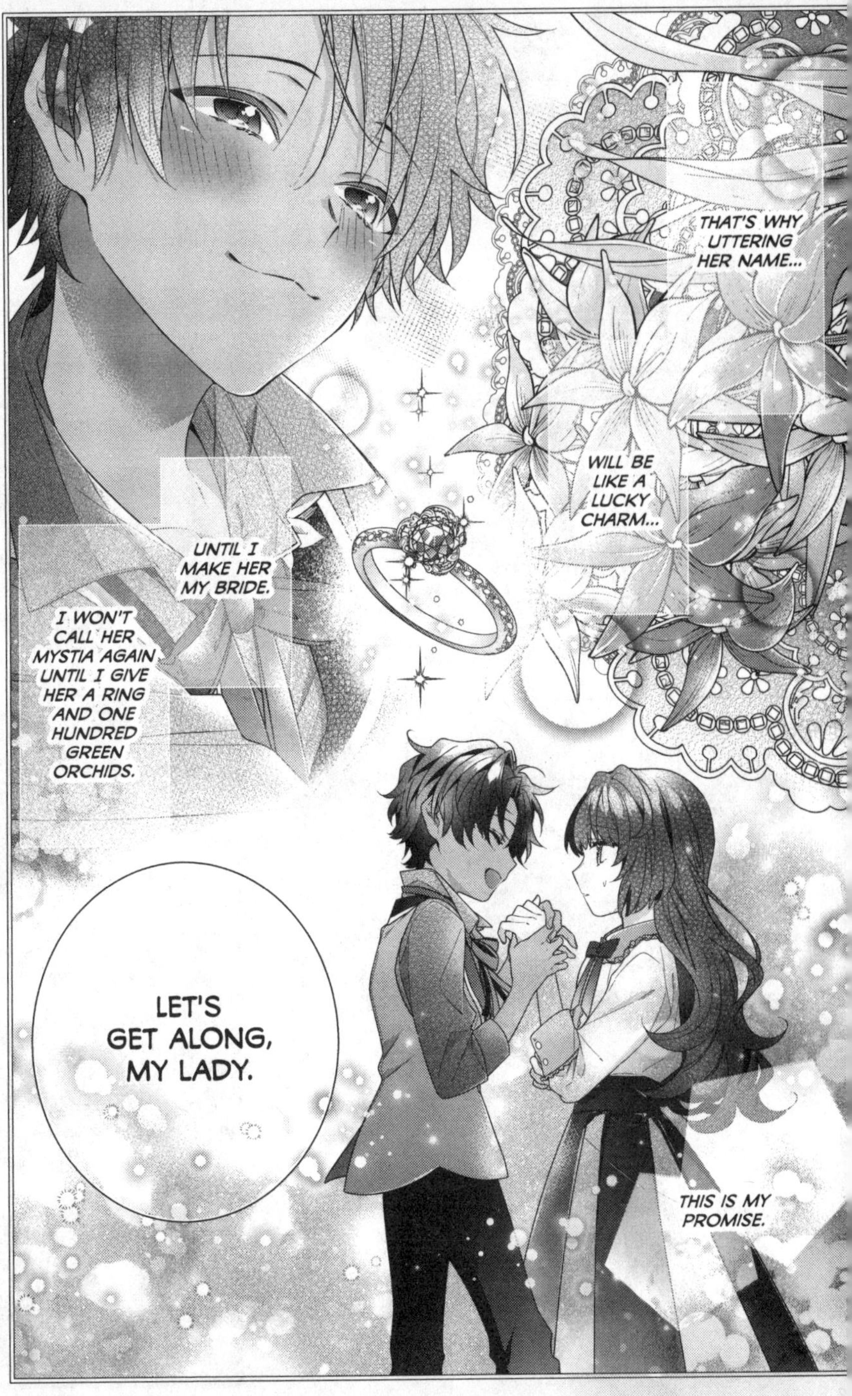
THAT'S WHY UTTERING HER NAME...
WILL BE LIKE A LUCKY CHARM...
UNTIL I MAKE HER MY BRIDE.
I WON'T CALL HER MYSTIA AGAIN UNTIL I GIVE HER A RING AND ONE HUNDRED GREEN ORCHIDS.
LET'S GET ALONG, MY LADY.
THIS IS MY PROMISE.

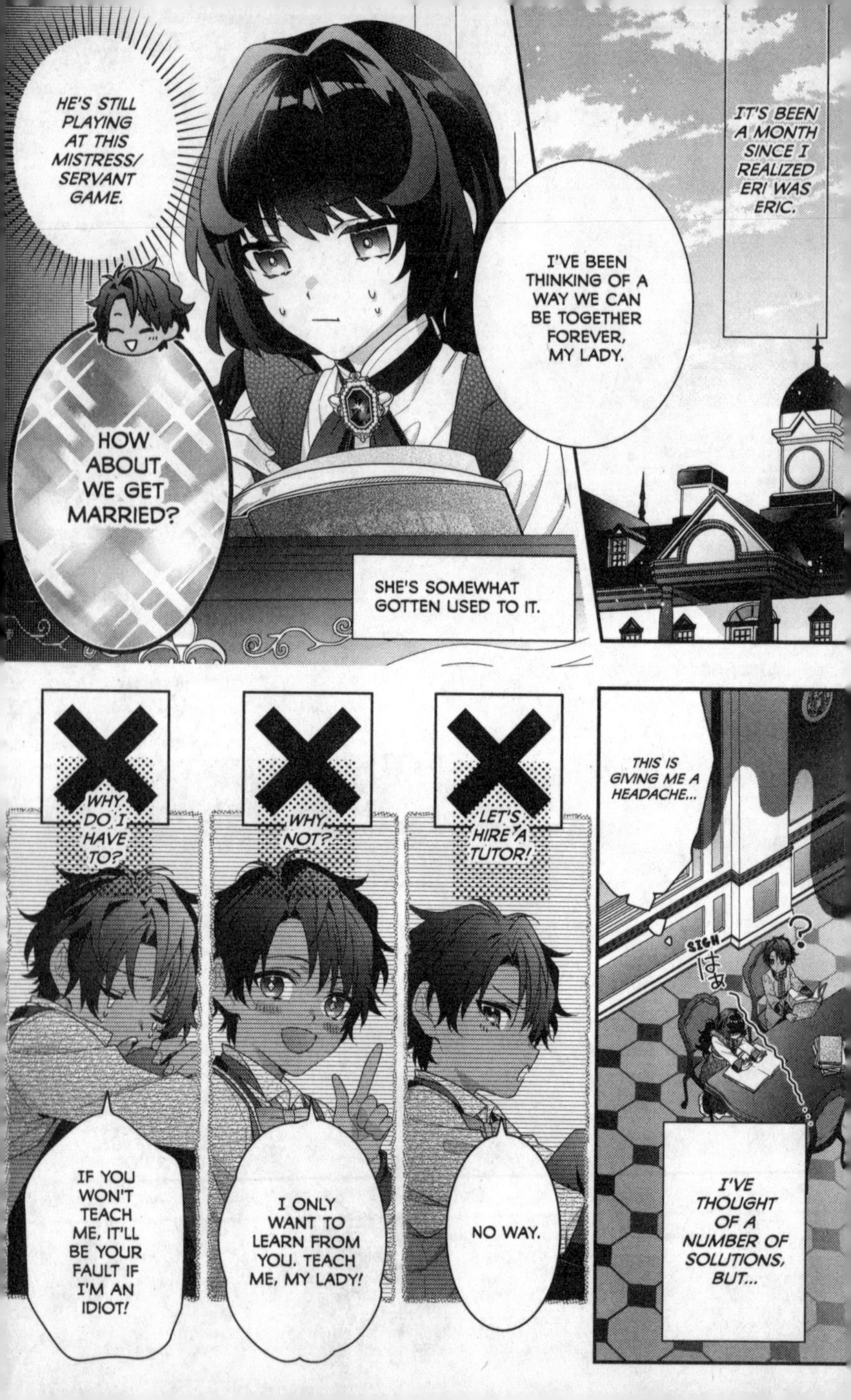
IT'S BEEN A MONTH SINCE I REALIZED ERI WAS ERIC.
I'VE BEEN THINKING OF A WAY WE CAN BE TOGETHER FOREVER, MY LADY.
HOW ABOUT WE GET MARRIED?
HE'S STILL PLAYING AT THIS MISTRESS/ SERVANT GAME.
SHE'S SOMEWHAT GOTTEN USED TO IT.
THIS IS GIVING ME A HEADACHE...
SIGH
はぁ
I'VE THOUGHT OF A NUMBER OF SOLUTIONS, BUT...
LET'S HIRE A TUTOR!
NO WAY.
WHY NOT?
I ONLY WANT TO LEARN FROM YOU. TEACH ME, MY LADY!
WHY DO I HAVE TO?
IF YOU WON'T TEACH ME, IT'LL BE YOUR FAULT IF I'M AN IDIOT!

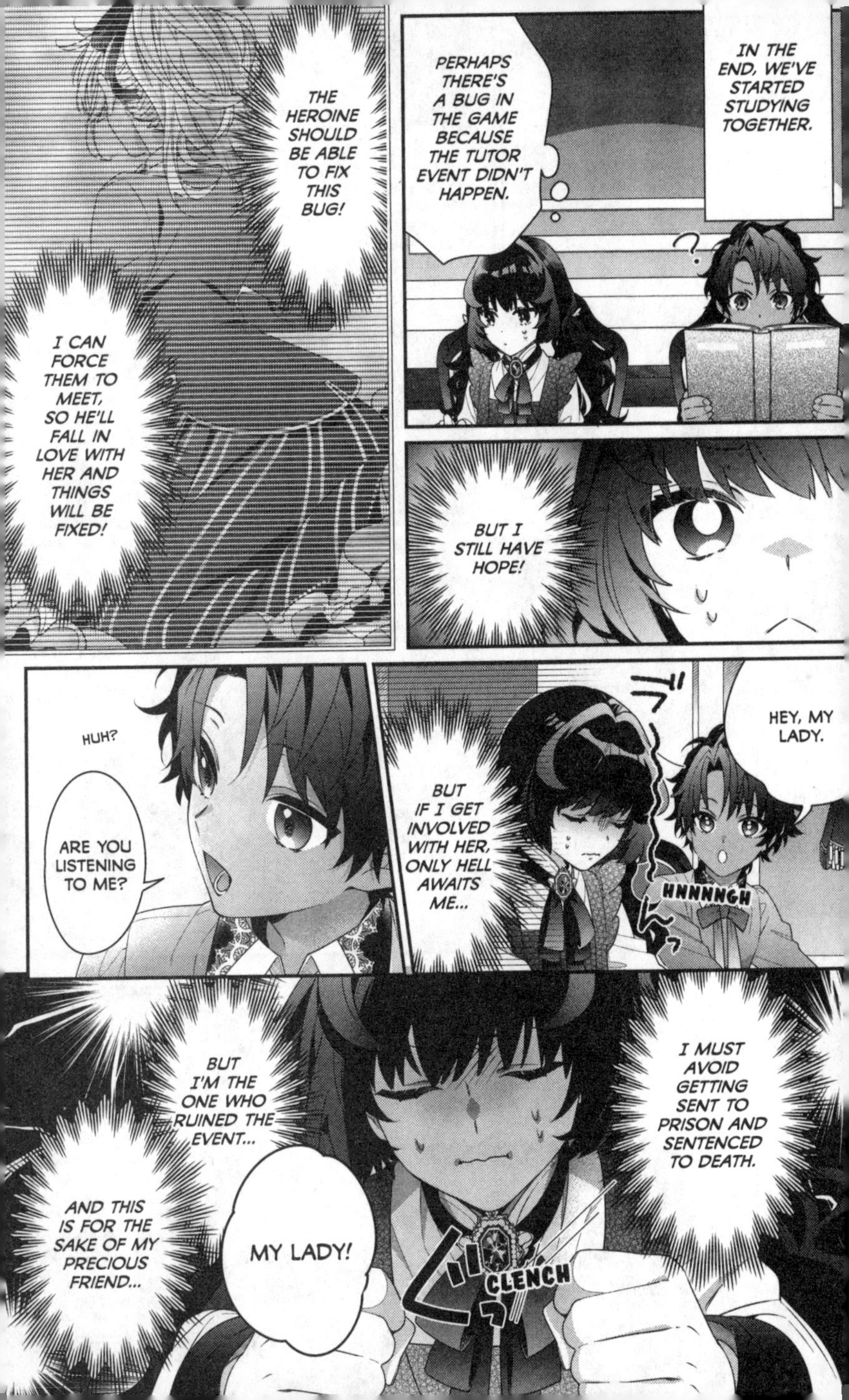
IN THE END, WE'VE STARTED STUDYING TOGETHER.
PERHAPS THERE'S A BUG IN THE GAME BECAUSE THE TUTOR EVENT DIDN'T HAPPEN.
BUT I STILL HAVE HOPE!
THE HEROINE SHOULD BE ABLE TO FIX THIS BUG!
I CAN FORCE THEM TO MEET, SO HE'LL FALL IN LOVE WITH HER AND THINGS WILL BE FIXED!
HEY, MY LADY.
HNNNNGH
BUT IF I GET INVOLVED WITH HER, ONLY HELL AWAITS ME...
HUH?
ARE YOU LISTENING TO ME?
I MUST AVOID GETTING SENT TO PRISON AND SENTENCED TO DEATH.
CLENCH
MY LADY!
BUT I'M THE ONE WHO RUINED THE EVENT...
AND THIS IS FOR THE SAKE OF MY PRECIOUS FRIEND...

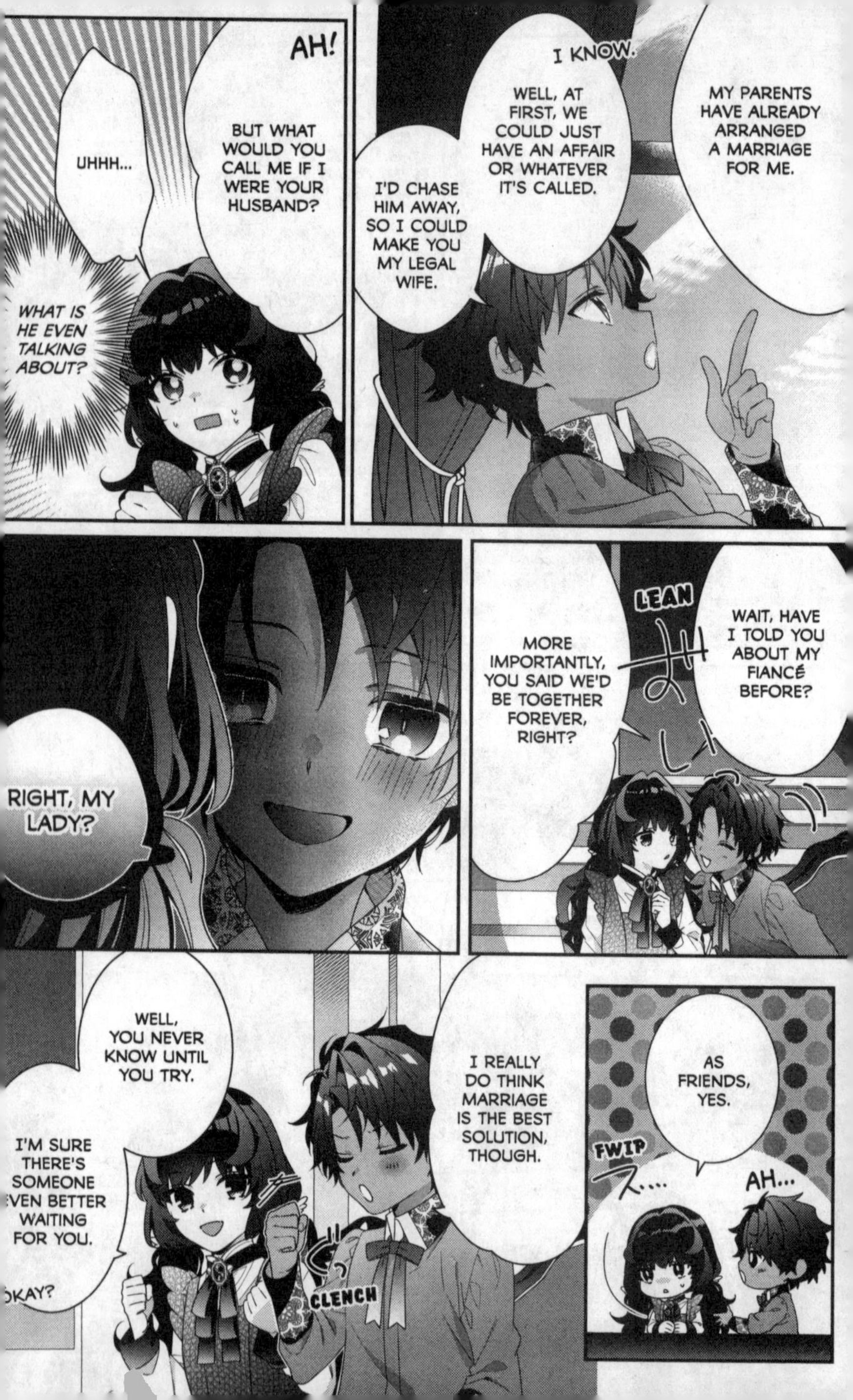
MY PARENTS HAVE ALREADY ARRANGED A MARRIAGE FOR ME.
I KNOW.
WELL, AT FIRST, WE COULD JUST HAVE AN AFFAIR OR WHATEVER IT'S CALLED.
I'D CHASE HIM AWAY, SO I COULD MAKE YOU MY LEGAL WIFE.
AH!
BUT WHAT WOULD YOU CALL ME IF I WERE YOUR HUSBAND?
UHHH...
WHAT IS HE EVEN TALKING ABOUT?
WAIT, HAVE I TOLD YOU ABOUT MY FIANCÉ BEFORE?
LEAN
MORE IMPORTANTLY, YOU SAID WE'D BE TOGETHER FOREVER, RIGHT?
RIGHT, MY LADY?
AS FRIENDS, YES.
FWIP
AH...
I REALLY DO THINK MARRIAGE IS THE BEST SOLUTION, THOUGH.
WELL, YOU NEVER KNOW UNTIL YOU TRY.
I'M SURE THERE'S SOMEONE EVEN BETTER WAITING FOR YOU.
OKAY?
CLENCH

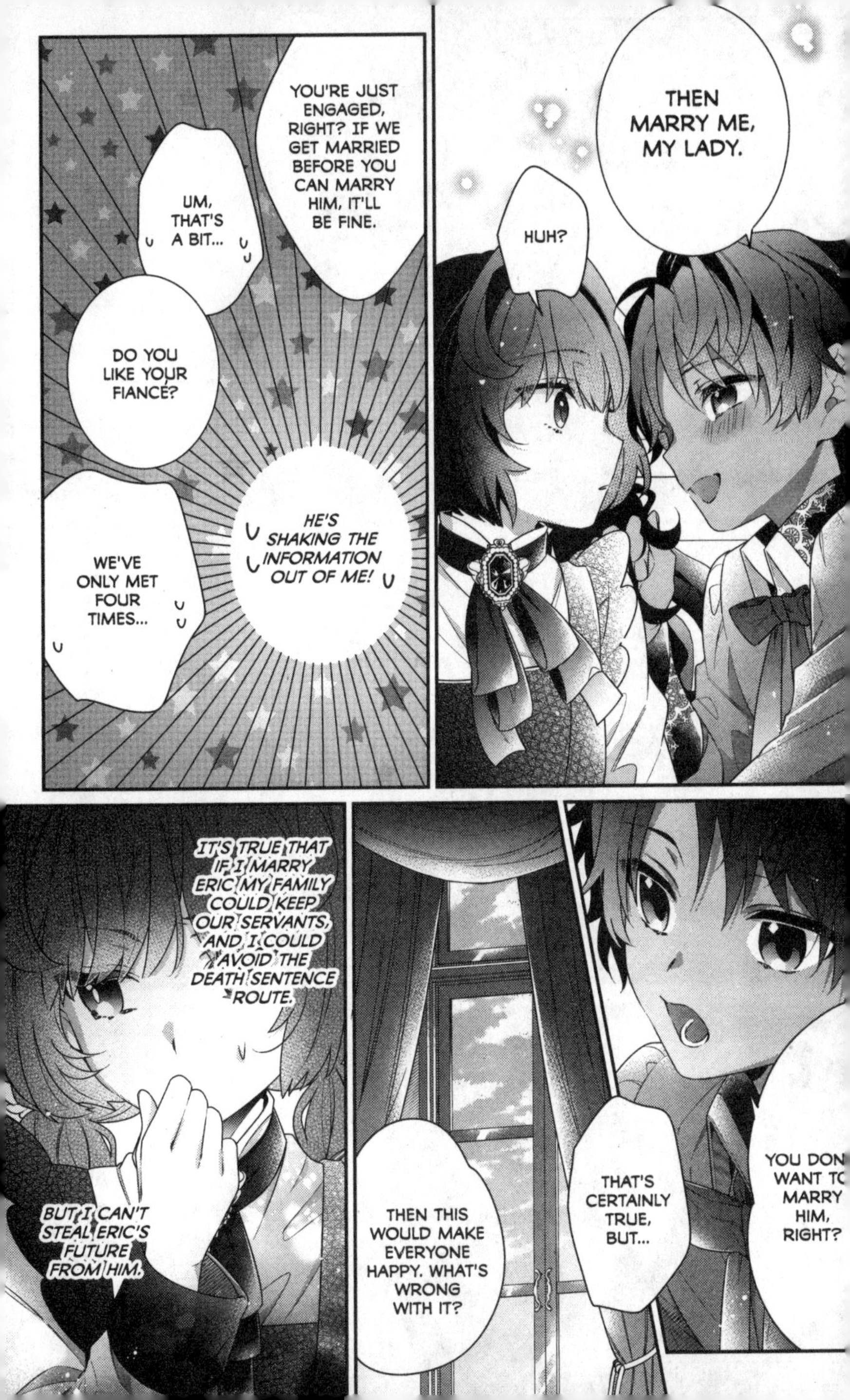
THEN MARRY ME, MY LADY.
HUH?
YOU'RE JUST ENGAGED, RIGHT? IF WE GET MARRIED BEFORE YOU CAN MARRY HIM, IT'LL BE FINE.
UM, THAT'S A BIT...
DO YOU LIKE YOUR FIANCE?
HE'S SHAKING THE INFORMATION OUT OF ME!
WE'VE ONLY MET FOUR TIMES...
YOU DON WANT TO MARRY HIM, RIGHT?
THAT'S CERTAINLY TRUE, BUT...
THEN THIS WOULD MAKE EVERYONE HAPPY. WHAT'S WRONG WITH IT?
IT'S TRUE THAT IF I MARRY ERIC MY FAMILY COULD KEEP OUR SERVANTS, AND I COULD AVOID THE DEATH SENTENCE ROUTE.
BUT I CAN'T STEAL ERIC'S FUTURE FROM HIM.

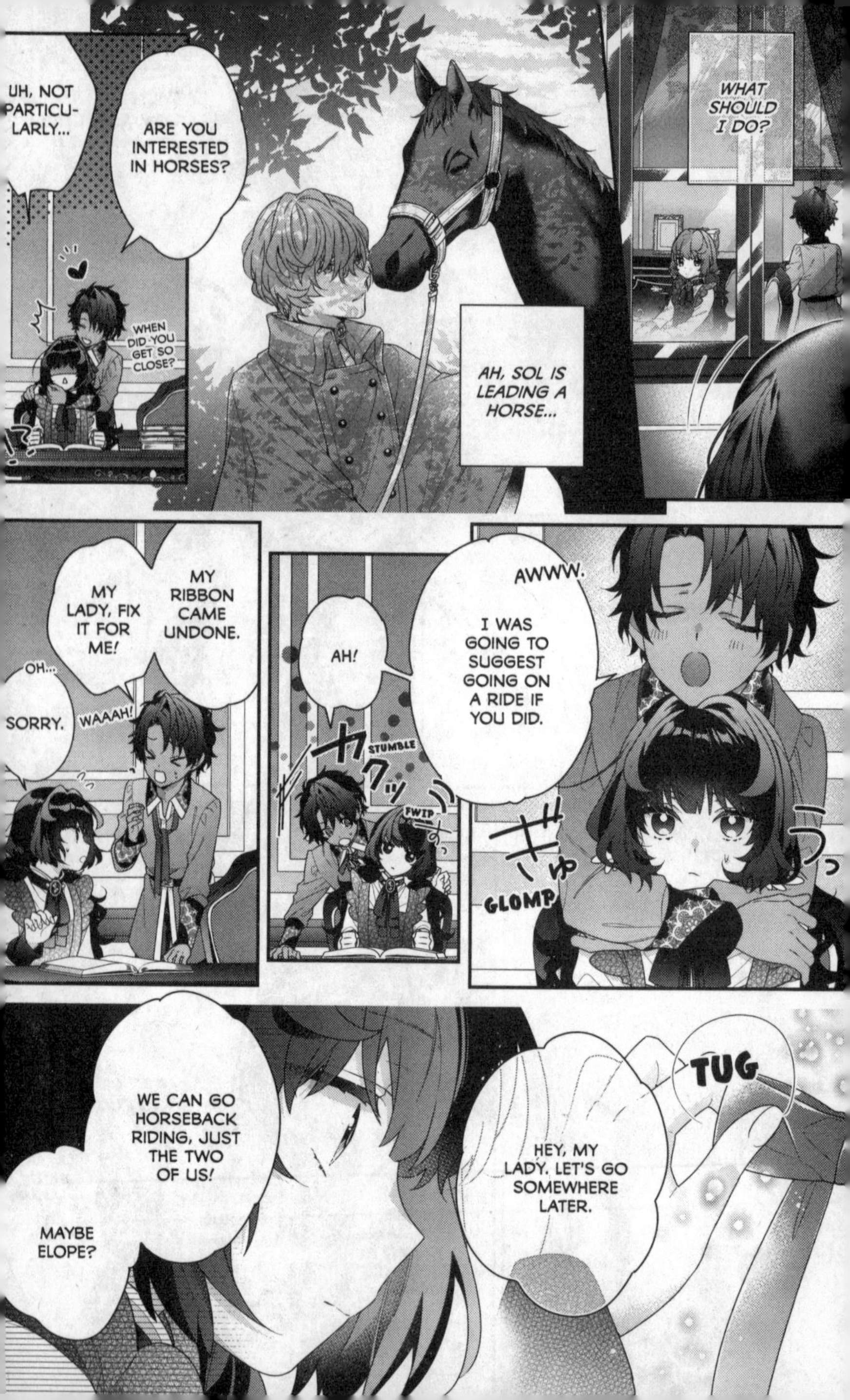
WHAT SHOULD I DO?
AH, SOL IS LEADING A HORSE...
ARE YOU INTERESTED IN HORSES?
UH, NOT PARTICULARLY...
WHEN DID YOU GET SO CLOSE?
AWWW.
I WAS GOING TO SUGGEST GOING ON A RIDE IF YOU DID.
GLOMP
AH!
STUMBLE
FWIP
MY RIBBON CAME UNDONE.
MY LADY, FIX IT FOR ME!
WAAAH!
OH...
SORRY.
TUG
HEY, MY LADY. LET'S GO SOMEWHERE LATER.
WE CAN GO HORSEBACK RIDING, JUST THE TWO OF US!
MAYBE ELOPE?

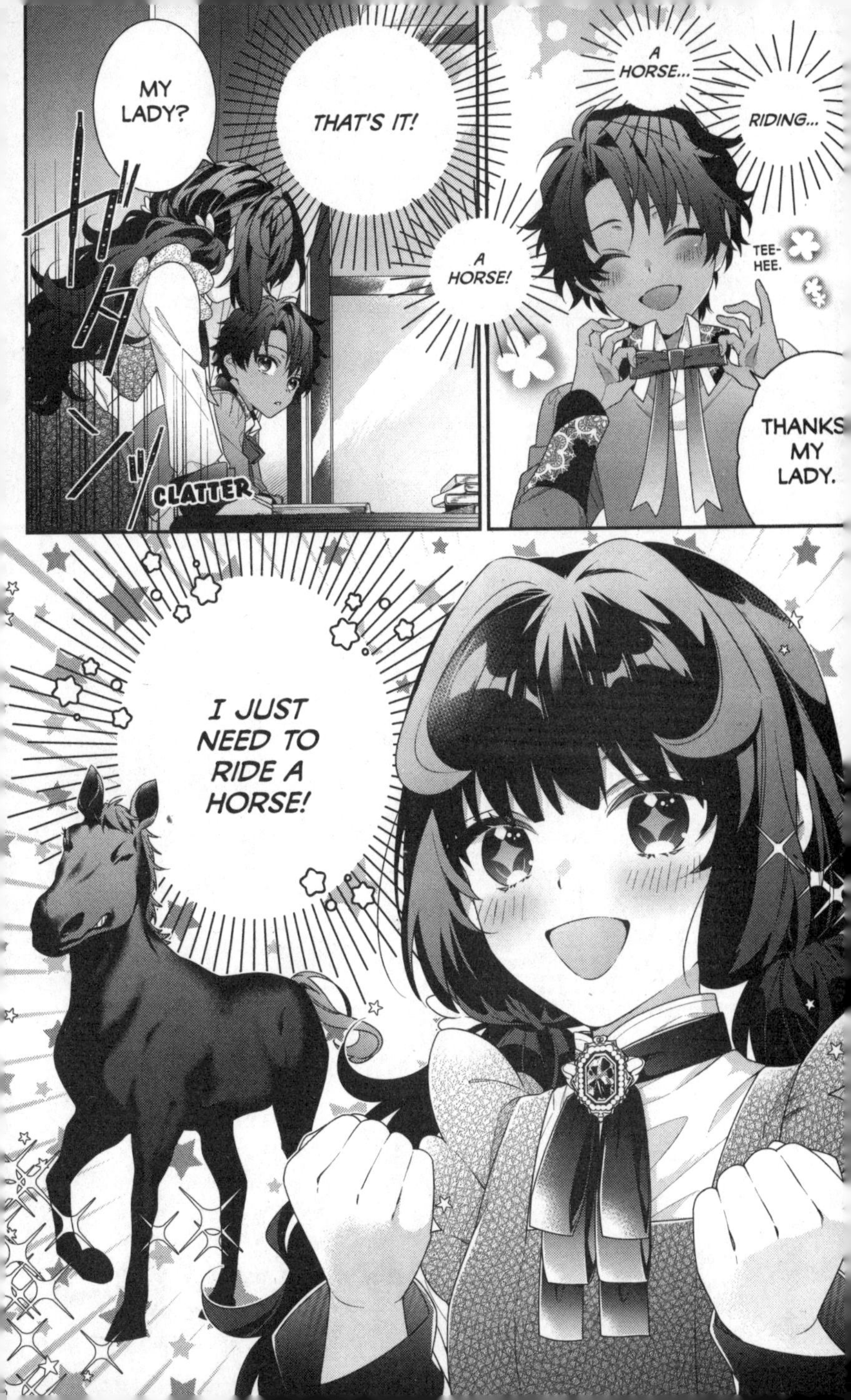
A HORSE...
RIDING...
TEE-HEE.
THANKS MY LADY.
THAT'S IT!
MY LADY?
A HORSE!
CLATTER
I JUST NEED TO RIDE A HORSE!

I was REINCARNATED as the Villainess in an OTOME GAME but the boys love me anyway!

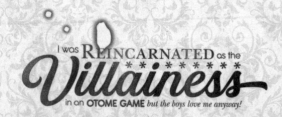

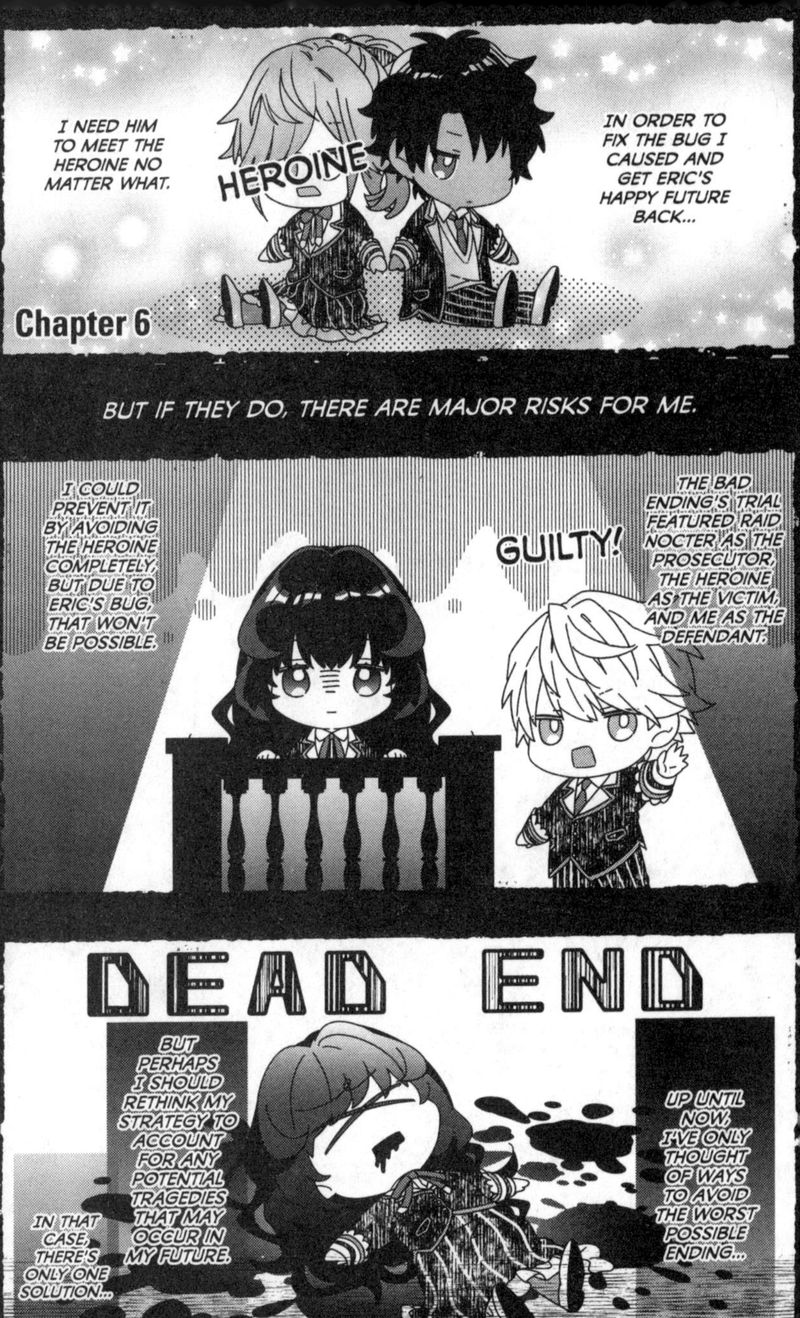
IN ORDER TO FIX THE BUG I CAUSED AND GET ERIC'S HAPPY FUTURE BACK...
HEROINE
I NEED HIM TO MEET THE HEROINE NO MATTER WHAT.
Chapter 6
BUT IF THEY DO, THERE ARE MAJOR RISKS FOR ME.
THE BAD ENDING'S TRIAL FEATURED RAID NOCTER AS THE PROSECUTOR, THE HEROINE AS THE VICTIM, AND ME AS THE DEFENDANT.
GUILTY!
I COULD PREVENT IT BY AVOIDING THE HEROINE COMPLETELY, BUT DUE TO ERIC'S BUG, THAT WON'T BE POSSIBLE.
DEAD END
UP UNTIL NOW, I'VE ONLY THOUGHT OF WAYS TO AVOID THE WORST POSSIBLE ENDING...
BUT PERHAPS I SHOULD RETHINK MY STRATEGY TO ACCOUNT FOR ANY POTENTIAL TRAGEDIES THAT MAY OCCUR IN MY FUTURE.
IN THAT CASE, THERE'S ONLY ONE SOLUTION...

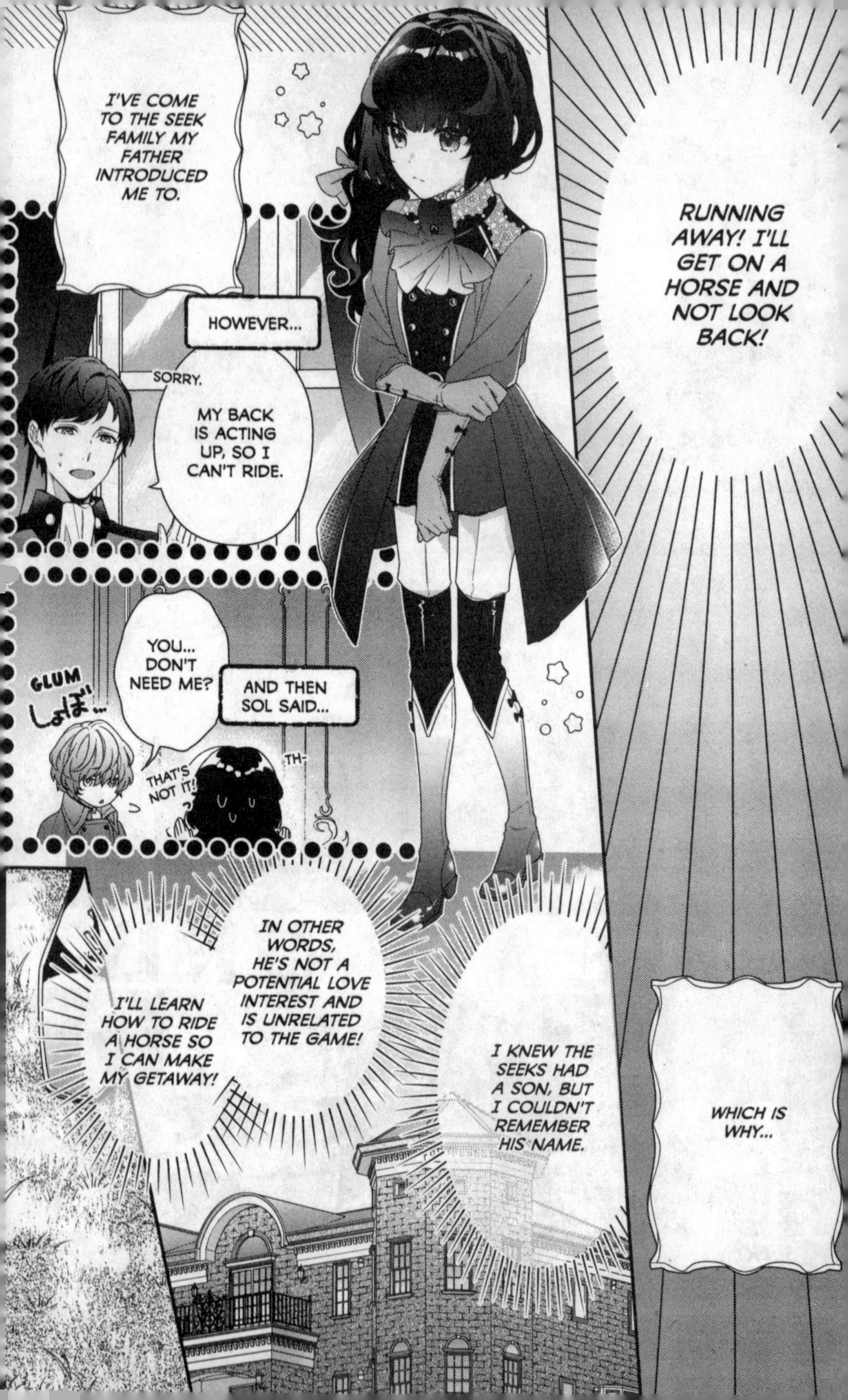
RUNNING AWAY! I'LL GET ON A HORSE AND NOT LOOK BACK!
WHICH IS WHY...
I'VE COME TO THE SEEK FAMILY MY FATHER INTRODUCED ME TO.
HOWEVER...
SORRY.
MY BACK IS ACTING UP, SO I CAN'T RIDE.
AND THEN SOL SAID...
YOU... DON'T NEED ME?
GLUM
しょぼ...
TH-
THAT'S NOT IT!
I KNEW THE SEEKS HAD A SON, BUT I COULDN'T REMEMBER HIS NAME.
IN OTHER WORDS, HE'S NOT A POTENTIAL LOVE INTEREST AND IS UNRELATED TO THE GAME!
I'LL LEARN HOW TO RIDE A HORSE SO I CAN MAKE MY GETAWAY!

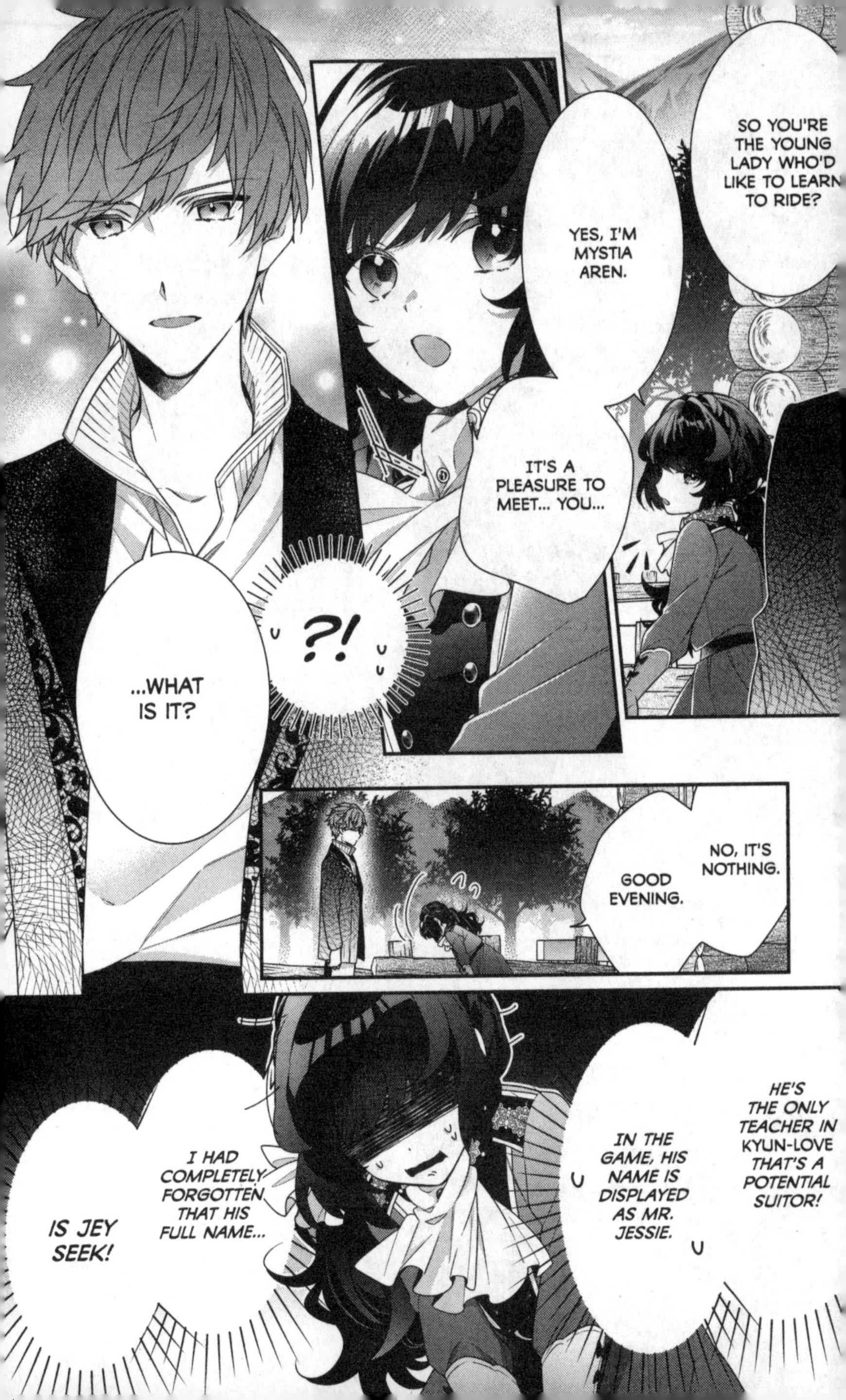
SO YOU'RE THE YOUNG LADY WHO'D LIKE TO LEARN TO RIDE?
YES, I'M MYSTIA AREN.
IT'S A PLEASURE TO MEET... YOU...
?!
...WHAT IS IT?
NO, IT'S NOTHING.
GOOD EVENING.
HE'S THE ONLY TEACHER IN KYUN-LOVE THAT'S A POTENTIAL SUITOR!
IN THE GAME, HIS NAME IS DISPLAYED AS MR. JESSIE.
I HAD COMPLETELY FORGOTTEN THAT HIS FULL NAME...
IS JEY SEEK!

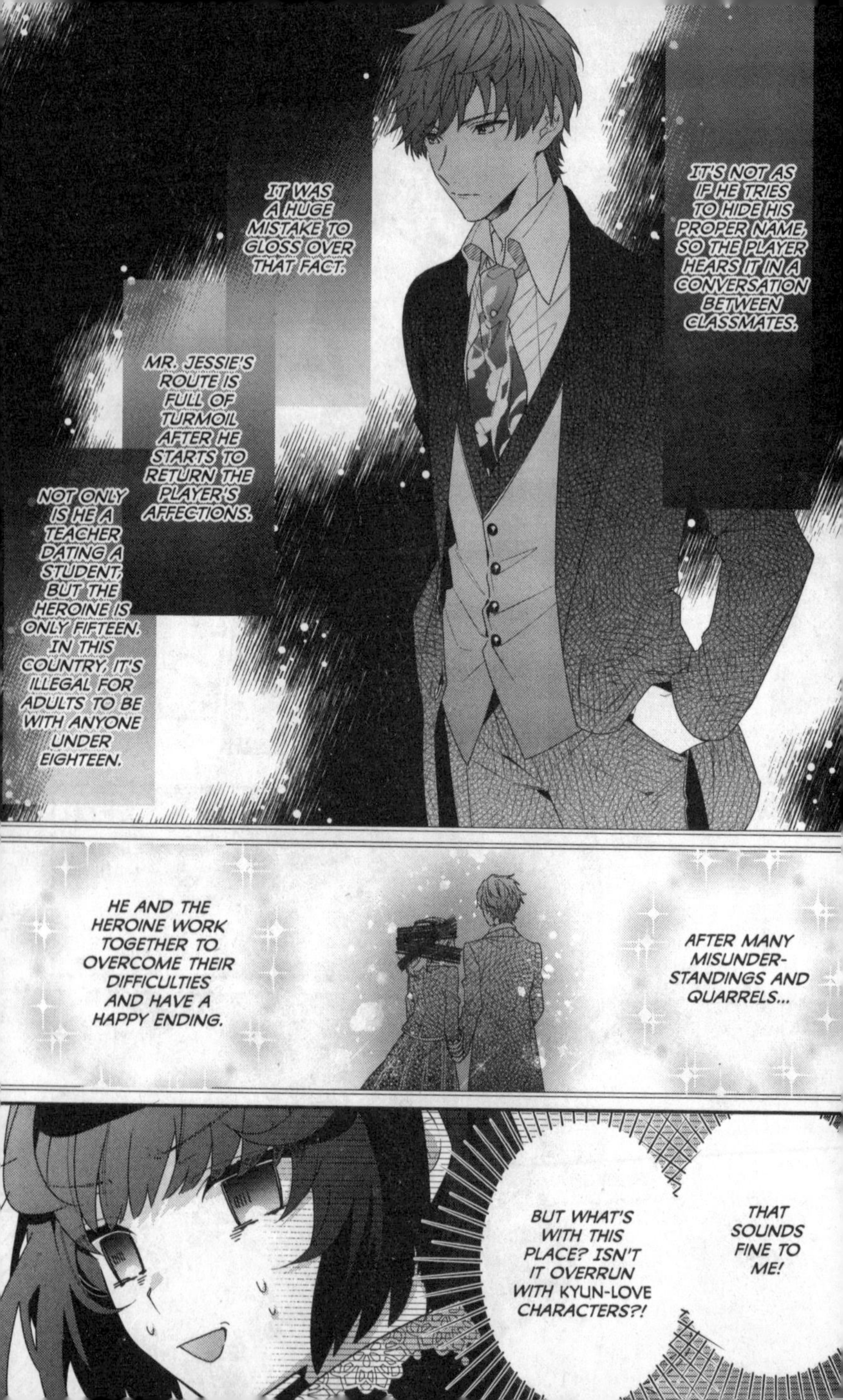
IT'S NOT AS IF HE TRIES TO HIDE HIS PROPER NAME, SO THE PLAYER HEARS IT IN A CONVERSATION BETWEEN CLASSMATES.
IT WAS A HUGE MISTAKE TO GLOSS OVER THAT FACT.
MR. JESSIE'S ROUTE IS FULL OF TURMOIL AFTER HE STARTS TO RETURN THE PLAYER'S AFFECTIONS.
NOT ONLY IS HE A TEACHER DATING A STUDENT, BUT THE HEROINE IS ONLY FIFTEEN. IN THIS COUNTRY, IT'S ILLEGAL FOR ADULTS TO BE WITH ANYONE UNDER EIGHTEEN.
AFTER MANY MISUNDER-STANDINGS AND QUARRELS...
HE AND THE HEROINE WORK TOGETHER TO OVERCOME THEIR DIFFICULTIES AND HAVE A HAPPY ENDING.
THAT SOUNDS FINE TO ME!
BUT WHAT'S WITH THIS PLACE? ISN'T IT OVERRUN WITH KYUN-LOVE CHARACTERS?!

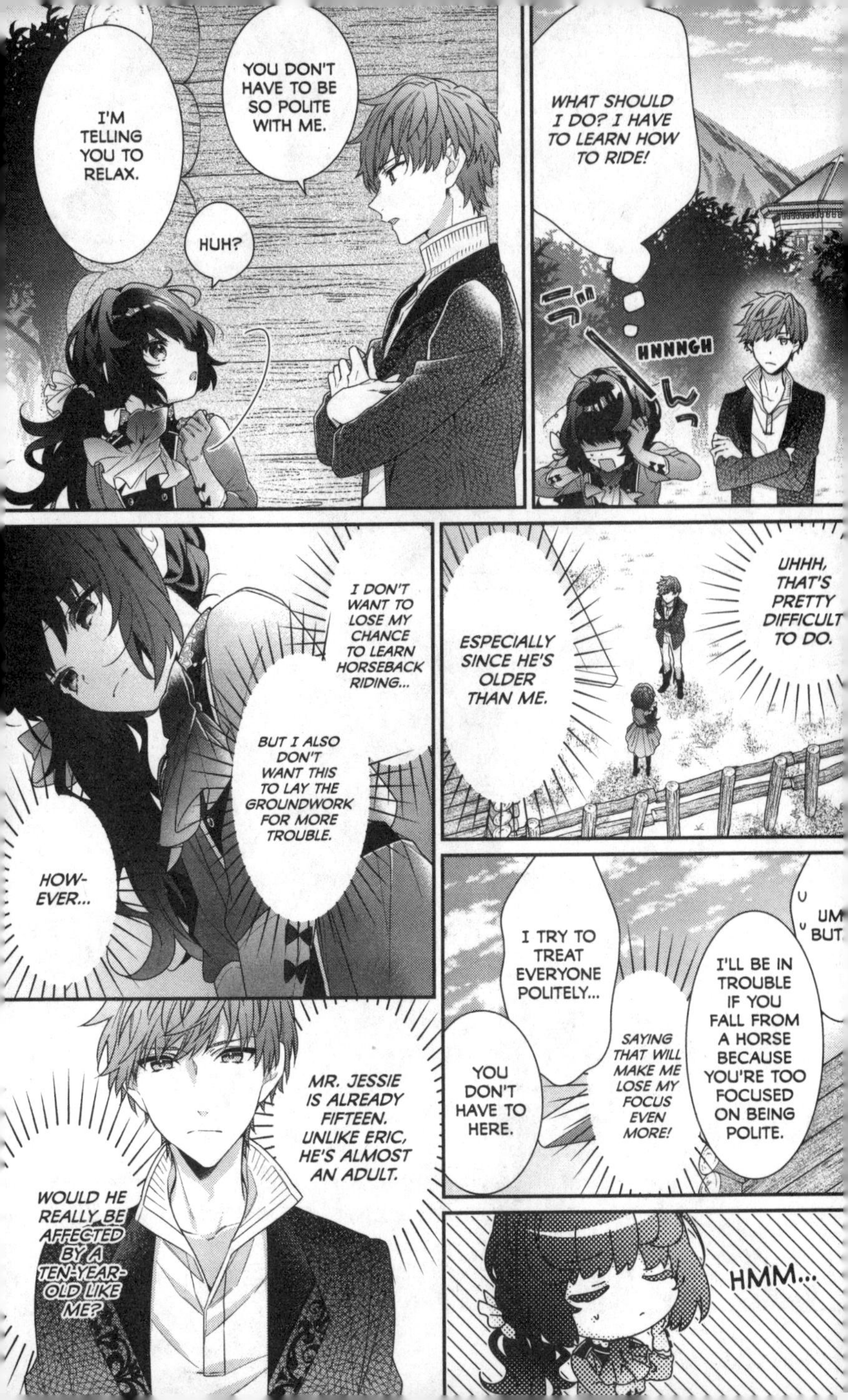
WHAT SHOULD I DO? I HAVE TO LEARN HOW TO RIDE!
HNNNGH
YOU DON'T HAVE TO BE SO POLITE WITH ME.
I'M TELLING YOU TO RELAX.
HUH?
UHHH, THAT'S PRETTY DIFFICULT TO DO.
ESPECIALLY SINCE HE'S OLDER THAN ME.
I DON'T WANT TO LOSE MY CHANCE TO LEARN HORSEBACK RIDING...
BUT I ALSO DON'T WANT THIS TO LAY THE GROUNDWORK FOR MORE TROUBLE.
HOW-EVER...
UM BUT.
I TRY TO TREAT EVERYONE POLITELY...
YOU DON'T HAVE TO HERE.
I'LL BE IN TROUBLE IF YOU FALL FROM A HORSE BECAUSE YOU'RE TOO FOCUSED ON BEING POLITE.
SAYING THAT WILL MAKE ME LOSE MY FOCUS EVEN MORE!
HMM...
MR. JESSIE IS ALREADY FIFTEEN. UNLIKE ERIC, HE'S ALMOST AN ADULT.
WOULD HE REALLY BE AFFECTED BY A TEN-YEAR-OLD LIKE ME?

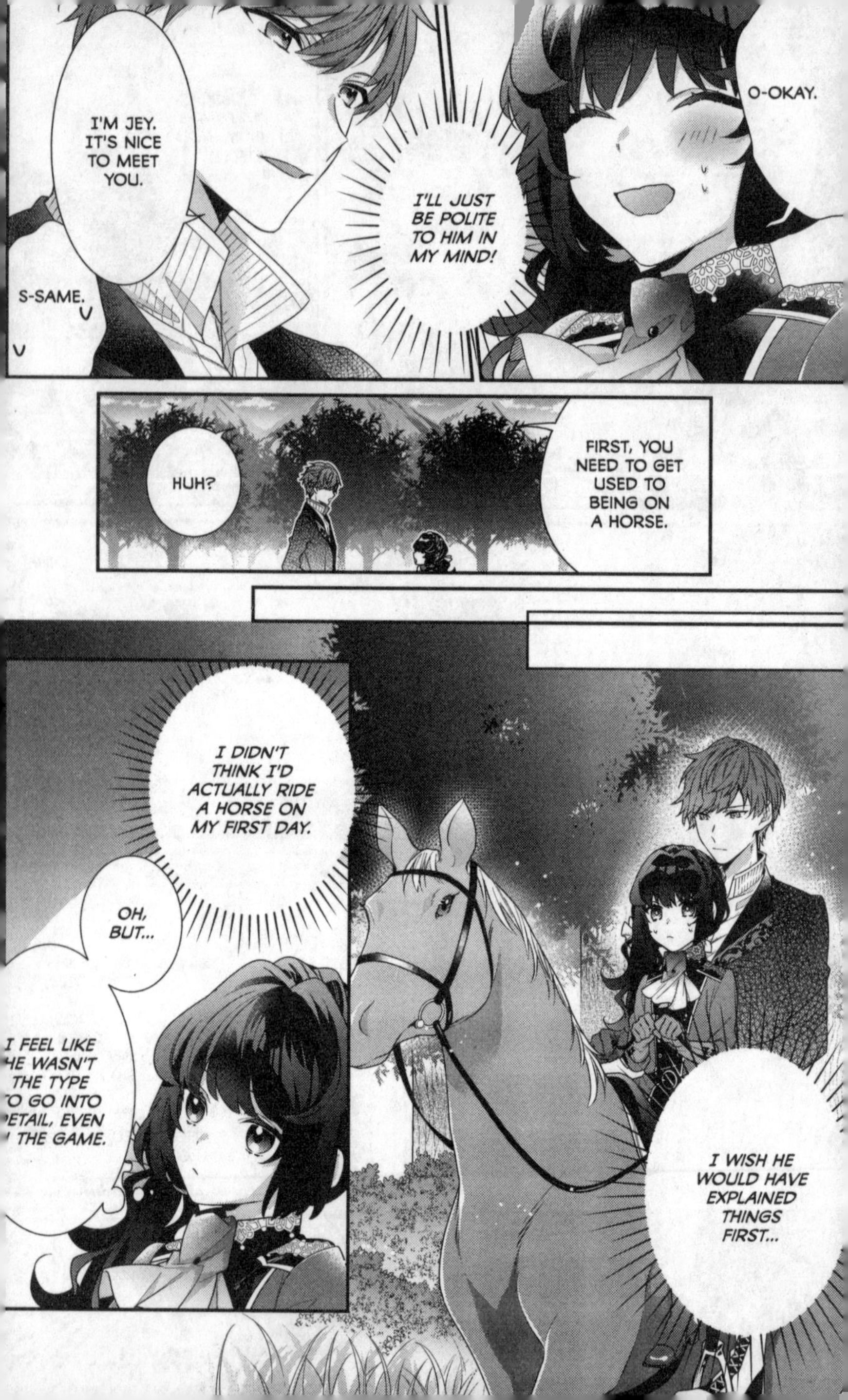
O-OKAY.
I'LL JUST BE POLITE TO HIM IN MY MIND!
I'M JEY. IT'S NICE TO MEET YOU.
S-SAME.
FIRST, YOU NEED TO GET USED TO BEING ON A HORSE.
HUH?
I DIDN'T THINK I'D ACTUALLY RIDE A HORSE ON MY FIRST DAY.
I WISH HE WOULD HAVE EXPLAINED THINGS FIRST...
OH, BUT...
I FEEL LIKE HE WASN'T THE TYPE TO GO INTO DETAIL, EVEN IN THE GAME.

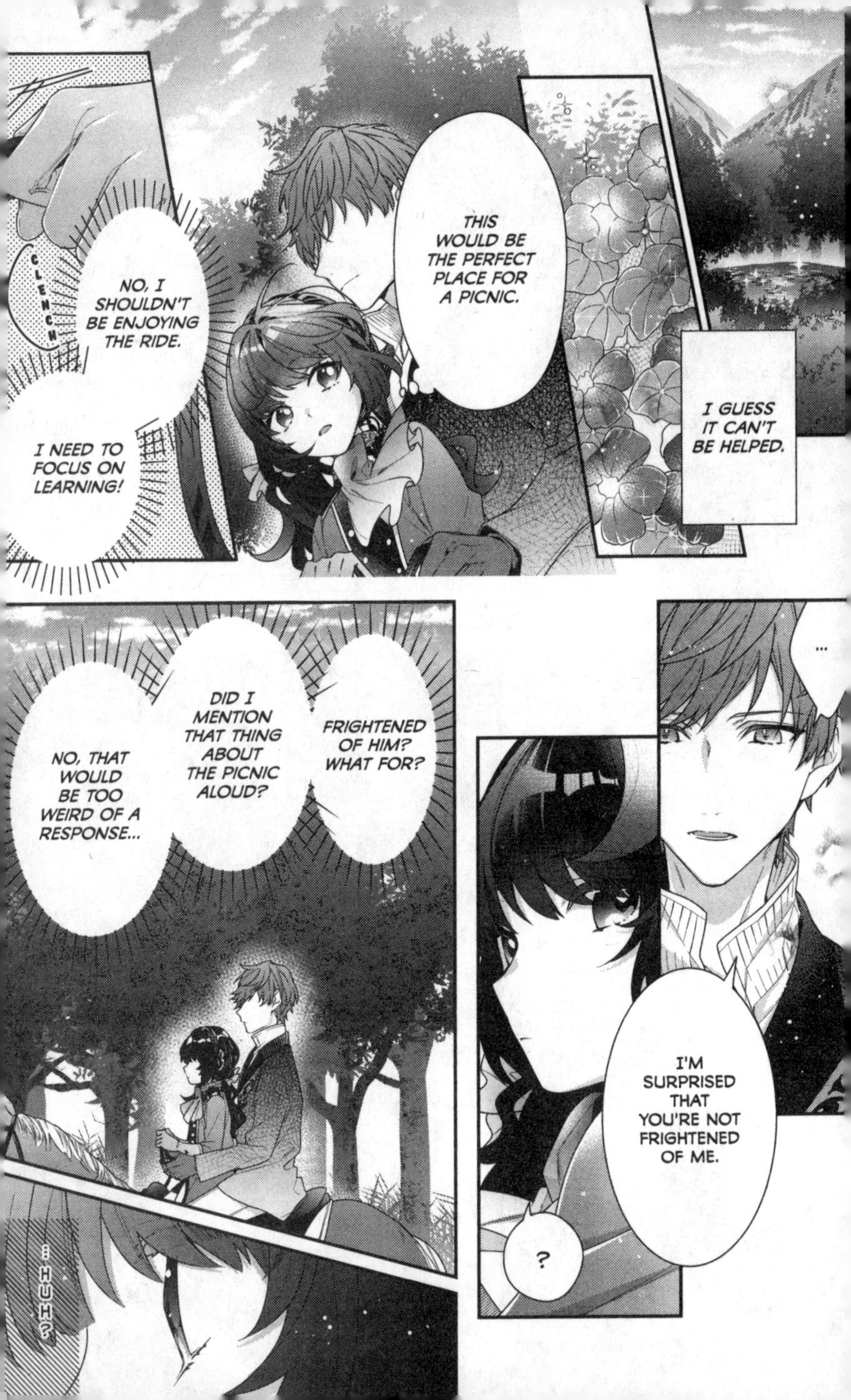
I GUESS IT CAN'T BE HELPED.
THIS WOULD BE THE PERFECT PLACE FOR A PICNIC.
NO, I SHOULDN'T BE ENJOYING THE RIDE.
CLENCH
I NEED TO FOCUS ON LEARNING!
...
I'M SURPRISED THAT YOU'RE NOT FRIGHTENED OF ME.
?
FRIGHTENED OF HIM? WHAT FOR?
DID I MENTION THAT THING ABOUT THE PICNIC ALOUD?
NO, THAT WOULD BE TOO WEIRD OF A RESPONSE...
...HUH?

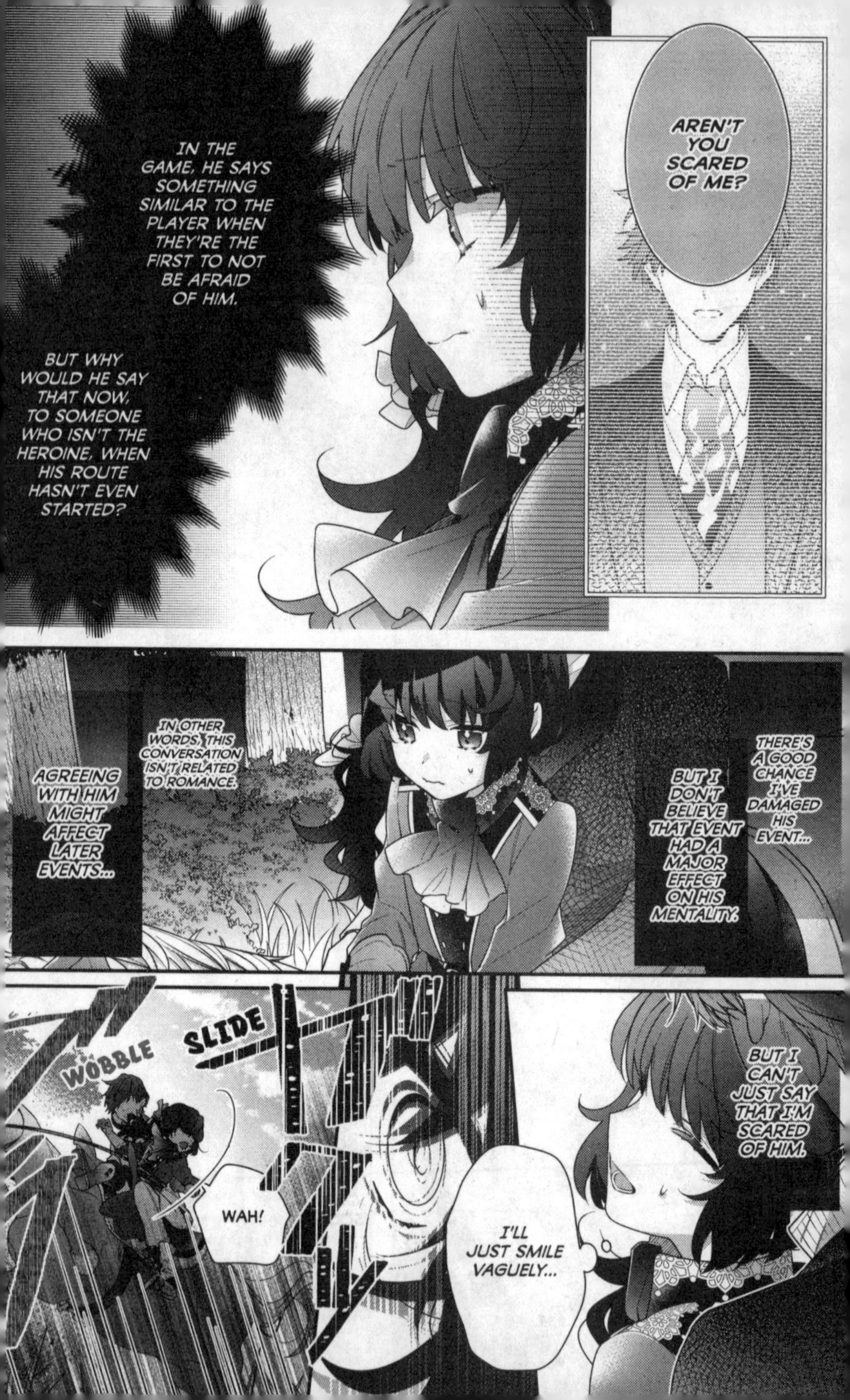
AREN'T YOU SCARED OF ME?
IN THE GAME, HE SAYS SOMETHING SIMILAR TO THE PLAYER WHEN THEY'RE THE FIRST TO NOT BE AFRAID OF HIM.
BUT WHY WOULD HE SAY THAT NOW, TO SOMEONE WHO ISN'T THE HEROINE, WHEN HIS ROUTE HASN'T EVEN STARTED?
THERE'S A GOOD CHANCE I'VE DAMAGED HIS EVENT...
BUT I DON'T BELIEVE THAT EVENT HAD A MAJOR EFFECT ON HIS MENTALITY.
IN OTHER WORDS, THIS CONVERSATION ISN'T RELATED TO ROMANCE.
AGREEING WITH HIM MIGHT AFFECT LATER EVENTS...
BUT I CAN'T JUST SAY THAT I'M SCARED OF HIM.
I'LL JUST SMILE VAGUELY...
SLIDE
WOBBLE
WAH!

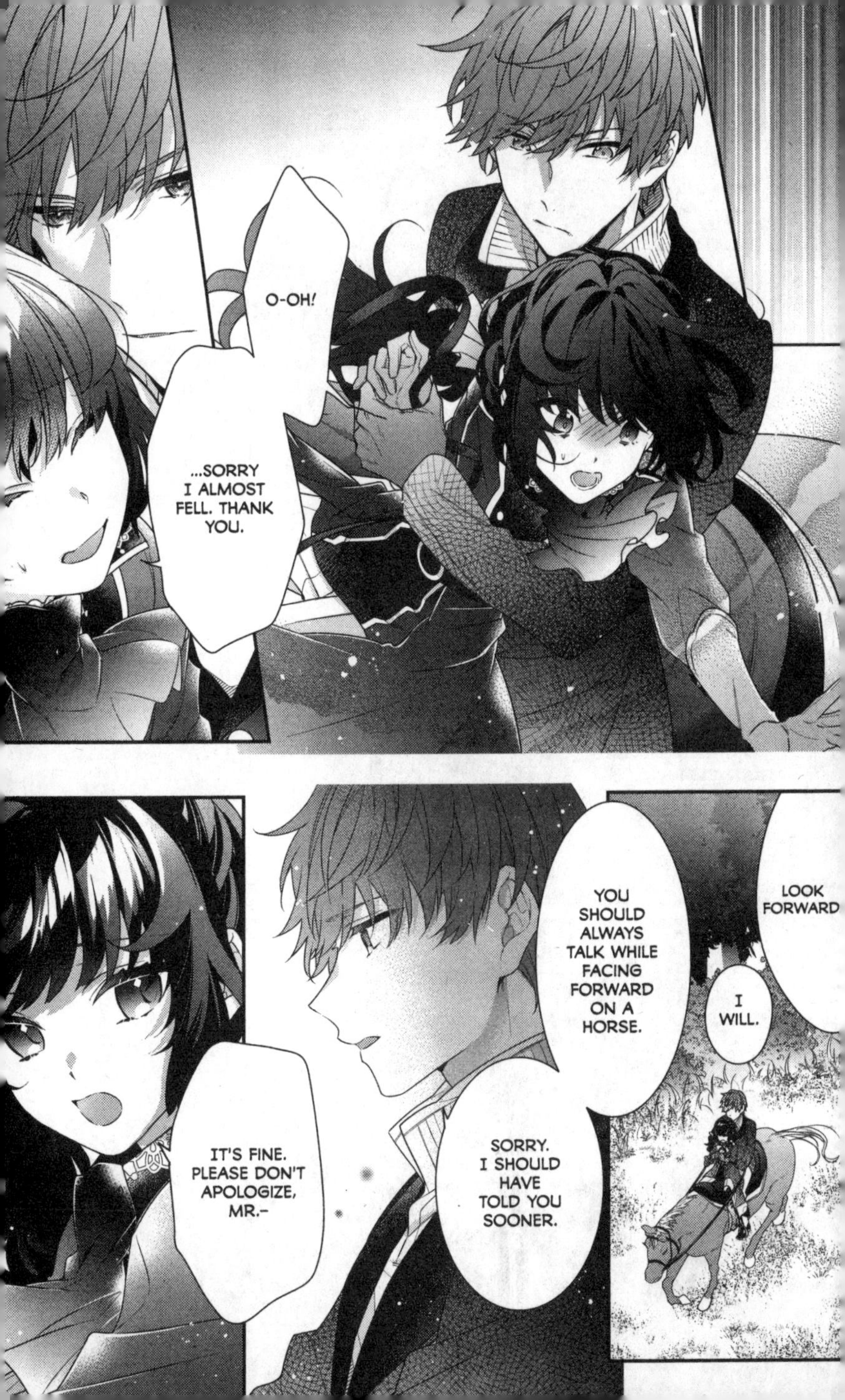
O-OH!
...SORRY I ALMOST FELL. THANK YOU.
LOOK FORWARD
I WILL.
YOU SHOULD ALWAYS TALK WHILE FACING FORWARD ON A HORSE.
SORRY. I SHOULD HAVE TOLD YOU SOONER.
IT'S FINE. PLEASE DON'T APOLOGIZE, MR.-

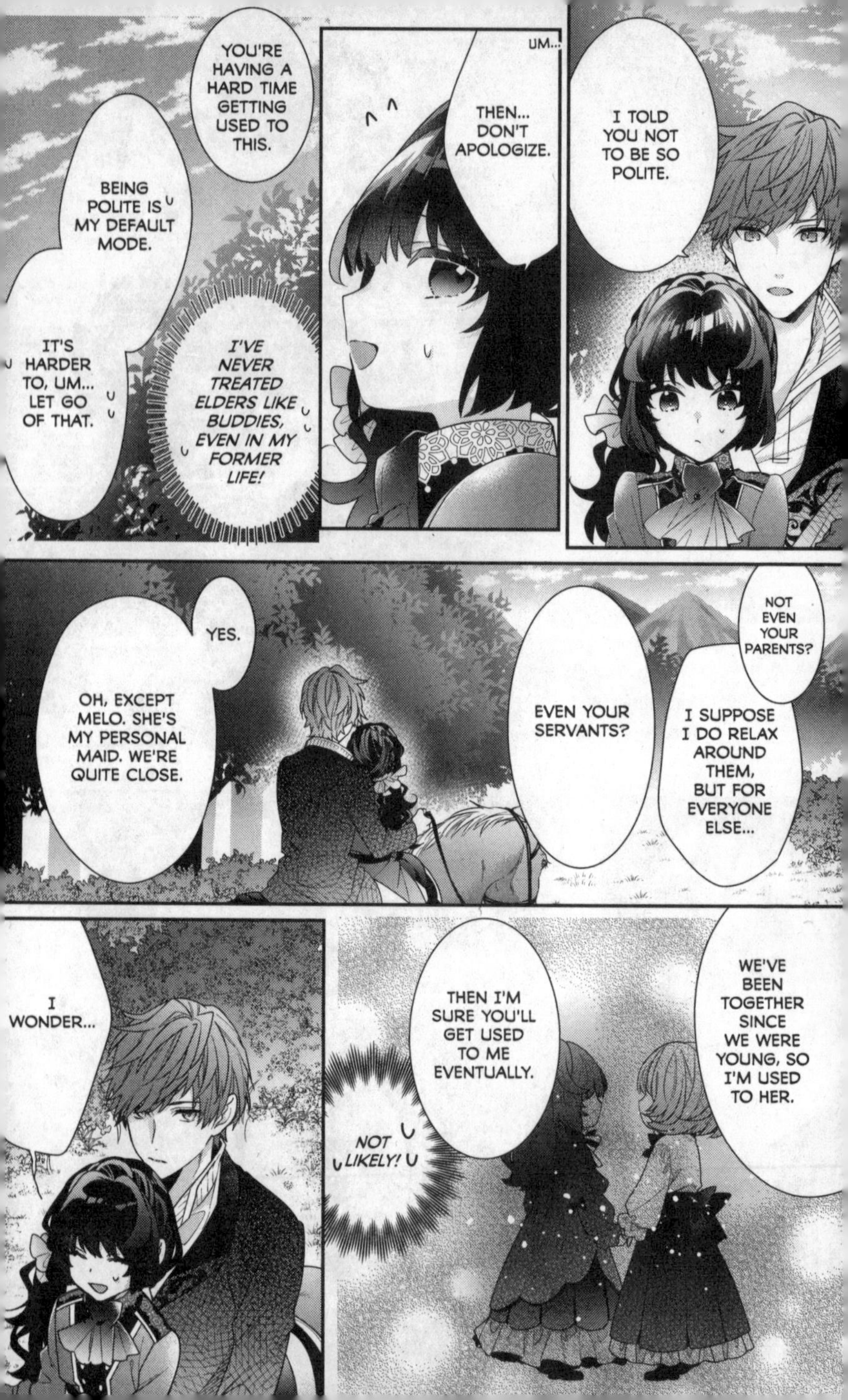

I TOLD YOU NOT TO BE SO POLITE.
UM...
THEN... DON'T APOLOGIZE.
YOU'RE HAVING A HARD TIME GETTING USED TO THIS.
BEING POLITE IS MY DEFAULT MODE.
IT'S HARDER TO, UM... LET GO OF THAT.
I'VE NEVER TREATED ELDERS LIKE BUDDIES, EVEN IN MY FORMER LIFE!
NOT EVEN YOUR PARENTS?
I SUPPOSE I DO RELAX AROUND THEM, BUT FOR EVERYONE ELSE...
EVEN YOUR SERVANTS?
YES.
OH, EXCEPT MELO. SHE'S MY PERSONAL MAID. WE'RE QUITE CLOSE.
WE'VE BEEN TOGETHER SINCE WE WERE YOUNG, SO I'M USED TO HER.
THEN I'M SURE YOU'LL GET USED TO ME EVENTUALLY.
NOT LIKELY!
I WONDER...

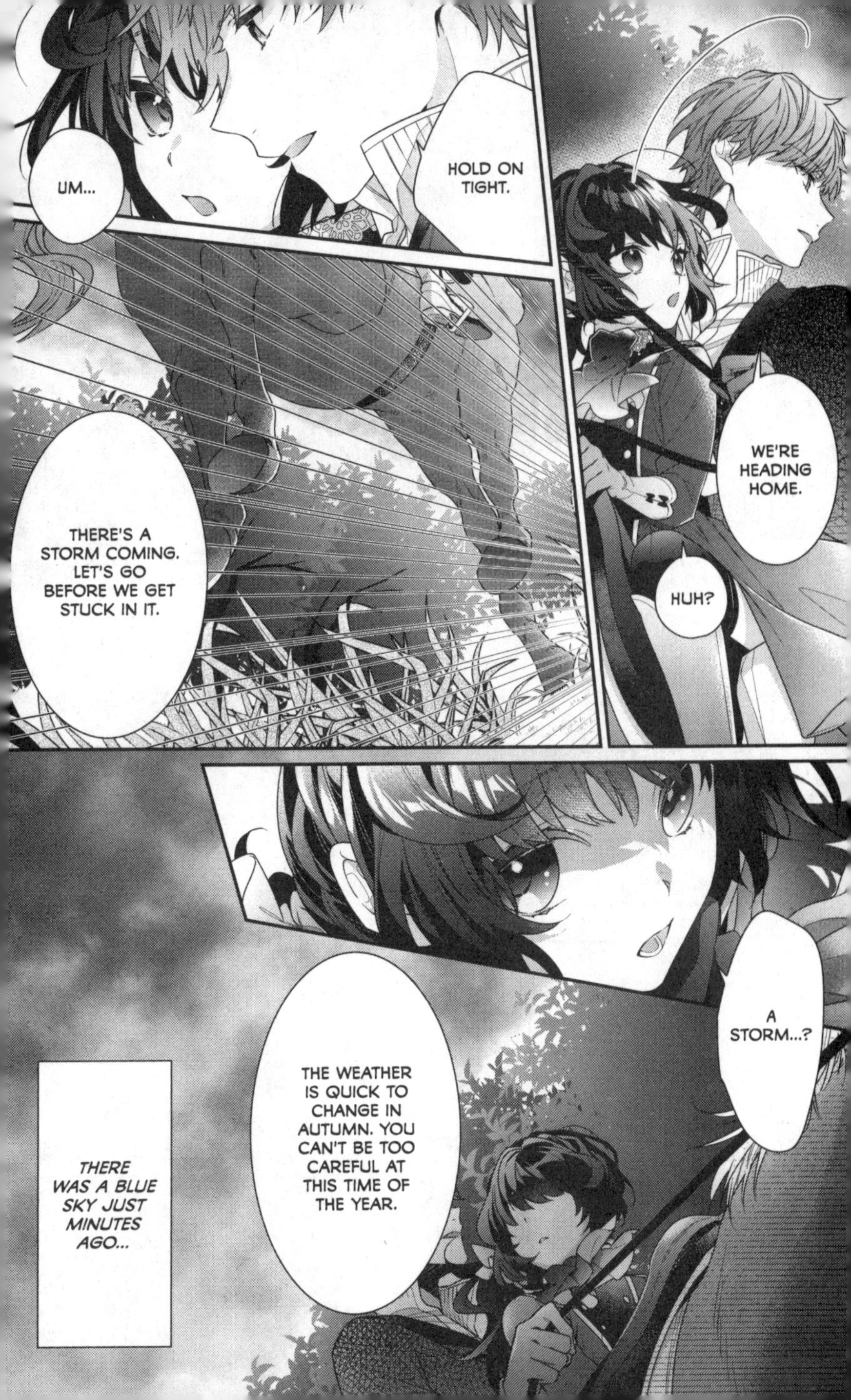
WE'RE HEADING HOME.
HUH?
HOLD ON TIGHT.
UM...
THERE'S A STORM COMING. LET'S GO BEFORE WE GET STUCK IN IT.
A STORM...?
THE WEATHER IS QUICK TO CHANGE IN AUTUMN. YOU CAN'T BE TOO CAREFUL AT THIS TIME OF THE YEAR.
THERE WAS A BLUE SKY JUST MINUTES AGO...

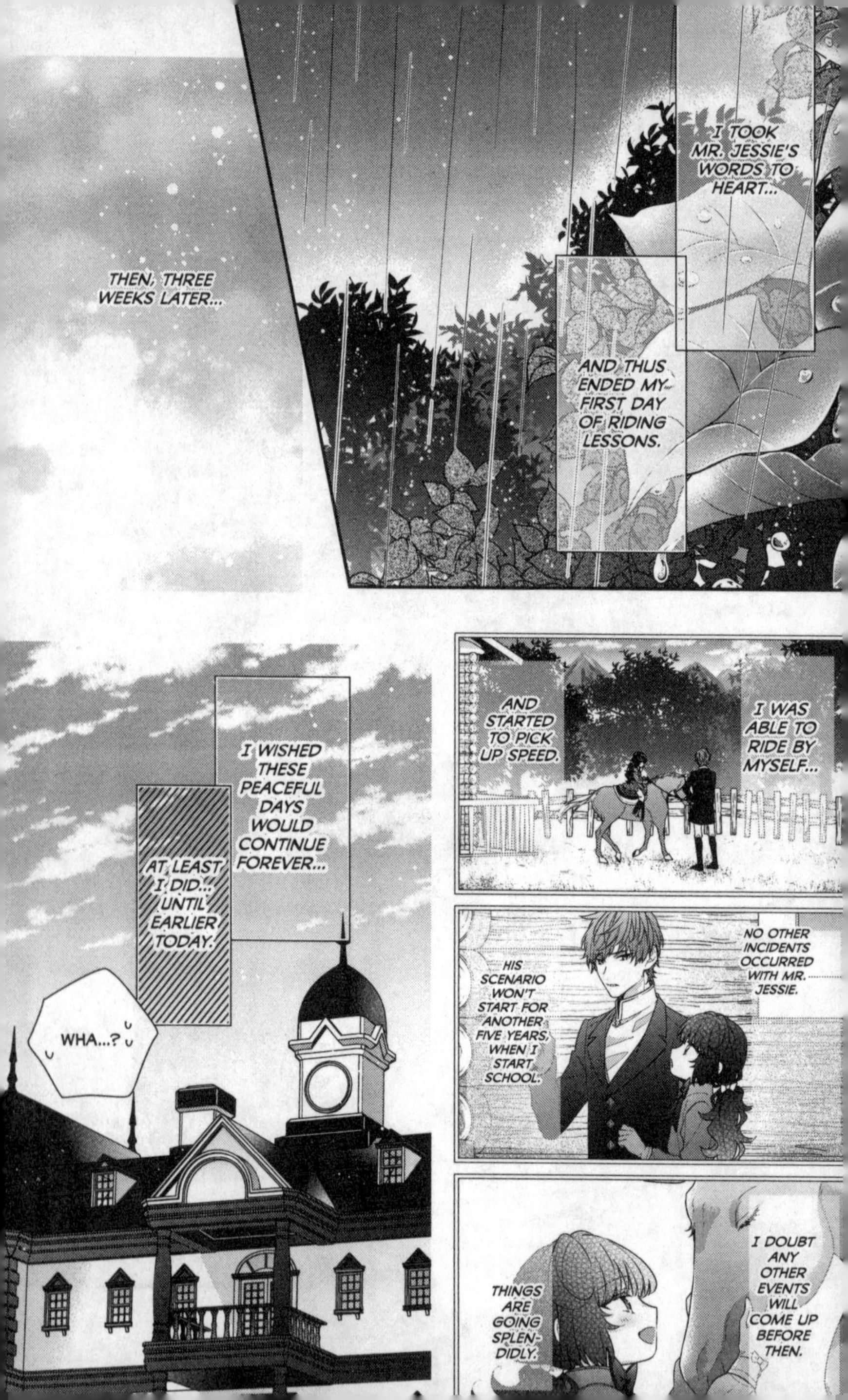
I TOOK MR. JESSIE'S WORDS TO HEART...
AND THUS ENDED MY FIRST DAY OF RIDING LESSONS.
THEN, THREE WEEKS LATER...
I WAS ABLE TO RIDE BY MYSELF...
AND STARTED TO PICK UP SPEED.
NO OTHER INCIDENTS OCCURRED WITH MR. JESSIE.
HIS SCENARIO WON'T START FOR ANOTHER FIVE YEARS, WHEN I START SCHOOL.
I DOUBT ANY OTHER EVENTS WILL COME UP BEFORE THEN.
THINGS ARE GOING SPLENDIDLY.
I WISHED THESE PEACEFUL DAYS WOULD CONTINUE FOREVER...
AT LEAST I DID... UNTIL EARLIER TODAY.
WHA...?

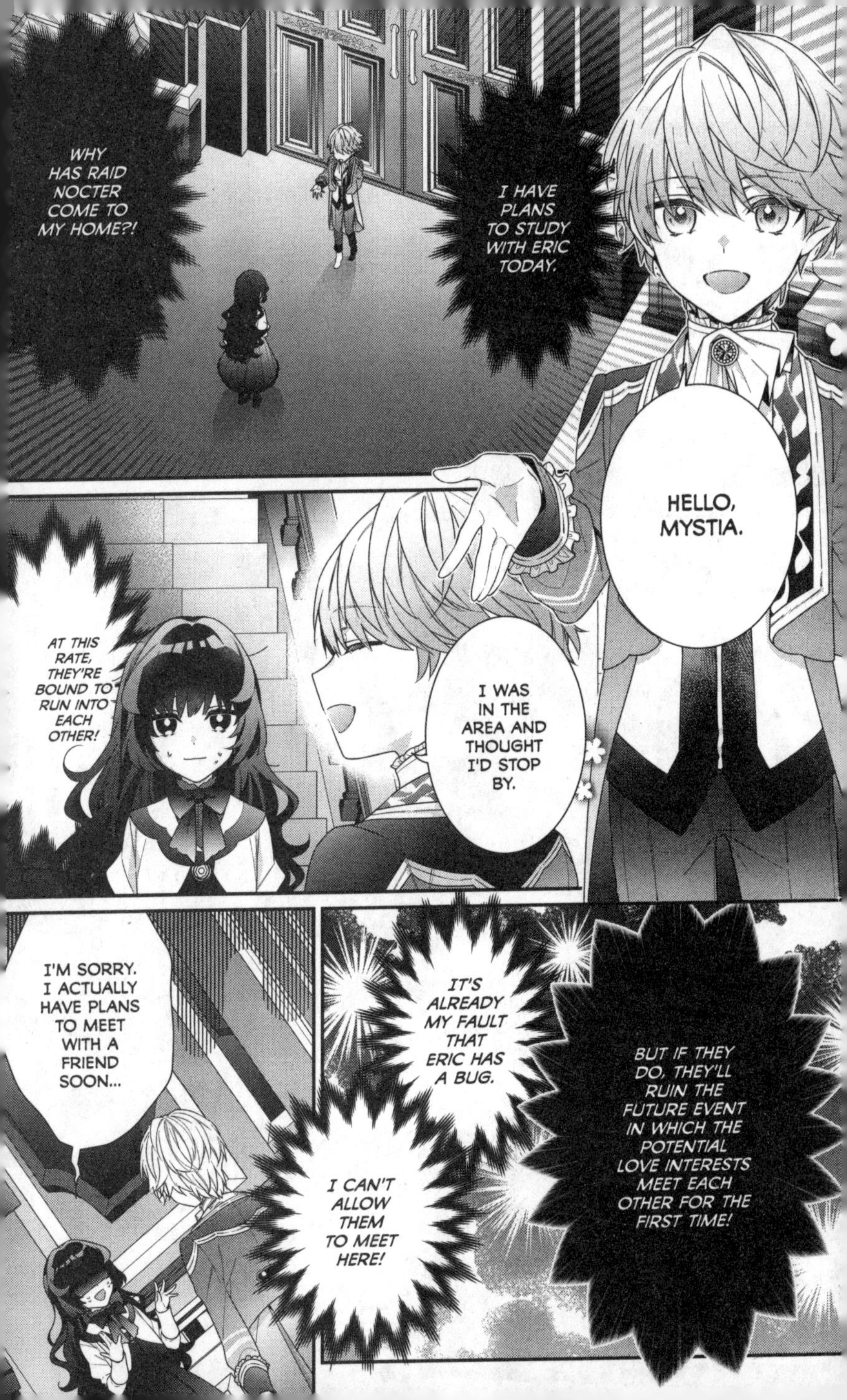
I HAVE PLANS TO STUDY WITH ERIC TODAY.
WHY HAS RAID NOCTER COME TO MY HOME?!
HELLO, MYSTIA.
I WAS IN THE AREA AND THOUGHT I'D STOP BY.
AT THIS RATE, THEY'RE BOUND TO RUN INTO EACH OTHER!
BUT IF THEY DO, THEY'LL RUIN THE FUTURE EVENT IN WHICH THE POTENTIAL LOVE INTERESTS MEET EACH OTHER FOR THE FIRST TIME!
IT'S ALREADY MY FAULT THAT ERIC HAS A BUG.
I CAN'T ALLOW THEM TO MEET HERE!
I'M SORRY. I ACTUALLY HAVE PLANS TO MEET WITH A FRIEND SOON...

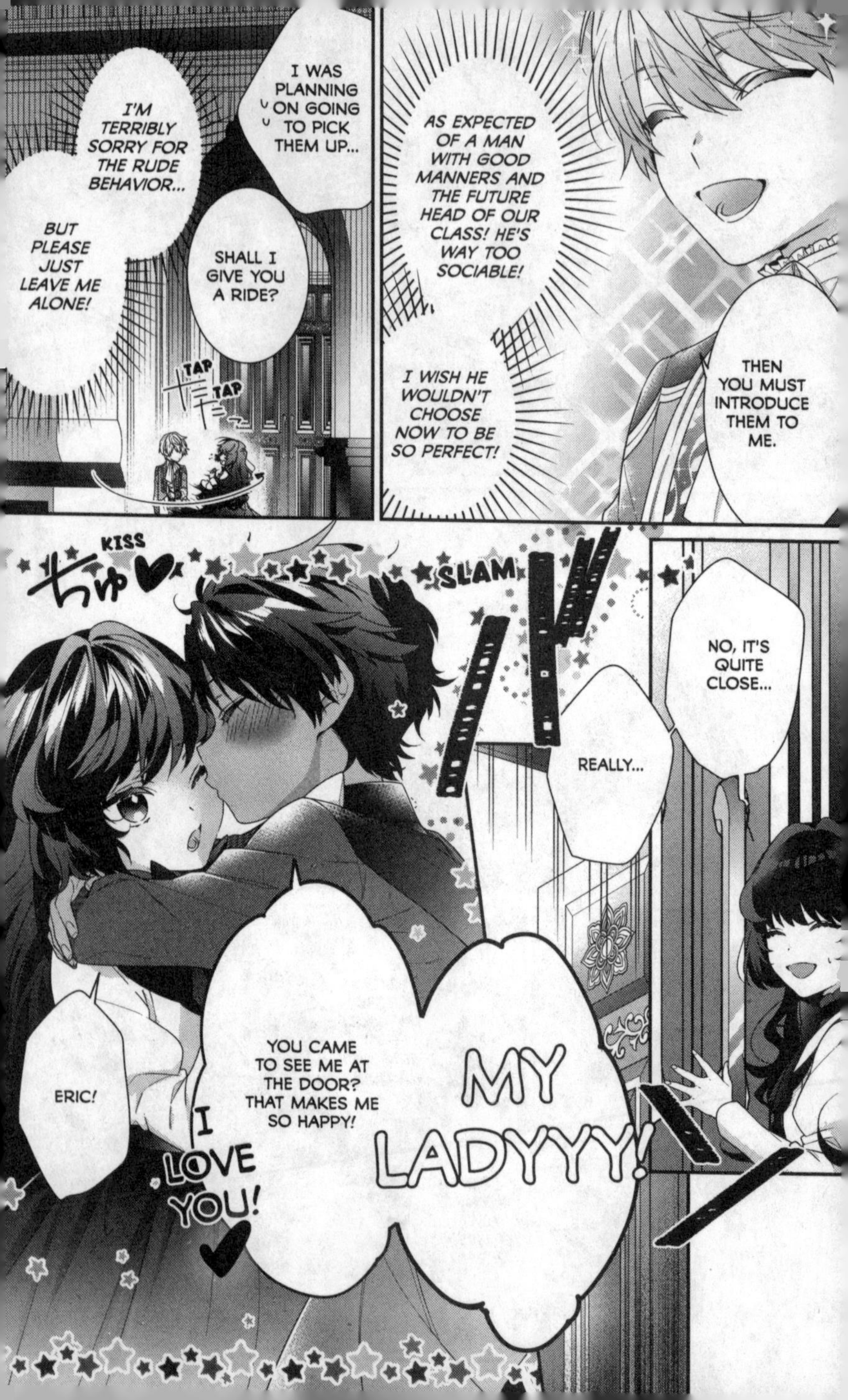
AS EXPECTED OF A MAN WITH GOOD MANNERS AND THE FUTURE HEAD OF OUR CLASS! HE'S WAY TOO SOCIABLE!
THEN YOU MUST INTRODUCE THEM TO ME.
I WISH HE WOULDN'T CHOOSE NOW TO BE SO PERFECT!
I WAS PLANNING ON GOING TO PICK THEM UP...
I'M TERRIBLY SORRY FOR THE RUDE BEHAVIOR...
SHALL I GIVE YOU A RIDE?
BUT PLEASE JUST LEAVE ME ALONE!
TAP
TAP
NO, IT'S QUITE CLOSE...
REALLY...
SLAM
MY LADYYY!
YOU CAME TO SEE ME AT THE DOOR? THAT MAKES ME SO HAPPY!
I LOVE YOU!
KISS
ちゅ
ERIC!

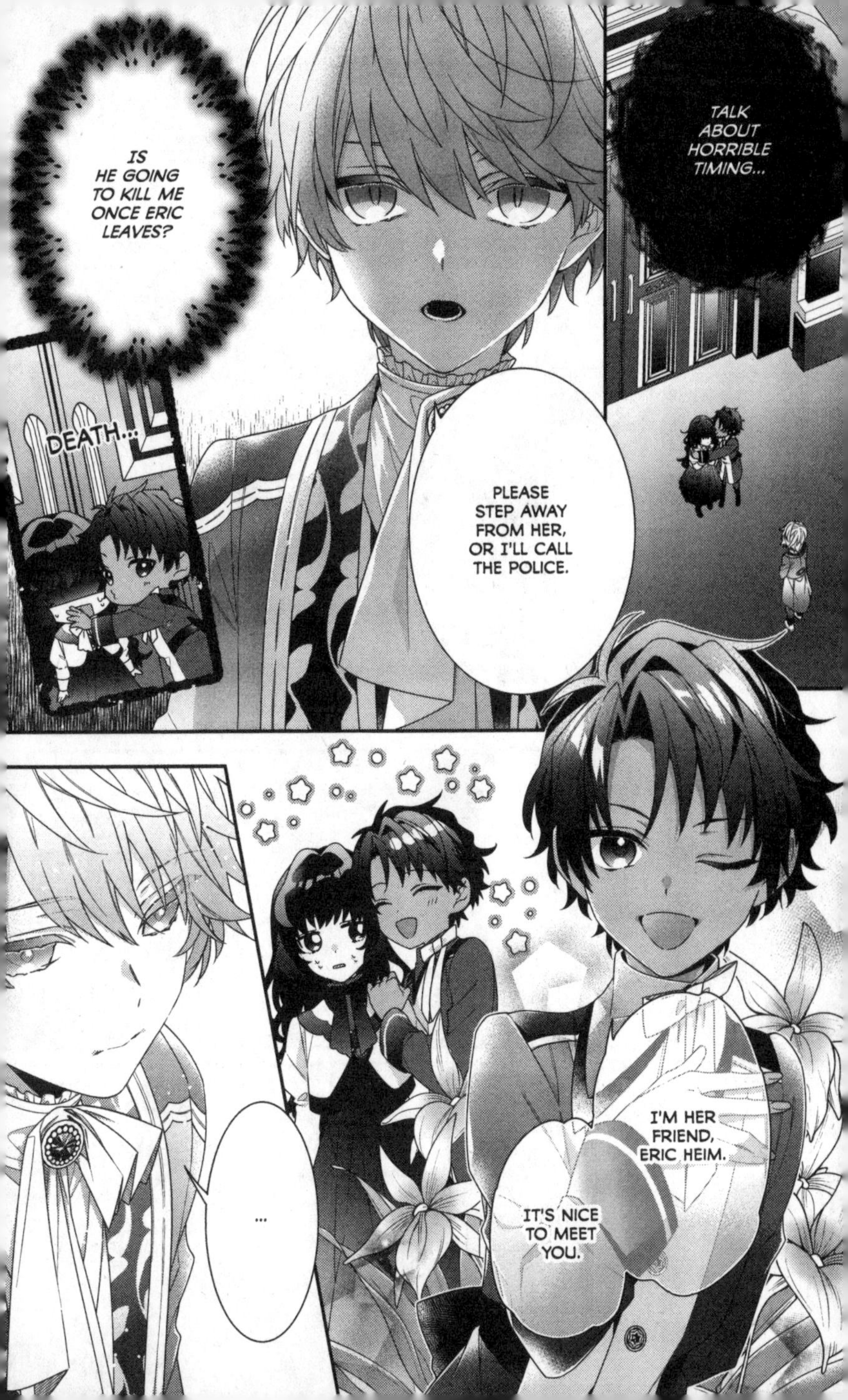
TALK ABOUT HORRIBLE TIMING...
PLEASE STEP AWAY FROM HER, OR I'LL CALL THE POLICE.
IS HE GOING TO KILL ME ONCE ERIC LEAVES?
DEATH...
I'M HER FRIEND, ERIC HEIM.
IT'S NICE TO MEET YOU.
...

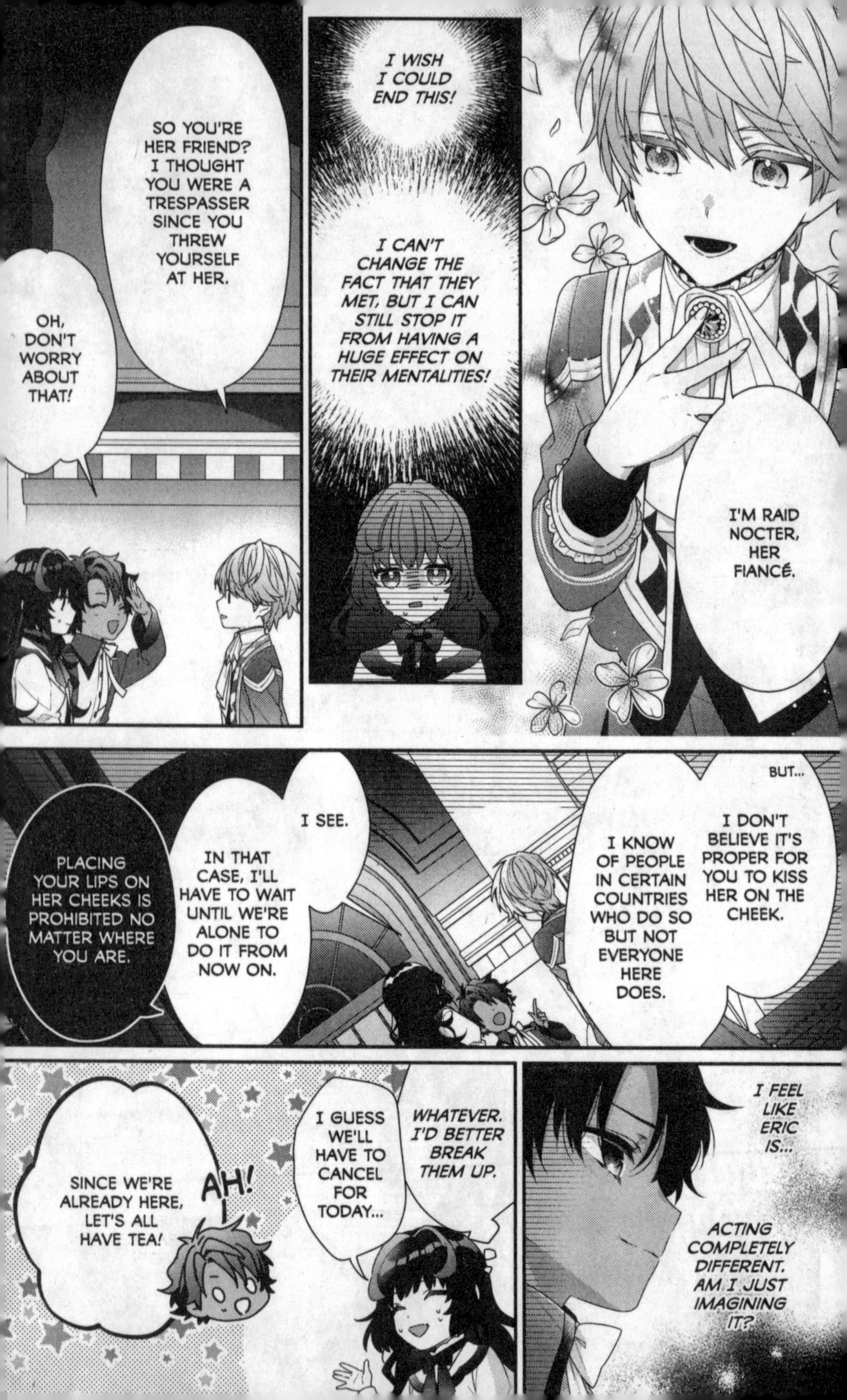
I'M RAID NOCTER, HER FIANCÉ.
I WISH I COULD END THIS!
I CAN'T CHANGE THE FACT THAT THEY MET, BUT I CAN STILL STOP IT FROM HAVING A HUGE EFFECT ON THEIR MENTALITIES!
SO YOU'RE HER FRIEND? I THOUGHT YOU WERE A TRESPASSER SINCE YOU THREW YOURSELF AT HER.
OH, DON'T WORRY ABOUT THAT!
BUT...
I DON'T BELIEVE IT'S PROPER FOR YOU TO KISS HER ON THE CHEEK.
I KNOW OF PEOPLE IN CERTAIN COUNTRIES WHO DO SO BUT NOT EVERYONE HERE DOES.
I SEE.
IN THAT CASE, I'LL HAVE TO WAIT UNTIL WE'RE ALONE TO DO IT FROM NOW ON.
PLACING YOUR LIPS ON HER CHEEKS IS PROHIBITED NO MATTER WHERE YOU ARE.
I FEEL LIKE ERIC IS...
ACTING COMPLETELY DIFFERENT. AM I JUST IMAGINING IT?
WHATEVER. I'D BETTER BREAK THEM UP.
I GUESS WE'LL HAVE TO CANCEL FOR TODAY...
AH!
SINCE WE'RE ALREADY HERE, LET'S ALL HAVE TEA!

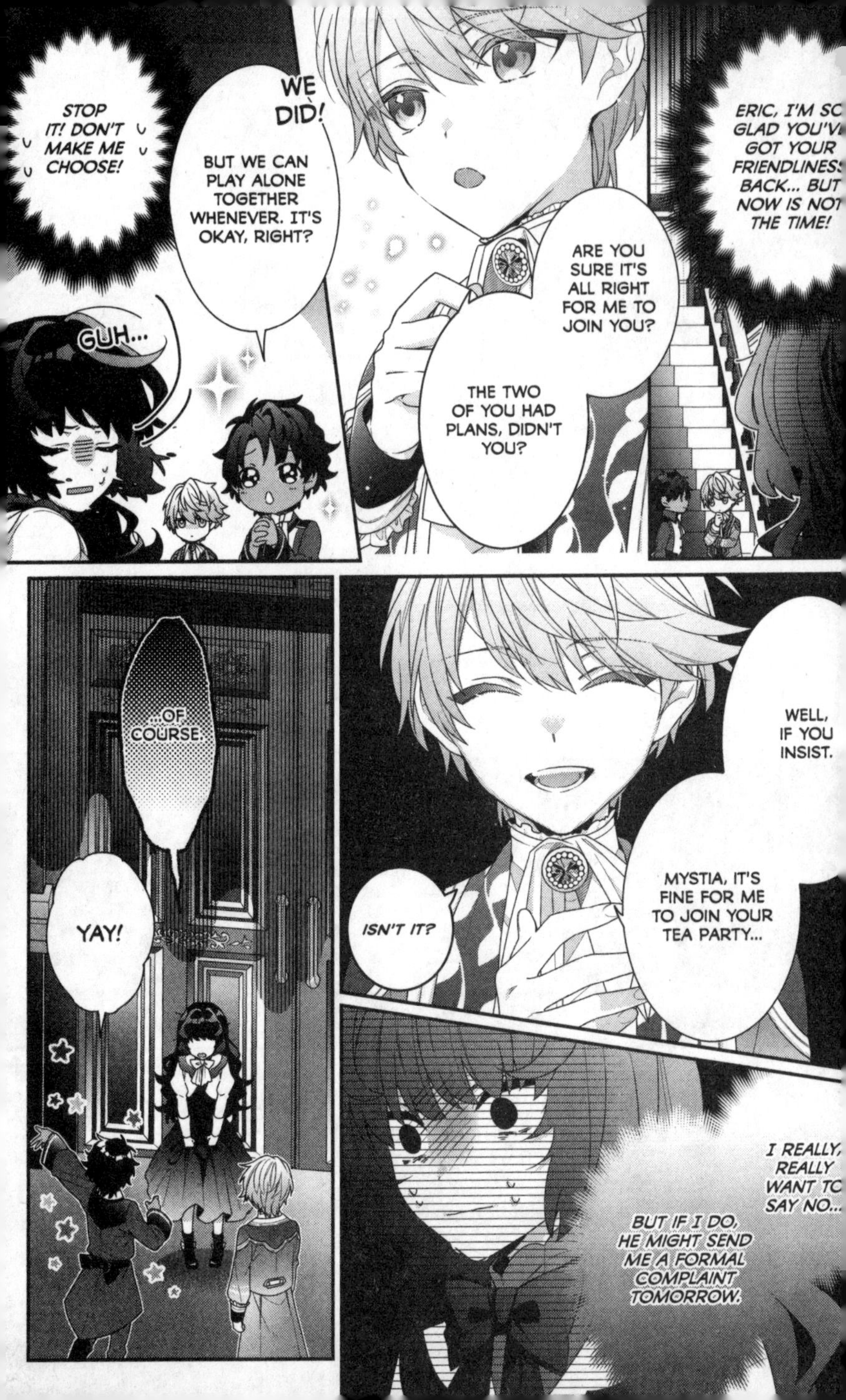
ERIC, I'M SO GLAD YOU'VE GOT YOUR FRIENDLINESS BACK... BUT NOW IS NOT THE TIME!
ARE YOU SURE IT'S ALL RIGHT FOR ME TO JOIN YOU?
THE TWO OF YOU HAD PLANS, DIDN'T YOU?
WE DID!
BUT WE CAN PLAY ALONE TOGETHER WHENEVER. IT'S OKAY, RIGHT?
STOP IT! DON'T MAKE ME CHOOSE!
GUH...
WELL, IF YOU INSIST.
MYSTIA, IT'S FINE FOR ME TO JOIN YOUR TEA PARTY...
ISN'T IT?
I REALLY, REALLY WANT TO SAY NO...
BUT IF I DO, HE MIGHT SEND ME A FORMAL COMPLAINT TOMORROW.
...OF COURSE.
YAY!

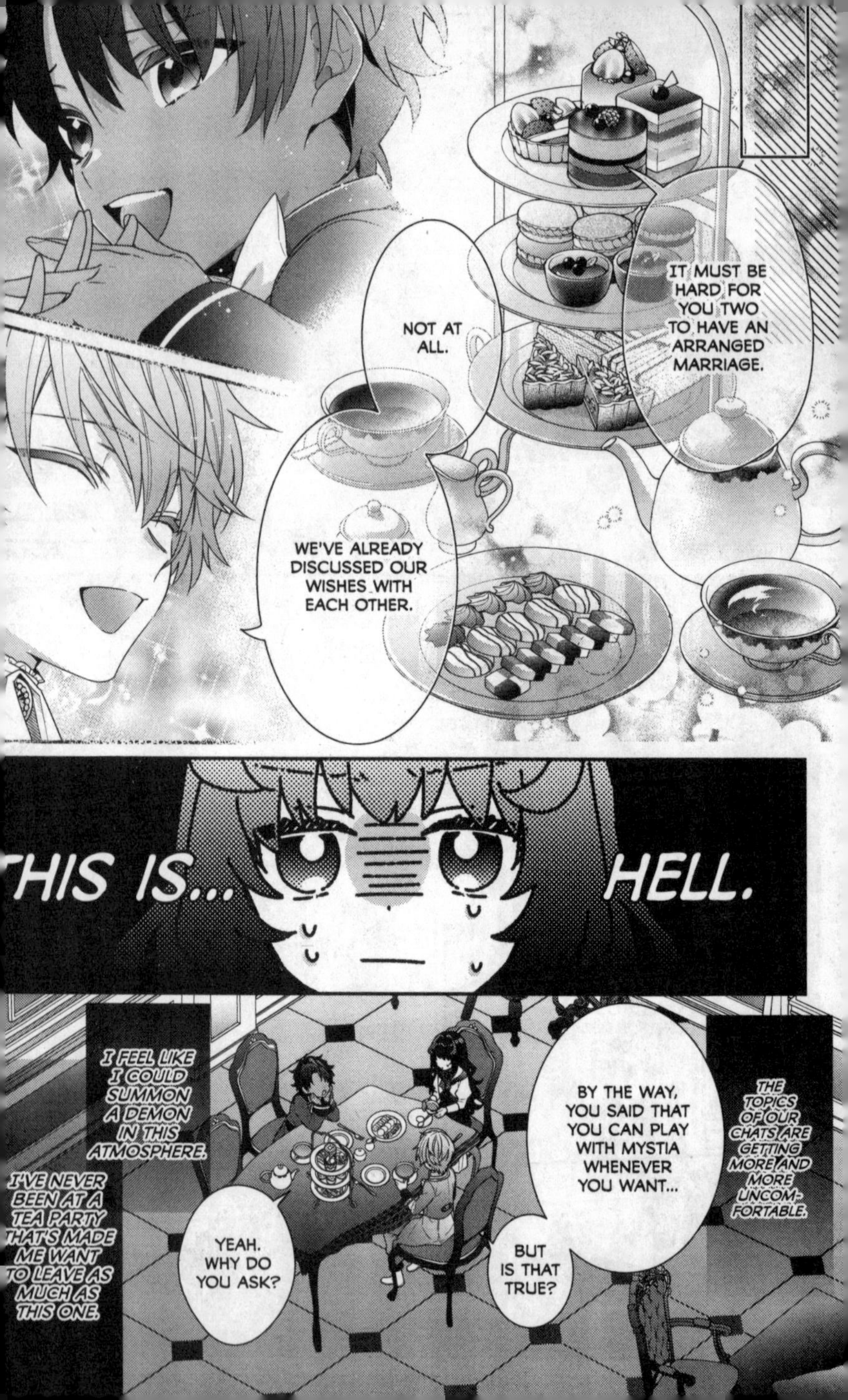
IT MUST BE HARD FOR YOU TWO TO HAVE AN ARRANGED MARRIAGE.
NOT AT ALL.
WE'VE ALREADY DISCUSSED OUR WISHES WITH EACH OTHER.
THIS IS... HELL.
THE TOPICS OF OUR CHATS ARE GETTING MORE AND MORE UNCOM-FORTABLE.
BY THE WAY, YOU SAID THAT YOU CAN PLAY WITH MYSTIA WHENEVER YOU WANT...
BUT IS THAT TRUE?
YEAH. WHY DO YOU ASK?
I FEEL LIKE I COULD SUMMON A DEMON IN THIS ATMOSPHERE.
I'VE NEVER BEEN AT A TEA PARTY THAT'S MADE ME WANT TO LEAVE AS MUCH AS THIS ONE.

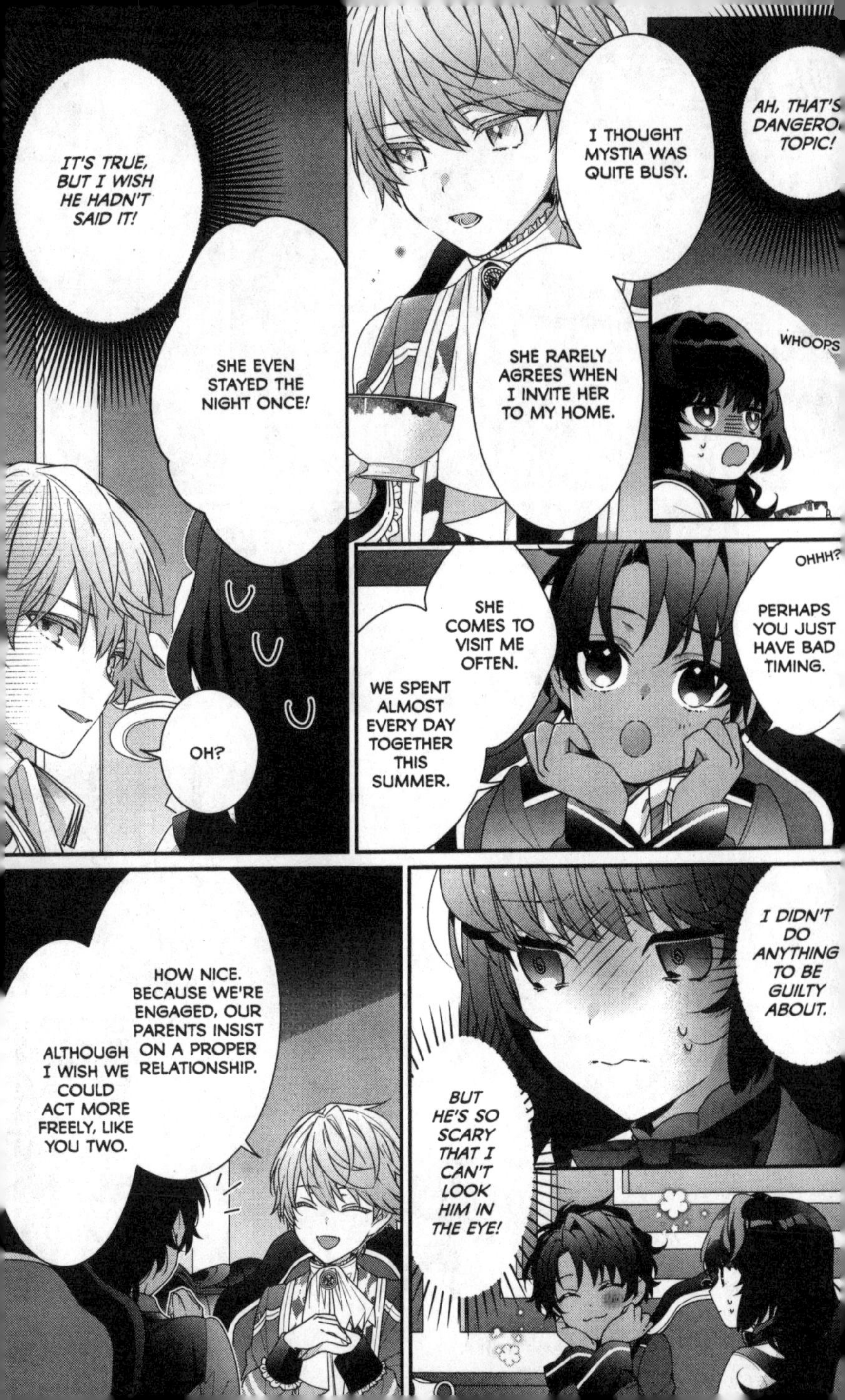
AH, THAT'S DANGERO TOPIC!
WHOOPS
I THOUGHT MYSTIA WAS QUITE BUSY.
SHE RARELY AGREES WHEN I INVITE HER TO MY HOME.
IT'S TRUE, BUT I WISH HE HADN'T SAID IT!
SHE EVEN STAYED THE NIGHT ONCE!
OH?
OHHH?
PERHAPS YOU JUST HAVE BAD TIMING.
SHE COMES TO VISIT ME OFTEN.
WE SPENT ALMOST EVERY DAY TOGETHER THIS SUMMER.
I DIDN'T DO ANYTHING TO BE GUILTY ABOUT.
BUT HE'S SO SCARY THAT I CAN'T LOOK HIM IN THE EYE!
HOW NICE. BECAUSE WE'RE ENGAGED, OUR PARENTS INSIST ON A PROPER RELATIONSHIP.
ALTHOUGH I WISH WE COULD ACT MORE FREELY, LIKE YOU TWO.

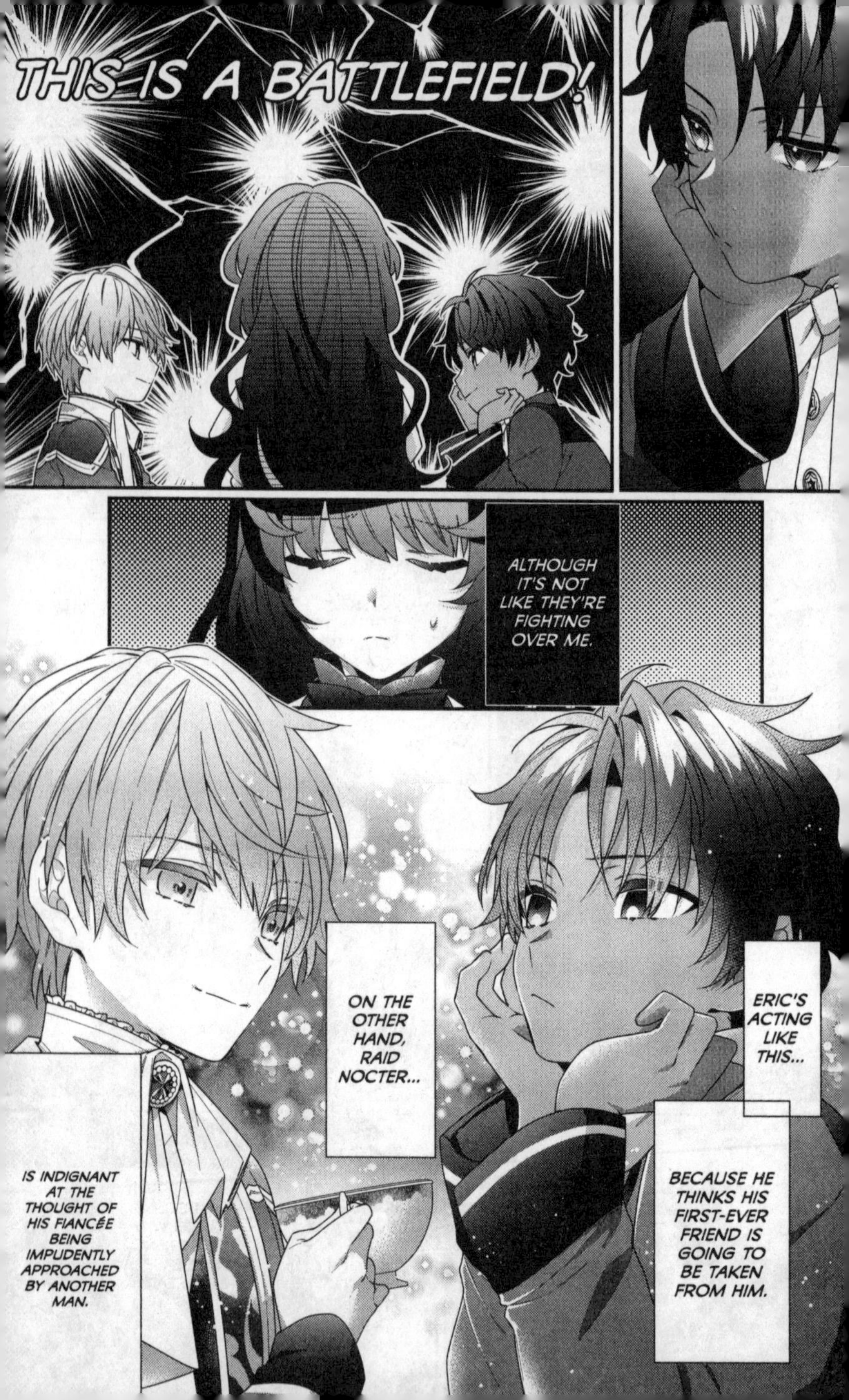
THIS IS A BATTLEFIELD!
ALTHOUGH IT'S NOT LIKE THEY'RE FIGHTING OVER ME.
ERIC'S ACTING LIKE THIS...
BECAUSE HE THINKS HIS FIRST-EVER FRIEND IS GOING TO BE TAKEN FROM HIM.
ON THE OTHER HAND, RAID NOCTER...
IS INDIGNANT AT THE THOUGHT OF HIS FIANCÉE BEING IMPUDENTLY APPROACHED BY ANOTHER MAN.

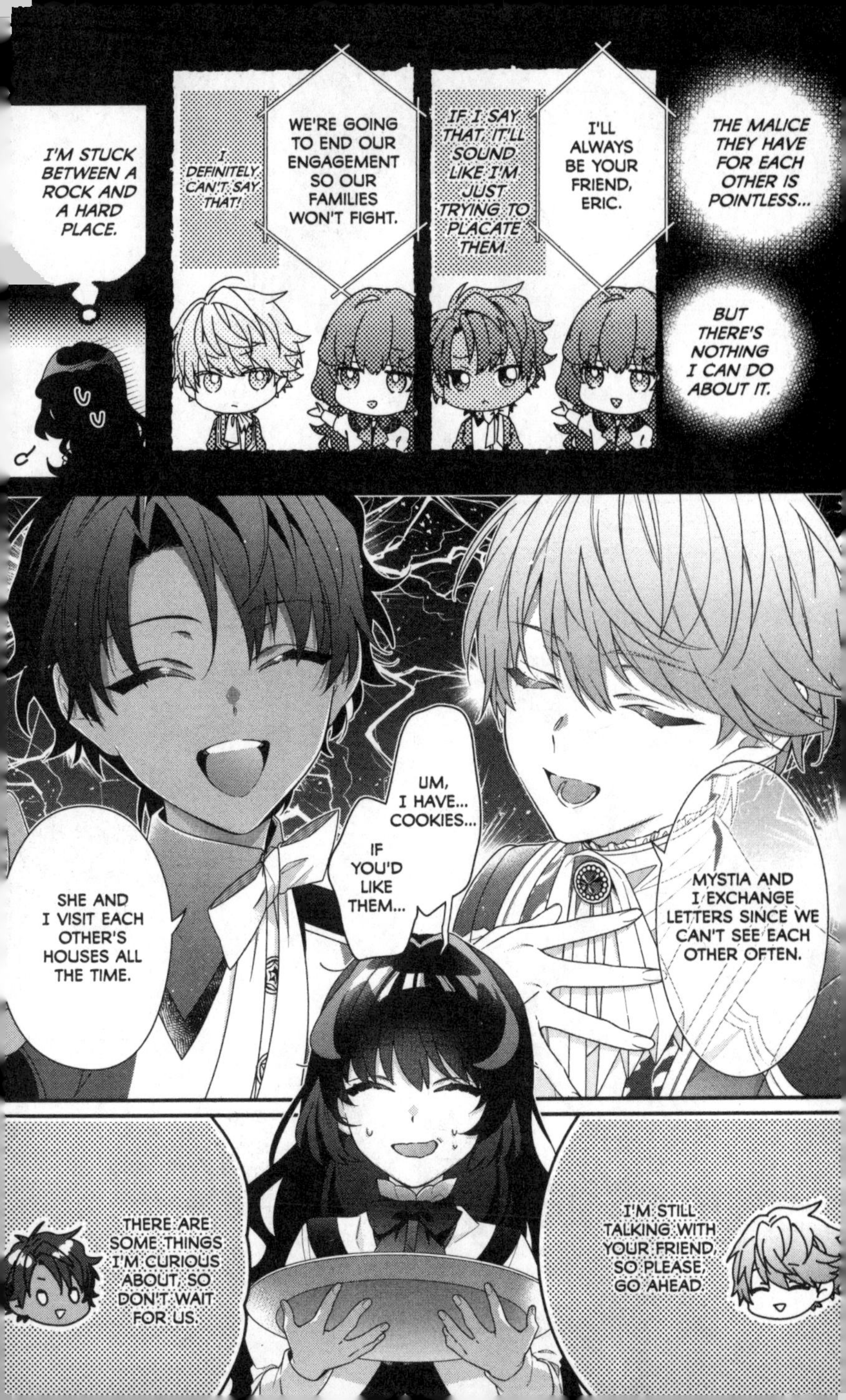
THE MALICE THEY HAVE FOR EACH OTHER IS POINTLESS...
BUT THERE'S NOTHING I CAN DO ABOUT IT.
I'LL ALWAYS BE YOUR FRIEND, ERIC.
IF I SAY THAT, IT'LL SOUND LIKE I'M JUST TRYING TO PLACATE THEM.
WE'RE GOING TO END OUR ENGAGEMENT SO OUR FAMILIES WON'T FIGHT.
I DEFINITELY CAN'T SAY THAT!
I'M STUCK BETWEEN A ROCK AND A HARD PLACE.
MYSTIA AND I EXCHANGE LETTERS SINCE WE CAN'T SEE EACH OTHER OFTEN.
SHE AND I VISIT EACH OTHER'S HOUSES ALL THE TIME.
UM, I HAVE... COOKIES...
IF YOU'D LIKE THEM...
I'M STILL TALKING WITH YOUR FRIEND, SO PLEASE GO AHEAD.
THERE ARE SOME THINGS I'M CURIOUS ABOUT, SO DON'T WAIT FOR US.

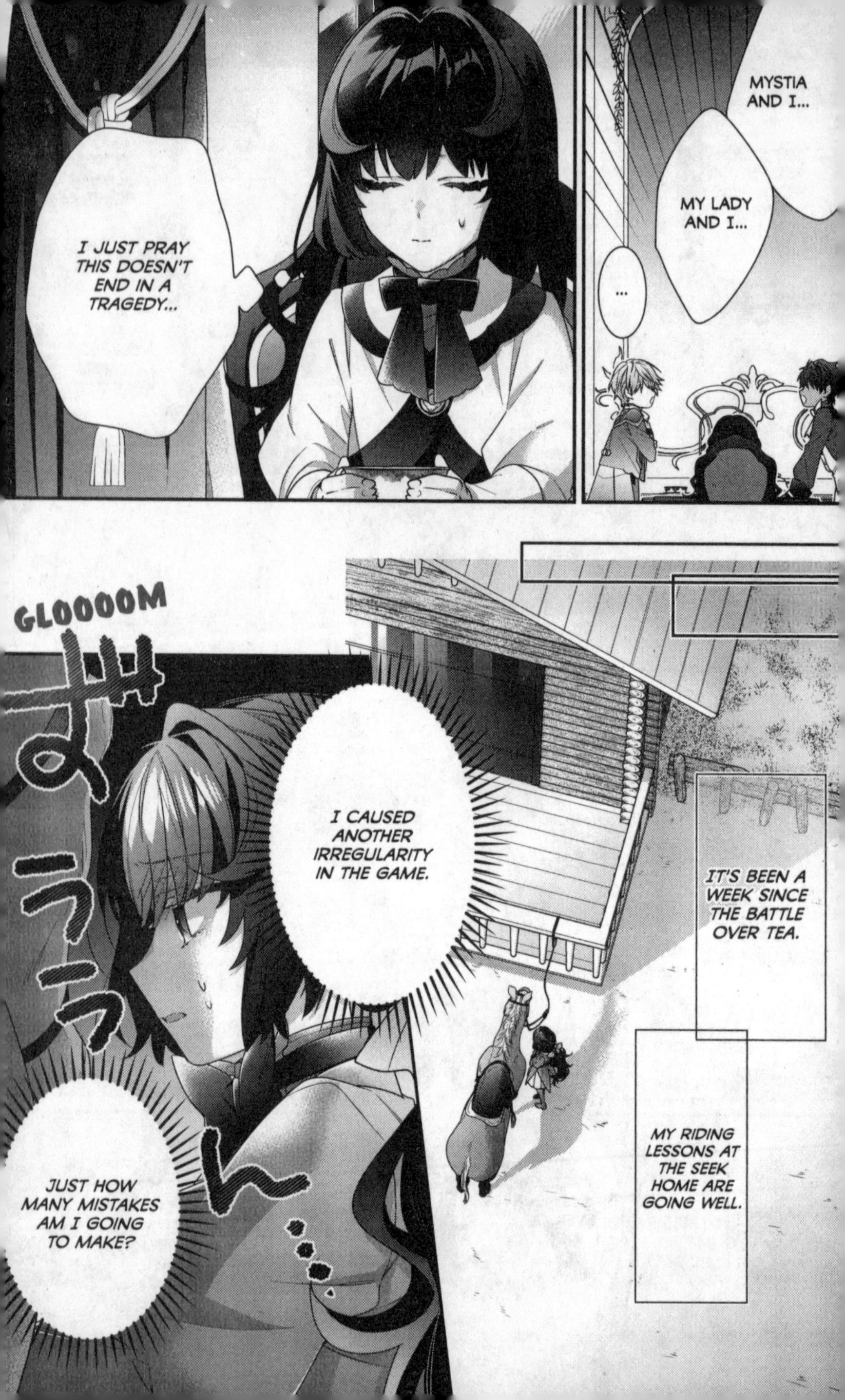
MYSTIA AND I...
MY LADY AND I...
...
I JUST PRAY THIS DOESN'T END IN A TRAGEDY...
IT'S BEEN A WEEK SINCE THE BATTLE OVER TEA.
MY RIDING LESSONS AT THE SEEK HOME ARE GOING WELL.
GLOOOOM
ずうん…
I CAUSED ANOTHER IRREGULARITY IN THE GAME.
JUST HOW MANY MISTAKES AM I GOING TO MAKE?

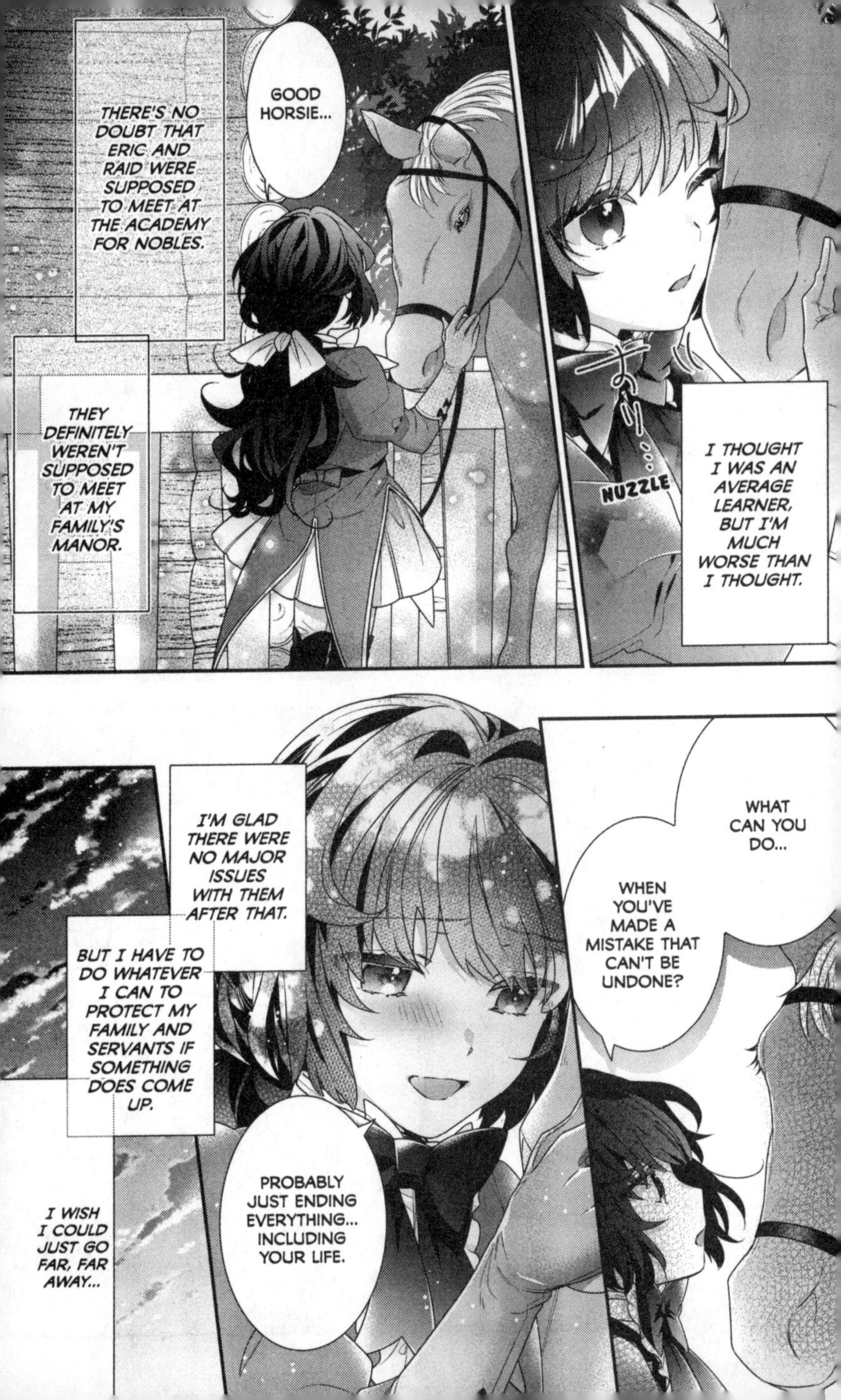
NUZZLE
I THOUGHT I WAS AN AVERAGE LEARNER, BUT I'M MUCH WORSE THAN I THOUGHT.
GOOD HORSIE...
THERE'S NO DOUBT THAT ERIC AND RAID WERE SUPPOSED TO MEET AT THE ACADEMY FOR NOBLES.
THEY DEFINITELY WEREN'T SUPPOSED TO MEET AT MY FAMILY'S MANOR.
WHAT CAN YOU DO...
WHEN YOU'VE MADE A MISTAKE THAT CAN'T BE UNDONE?
PROBABLY JUST ENDING EVERYTHING... INCLUDING YOUR LIFE.
I'M GLAD THERE WERE NO MAJOR ISSUES WITH THEM AFTER THAT.
BUT I HAVE TO DO WHATEVER I CAN TO PROTECT MY FAMILY AND SERVANTS IF SOMETHING DOES COME UP.
I WISH I COULD JUST GO FAR, FAR AWAY...

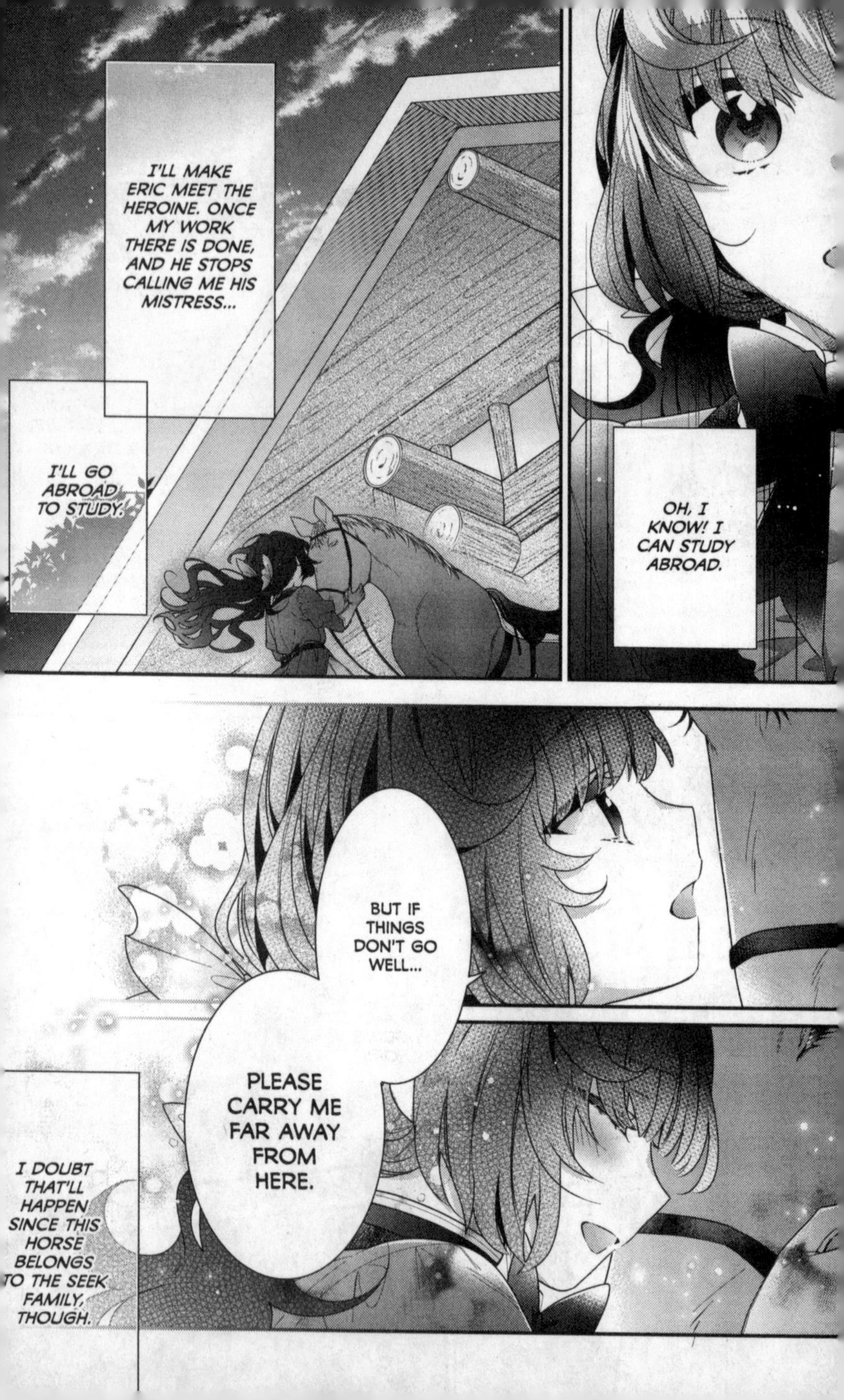
OH, I KNOW! I CAN STUDY ABROAD.
I'LL MAKE ERIC MEET THE HEROINE. ONCE MY WORK THERE IS DONE, AND HE STOPS CALLING ME HIS MISTRESS...
I'LL GO ABROAD TO STUDY.
BUT IF THINGS DON'T GO WELL...
PLEASE CARRY ME FAR AWAY FROM HERE.
I DOUBT THAT'LL HAPPEN SINCE THIS HORSE BELONGS TO THE SEEK FAMILY, THOUGH.

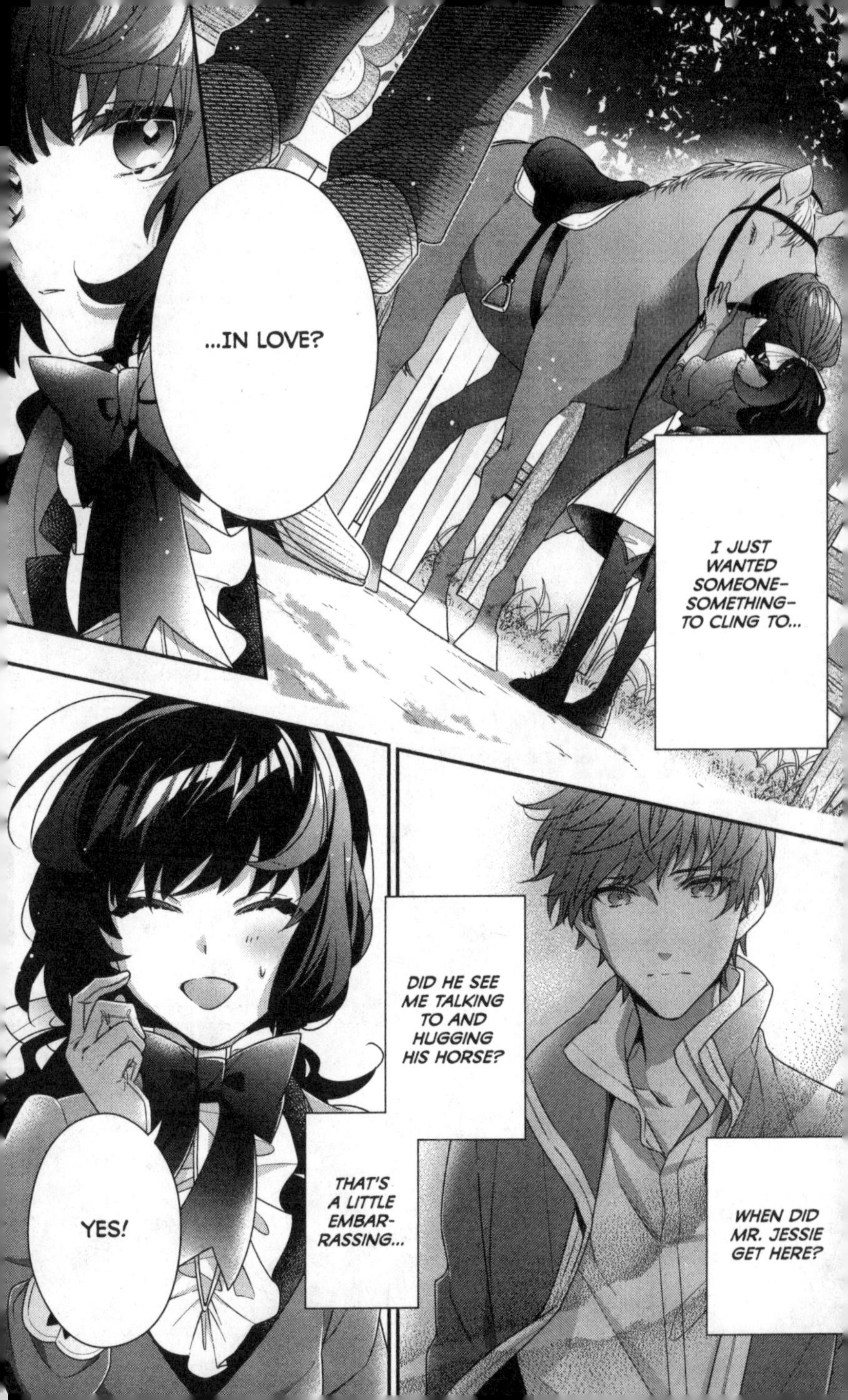
I JUST WANTED SOMEONE-SOMETHING-TO CLING TO...
...IN LOVE?
WHEN DID MR. JESSIE GET HERE?
DID HE SEE ME TALKING TO AND HUGGING HIS HORSE?
THAT'S A LITTLE EMBAR-RASSING...
YES!

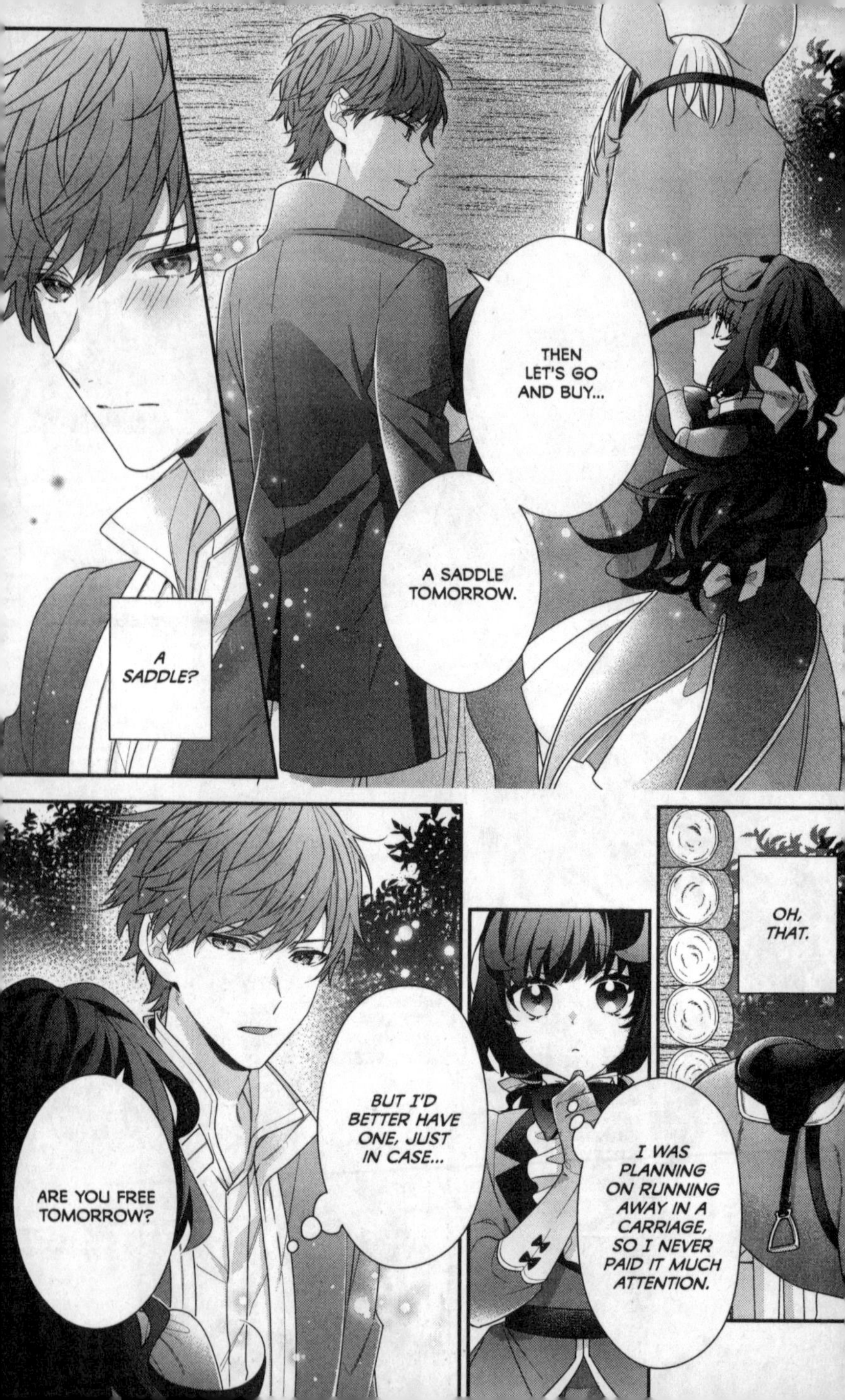
THEN LET'S GO AND BUY...
A SADDLE TOMORROW.
A SADDLE?
OH, THAT.
I WAS PLANNING ON RUNNING AWAY IN A CARRIAGE, SO I NEVER PAID IT MUCH ATTENTION.
BUT I'D BETTER HAVE ONE, JUST IN CASE...
ARE YOU FREE TOMORROW?

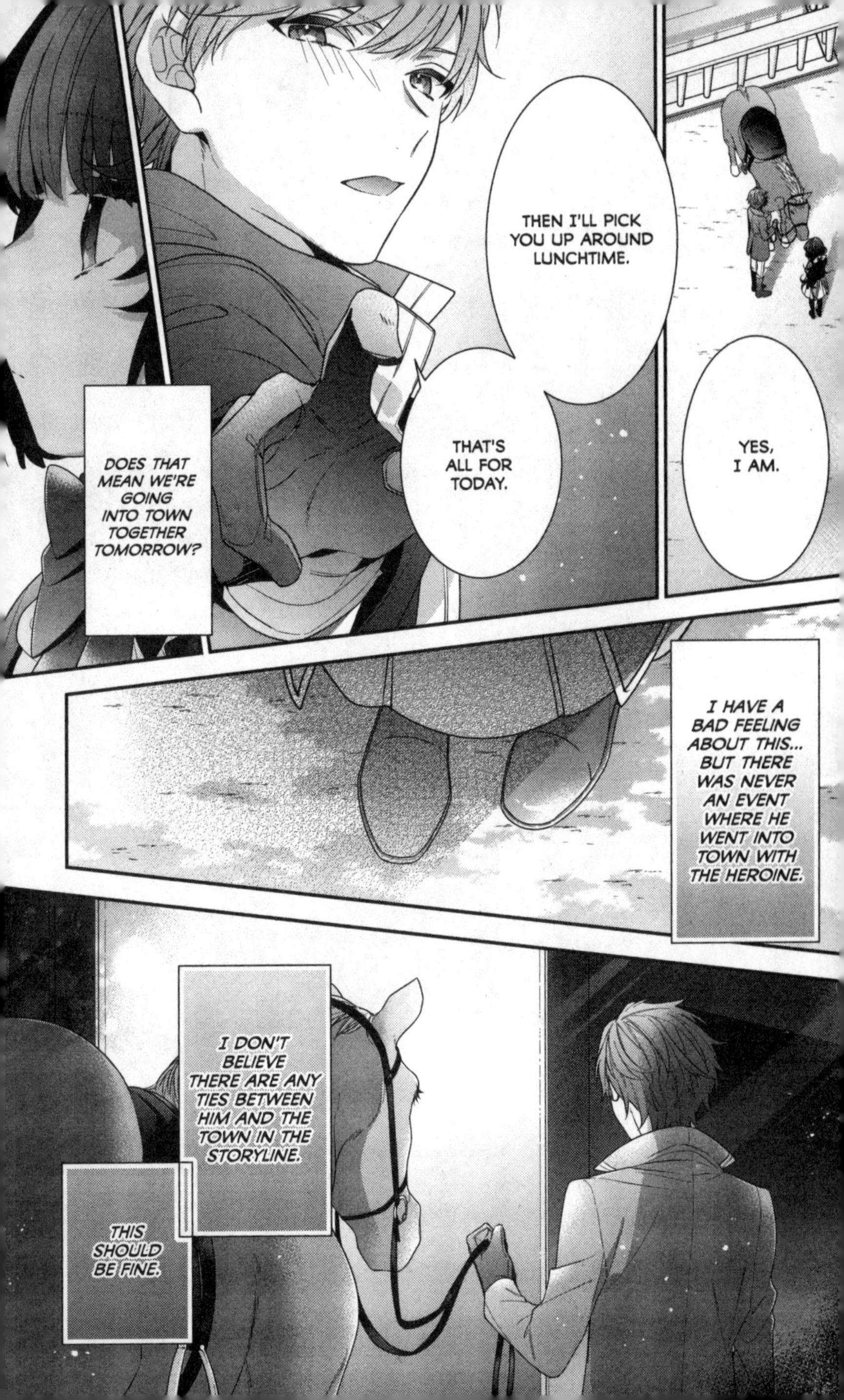
YES, I AM.
THEN I'LL PICK YOU UP AROUND LUNCHTIME.
THAT'S ALL FOR TODAY.
DOES THAT MEAN WE'RE GOING INTO TOWN TOGETHER TOMORROW?
I HAVE A BAD FEELING ABOUT THIS... BUT THERE WAS NEVER AN EVENT WHERE HE WENT INTO TOWN WITH THE HEROINE.
I DON'T BELIEVE THERE ARE ANY TIES BETWEEN HIM AND THE TOWN IN THE STORYLINE.
THIS SHOULD BE FINE.

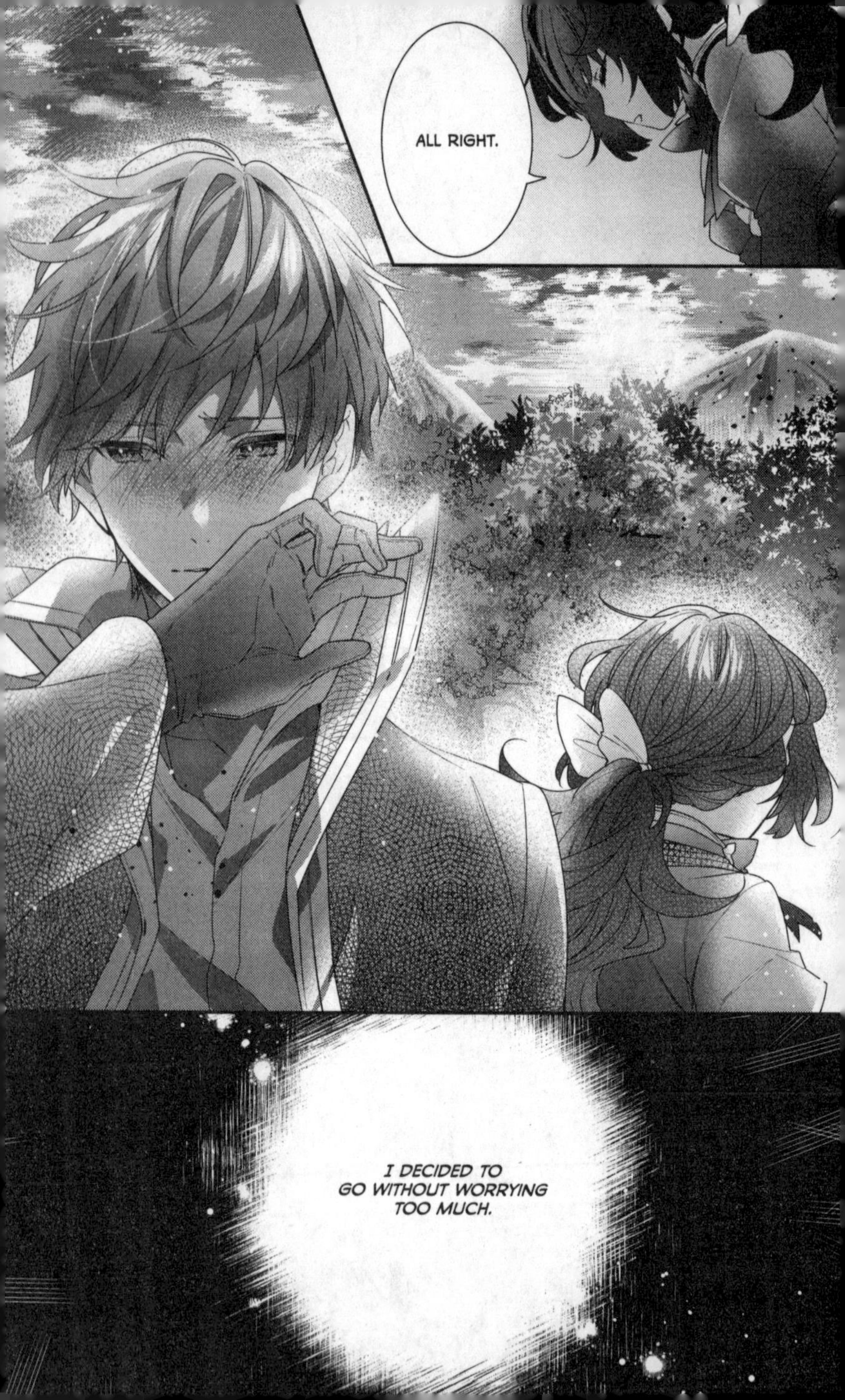
ALL RIGHT.
I DECIDED TO GO WITHOUT WORRYING TOO MUCH.

I was REINCARNATED as the

Villainess
****

in an OTOME GAME *but the boys love me anyway!*

I was REINCARNATED as the Villainess ********** in an OTOME GAME *but the boys love me anyway!*

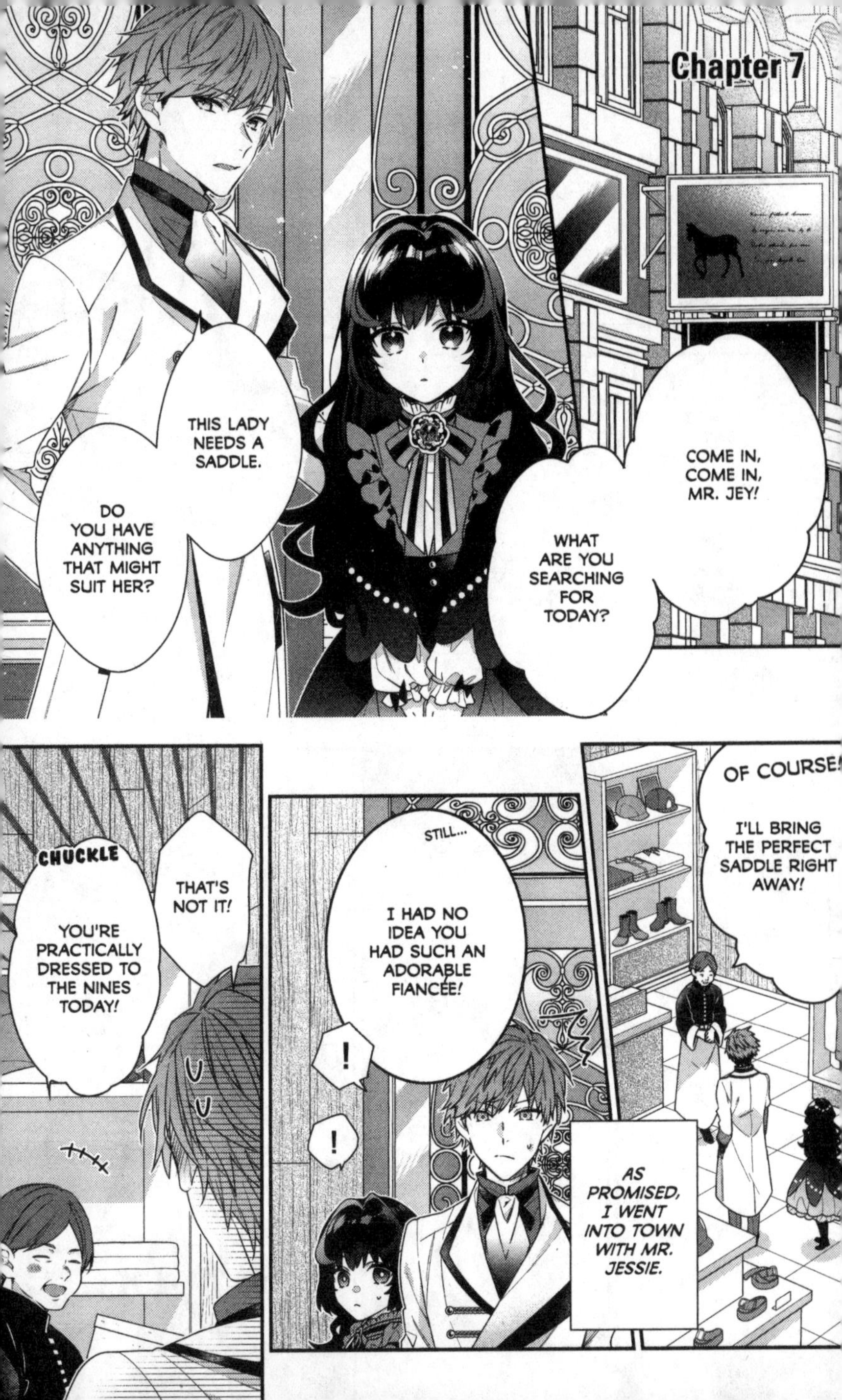
Chapter 7
COME IN, COME IN, MR. JEY!
WHAT ARE YOU SEARCHING FOR TODAY?
THIS LADY NEEDS A SADDLE.
DO YOU HAVE ANYTHING THAT MIGHT SUIT HER?
OF COURSE!
I'LL BRING THE PERFECT SADDLE RIGHT AWAY!
AS PROMISED, I WENT INTO TOWN WITH MR. JESSIE.
STILL...
I HAD NO IDEA YOU HAD SUCH AN ADORABLE FIANCÉE!
!
!
THAT'S NOT IT!
CHUCKLE
YOU'RE PRACTICALLY DRESSED TO THE NINES TODAY!

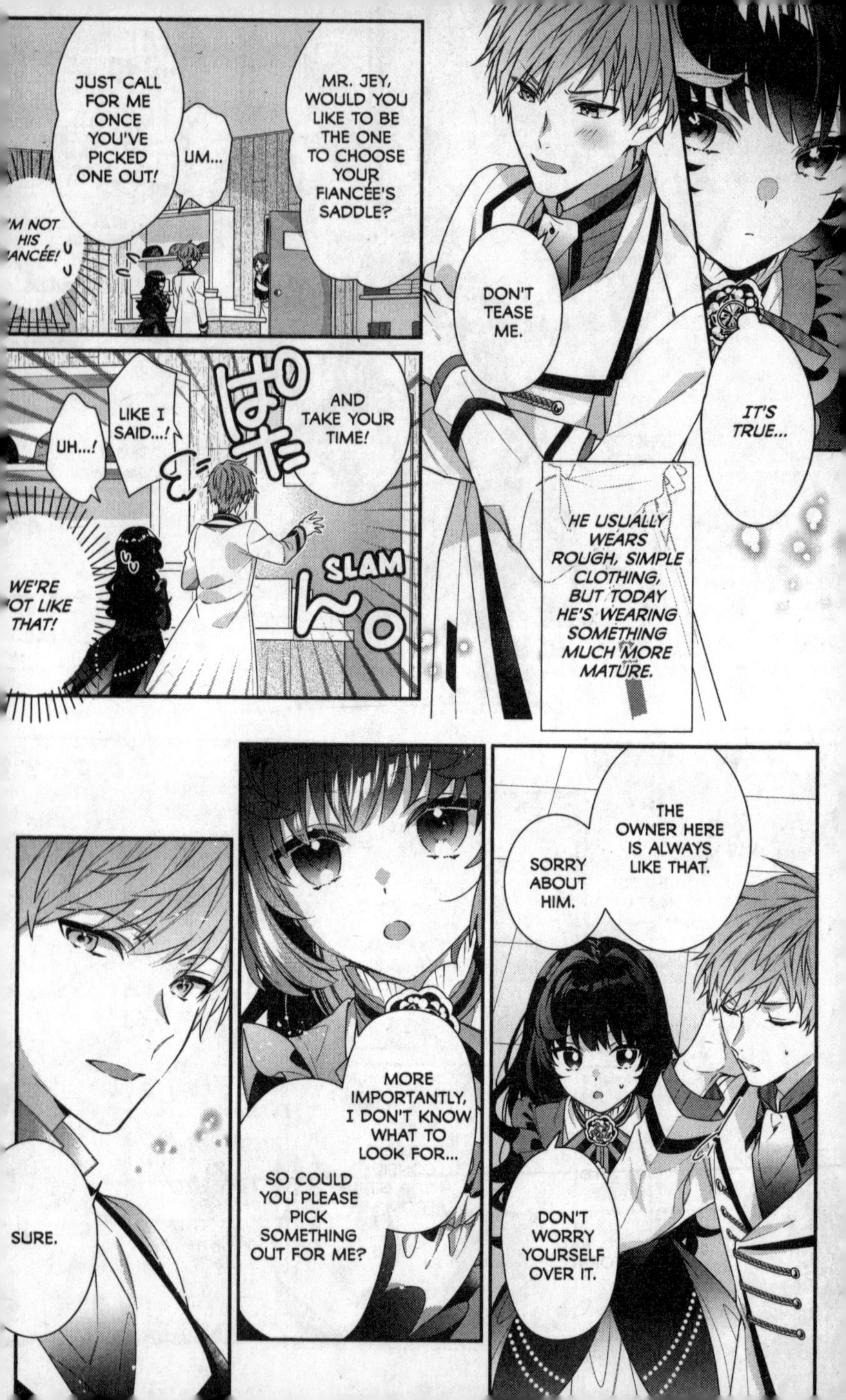
DON'T TEASE ME.
IT'S TRUE...
HE USUALLY WEARS ROUGH, SIMPLE CLOTHING, BUT TODAY HE'S WEARING SOMETHING MUCH MORE MATURE.
MR. JEY, WOULD YOU LIKE TO BE THE ONE TO CHOOSE YOUR FIANCÉE'S SADDLE?
UM...
JUST CALL FOR ME ONCE YOU'VE PICKED ONE OUT!
'M NOT HIS ANCÉE!
AND TAKE YOUR TIME!
ぱた
SLAM
ん。
LIKE I SAID...!
UH...!
WE'RE OT LIKE THAT!
THE OWNER HERE IS ALWAYS LIKE THAT.
SORRY ABOUT HIM.
DON'T WORRY YOURSELF OVER IT.
MORE IMPORTANTLY, I DON'T KNOW WHAT TO LOOK FOR...
SO COULD YOU PLEASE PICK SOMETHING OUT FOR ME?
SURE.

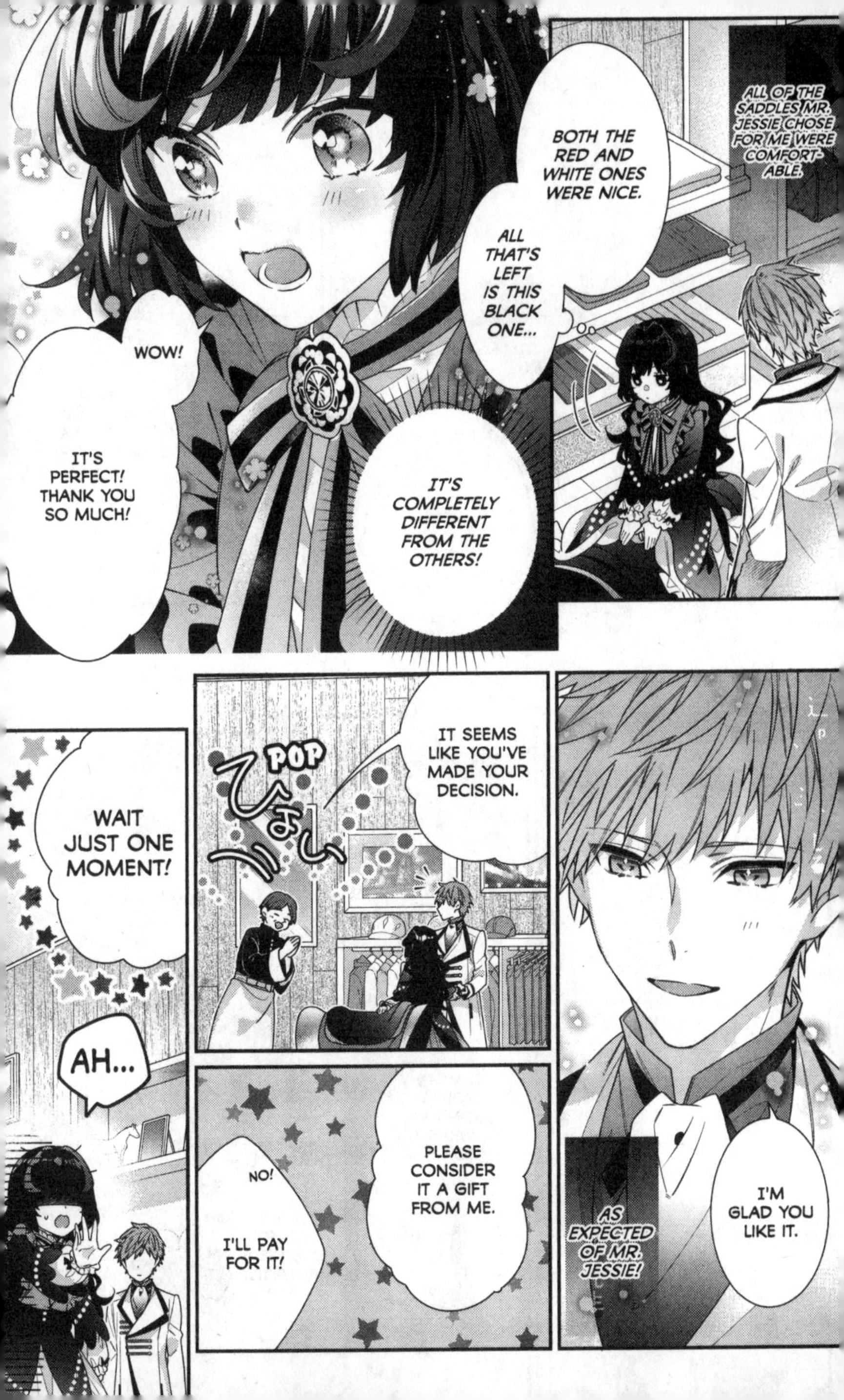
ALL OF THE SADDLES MR. JESSIE CHOSE FOR ME WERE COMFORTABLE.
BOTH THE RED AND WHITE ONES WERE NICE.
ALL THAT'S LEFT IS THIS BLACK ONE...
IT'S COMPLETELY DIFFERENT FROM THE OTHERS!
WOW!
IT'S PERFECT! THANK YOU SO MUCH!
I'M GLAD YOU LIKE IT.
AS EXPECTED OF MR. JESSIE!
IT SEEMS LIKE YOU'VE MADE YOUR DECISION.
POP
ひょい
PLEASE CONSIDER IT A GIFT FROM ME.
NO!
I'LL PAY FOR IT!
WAIT JUST ONE MOMENT!
AH...

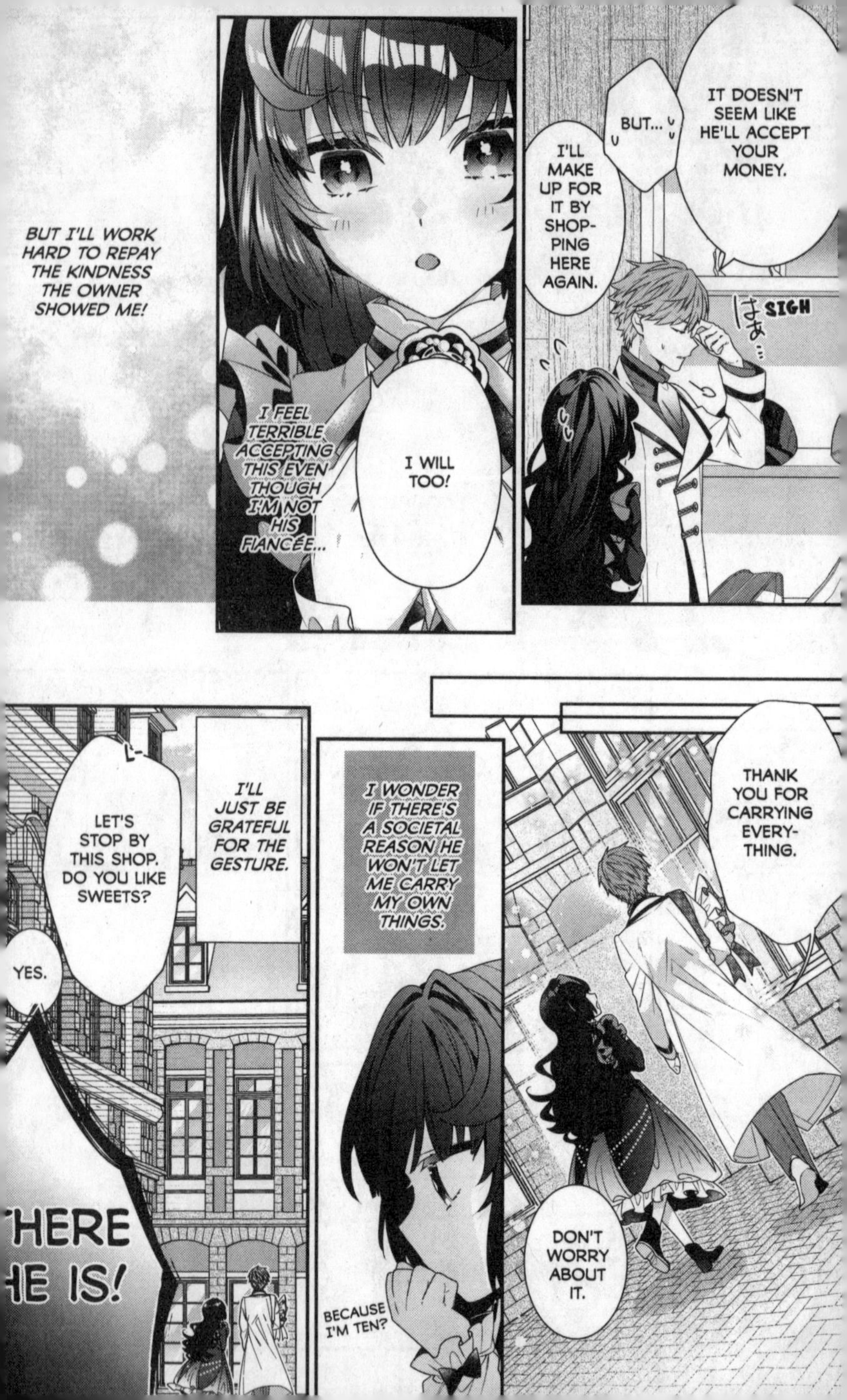
IT DOESN'T SEEM LIKE HE'LL ACCEPT YOUR MONEY.
BUT...
I'LL MAKE UP FOR IT BY SHOP-PING HERE AGAIN.
はぁ… SIGH
I FEEL TERRIBLE ACCEPTING THIS EVEN THOUGH I'M NOT HIS FIANCÉE...
I WILL TOO!
BUT I'LL WORK HARD TO REPAY THE KINDNESS THE OWNER SHOWED ME!
THANK YOU FOR CARRYING EVERY-THING.
DON'T WORRY ABOUT IT.
I WONDER IF THERE'S A SOCIETAL REASON HE WON'T LET ME CARRY MY OWN THINGS.
BECAUSE I'M TEN?
I'LL JUST BE GRATEFUL FOR THE GESTURE.
LET'S STOP BY THIS SHOP. DO YOU LIKE SWEETS?
YES.
HERE
E IS!

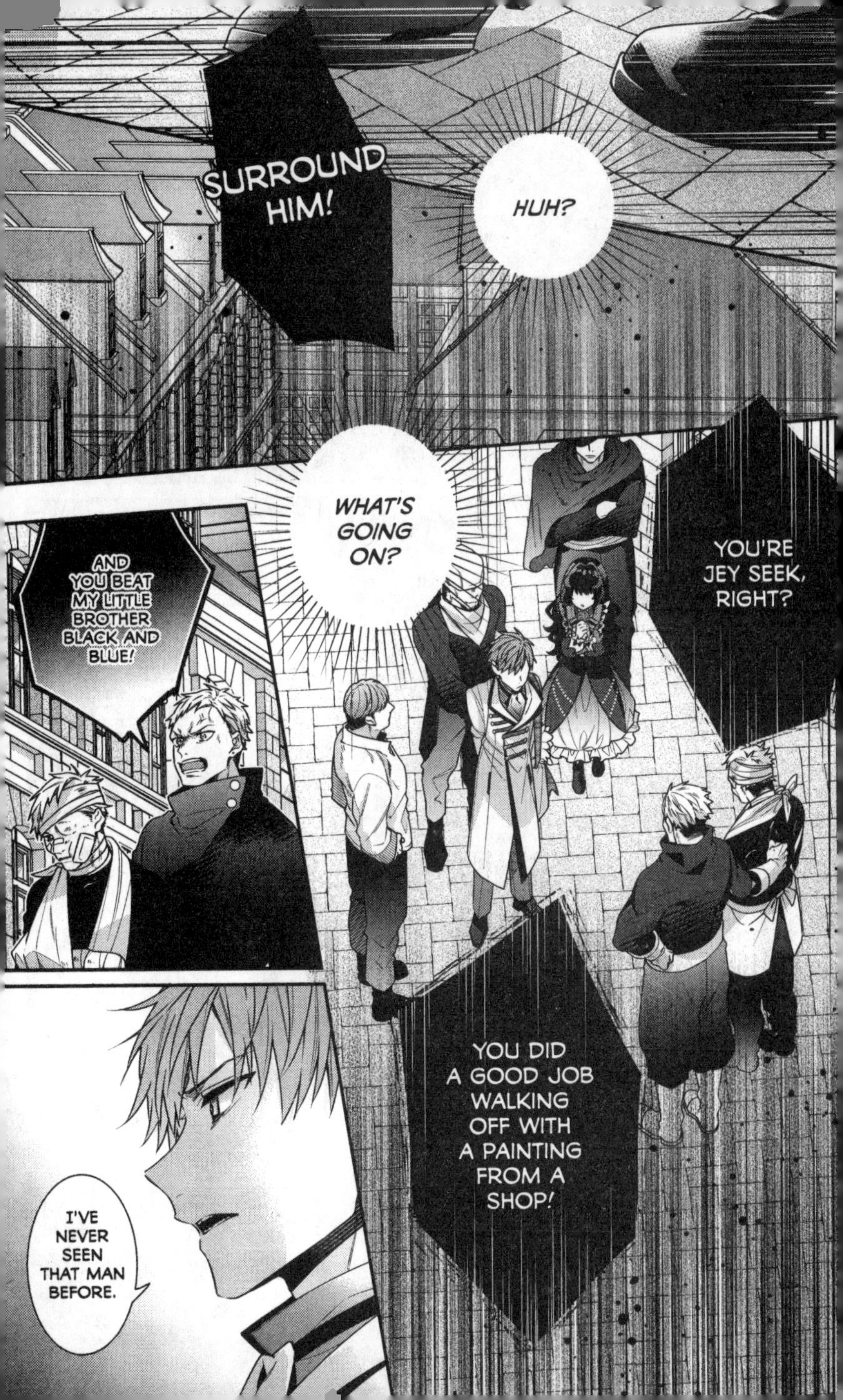
SURROUND HIM!
HUH?
WHAT'S GOING ON?
YOU'RE JEY SEEK, RIGHT?
YOU DID A GOOD JOB WALKING OFF WITH A PAINTING FROM A SHOP!
AND YOU BEAT MY LITTLE BROTHER BLACK AND BLUE!
I'VE NEVER SEEN THAT MAN BEFORE.

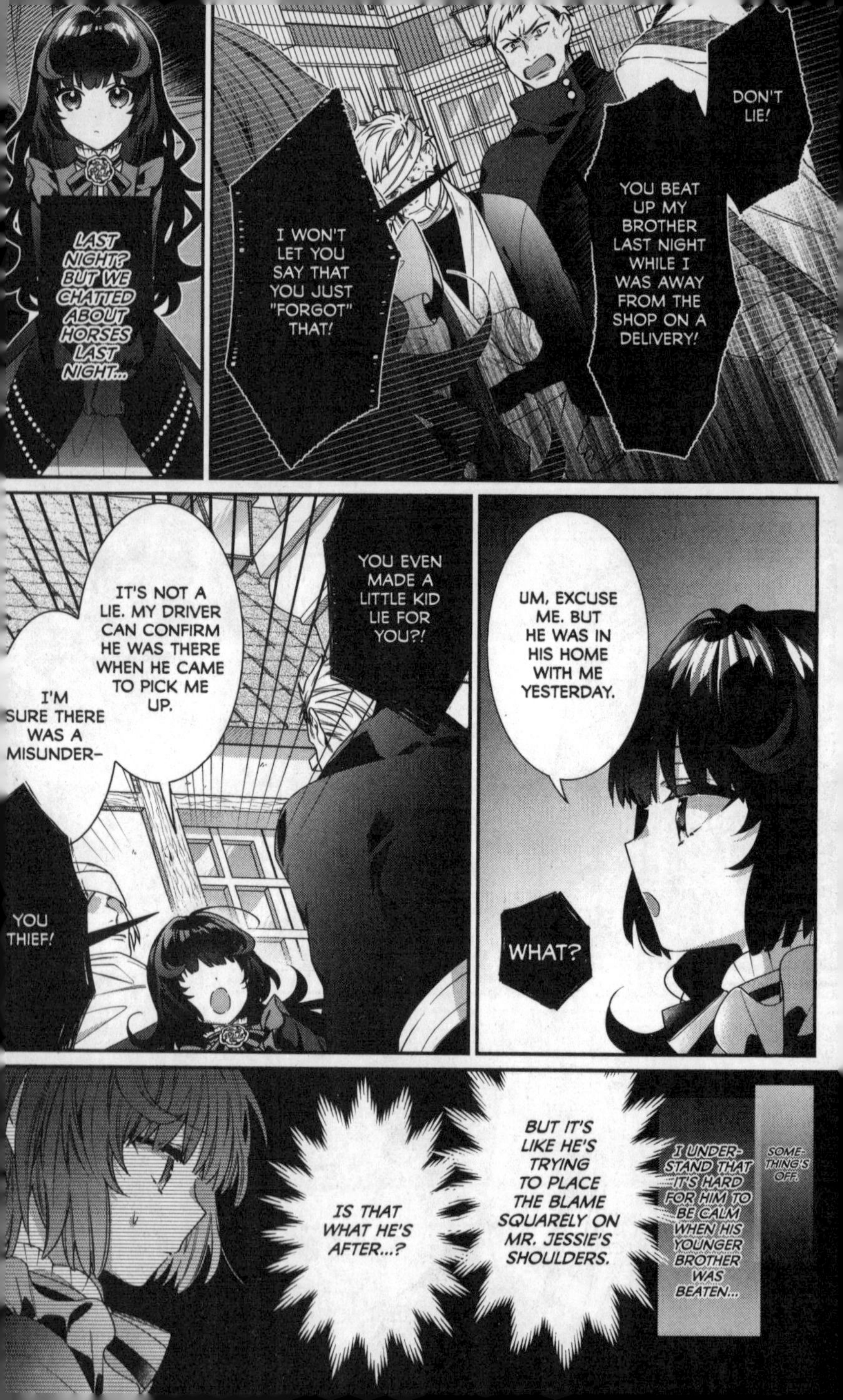

DON'T LIE!
YOU BEAT UP MY BROTHER LAST NIGHT WHILE I WAS AWAY FROM THE SHOP ON A DELIVERY!
I WON'T LET YOU SAY THAT YOU JUST "FORGOT" THAT!
LAST NIGHT? BUT WE CHATTED ABOUT HORSES LAST NIGHT...
UM, EXCUSE ME. BUT HE WAS IN HIS HOME WITH ME YESTERDAY.
WHAT?
YOU EVEN MADE A LITTLE KID LIE FOR YOU?!
IT'S NOT A LIE. MY DRIVER CAN CONFIRM HE WAS THERE WHEN HE CAME TO PICK ME UP.
I'M SURE THERE WAS A MISUNDER-
YOU THIEF!
SOME-THING'S OFF.
I UNDER-STAND THAT IT'S HARD FOR HIM TO BE CALM WHEN HIS YOUNGER BROTHER WAS BEATEN...
BUT IT'S LIKE HE'S TRYING TO PLACE THE BLAME SQUARELY ON MR. JESSIE'S SHOULDERS.
IS THAT WHAT HE'S AFTER...?

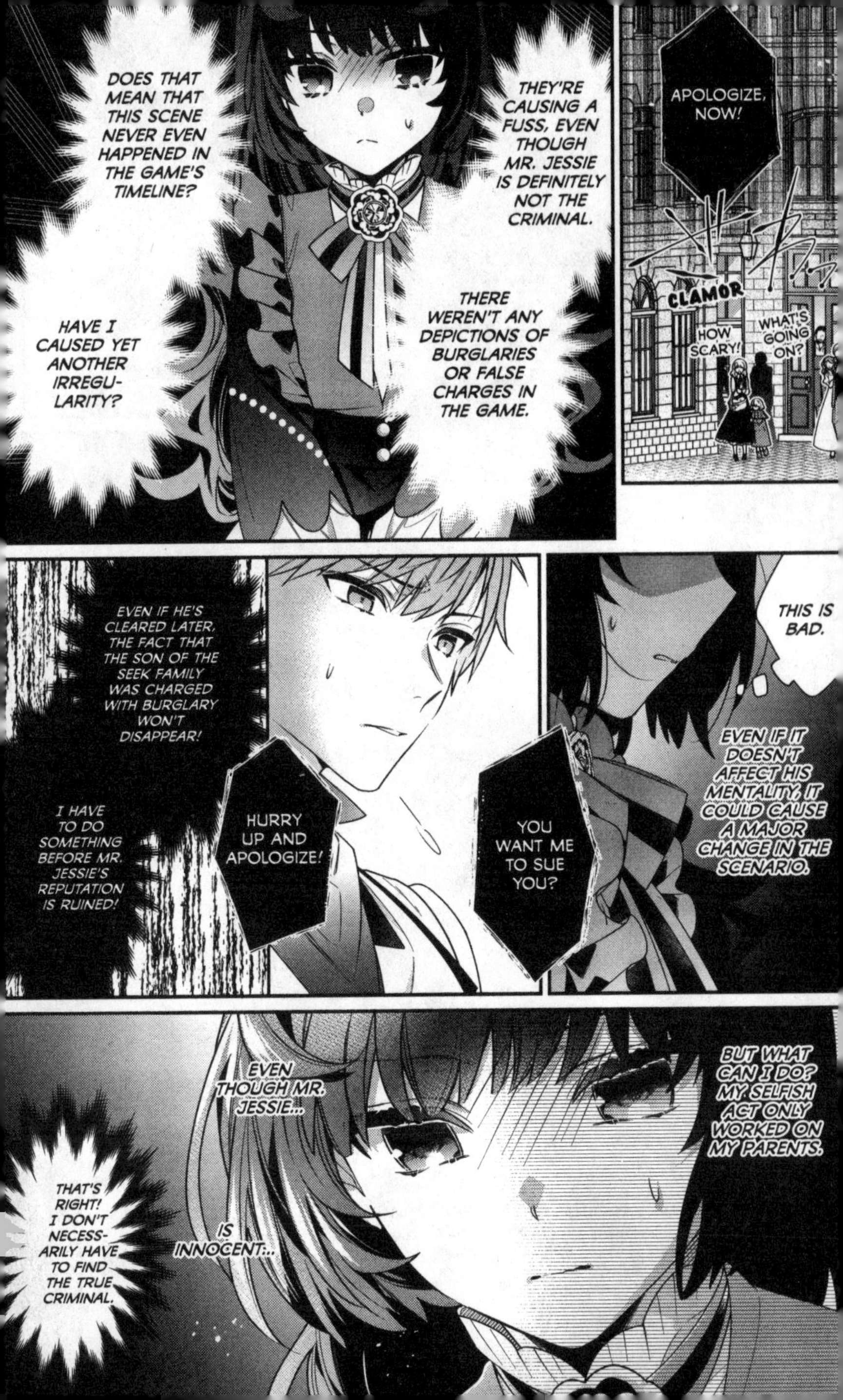
APOLOGIZE, NOW!
CLAMOR
WHAT'S GOING ON?
HOW SCARY!
THEY'RE CAUSING A FUSS, EVEN THOUGH MR. JESSIE IS DEFINITELY NOT THE CRIMINAL.
DOES THAT MEAN THAT THIS SCENE NEVER EVEN HAPPENED IN THE GAME'S TIMELINE?
THERE WEREN'T ANY DEPICTIONS OF BURGLARIES OR FALSE CHARGES IN THE GAME.
HAVE I CAUSED YET ANOTHER IRREGU-LARITY?
THIS IS BAD.
EVEN IF IT DOESN'T AFFECT HIS MENTALITY, IT COULD CAUSE A MAJOR CHANGE IN THE SCENARIO.
YOU WANT ME TO SUE YOU?
HURRY UP AND APOLOGIZE!
EVEN IF HE'S CLEARED LATER, THE FACT THAT THE SON OF THE SEEK FAMILY WAS CHARGED WITH BURGLARY WON'T DISAPPEAR!
I HAVE TO DO SOMETHING BEFORE MR. JESSIE'S REPUTATION IS RUINED!
BUT WHAT CAN I DO? MY SELFISH ACT ONLY WORKED ON MY PARENTS.
EVEN THOUGH MR. JESSIE...
IS INNOCENT...
THAT'S RIGHT! I DON'T NECESS-ARILY HAVE TO FIND THE TRUE CRIMINAL.

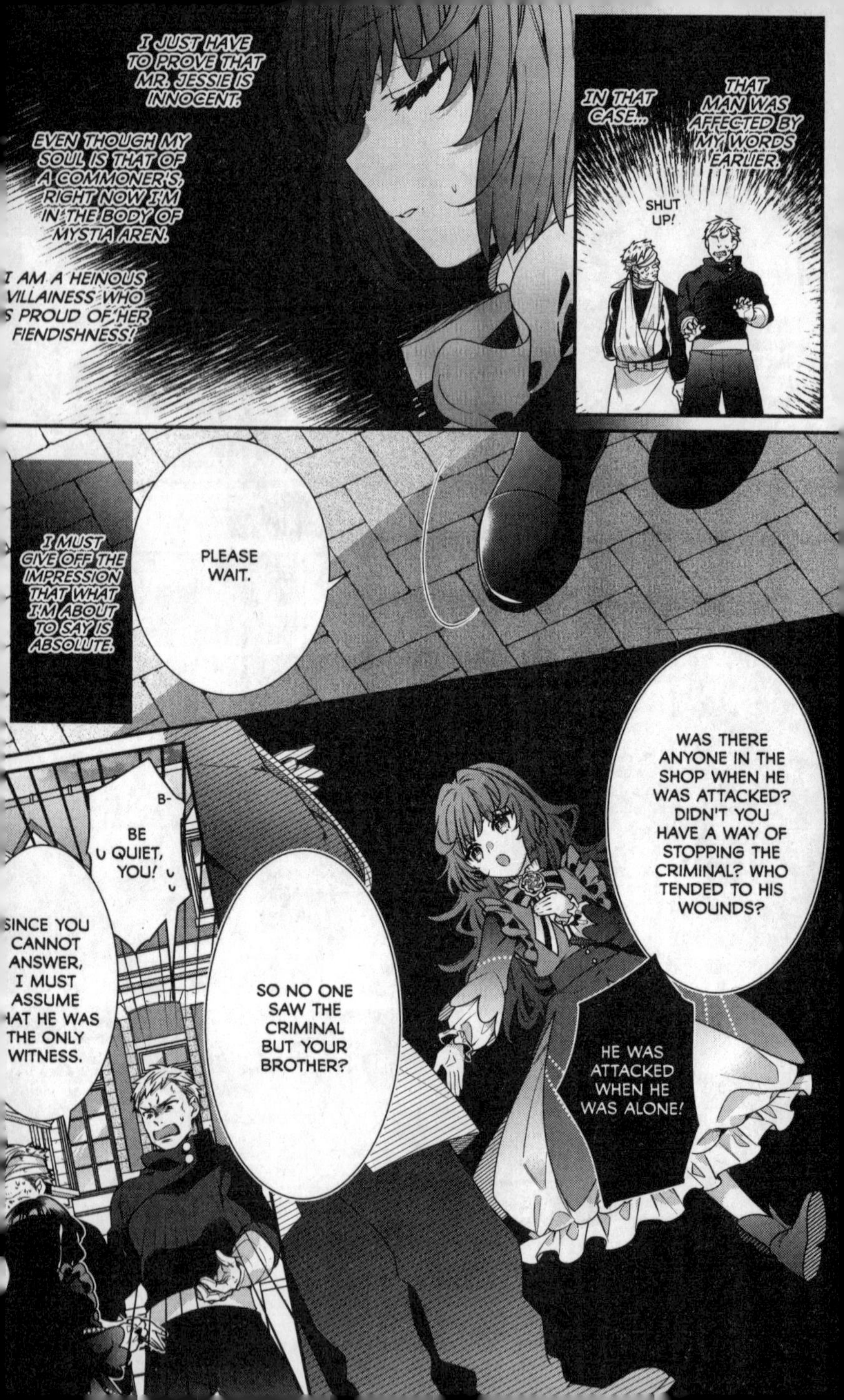
THAT MAN WAS AFFECTED BY MY WORDS EARLIER.
IN THAT CASE...
SHUT UP!
I JUST HAVE TO PROVE THAT MR. JESSIE IS INNOCENT.
EVEN THOUGH MY SOUL IS THAT OF A COMMONER'S, RIGHT NOW I'M IN THE BODY OF MYSTIA AREN.
I AM A HEINOUS VILLAINESS WHO S PROUD OF HER FIENDISHNESS!
PLEASE WAIT.
I MUST GIVE OFF THE IMPRESSION THAT WHAT I'M ABOUT TO SAY IS ABSOLUTE.
WAS THERE ANYONE IN THE SHOP WHEN HE WAS ATTACKED? DIDN'T YOU HAVE A WAY OF STOPPING THE CRIMINAL? WHO TENDED TO HIS WOUNDS?
HE WAS ATTACKED WHEN HE WAS ALONE!
SO NO ONE SAW THE CRIMINAL BUT YOUR BROTHER?
B- BE QUIET, YOU!
SINCE YOU CANNOT ANSWER, I MUST ASSUME HAT HE WAS THE ONLY WITNESS.

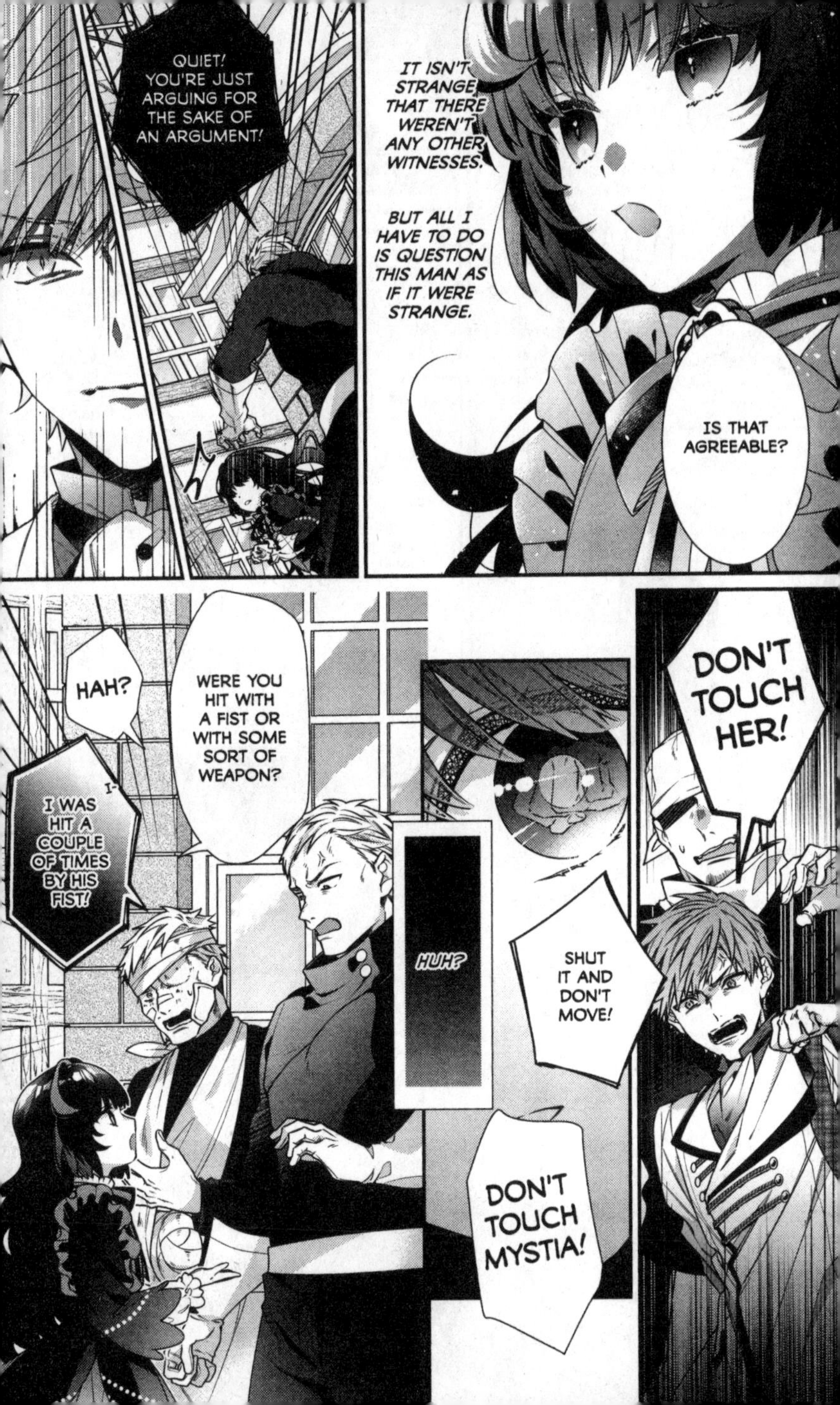
IT ISN'T STRANGE THAT THERE WEREN'T ANY OTHER WITNESSES.
BUT ALL I HAVE TO DO IS QUESTION THIS MAN AS IF IT WERE STRANGE.
IS THAT AGREEABLE?
QUIET! YOU'RE JUST ARGUING FOR THE SAKE OF AN ARGUMENT!
DON'T TOUCH HER!
SHUT IT AND DON'T MOVE!
DON'T TOUCH MYSTIA!
HUH?
WERE YOU HIT WITH A FIST OR WITH SOME SORT OF WEAPON?
HAH?
I- I WAS HIT A COUPLE OF TIMES BY HIS FIST!

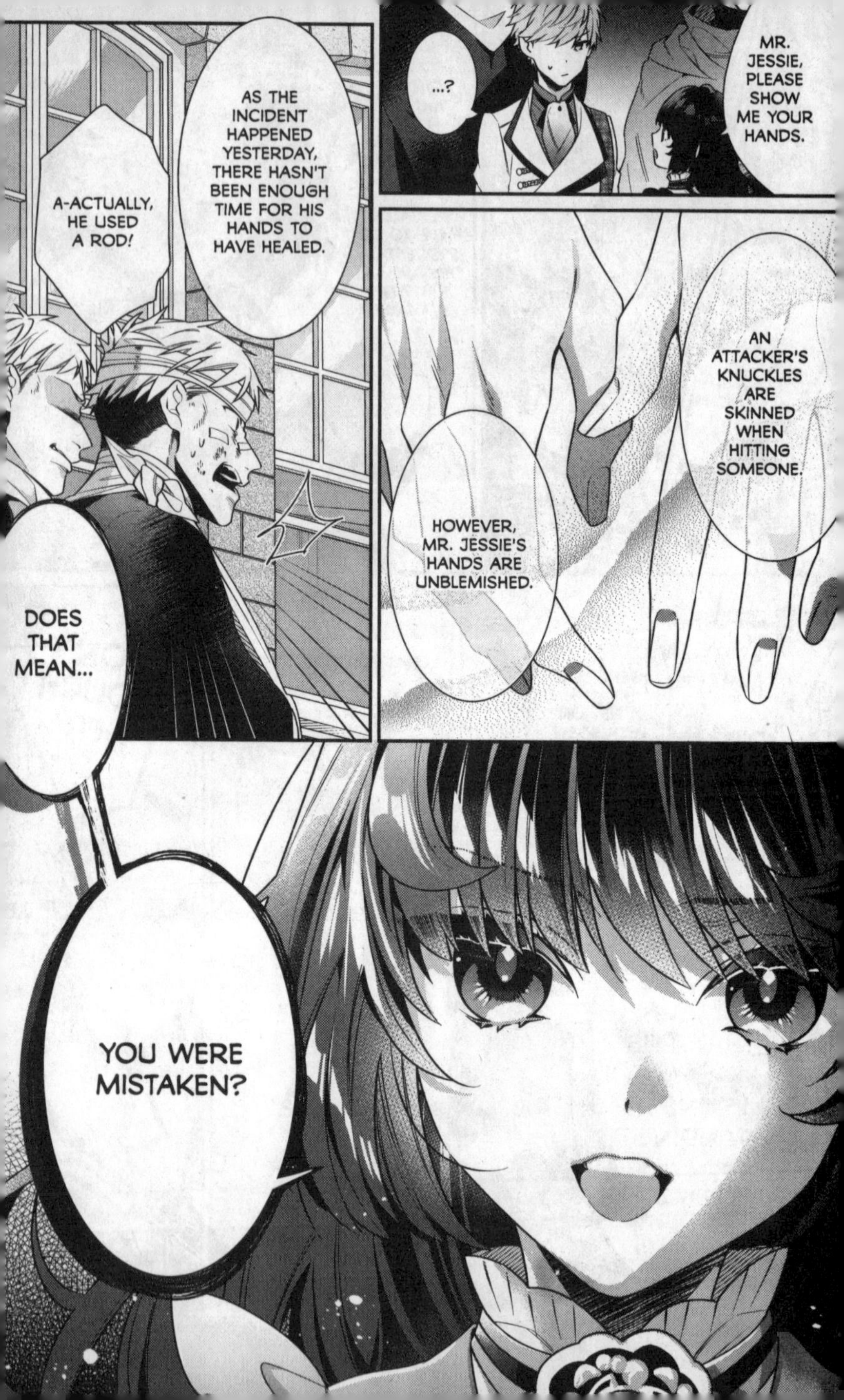
MR. JESSIE, PLEASE SHOW ME YOUR HANDS.
...?
AN ATTACKER'S KNUCKLES ARE SKINNED WHEN HITTING SOMEONE.
HOWEVER, MR. JESSIE'S HANDS ARE UNBLEMISHED.
AS THE INCIDENT HAPPENED YESTERDAY, THERE HASN'T BEEN ENOUGH TIME FOR HIS HANDS TO HAVE HEALED.
A-ACTUALLY, HE USED A ROD!
DOES THAT MEAN...
YOU WERE MISTAKEN?

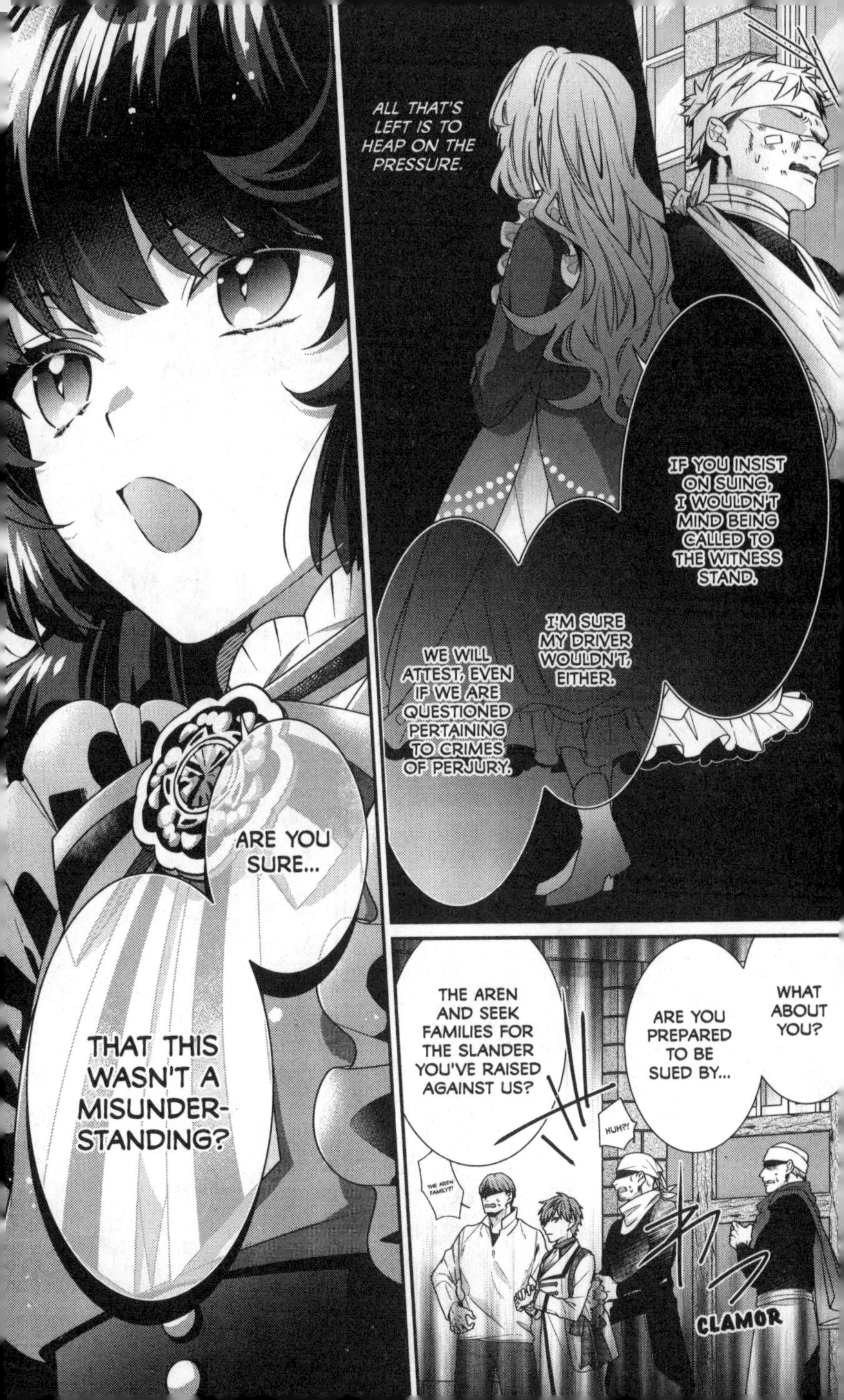
ALL THAT'S LEFT IS TO HEAP ON THE PRESSURE.
IF YOU INSIST ON SUING, I WOULDN'T MIND BEING CALLED TO THE WITNESS STAND.
I'M SURE MY DRIVER WOULDN'T, EITHER.
WE WILL ATTEST, EVEN IF WE ARE QUESTIONED PERTAINING TO CRIMES OF PERJURY.
WHAT ABOUT YOU?
ARE YOU PREPARED TO BE SUED BY...
THE AREN AND SEEK FAMILIES FOR THE SLANDER YOU'VE RAISED AGAINST US?
HUH?!
THE AREN FAMILY?!
CLAMOR
ARE YOU SURE...
THAT THIS WASN'T A MISUNDER-STANDING?

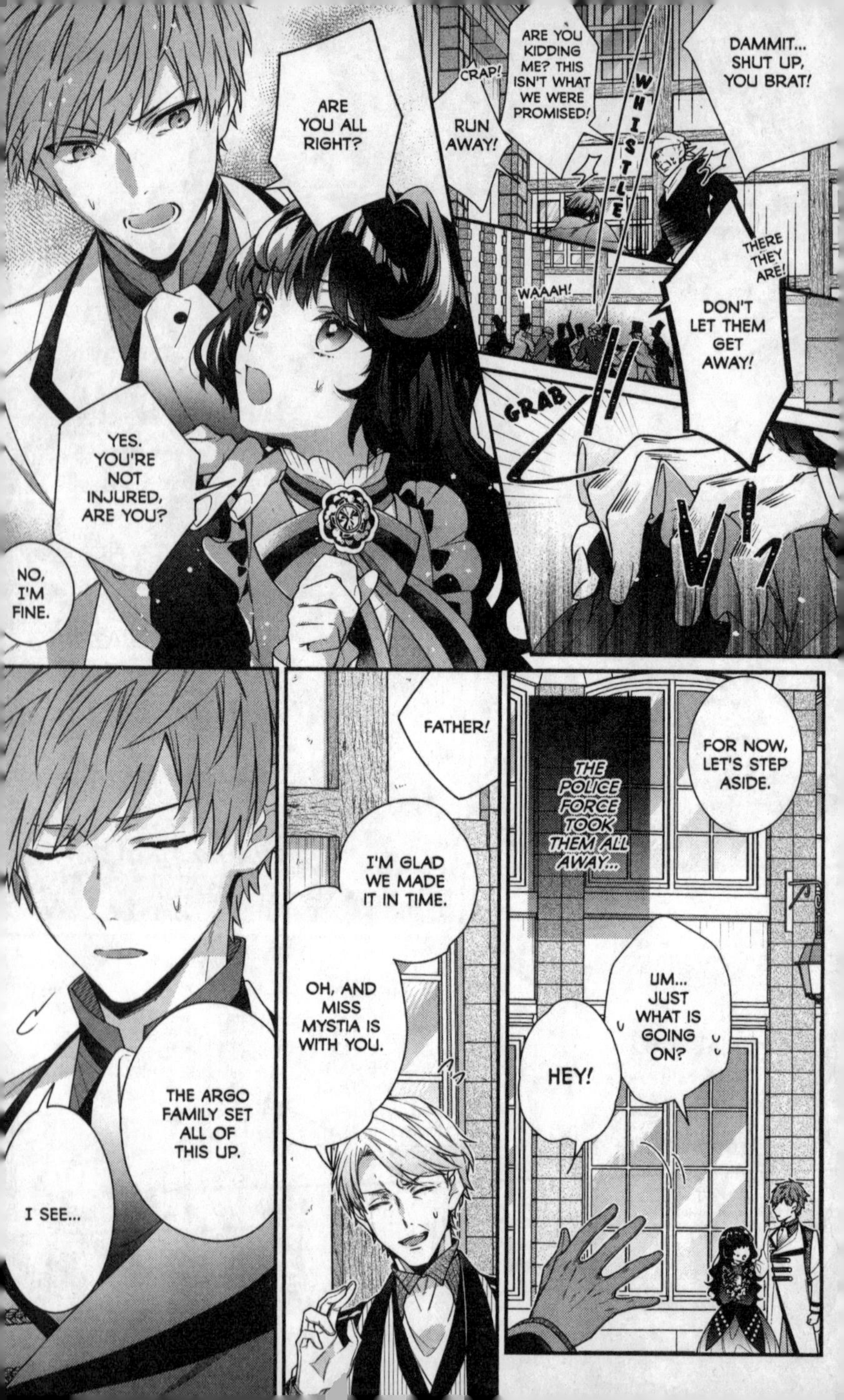
DAMMIT... SHUT UP, YOU BRAT!
ARE YOU KIDDING ME? THIS ISN'T WHAT WE WERE PROMISED!
CRAP!
RUN AWAY!
WHISTLE
THERE THEY ARE!
DON'T LET THEM GET AWAY!
WAAAH!
GRAB
ARE YOU ALL RIGHT?
YES. YOU'RE NOT INJURED, ARE YOU?
NO, I'M FINE.
FOR NOW, LET'S STEP ASIDE.
THE POLICE FORCE TOOK THEM ALL AWAY...
UM... JUST WHAT IS GOING ON?
HEY!
FATHER!
I'M GLAD WE MADE IT IN TIME.
OH, AND MISS MYSTIA IS WITH YOU.
THE ARGO FAMILY SET ALL OF THIS UP.
I SEE...

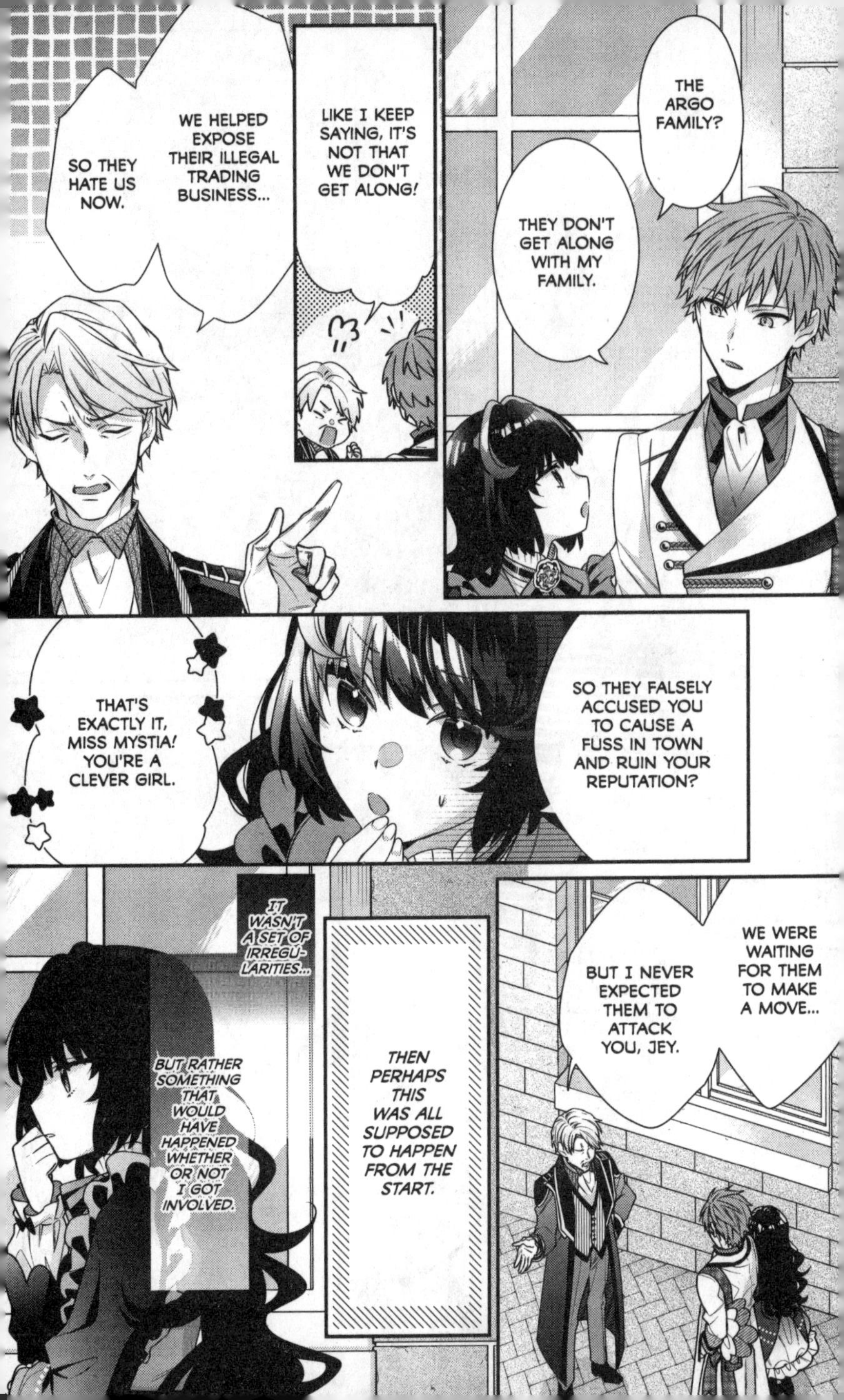
THE ARGO FAMILY?
THEY DON'T GET ALONG WITH MY FAMILY.
LIKE I KEEP SAYING, IT'S NOT THAT WE DON'T GET ALONG!
WE HELPED EXPOSE THEIR ILLEGAL TRADING BUSINESS...
SO THEY HATE US NOW.
SO THEY FALSELY ACCUSED YOU TO CAUSE A FUSS IN TOWN AND RUIN YOUR REPUTATION?
THAT'S EXACTLY IT, MISS MYSTIA! YOU'RE A CLEVER GIRL.
WE WERE WAITING FOR THEM TO MAKE A MOVE...
BUT I NEVER EXPECTED THEM TO ATTACK YOU, JEY.
THEN PERHAPS THIS WAS ALL SUPPOSED TO HAPPEN FROM THE START.
IT WASN'T A SET OF IRREGU-LARITIES...
BUT RATHER SOMETHING THAT WOULD HAVE HAPPENED WHETHER OR NOT I GOT INVOLVED.

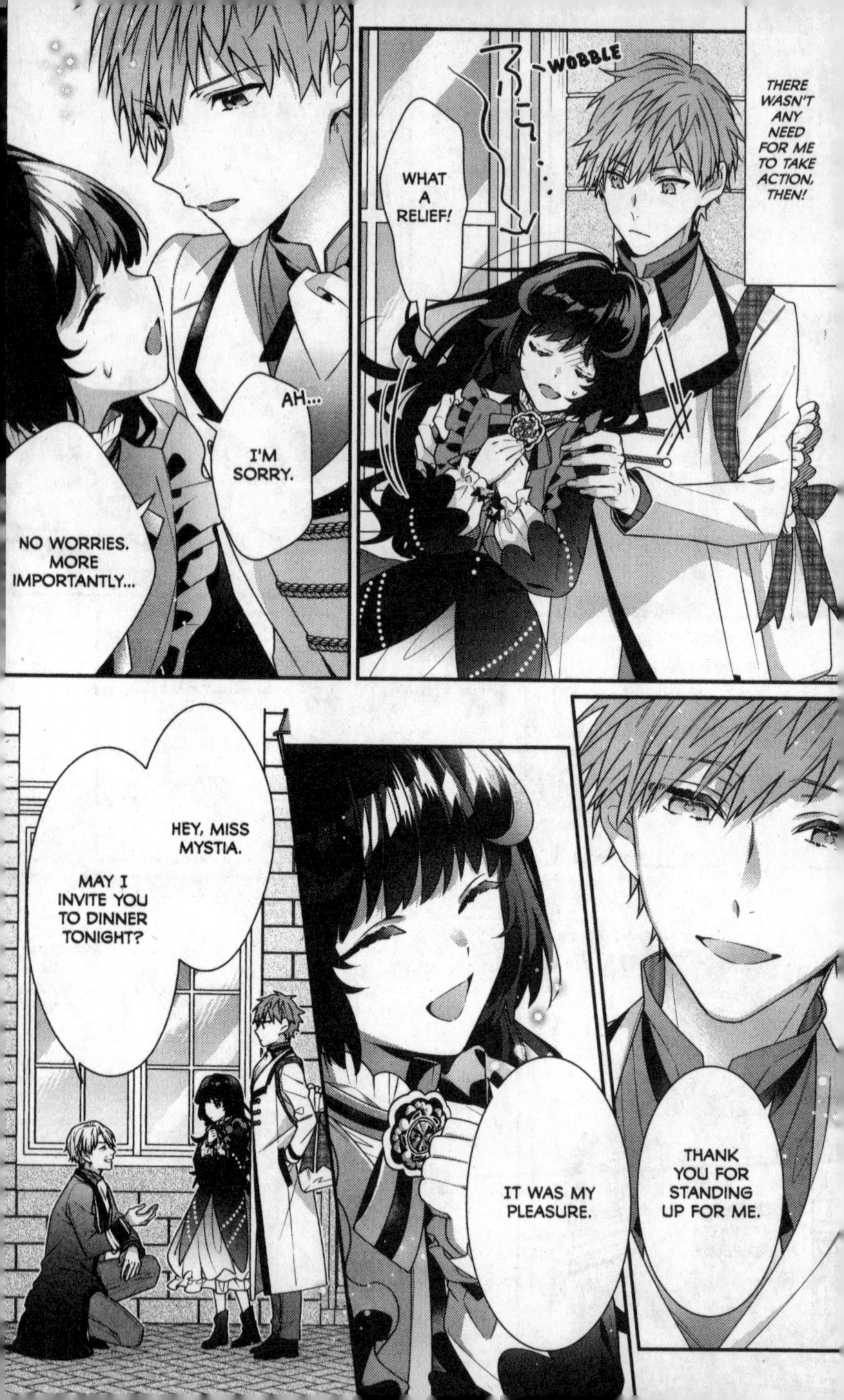
THERE WASN'T ANY NEED FOR ME TO TAKE ACTION, THEN!
WOBBLE
WHAT A RELIEF!
AH...
I'M SORRY.
NO WORRIES. MORE IMPORTANTLY...
THANK YOU FOR STANDING UP FOR ME.
IT WAS MY PLEASURE.
HEY, MISS MYSTIA.
MAY I INVITE YOU TO DINNER TONIGHT?

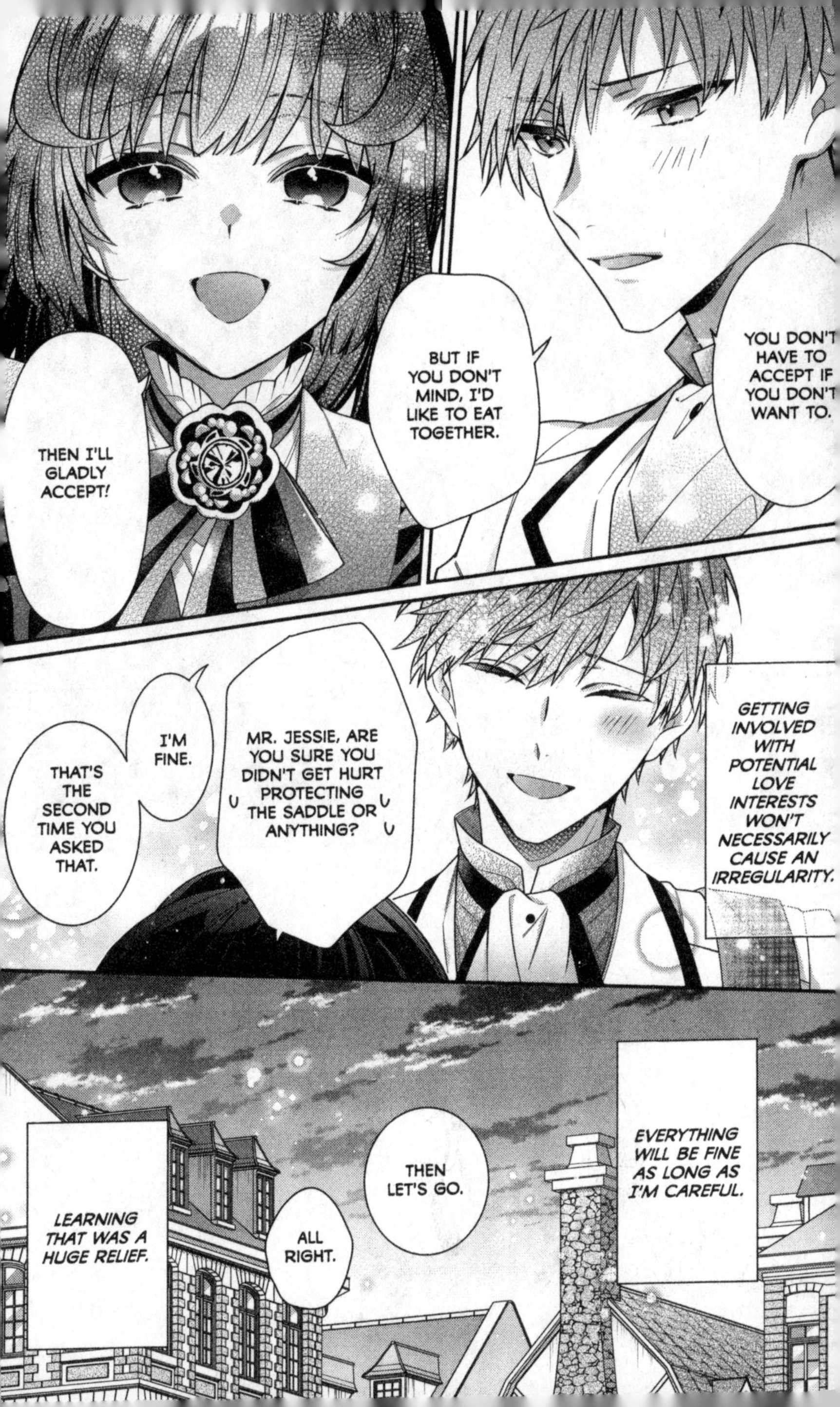
YOU DON'T HAVE TO ACCEPT IF YOU DON'T WANT TO.
BUT IF YOU DON'T MIND, I'D LIKE TO EAT TOGETHER.
THEN I'LL GLADLY ACCEPT!
GETTING INVOLVED WITH POTENTIAL LOVE INTERESTS WON'T NECESSARILY CAUSE AN IRREGULARITY.
MR. JESSIE, ARE YOU SURE YOU DIDN'T GET HURT PROTECTING THE SADDLE OR ANYTHING?
I'M FINE.
THAT'S THE SECOND TIME YOU ASKED THAT.
EVERYTHING WILL BE FINE AS LONG AS I'M CAREFUL.
THEN LET'S GO.
ALL RIGHT.
LEARNING THAT WAS A HUGE RELIEF.

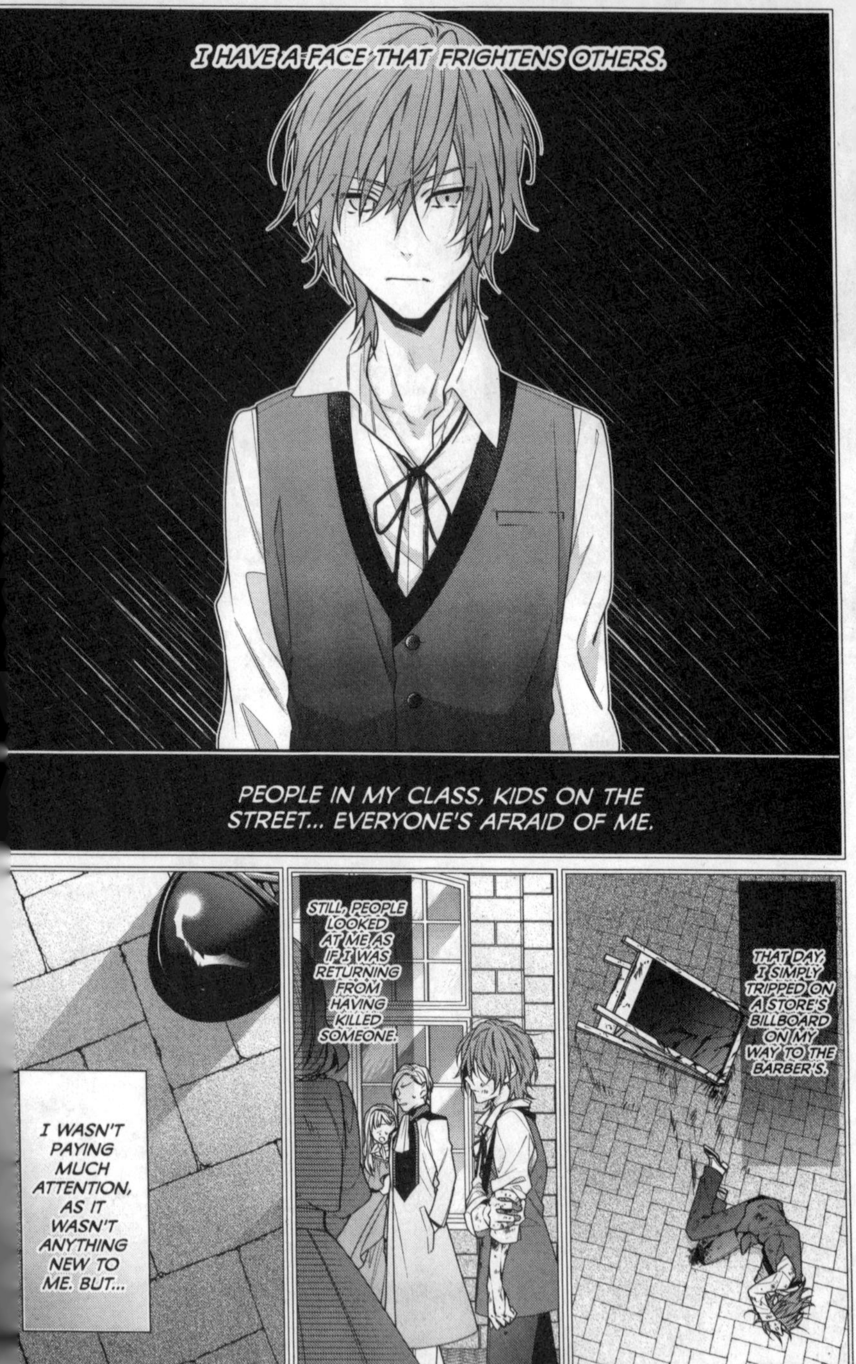
I HAVE A FACE THAT FRIGHTENS OTHERS.
PEOPLE IN MY CLASS, KIDS ON THE STREET... EVERYONE'S AFRAID OF ME.
THAT DAY, I SIMPLY TRIPPED ON A STORE'S BILLBOARD ON MY WAY TO THE BARBER'S.
STILL, PEOPLE LOOKED AT ME AS IF I WAS RETURNING FROM HAVING KILLED SOMEONE.
I WASN'T PAYING MUCH ATTENTION, AS IT WASN'T ANYTHING NEW TO ME. BUT...

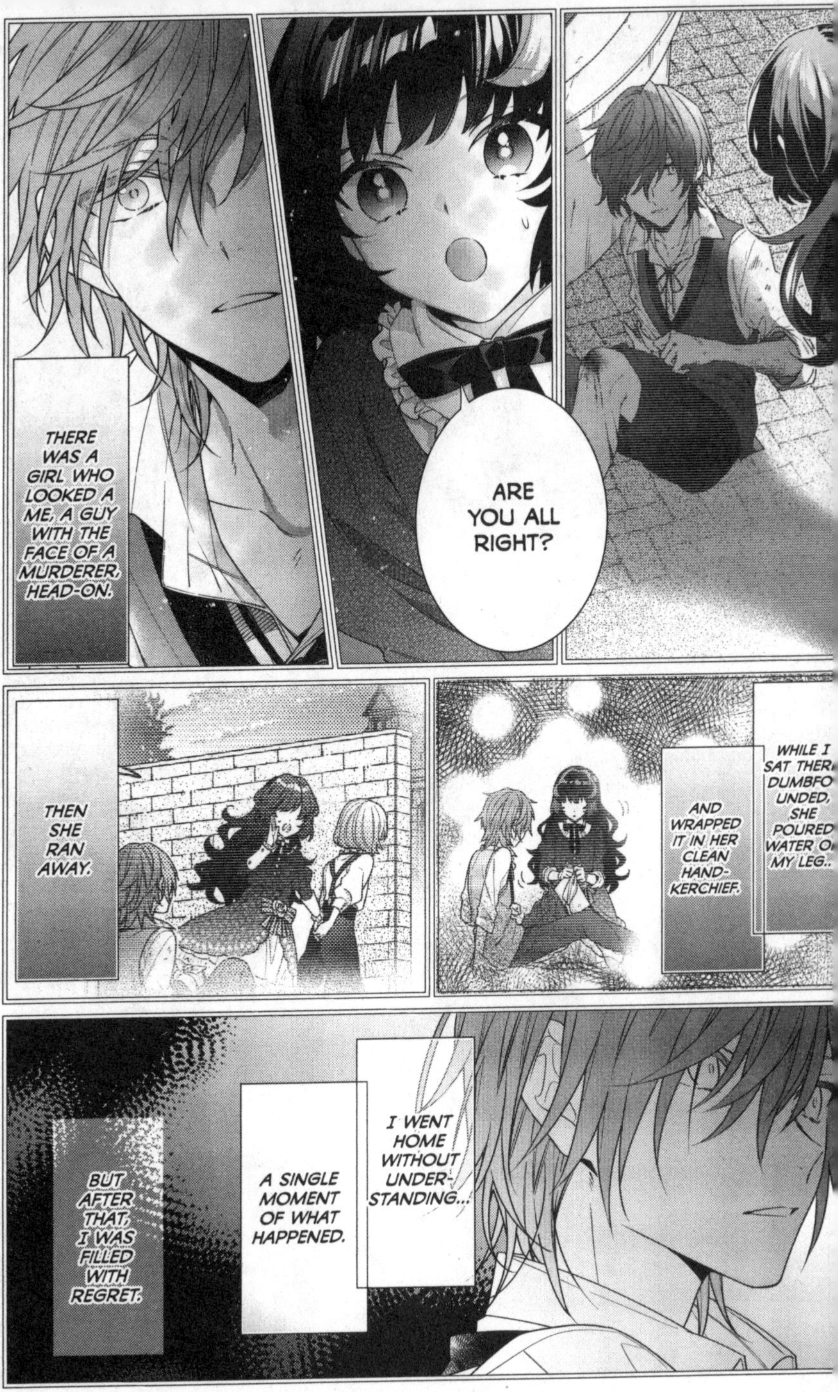
ARE YOU ALL RIGHT?
THERE WAS A GIRL WHO LOOKED A ME, A GUY WITH THE FACE OF A MURDERER, HEAD-ON.
WHILE I SAT THER DUMBFO UNDED, SHE POURED WATER O MY LEG...
AND WRAPPED IT IN HER CLEAN HAND-KERCHIEF.
THEN SHE RAN AWAY.
I WENT HOME WITHOUT UNDER-STANDING...
A SINGLE MOMENT OF WHAT HAPPENED.
BUT AFTER THAT, I WAS FILLED WITH REGRET.

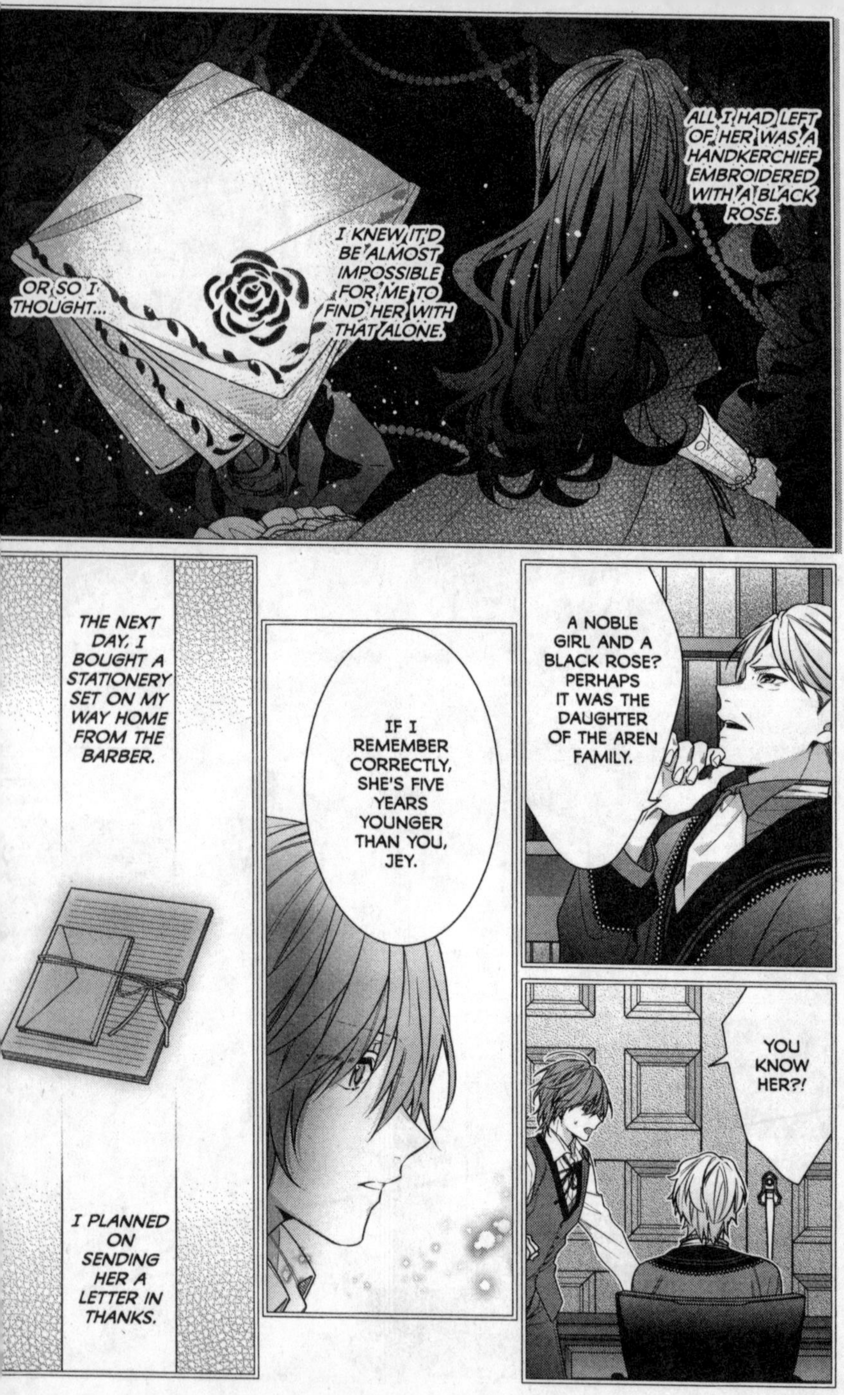
ALL I HAD LEFT OF HER WAS A HANDKERCHIEF EMBROIDERED WITH A BLACK ROSE.
I KNEW IT'D BE ALMOST IMPOSSIBLE FOR ME TO FIND HER WITH THAT ALONE.
OR SO I THOUGHT...
A NOBLE GIRL AND A BLACK ROSE? PERHAPS IT WAS THE DAUGHTER OF THE AREN FAMILY.
YOU KNOW HER?!
IF I REMEMBER CORRECTLY, SHE'S FIVE YEARS YOUNGER THAN YOU, JEY.
THE NEXT DAY, I BOUGHT A STATIONERY SET ON MY WAY HOME FROM THE BARBER.
I PLANNED ON SENDING HER A LETTER IN THANKS.

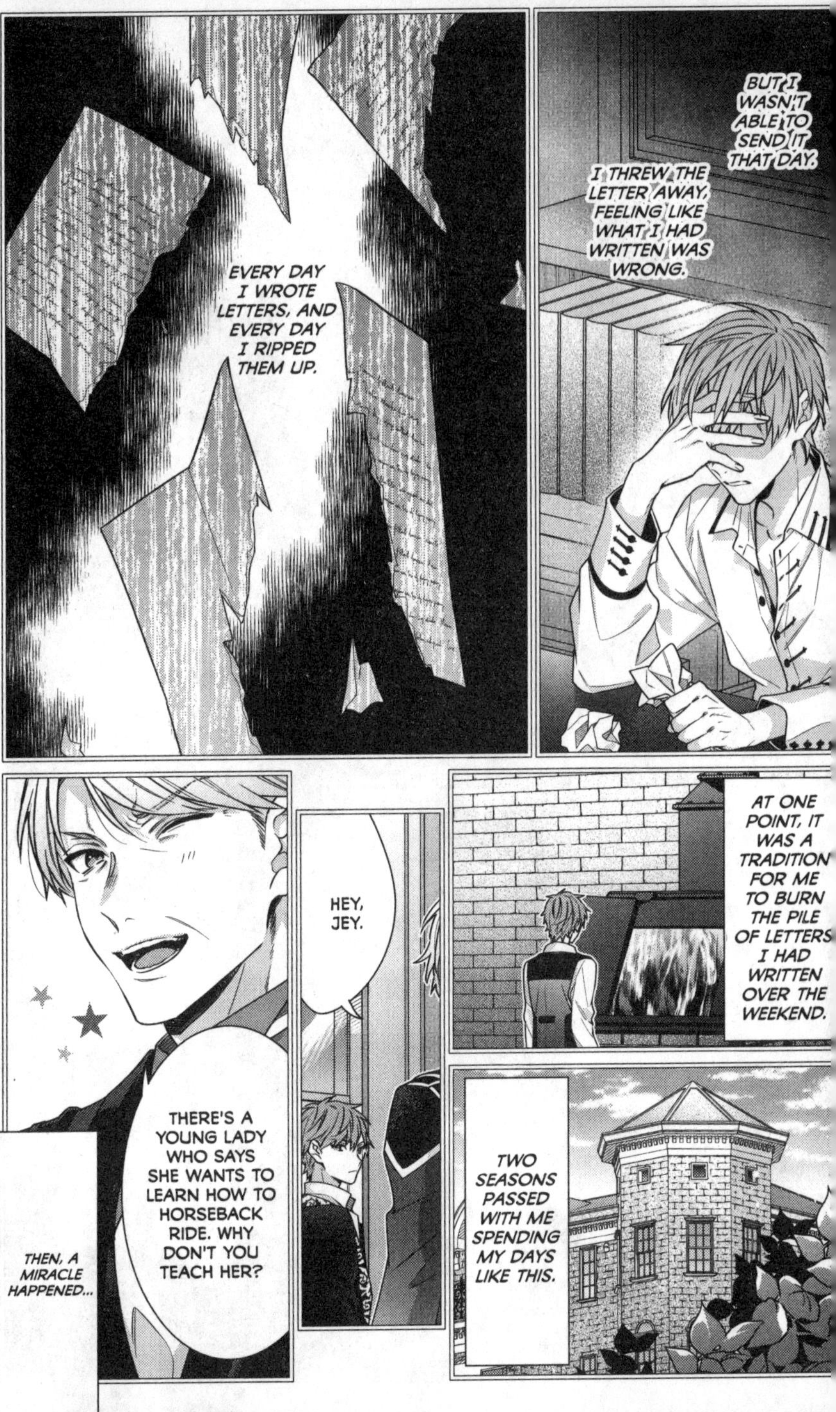
BUT I WASN'T ABLE TO SEND IT THAT DAY.
I THREW THE LETTER AWAY, FEELING LIKE WHAT I HAD WRITTEN WAS WRONG.
EVERY DAY I WROTE LETTERS, AND EVERY DAY I RIPPED THEM UP.
AT ONE POINT, IT WAS A TRADITION FOR ME TO BURN THE PILE OF LETTERS I HAD WRITTEN OVER THE WEEKEND.
TWO SEASONS PASSED WITH ME SPENDING MY DAYS LIKE THIS.
HEY, JEY.
THERE'S A YOUNG LADY WHO SAYS SHE WANTS TO LEARN HOW TO HORSEBACK RIDE. WHY DON'T YOU TEACH HER?
THEN, A MIRACLE HAPPENED...

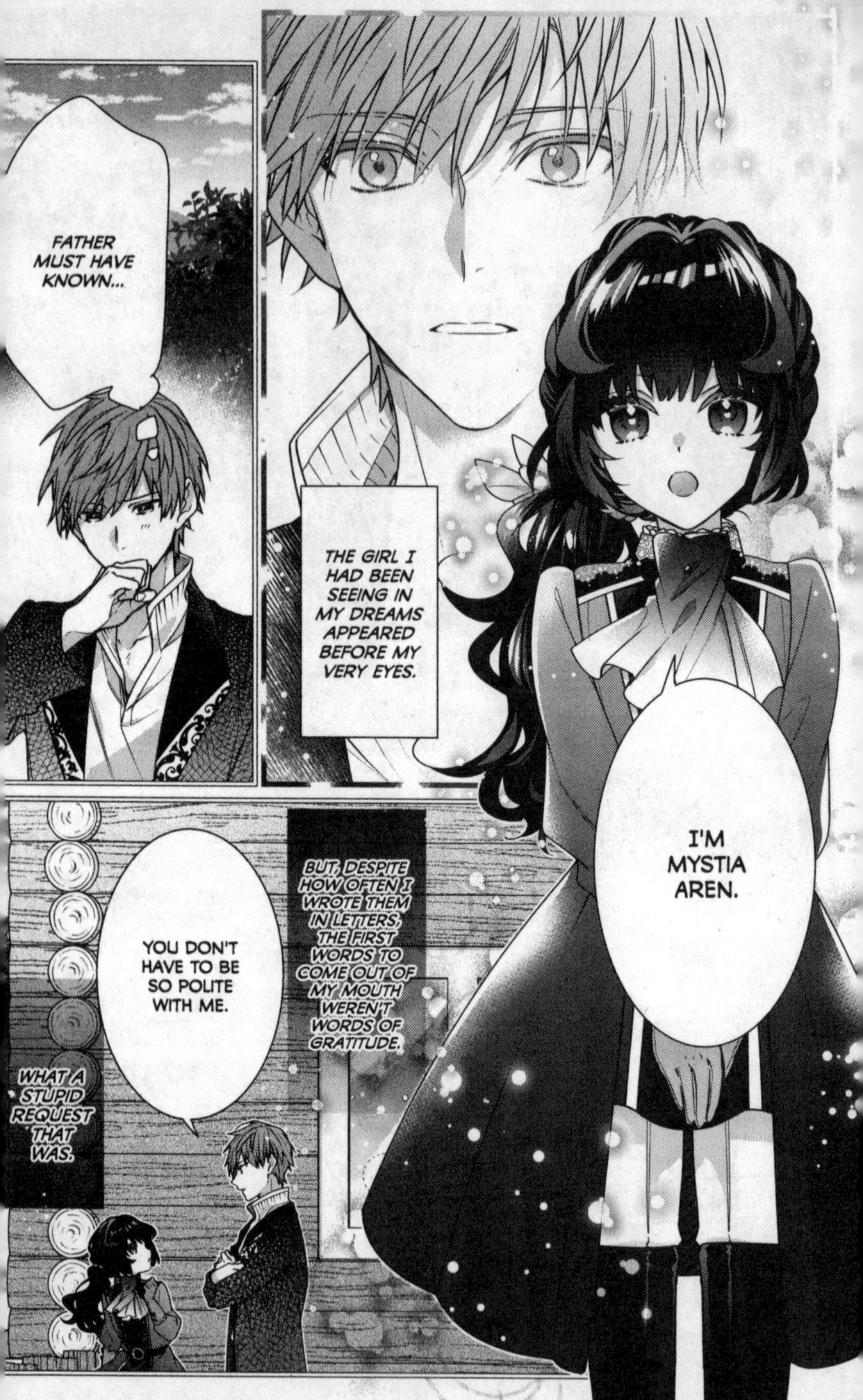
THE GIRL I HAD BEEN SEEING IN MY DREAMS APPEARED BEFORE MY VERY EYES.
I'M MYSTIA AREN.
FATHER MUST HAVE KNOWN...
BUT, DESPITE HOW OFTEN I WROTE THEM IN LETTERS, THE FIRST WORDS TO COME OUT OF MY MOUTH WEREN'T WORDS OF GRATITUDE.
YOU DON'T HAVE TO BE SO POLITE WITH ME.
WHAT A STUPID REQUEST THAT WAS.

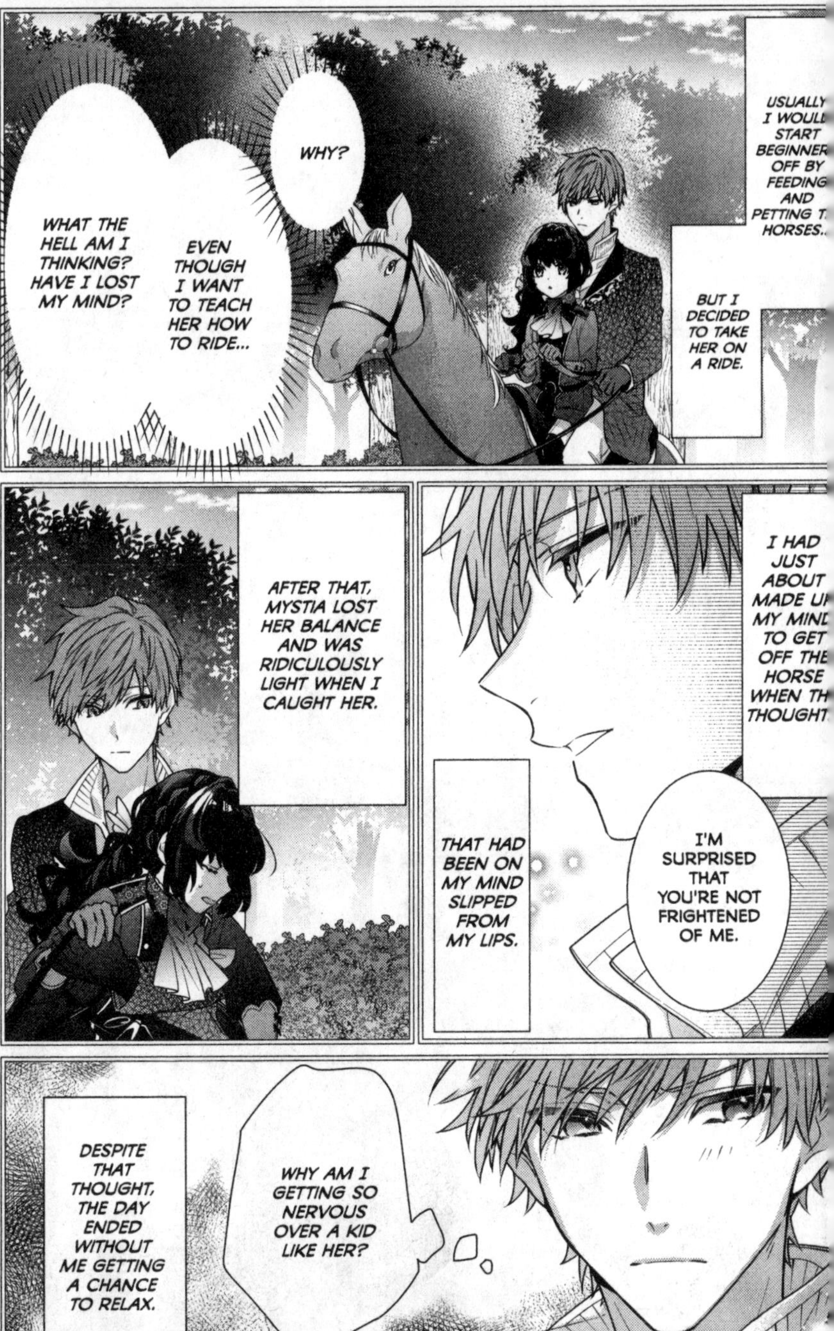
USUALLY I WOUL START BEGINNER OFF BY FEEDING AND PETTING T HORSES..
BUT I DECIDED TO TAKE HER ON A RIDE.
WHY?
EVEN THOUGH I WANT TO TEACH HER HOW TO RIDE...
WHAT THE HELL AM I THINKING? HAVE I LOST MY MIND?
I HAD JUST ABOUT MADE U MY MIN TO GET OFF THE HORSE WHEN TH THOUGHT
THAT HAD BEEN ON MY MIND SLIPPED FROM MY LIPS.
I'M SURPRISED THAT YOU'RE NOT FRIGHTENED OF ME.
AFTER THAT, MYSTIA LOST HER BALANCE AND WAS RIDICULOUSLY LIGHT WHEN I CAUGHT HER.
WHY AM I GETTING SO NERVOUS OVER A KID LIKE HER?
DESPITE THAT THOUGHT, THE DAY ENDED WITHOUT ME GETTING A CHANCE TO RELAX.

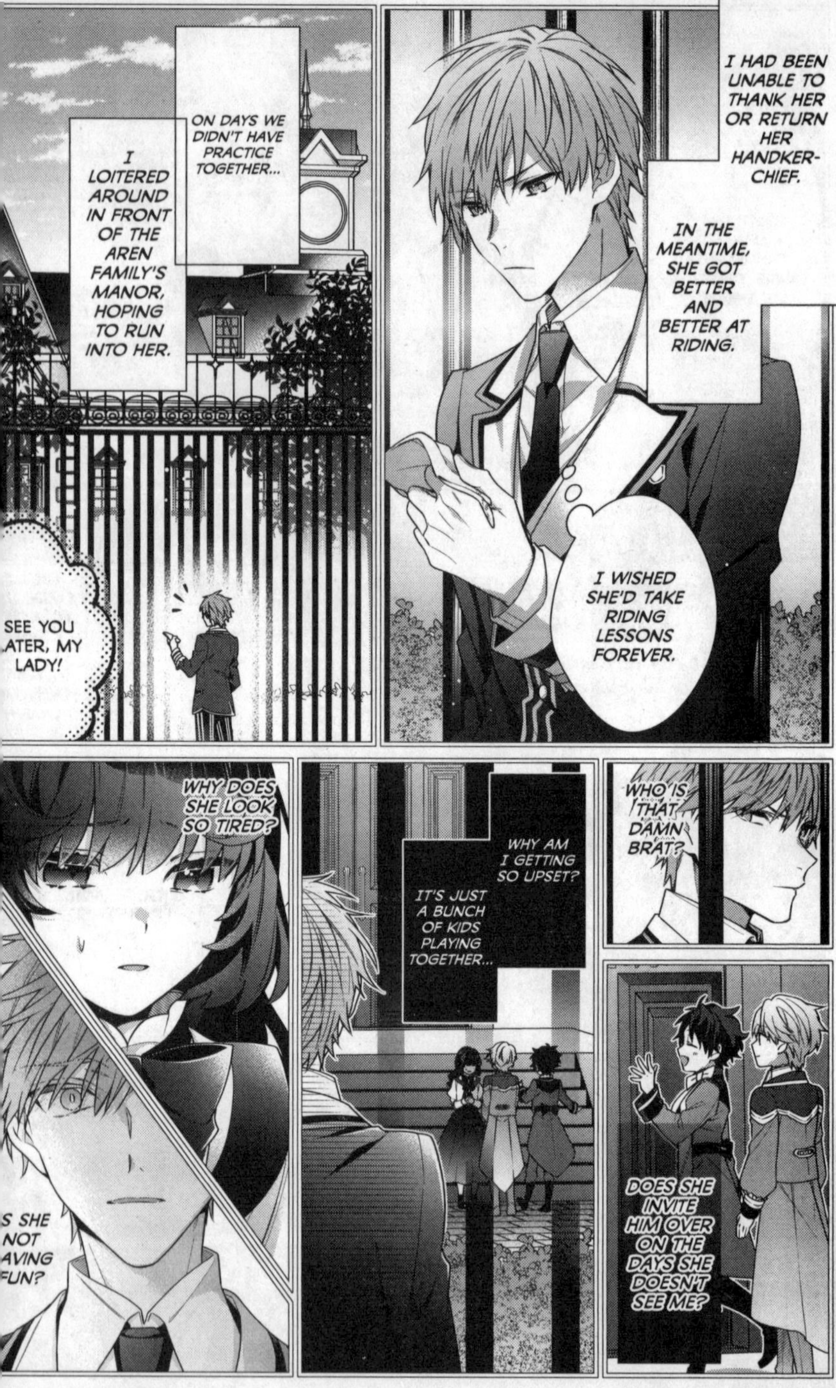
I HAD BEEN UNABLE TO THANK HER OR RETURN HER HANDKER-CHIEF.
IN THE MEANTIME, SHE GOT BETTER AND BETTER AT RIDING.
I WISHED SHE'D TAKE RIDING LESSONS FOREVER.
ON DAYS WE DIDN'T HAVE PRACTICE TOGETHER...
I LOITERED AROUND IN FRONT OF THE AREN FAMILY'S MANOR, HOPING TO RUN INTO HER.
SEE YOU ATER, MY LADY!
WHO IS THAT DAMN BRAT?
DOES SHE INVITE HIM OVER ON THE DAYS SHE DOESN'T SEE ME?
WHY AM I GETTING SO UPSET?
IT'S JUST A BUNCH OF KIDS PLAYING TOGETHER...
WHY DOES SHE LOOK SO TIRED?
S SHE NOT AVING FUN?

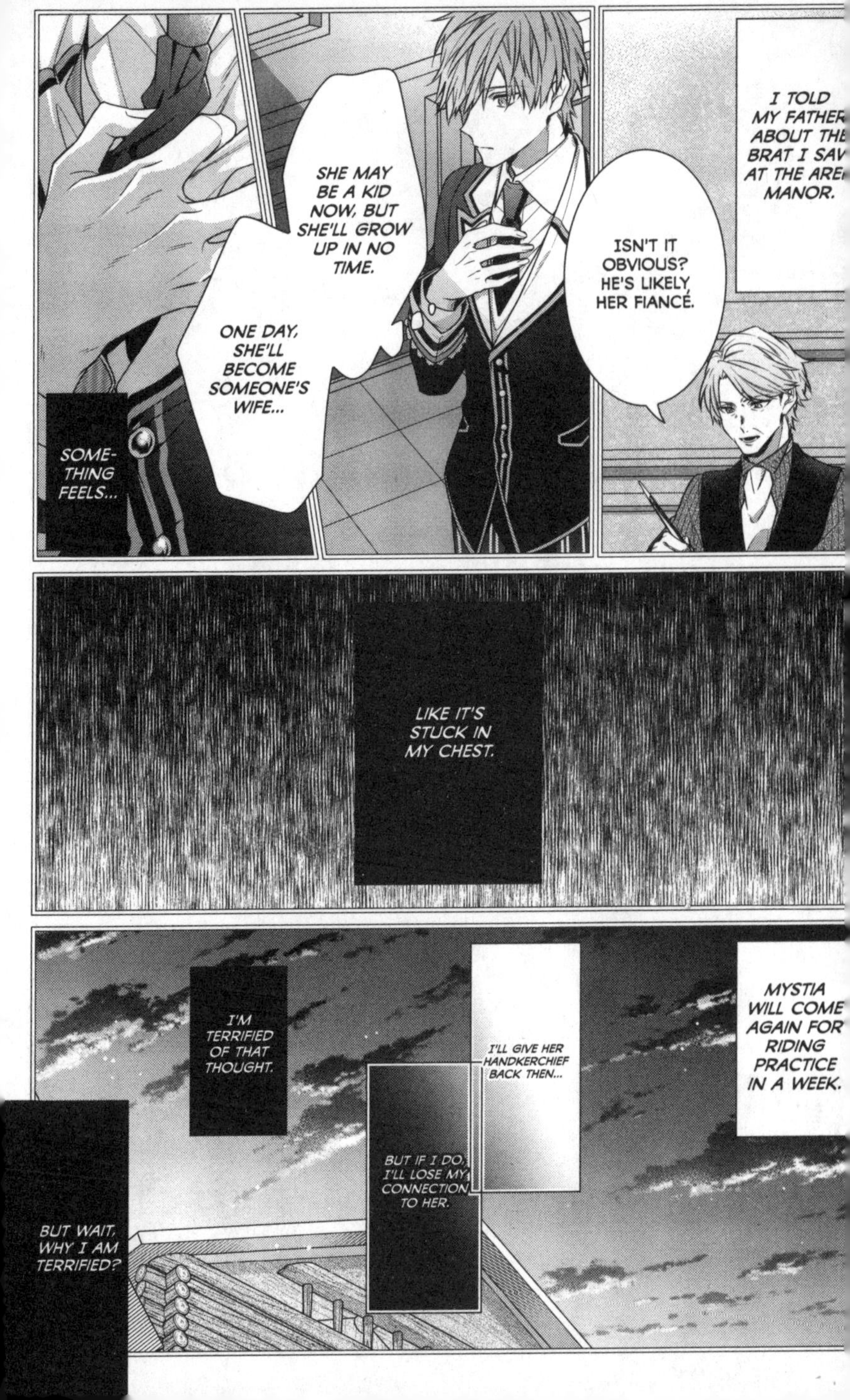
I TOLD MY FATHER ABOUT THE BRAT I SAW AT THE ARE MANOR.
ISN'T IT OBVIOUS? HE'S LIKELY HER FIANCÉ.
SHE MAY BE A KID NOW, BUT SHE'LL GROW UP IN NO TIME.
ONE DAY, SHE'LL BECOME SOMEONE'S WIFE...
SOME-THING FEELS...
LIKE IT'S STUCK IN MY CHEST.
MYSTIA WILL COME AGAIN FOR RIDING PRACTICE IN A WEEK.
I'LL GIVE HER HANDKERCHIEF BACK THEN...
BUT IF I DO, I'LL LOSE MY CONNECTION TO HER.
I'M TERRIFIED OF THAT THOUGHT.
BUT WAIT, WHY I AM TERRIFIED?

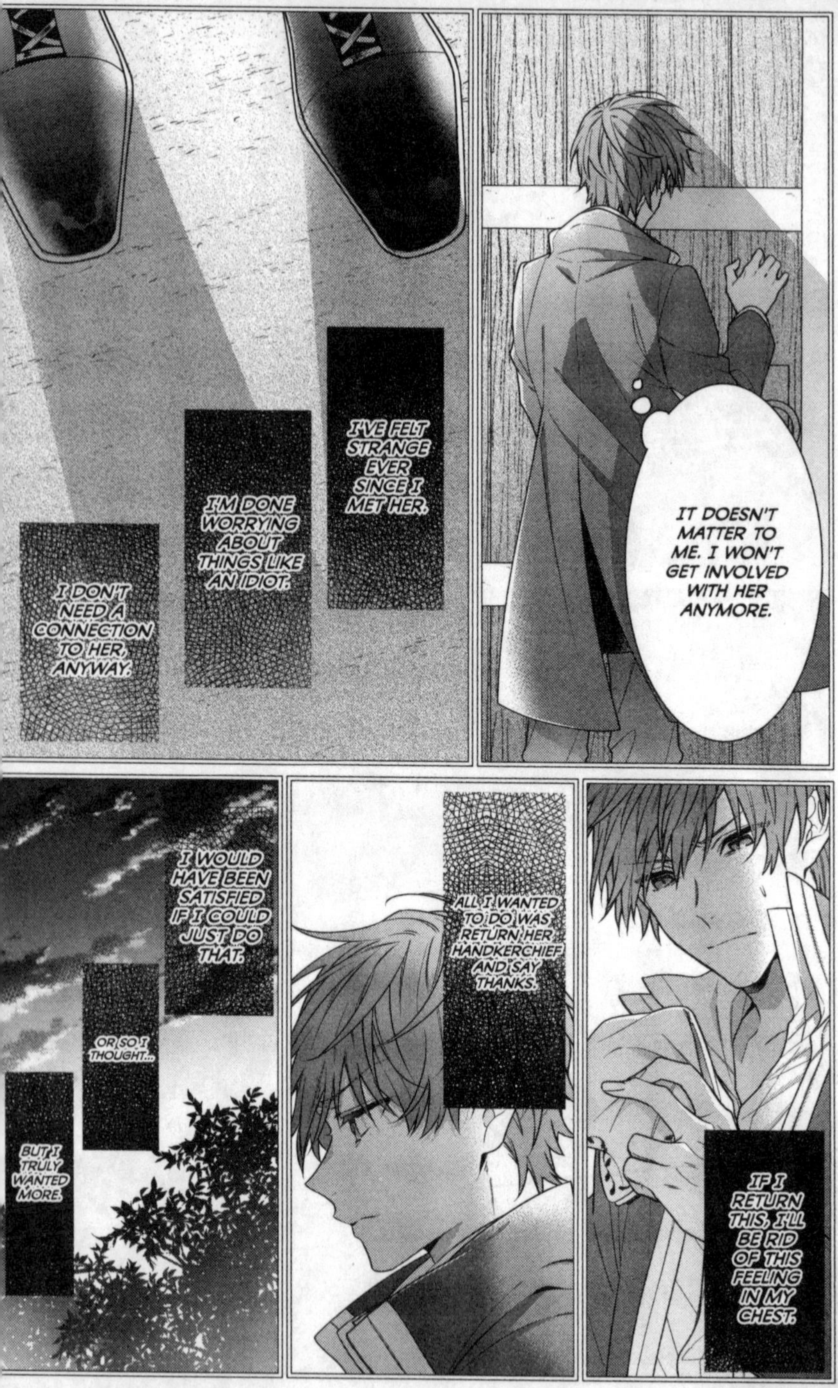
IT DOESN'T MATTER TO ME. I WON'T GET INVOLVED WITH HER ANYMORE.
I'VE FELT STRANGE EVER SINCE I MET HER.
I'M DONE WORRYING ABOUT THINGS LIKE AN IDIOT.
I DON'T NEED A CONNECTION TO HER, ANYWAY.
IF I RETURN THIS, I'LL BE RID OF THIS FEELING IN MY CHEST.
ALL I WANTED TO DO WAS RETURN HER HANDKERCHIEF AND SAY THANKS.
I WOULD HAVE BEEN SATISFIED IF I COULD JUST DO THAT.
OR SO I THOUGHT...
BUT I TRULY WANTED MORE.

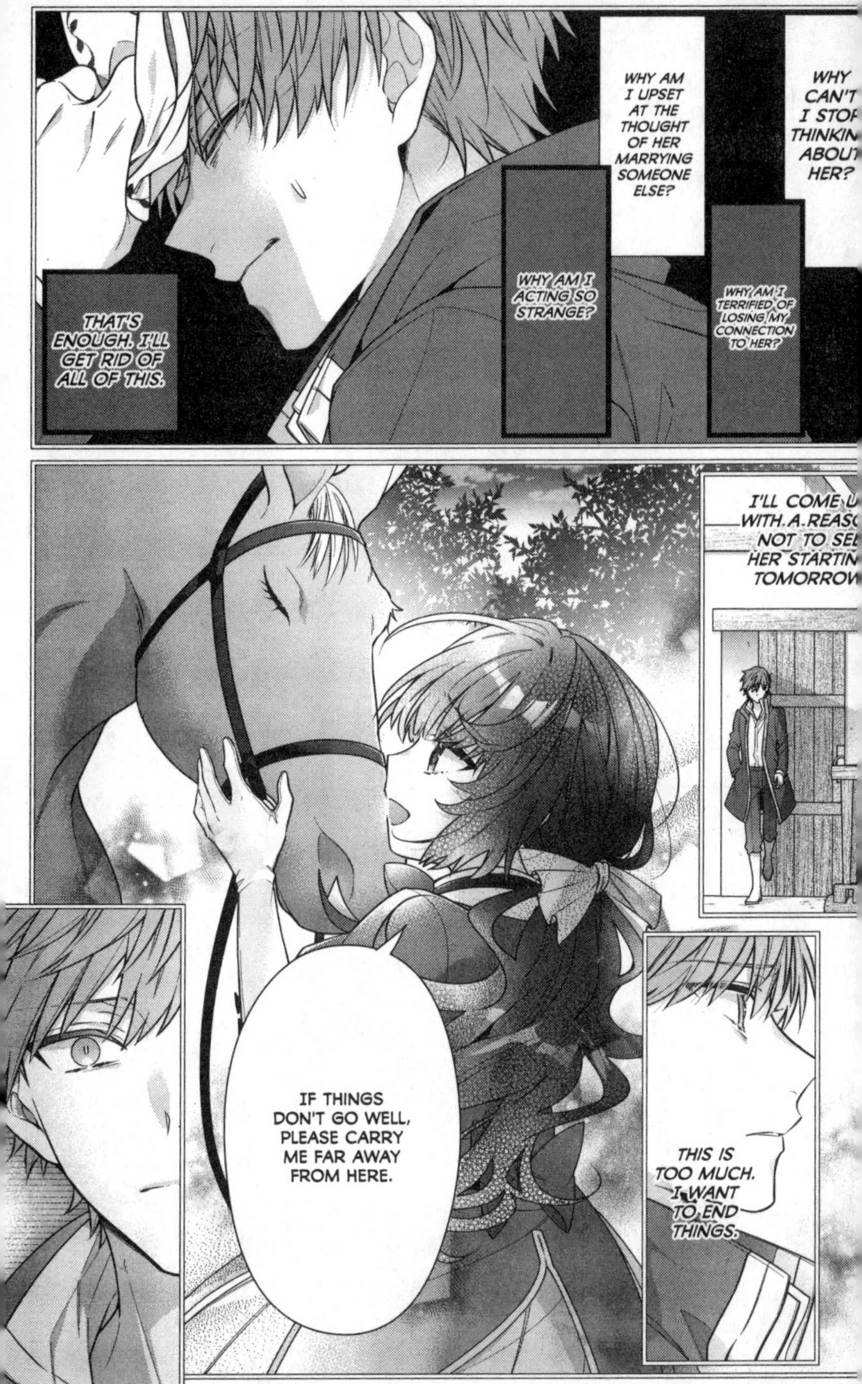
WHY CAN'T I STO THINKIN ABOUT HER?
WHY AM I UPSET AT THE THOUGHT OF HER MARRYING SOMEONE ELSE?
WHY AM I TERRIFIED OF LOSING MY CONNECTION TO HER?
WHY AM I ACTING SO STRANGE?
THAT'S ENOUGH. I'LL GET RID OF ALL OF THIS.
I'LL COME U WITH A REASO NOT TO SE HER STARTIN TOMORROW
IF THINGS DON'T GO WELL, PLEASE CARRY ME FAR AWAY FROM HERE.
THIS IS TOO MUCH. I WANT TO END THINGS.

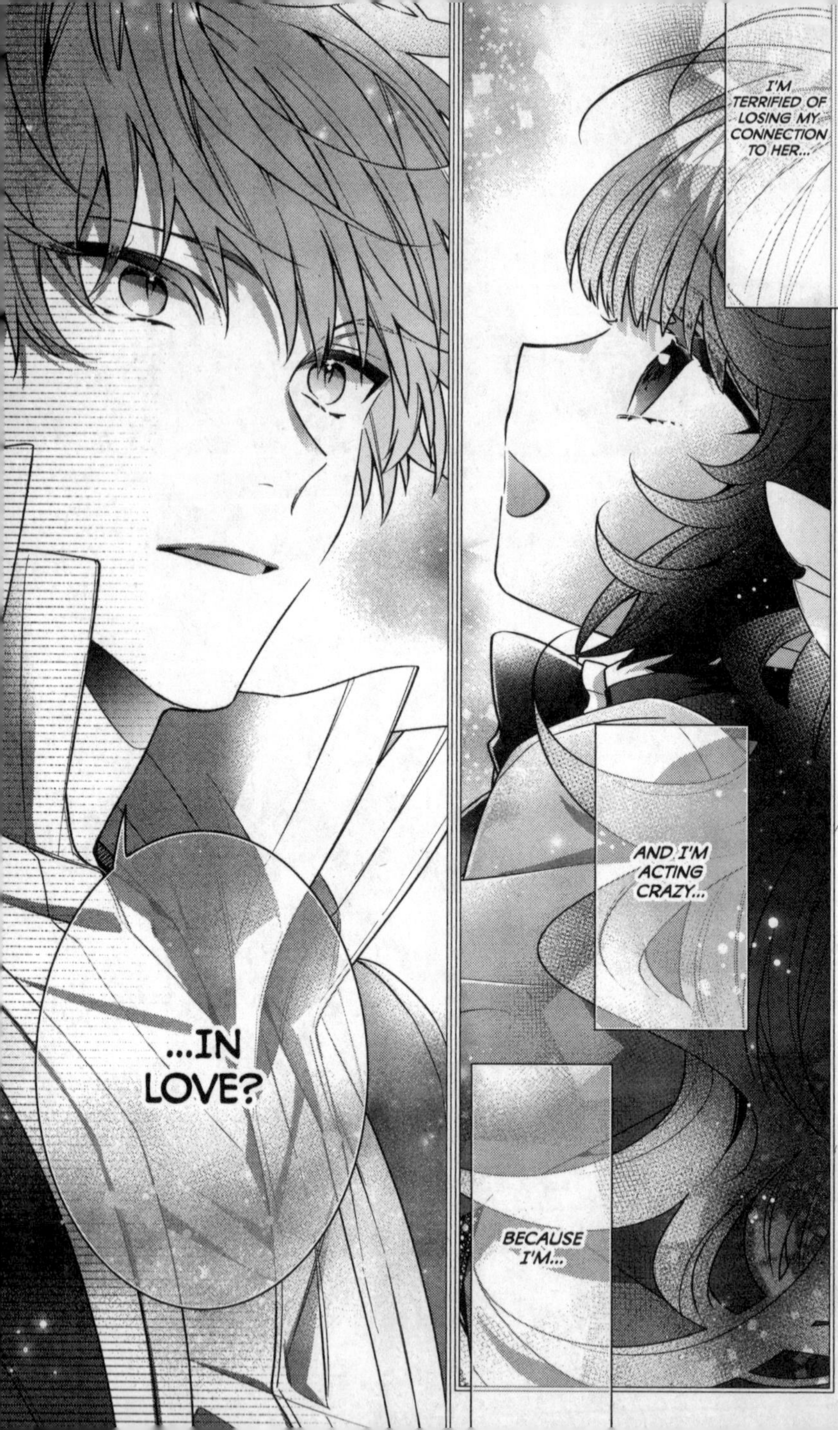
I'M TERRIFIED OF LOSING MY CONNECTION TO HER...
AND I'M ACTING CRAZY...
BECAUSE I'M...
...IN LOVE?

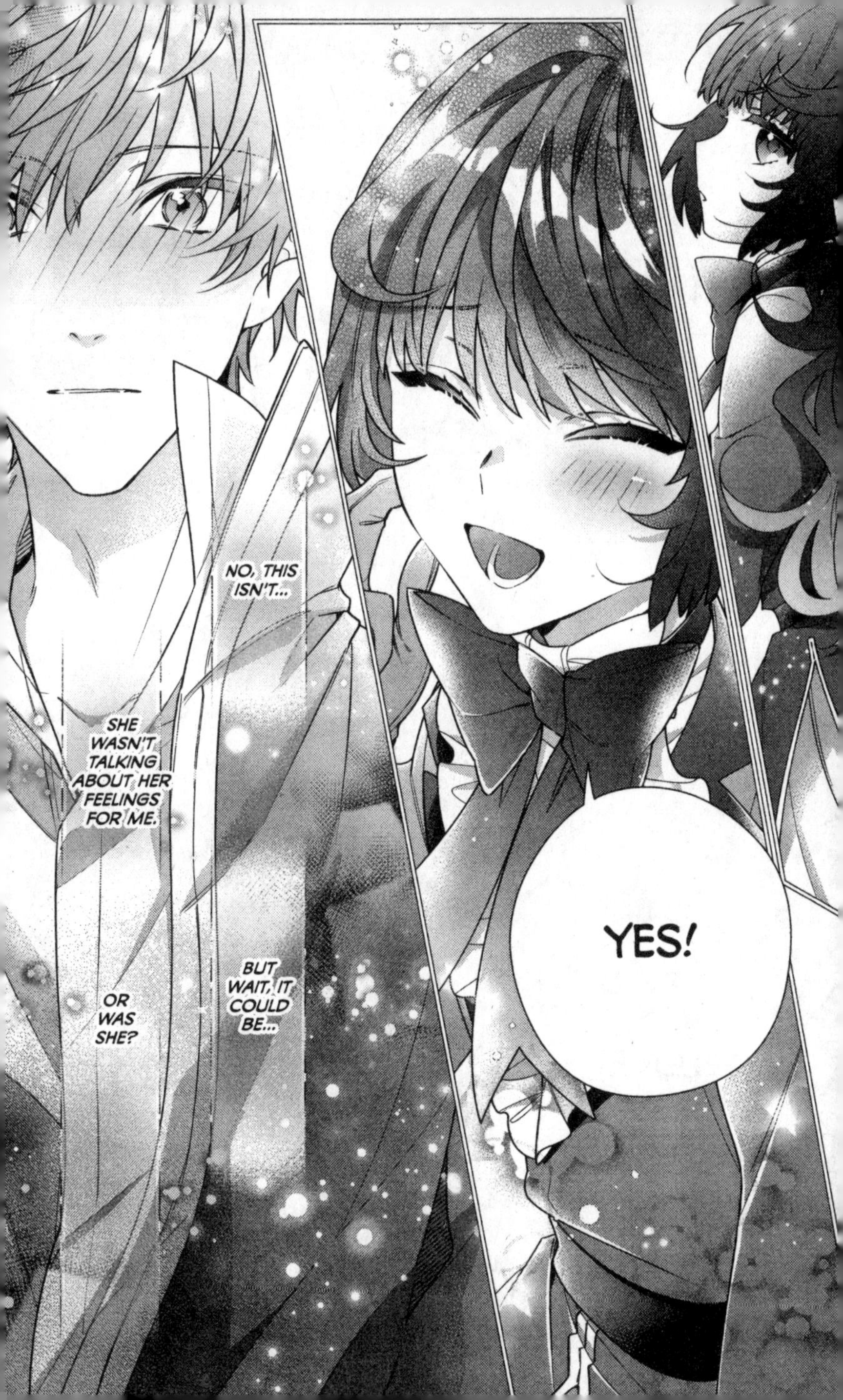
YES!
NO, THIS ISN'T...
SHE WASN'T TALKING ABOUT HER FEELINGS FOR ME.
BUT WAIT, IT COULD BE...
OR WAS SHE?

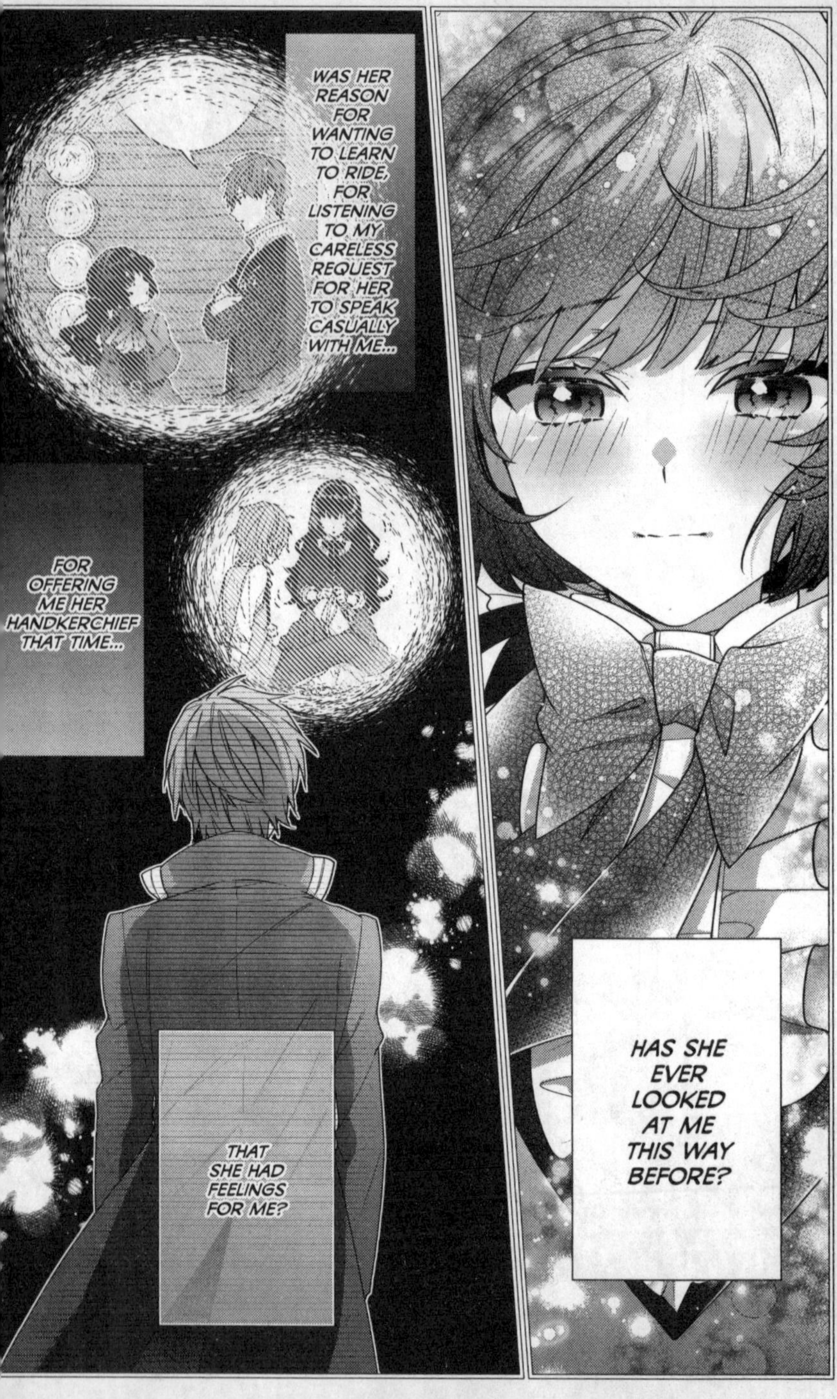
HAS SHE EVER LOOKED AT ME THIS WAY BEFORE?
WAS HER REASON FOR WANTING TO LEARN TO RIDE, FOR LISTENING TO MY CARELESS REQUEST FOR HER TO SPEAK CASUALLY WITH ME...
FOR OFFERING ME HER HANDKERCHIEF THAT TIME...
THAT SHE HAD FEELINGS FOR ME?

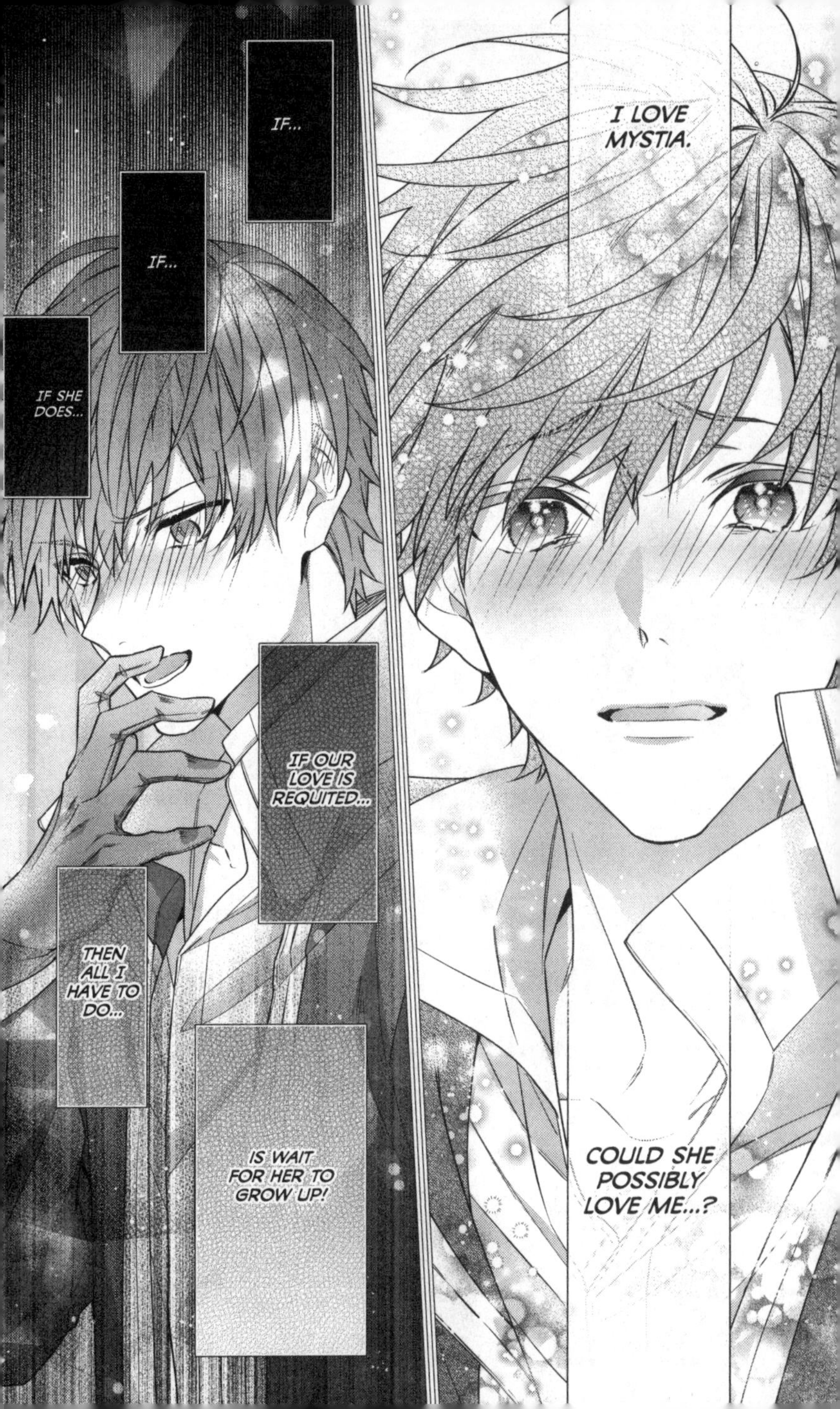
I LOVE MYSTIA.
COULD SHE POSSIBLY LOVE ME...?
IF...
IF...
IF SHE DOES...
IF OUR LOVE IS REQUITED...
THEN ALL I HAVE TO DO...
IS WAIT FOR HER TO GROW UP!

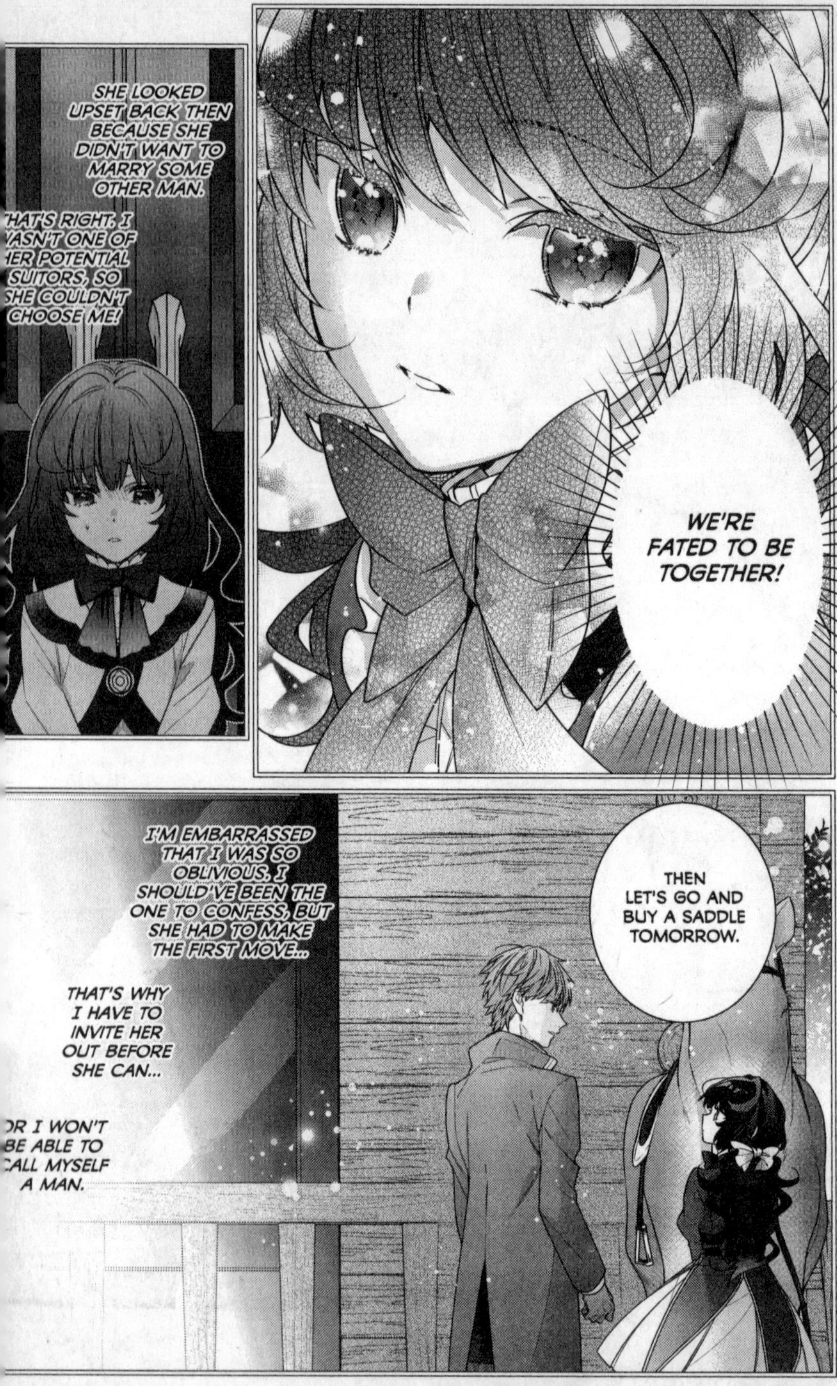
WE'RE FATED TO BE TOGETHER!
SHE LOOKED UPSET BACK THEN BECAUSE SHE DIDN'T WANT TO MARRY SOME OTHER MAN.
THAT'S RIGHT. I WASN'T ONE OF HER POTENTIAL SUITORS, SO SHE COULDN'T CHOOSE ME!
THEN LET'S GO AND BUY A SADDLE TOMORROW.
I'M EMBARRASSED THAT I WAS SO OBLIVIOUS. I SHOULD'VE BEEN THE ONE TO CONFESS, BUT SHE HAD TO MAKE THE FIRST MOVE...
THAT'S WHY I HAVE TO INVITE HER OUT BEFORE SHE CAN...
OR I WON'T BE ABLE TO CALL MYSELF A MAN.

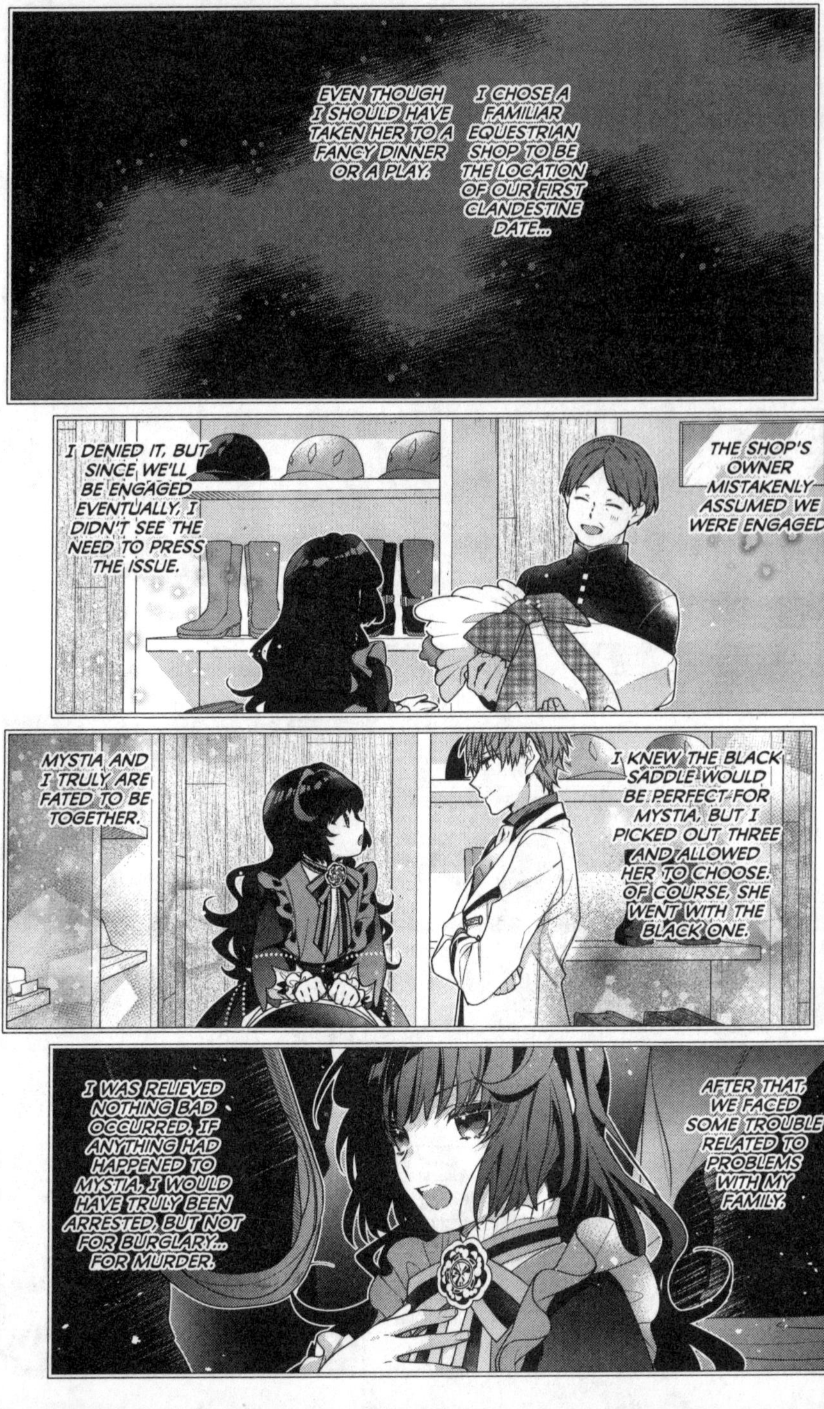
I CHOSE A FAMILIAR EQUESTRIAN SHOP TO BE THE LOCATION OF OUR FIRST CLANDESTINE DATE...
EVEN THOUGH I SHOULD HAVE TAKEN HER TO A FANCY DINNER OR A PLAY.
THE SHOP'S OWNER MISTAKENLY ASSUMED WE WERE ENGAGED.
I DENIED IT, BUT SINCE WE'LL BE ENGAGED EVENTUALLY, I DIDN'T SEE THE NEED TO PRESS THE ISSUE.
I KNEW THE BLACK SADDLE WOULD BE PERFECT FOR MYSTIA, BUT I PICKED OUT THREE AND ALLOWED HER TO CHOOSE. OF COURSE, SHE WENT WITH THE BLACK ONE.
MYSTIA AND I TRULY ARE FATED TO BE TOGETHER.
AFTER THAT, WE FACED SOME TROUBLE RELATED TO PROBLEMS WITH MY FAMILY.
I WAS RELIEVED NOTHING BAD OCCURRED. IF ANYTHING HAD HAPPENED TO MYSTIA, I WOULD HAVE TRULY BEEN ARRESTED, BUT NOT FOR BURGLARY... FOR MURDER.

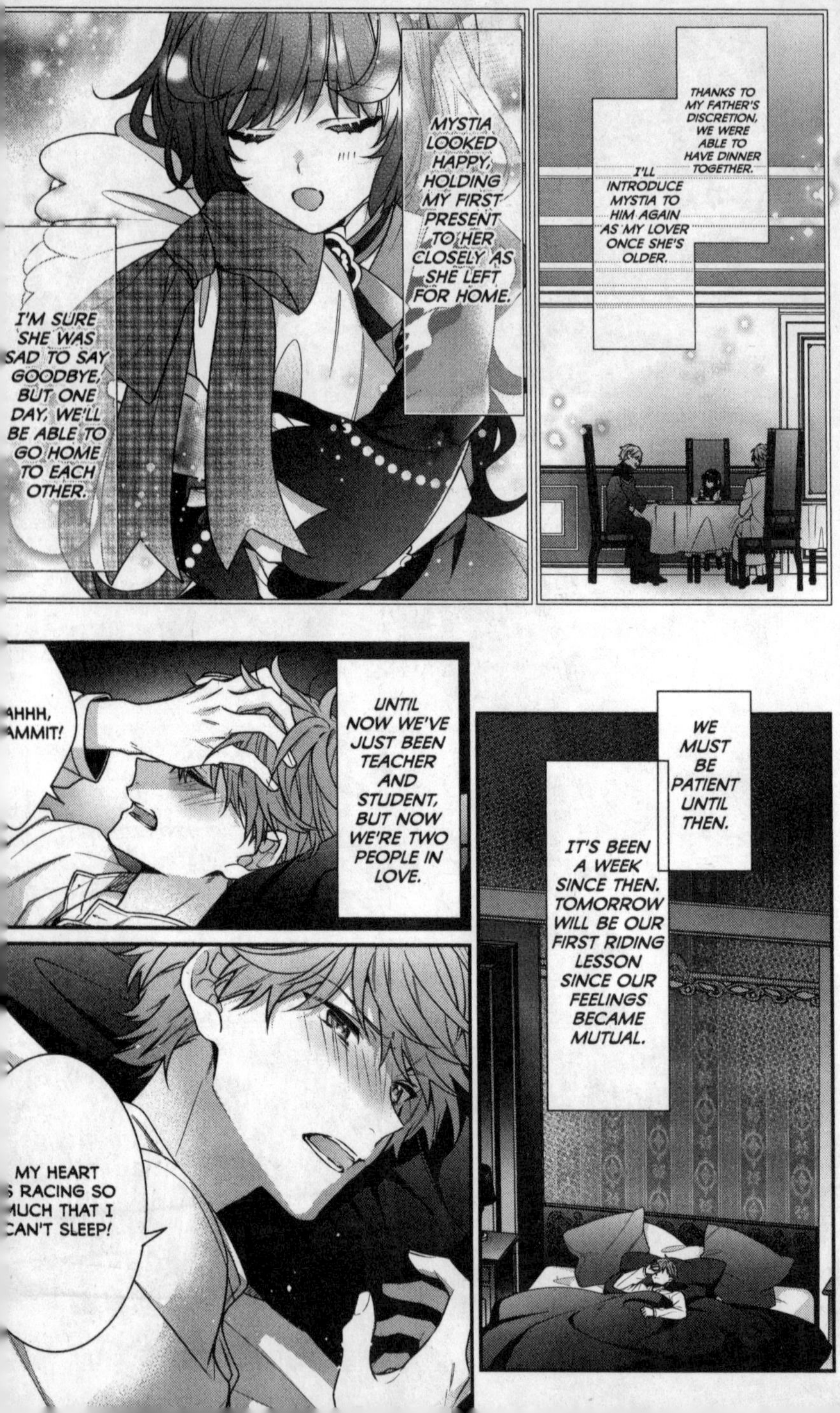
THANKS TO MY FATHER'S DISCRETION, WE WERE ABLE TO HAVE DINNER TOGETHER.
I'LL INTRODUCE MYSTIA TO HIM AGAIN AS MY LOVER ONCE SHE'S OLDER.
MYSTIA LOOKED HAPPY, HOLDING MY FIRST PRESENT TO HER CLOSELY AS SHE LEFT FOR HOME.
I'M SURE SHE WAS SAD TO SAY GOODBYE, BUT ONE DAY, WE'LL BE ABLE TO GO HOME TO EACH OTHER.
WE MUST BE PATIENT UNTIL THEN.
IT'S BEEN A WEEK SINCE THEN. TOMORROW WILL BE OUR FIRST RIDING LESSON SINCE OUR FEELINGS BECAME MUTUAL.
UNTIL NOW WE'VE JUST BEEN TEACHER AND STUDENT, BUT NOW WE'RE TWO PEOPLE IN LOVE.
AHHH, AMMIT!
MY HEART S RACING SO MUCH THAT I CAN'T SLEEP!

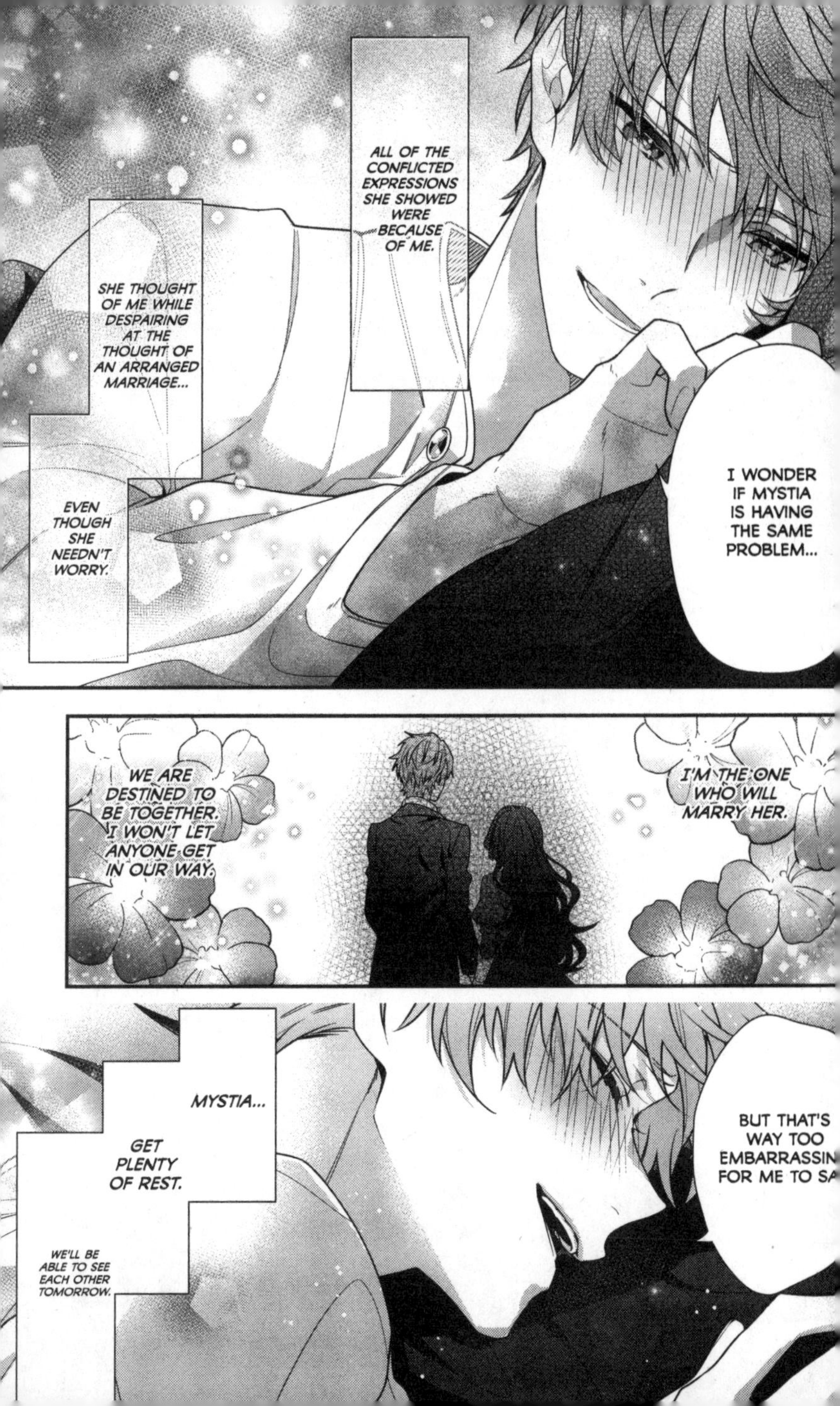
I WONDER IF MYSTIA IS HAVING THE SAME PROBLEM...
ALL OF THE CONFLICTED EXPRESSIONS SHE SHOWED WERE BECAUSE OF ME.
SHE THOUGHT OF ME WHILE DESPAIRING AT THE THOUGHT OF AN ARRANGED MARRIAGE...
EVEN THOUGH SHE NEEDN'T WORRY.
I'M THE ONE WHO WILL MARRY HER.
WE ARE DESTINED TO BE TOGETHER. I WON'T LET ANYONE GET IN OUR WAY.
BUT THAT'S WAY TOO EMBARRASSIN FOR ME TO SA
MYSTIA...
GET PLENTY OF REST.
WE'LL BE ABLE TO SEE EACH OTHER TOMORROW.

I was REINCARNATED as the Villainess in an OTOME GAME but the boys love me anyway!

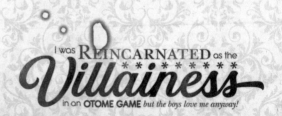

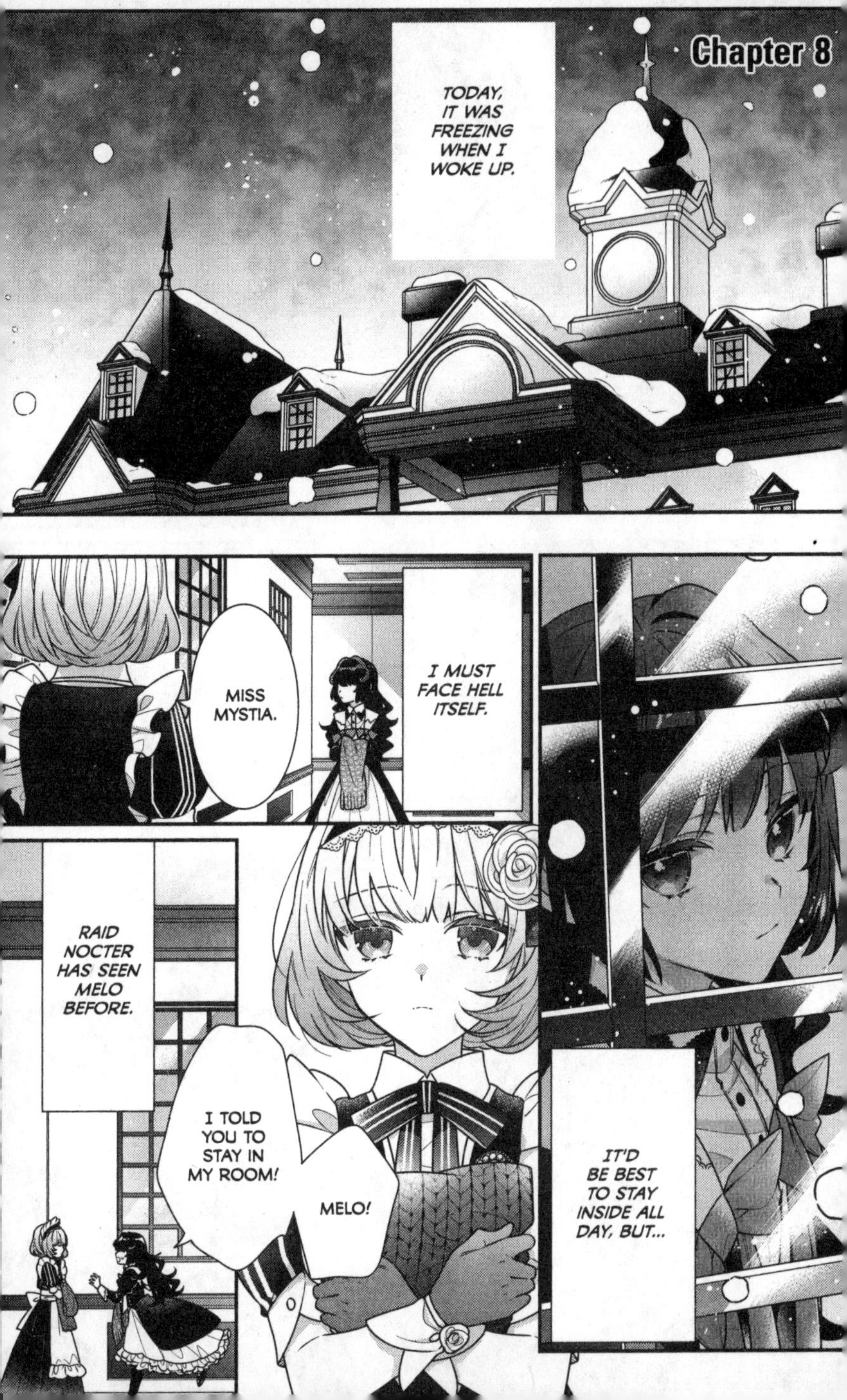
Chapter 8
TODAY, IT WAS FREEZING WHEN I WOKE UP.
IT'D BE BEST TO STAY INSIDE ALL DAY, BUT...
I MUST FACE HELL ITSELF.
MISS MYSTIA.
RAID NOCTER HAS SEEN MELO BEFORE.
MELO!
I TOLD YOU TO STAY IN MY ROOM!

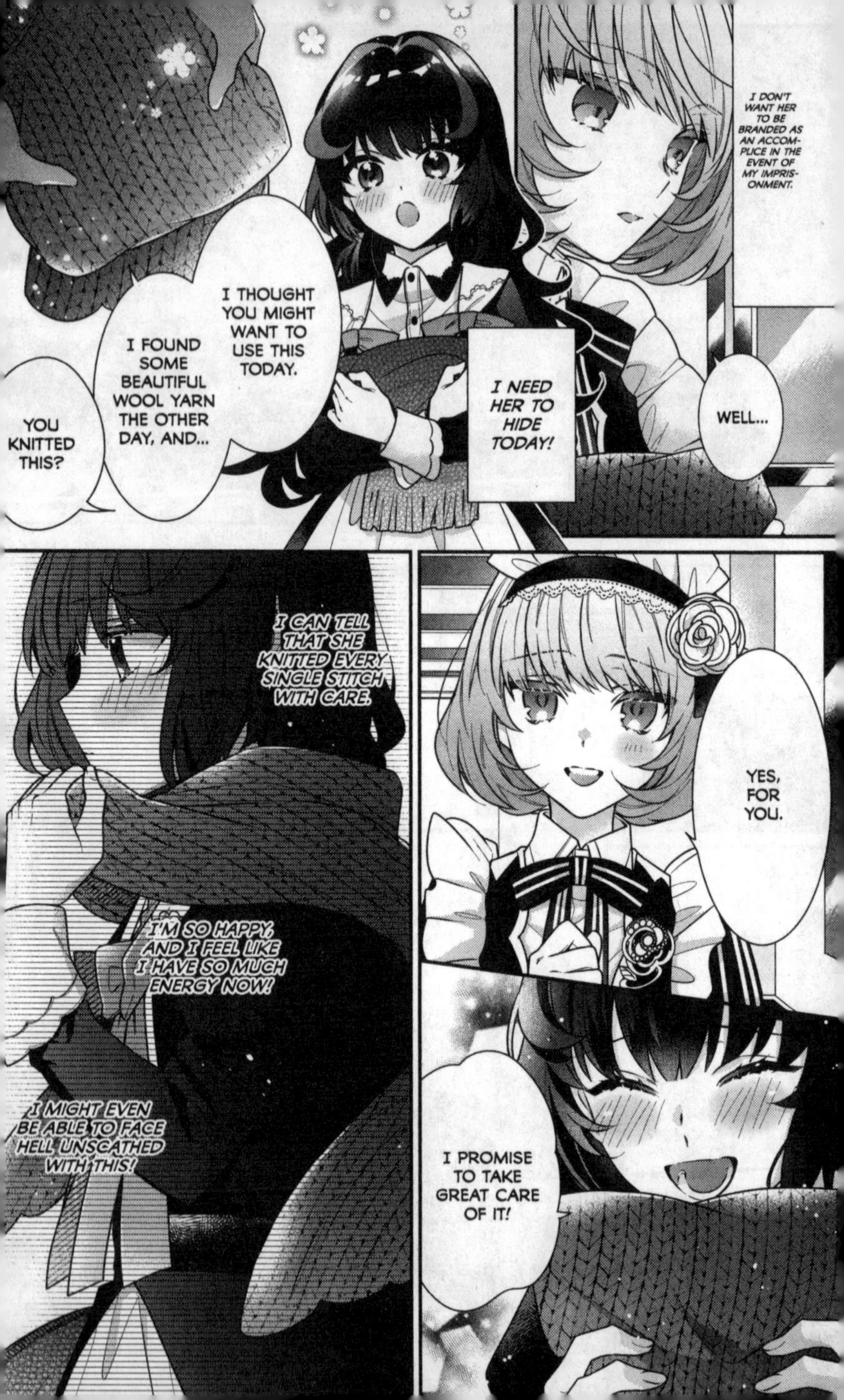
I DON'T WANT HER TO BE BRANDED AS AN ACCOMPLICE IN THE EVENT OF MY IMPRISONMENT.
WELL...
I NEED HER TO HIDE TODAY!
I THOUGHT YOU MIGHT WANT TO USE THIS TODAY.
I FOUND SOME BEAUTIFUL WOOL YARN THE OTHER DAY, AND...
YOU KNITTED THIS?
YES, FOR YOU.
I PROMISE TO TAKE GREAT CARE OF IT!
I CAN TELL THAT SHE KNITTED EVERY SINGLE STITCH WITH CARE.
I'M SO HAPPY, AND I FEEL LIKE I HAVE SO MUCH ENERGY NOW!
I MIGHT EVEN BE ABLE TO FACE HELL UNSCATHED WITH THIS!

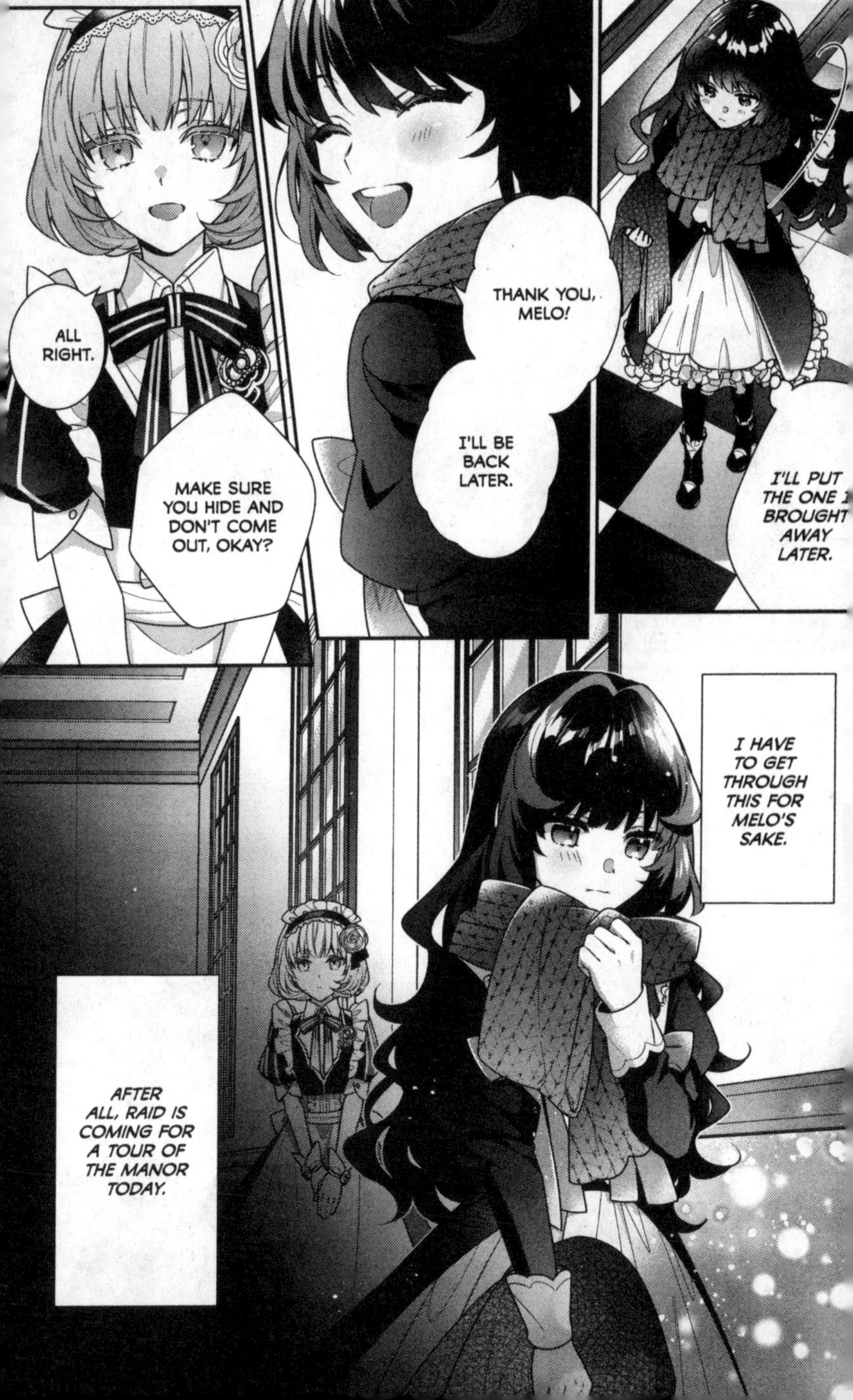
I'LL PUT THE ONE I BROUGHT AWAY LATER.
THANK YOU, MELO!
I'LL BE BACK LATER.
ALL RIGHT.
MAKE SURE YOU HIDE AND DON'T COME OUT, OKAY?
I HAVE TO GET THROUGH THIS FOR MELO'S SAKE.
AFTER ALL, RAID IS COMING FOR A TOUR OF THE MANOR TODAY.

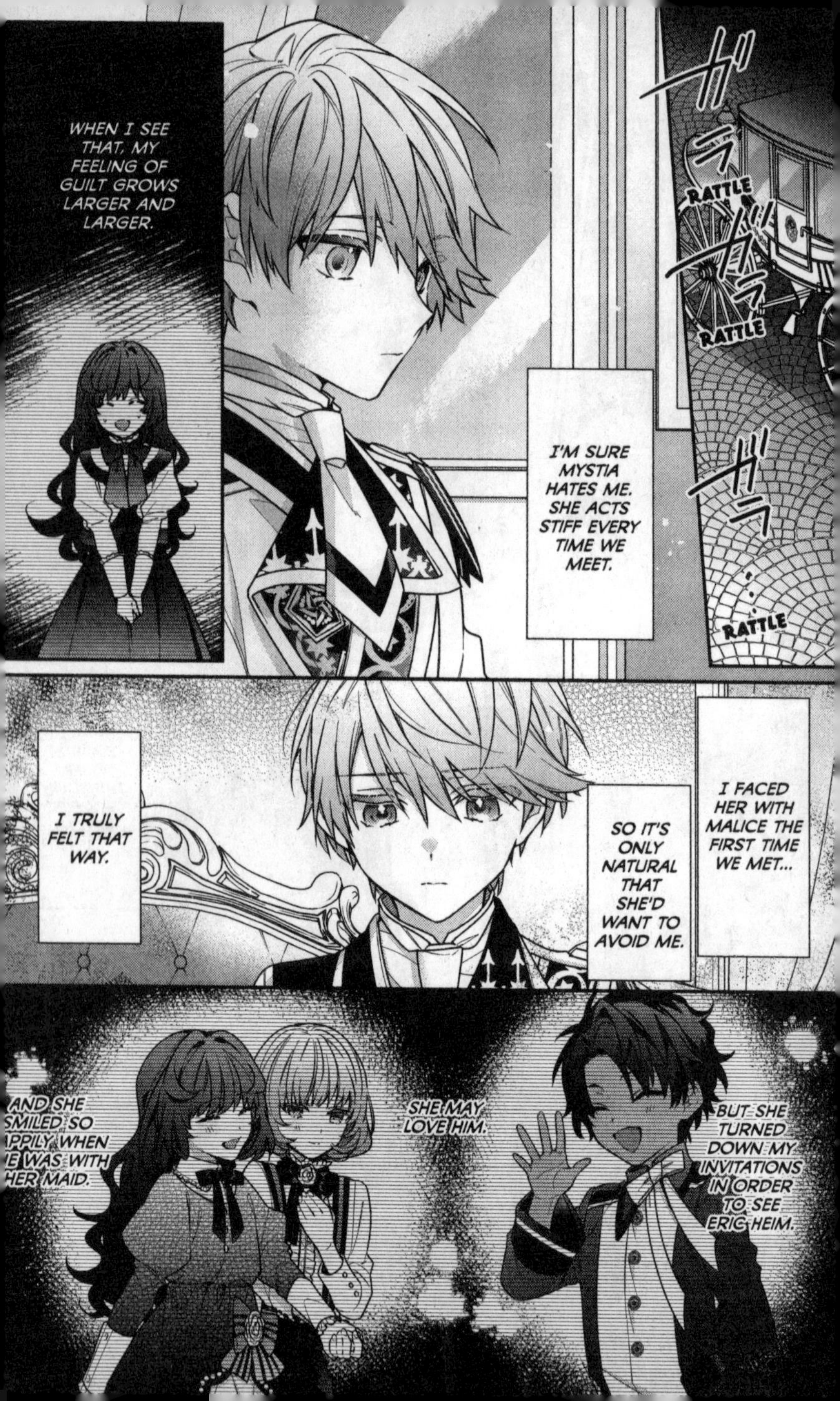
RATTLE
RATTLE
RATTLE
I'M SURE MYSTIA HATES ME. SHE ACTS STIFF EVERY TIME WE MEET.
WHEN I SEE THAT, MY FEELING OF GUILT GROWS LARGER AND LARGER.
I FACED HER WITH MALICE THE FIRST TIME WE MET...
SO IT'S ONLY NATURAL THAT SHE'D WANT TO AVOID ME.
I TRULY FELT THAT WAY.
BUT SHE TURNED DOWN MY INVITATIONS IN ORDER TO SEE ERIC HEIM.
SHE MAY LOVE HIM.
AND SHE SMILED SO APPILY WHEN E WAS WITH HER MAID.

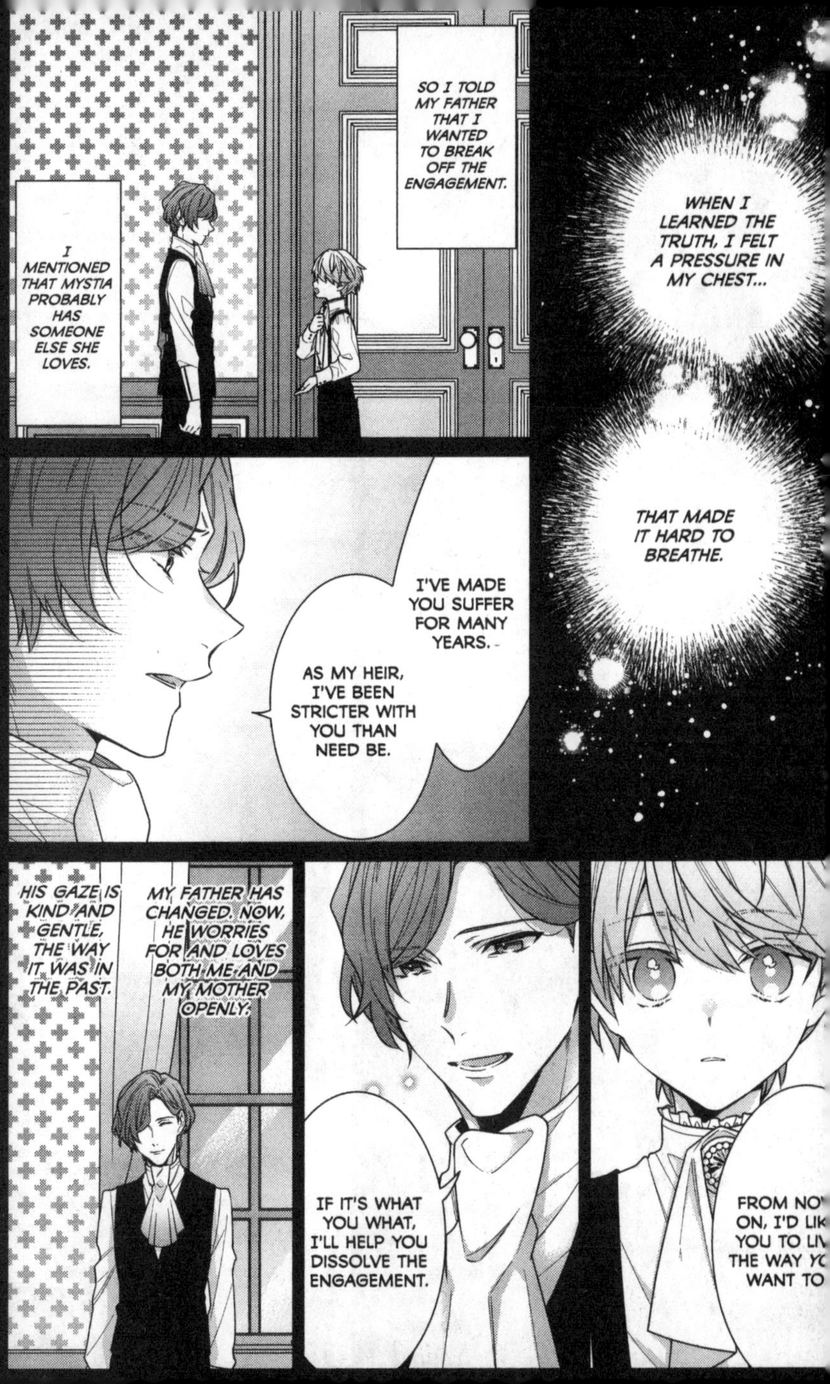
WHEN I LEARNED THE TRUTH, I FELT A PRESSURE IN MY CHEST...
THAT MADE IT HARD TO BREATHE.
SO I TOLD MY FATHER THAT I WANTED TO BREAK OFF THE ENGAGEMENT.
I MENTIONED THAT MYSTIA PROBABLY HAS SOMEONE ELSE SHE LOVES.
I'VE MADE YOU SUFFER FOR MANY YEARS.
AS MY HEIR, I'VE BEEN STRICTER WITH YOU THAN NEED BE.
FROM NO ON, I'D LIK YOU TO LI THE WAY Y WANT TO
IF IT'S WHAT YOU WHAT, I'LL HELP YOU DISSOLVE THE ENGAGEMENT.
MY FATHER HAS CHANGED. NOW, HE WORRIES FOR AND LOVES BOTH ME AND MY MOTHER OPENLY.
HIS GAZE IS KIND AND GENTLE, THE WAY IT WAS IN THE PAST.

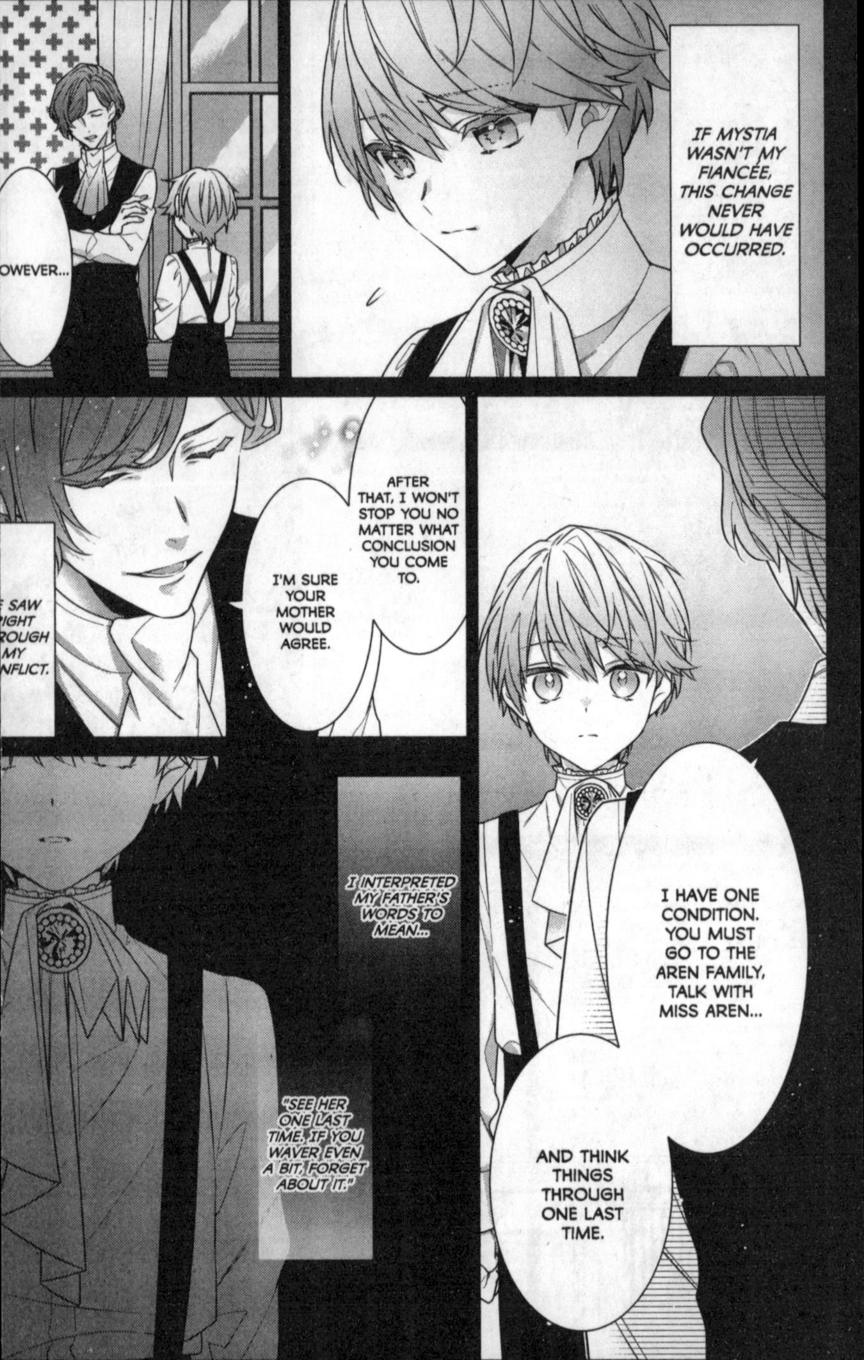
IF MYSTIA WASN'T MY FIANCÉE, THIS CHANGE NEVER WOULD HAVE OCCURRED.
OWEVER...
I HAVE ONE CONDITION. YOU MUST GO TO THE AREN FAMILY, TALK WITH MISS AREN...
AND THINK THINGS THROUGH ONE LAST TIME.
AFTER THAT, I WON'T STOP YOU NO MATTER WHAT CONCLUSION YOU COME TO.
I'M SURE YOUR MOTHER WOULD AGREE.
E SAW IGHT ROUGH MY NFLICT.
I INTERPRETED MY FATHER'S WORDS TO MEAN...
"SEE HER ONE LAST TIME. IF YOU WAVER EVEN A BIT, FORGET ABOUT IT."

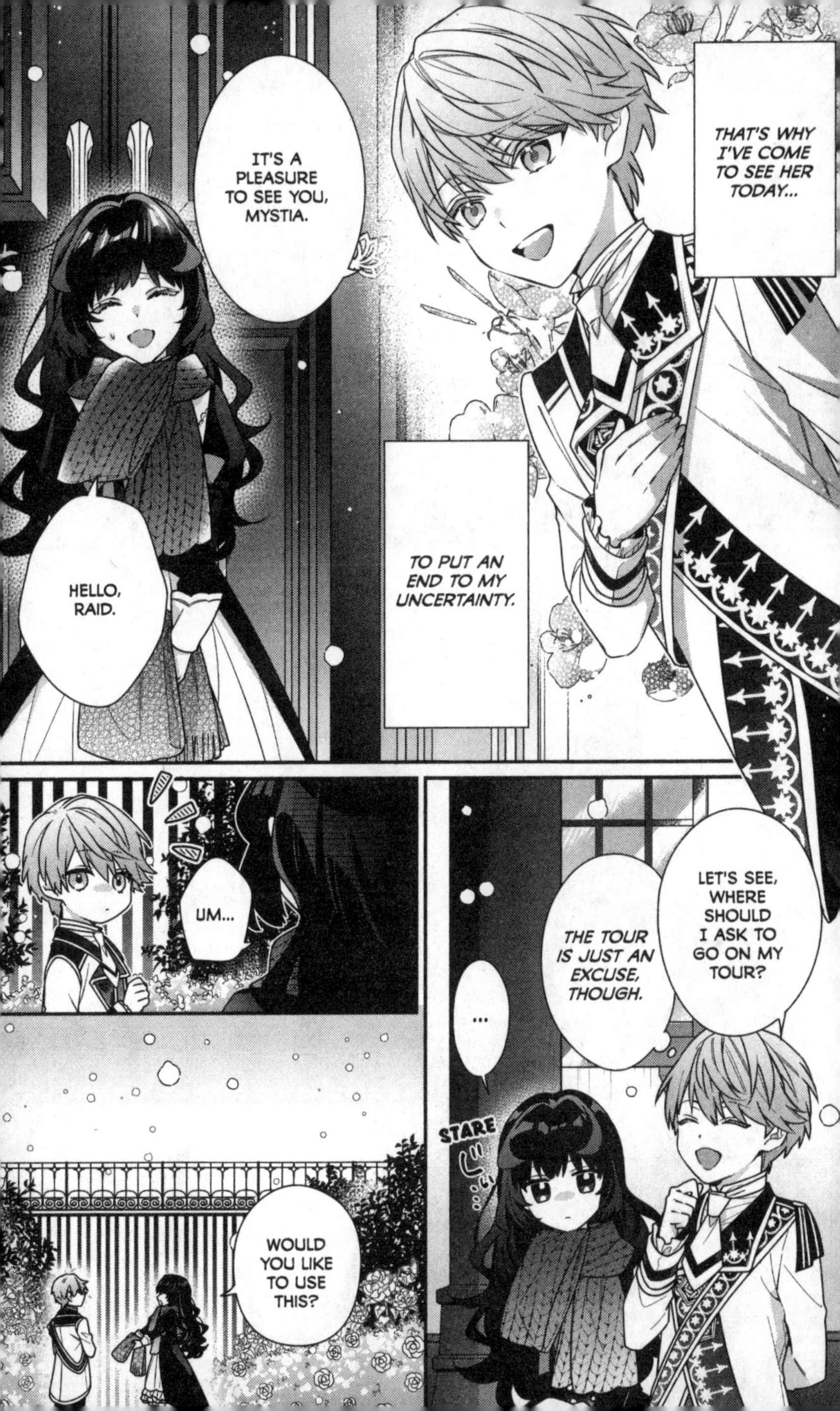
THAT'S WHY I'VE COME TO SEE HER TODAY...
TO PUT AN END TO MY UNCERTAINTY.
IT'S A PLEASURE TO SEE YOU, MYSTIA.
HELLO, RAID.
LET'S SEE, WHERE SHOULD I ASK TO GO ON MY TOUR?
THE TOUR IS JUST AN EXCUSE, THOUGH.
...
STARE
UM...
WOULD YOU LIKE TO USE THIS?

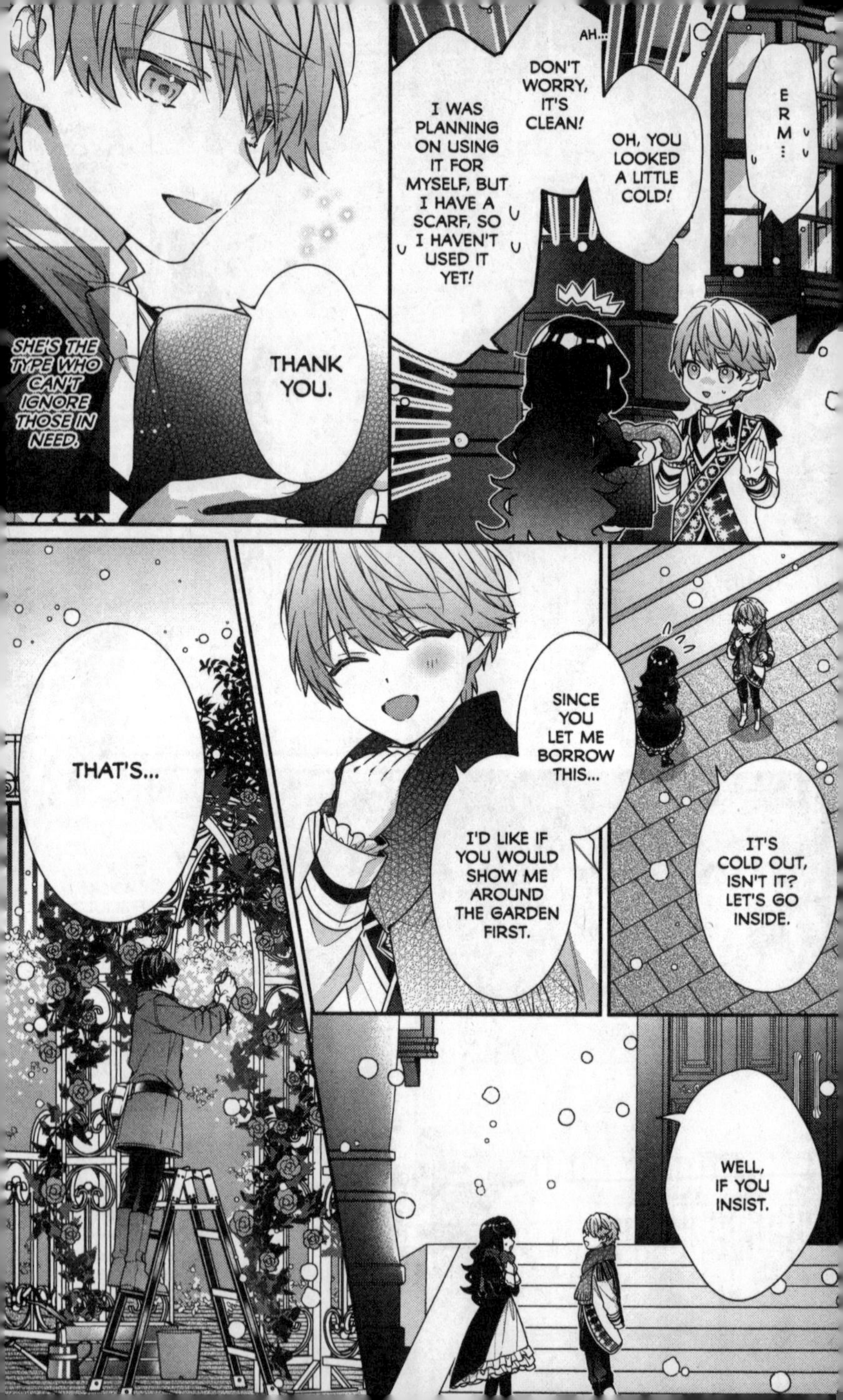
ERM...
OH, YOU LOOKED A LITTLE COLD!
DON'T WORRY, IT'S CLEAN!
I WAS PLANNING ON USING IT FOR MYSELF, BUT I HAVE A SCARF, SO I HAVEN'T USED IT YET!
AH...
THANK YOU.
SHE'S THE TYPE WHO CAN'T IGNORE THOSE IN NEED.
IT'S COLD OUT, ISN'T IT? LET'S GO INSIDE.
SINCE YOU LET ME BORROW THIS...
I'D LIKE IF YOU WOULD SHOW ME AROUND THE GARDEN FIRST.
WELL, IF YOU INSIST.
THAT'S...

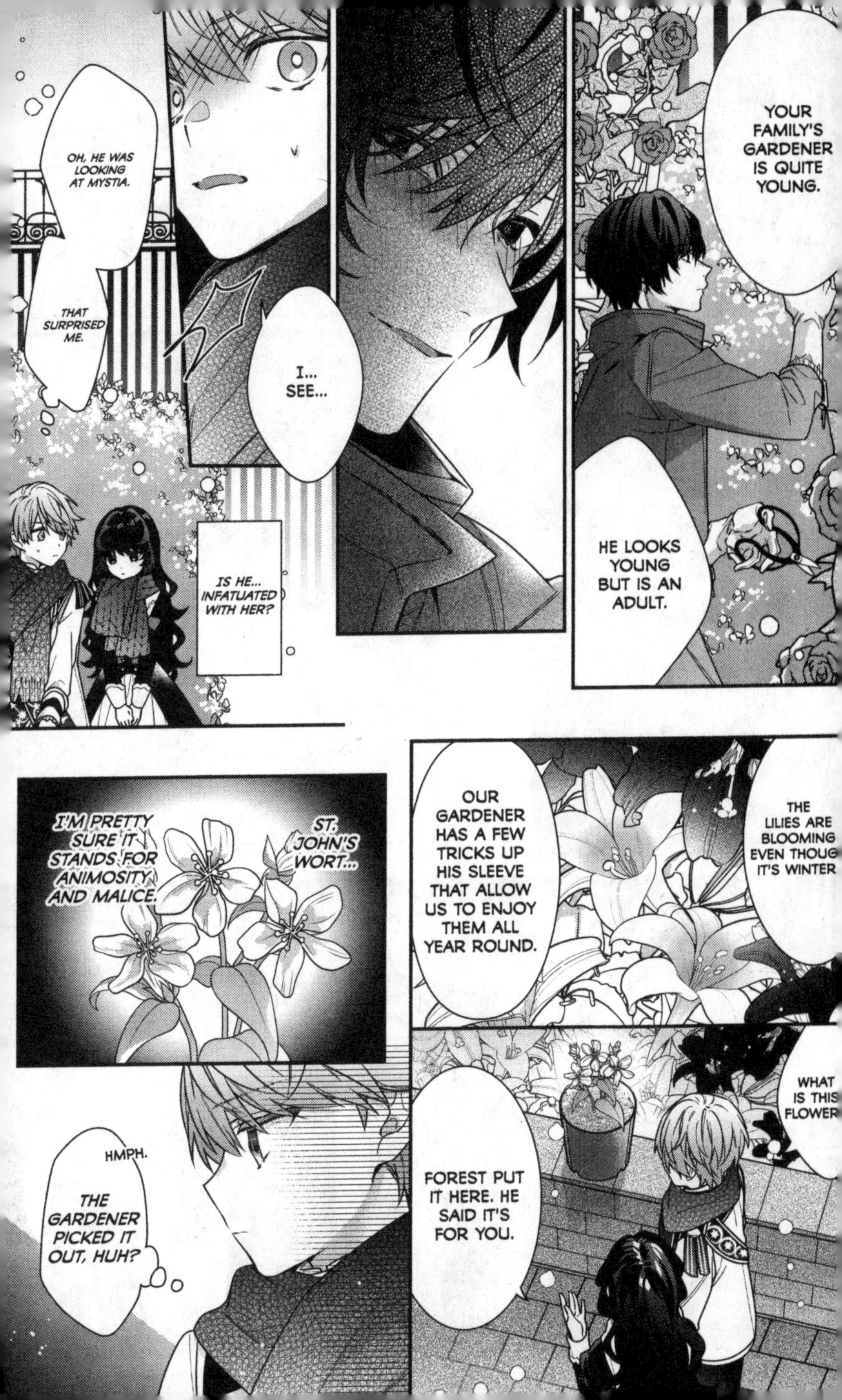
YOUR FAMILY'S GARDENER IS QUITE YOUNG.
HE LOOKS YOUNG BUT IS AN ADULT.
I... SEE...
OH, HE WAS LOOKING AT MYSTIA.
THAT SURPRISED ME.
IS HE... INFATUATED WITH HER?
THE LILIES ARE BLOOMING EVEN THOUG IT'S WINTER
OUR GARDENER HAS A FEW TRICKS UP HIS SLEEVE THAT ALLOW US TO ENJOY THEM ALL YEAR ROUND.
ST. JOHN'S WORT...
I'M PRETTY SURE IT STANDS FOR ANIMOSITY AND MALICE.
WHAT IS THIS FLOWER
FOREST PUT IT HERE. HE SAID IT'S FOR YOU.
HMPH.
THE GARDENER PICKED IT OUT, HUH?

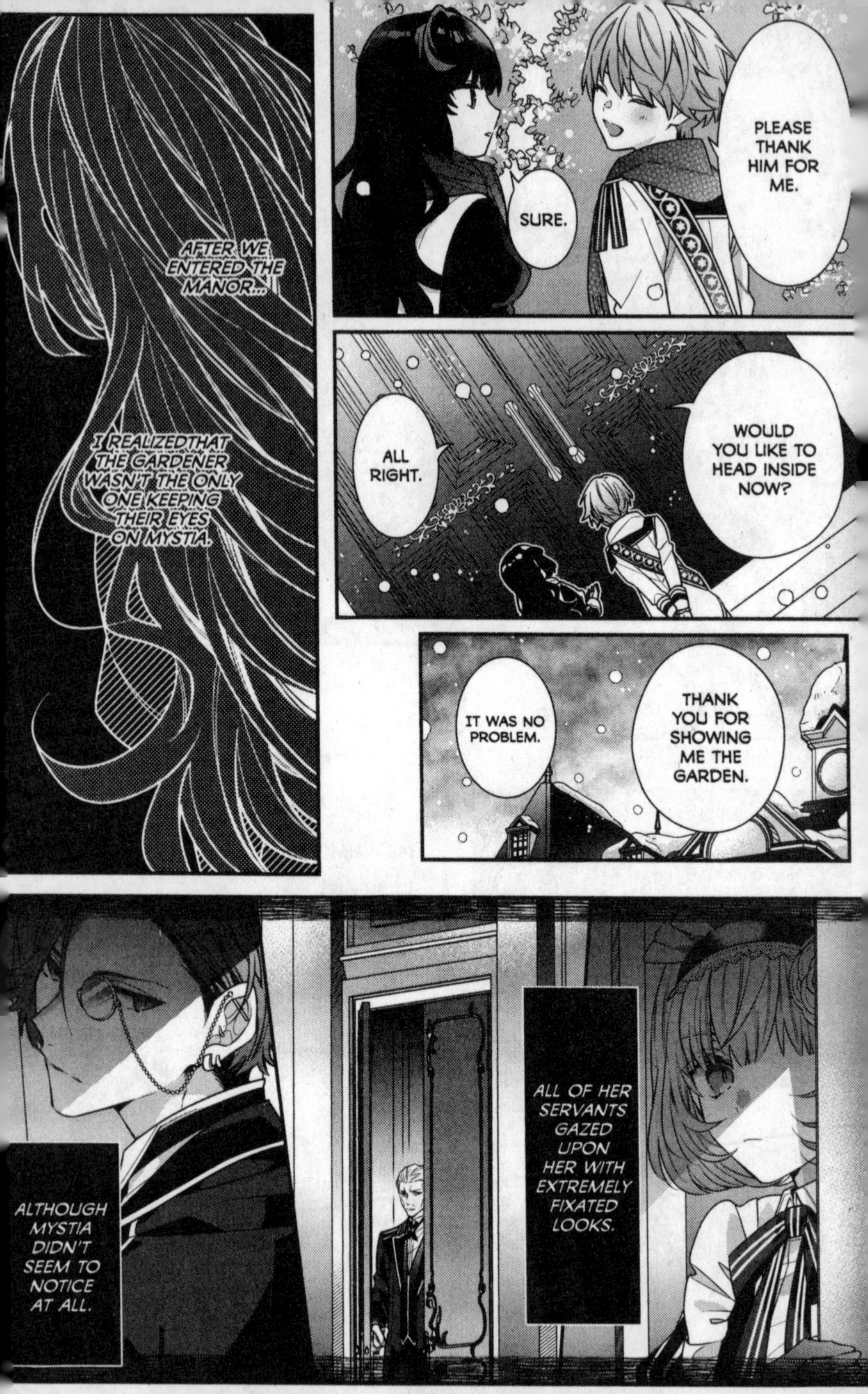
PLEASE THANK HIM FOR ME.
SURE.
WOULD YOU LIKE TO HEAD INSIDE NOW?
ALL RIGHT.
THANK YOU FOR SHOWING ME THE GARDEN.
IT WAS NO PROBLEM.
AFTER WE ENTERED THE MANOR...
I REALIZEDTHAT THE GARDENER WASN'T THE ONLY ONE KEEPING THEIR EYES ON MYSTIA.
ALL OF HER SERVANTS GAZED UPON HER WITH EXTREMELY FIXATED LOOKS.
ALTHOUGH MYSTIA DIDN'T SEEM TO NOTICE AT ALL.

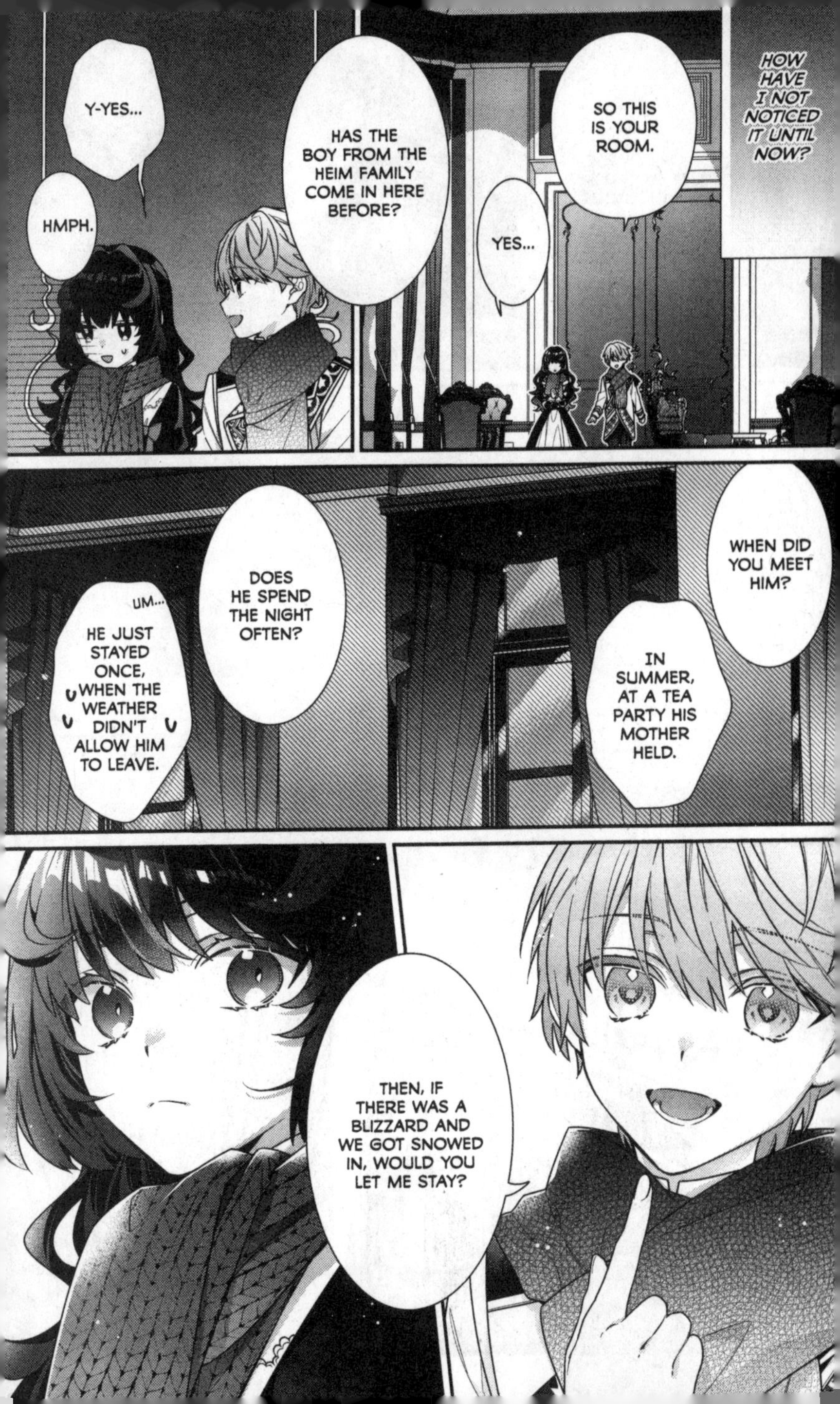

HOW HAVE I NOT NOTICED IT UNTIL NOW?
SO THIS IS YOUR ROOM.
YES...
HAS THE BOY FROM THE HEIM FAMILY COME IN HERE BEFORE?
Y-YES...
HMPH.
WHEN DID YOU MEET HIM?
IN SUMMER, AT A TEA PARTY HIS MOTHER HELD.
DOES HE SPEND THE NIGHT OFTEN?
UM...
HE JUST STAYED ONCE, WHEN THE WEATHER DIDN'T ALLOW HIM TO LEAVE.
THEN, IF THERE WAS A BLIZZARD AND WE GOT SNOWED IN, WOULD YOU LET ME STAY?

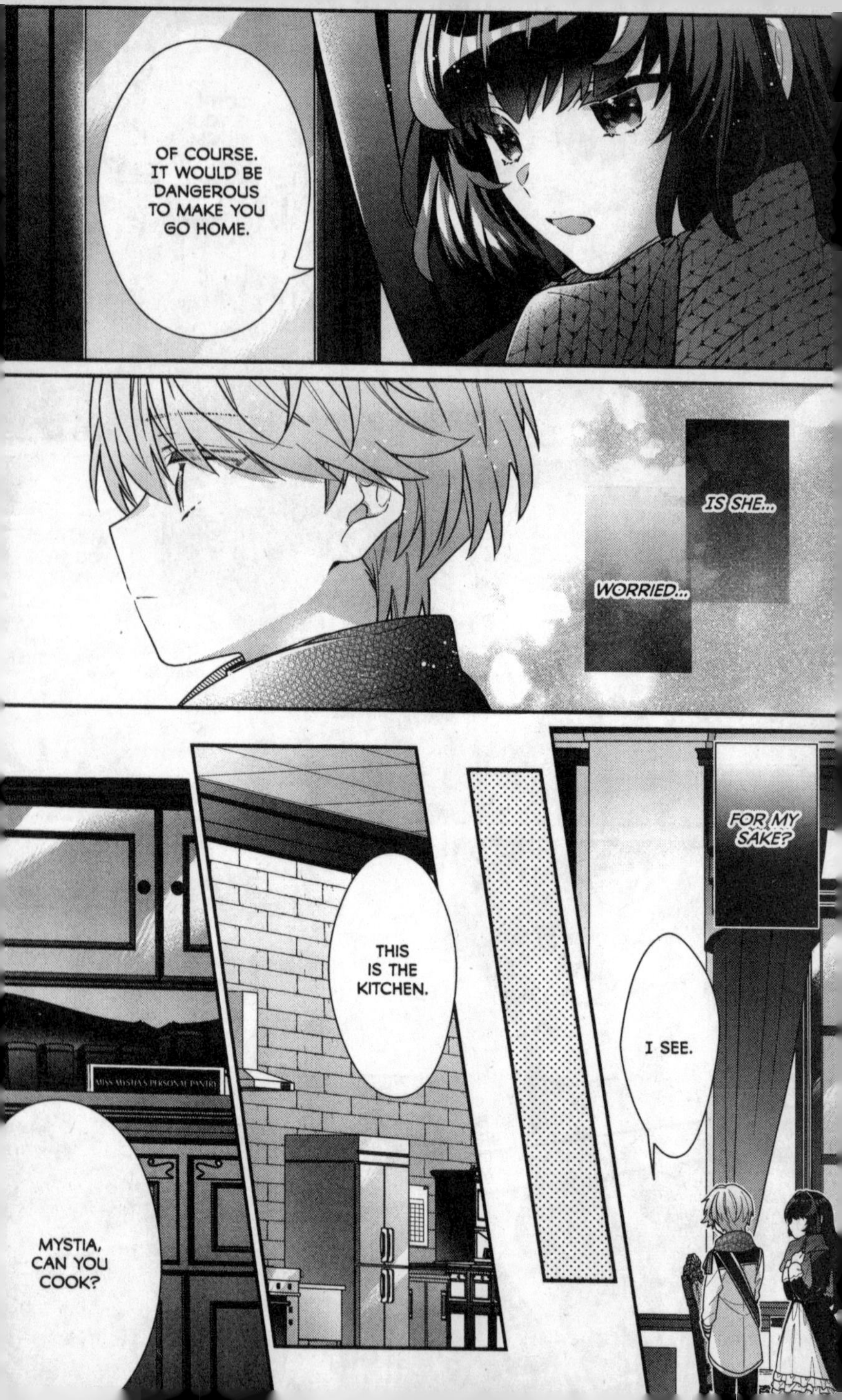
OF COURSE. IT WOULD BE DANGEROUS TO MAKE YOU GO HOME.
IS SHE...
WORRIED...
FOR MY SAKE?
I SEE.
THIS IS THE KITCHEN.
MISS MYSTIA'S PERSONAL PANTRY
MYSTIA, CAN YOU COOK?

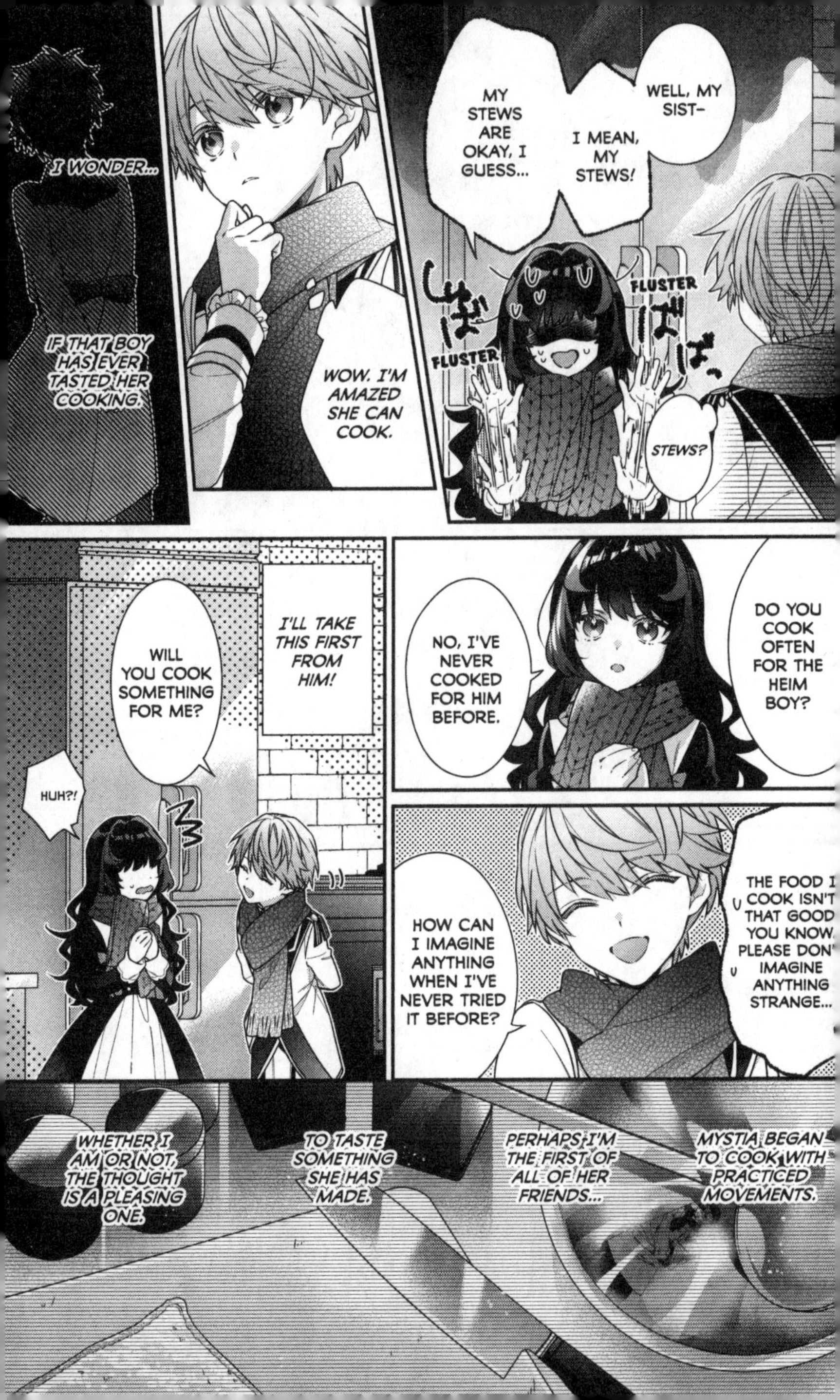
WELL, MY SIST–
I MEAN, MY STEWS!
MY STEWS ARE OKAY, I GUESS...
FLUSTER
FLUSTER
STEWS?
WOW. I'M AMAZED SHE CAN COOK.
I WONDER...
IF THAT BOY HAS EVER TASTED HER COOKING.
DO YOU COOK OFTEN FOR THE HEIM BOY?
NO, I'VE NEVER COOKED FOR HIM BEFORE.
THE FOOD I COOK ISN'T THAT GOOD YOU KNOW. PLEASE DON' IMAGINE ANYTHING STRANGE...
HOW CAN I IMAGINE ANYTHING WHEN I'VE NEVER TRIED IT BEFORE?
I'LL TAKE THIS FIRST FROM HIM!
WILL YOU COOK SOMETHING FOR ME?
HUH?!
MYSTIA BEGAN TO COOK WITH PRACTICED MOVEMENTS.
PERHAPS I'M THE FIRST OF ALL OF HER FRIENDS...
TO TASTE SOMETHING SHE HAS MADE.
WHETHER I AM OR NOT, THE THOUGHT IS A PLEASING ONE.

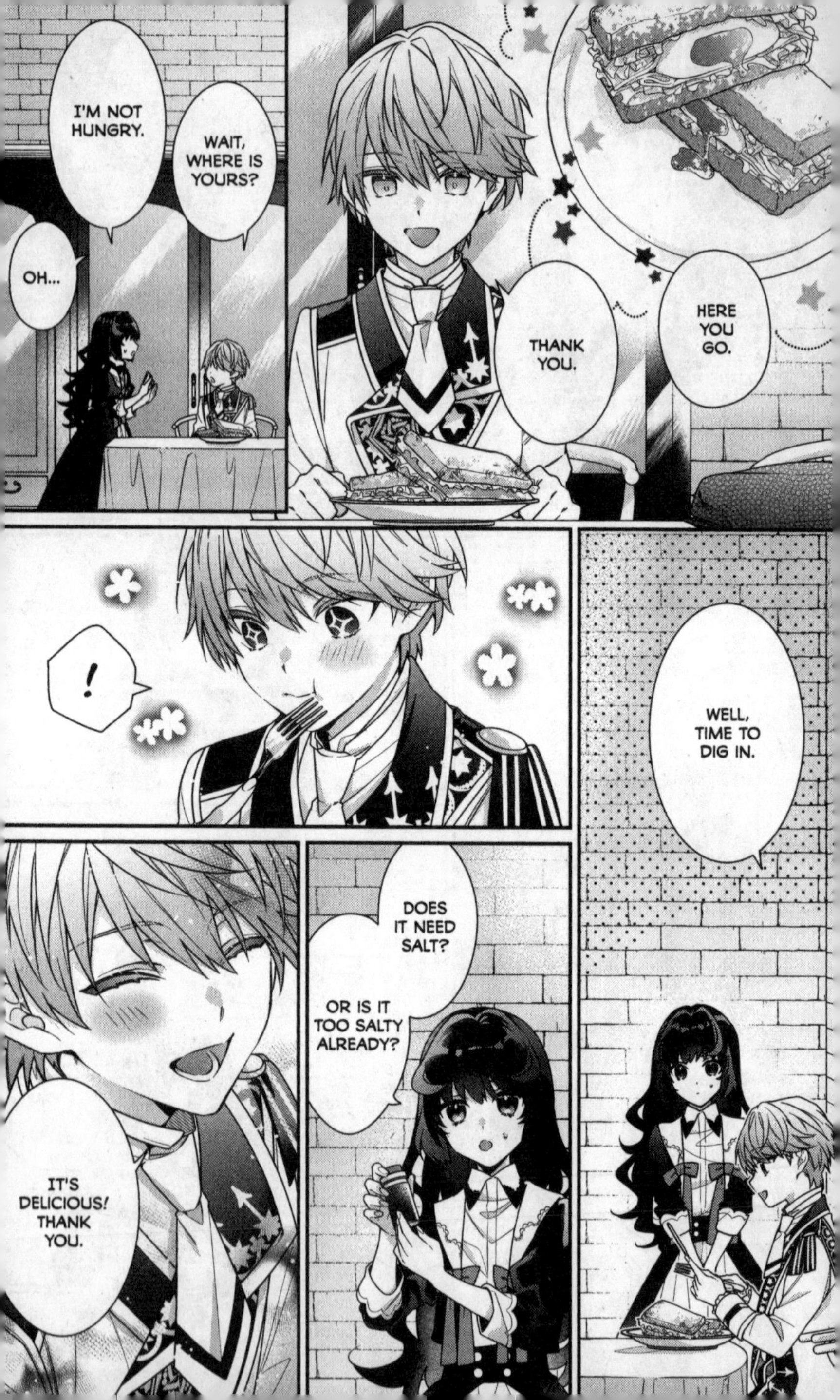
HERE YOU GO.
THANK YOU.
WAIT, WHERE IS YOURS?
I'M NOT HUNGRY.
OH...
WELL, TIME TO DIG IN.
!
DOES IT NEED SALT?
OR IS IT TOO SALTY ALREADY?
IT'S DELICIOUS! THANK YOU.

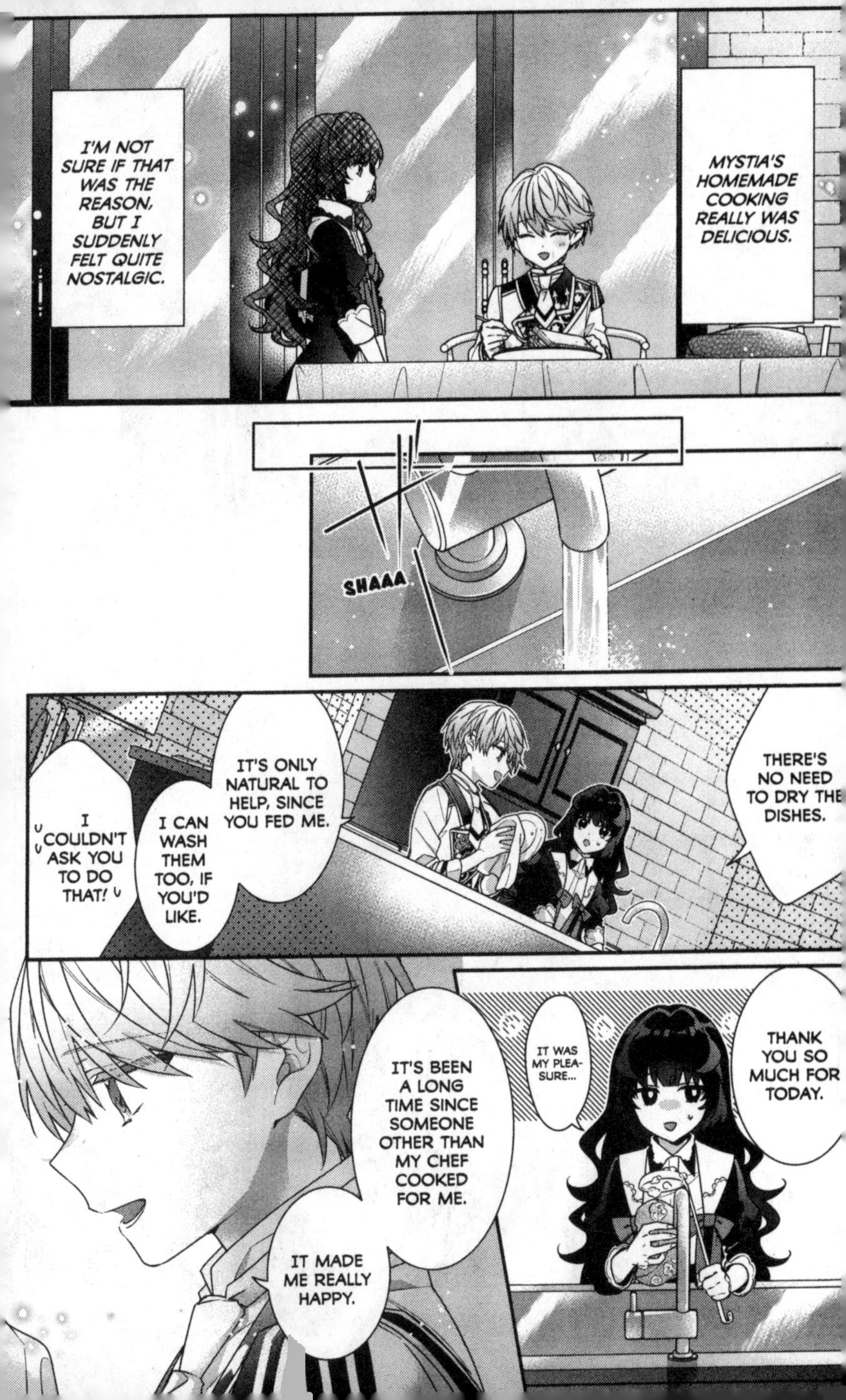
MYSTIA'S HOMEMADE COOKING REALLY WAS DELICIOUS.
I'M NOT SURE IF THAT WAS THE REASON, BUT I SUDDENLY FELT QUITE NOSTALGIC.
SHAAA
THERE'S NO NEED TO DRY THE DISHES.
IT'S ONLY NATURAL TO HELP, SINCE YOU FED ME.
I CAN WASH THEM TOO, IF YOU'D LIKE.
I COULDN'T ASK YOU TO DO THAT!
THANK YOU SO MUCH FOR TODAY.
IT WAS MY PLEA-SURE...
IT'S BEEN A LONG TIME SINCE SOMEONE OTHER THAN MY CHEF COOKED FOR ME.
IT MADE ME REALLY HAPPY.

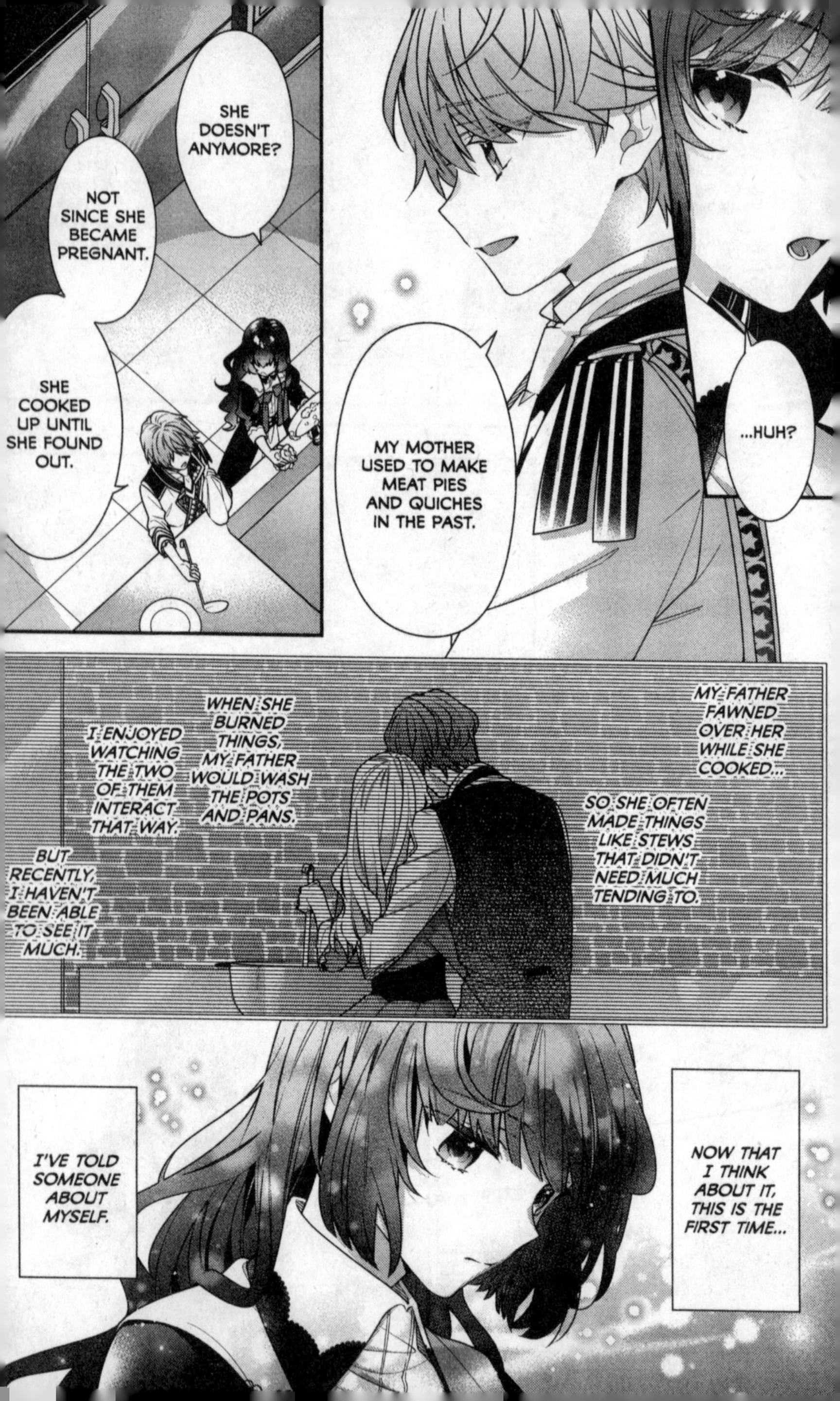
MY MOTHER USED TO MAKE MEAT PIES AND QUICHES IN THE PAST.
...HUH?
SHE DOESN'T ANYMORE?
NOT SINCE SHE BECAME PREGNANT.
SHE COOKED UP UNTIL SHE FOUND OUT.
MY FATHER FAWNED OVER HER WHILE SHE COOKED...
SO SHE OFTEN MADE THINGS LIKE STEWS THAT DIDN'T NEED MUCH TENDING TO.
WHEN SHE BURNED THINGS, MY FATHER WOULD WASH THE POTS AND PANS.
I ENJOYED WATCHING THE TWO OF THEM INTERACT THAT WAY.
BUT RECENTLY, I HAVEN'T BEEN ABLE TO SEE IT MUCH.
NOW THAT I THINK ABOUT IT, THIS IS THE FIRST TIME...
I'VE TOLD SOMEONE ABOUT MYSELF.

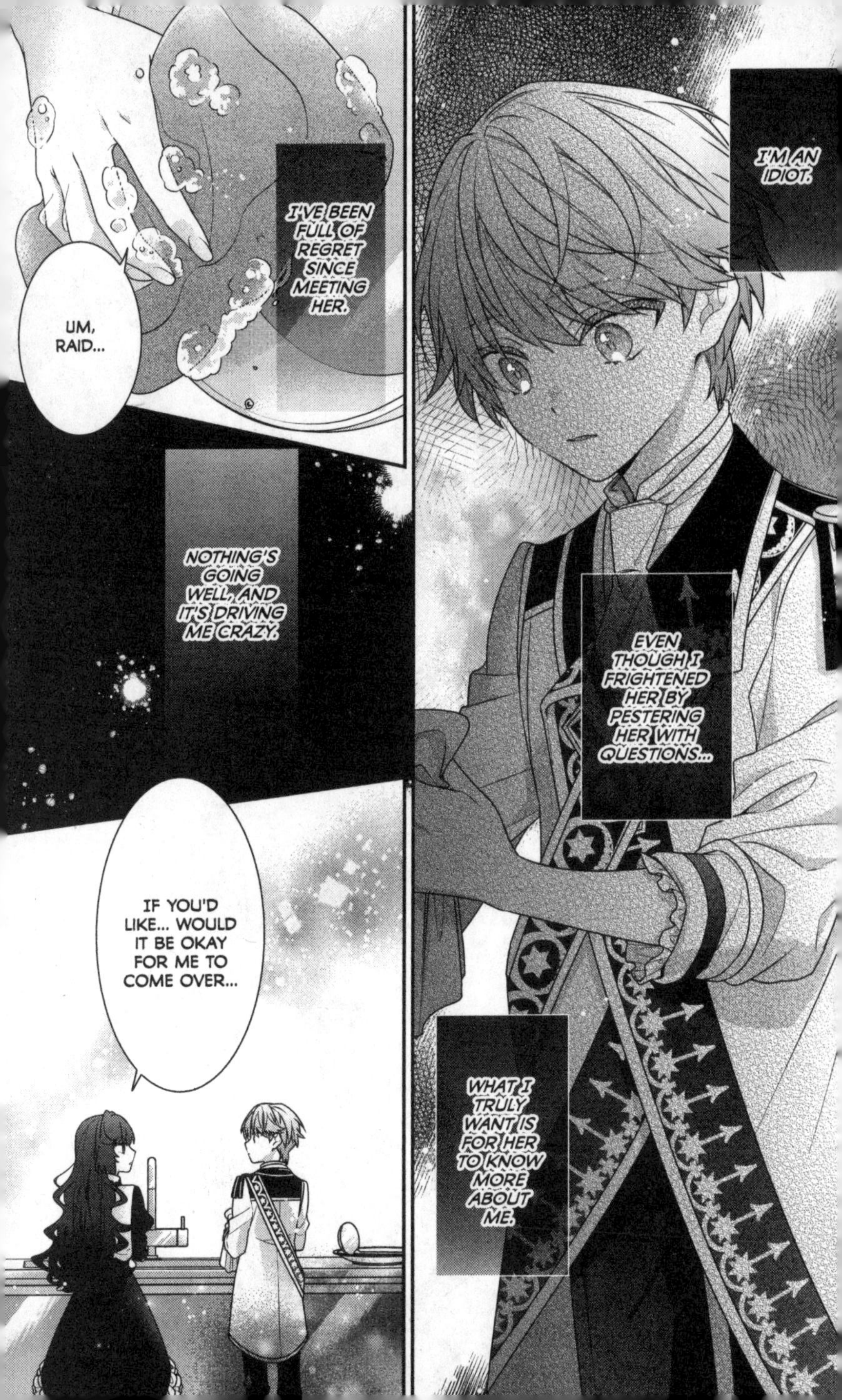
I'M AN IDIOT.
EVEN THOUGH I FRIGHTENED HER BY PESTERING HER WITH QUESTIONS...
WHAT I TRULY WANT IS FOR HER TO KNOW MORE ABOUT ME.
I'VE BEEN FULL OF REGRET SINCE MEETING HER.
UM, RAID...
NOTHING'S GOING WELL, AND IT'S DRIVING ME CRAZY.
IF YOU'D LIKE... WOULD IT BE OKAY FOR ME TO COME OVER...

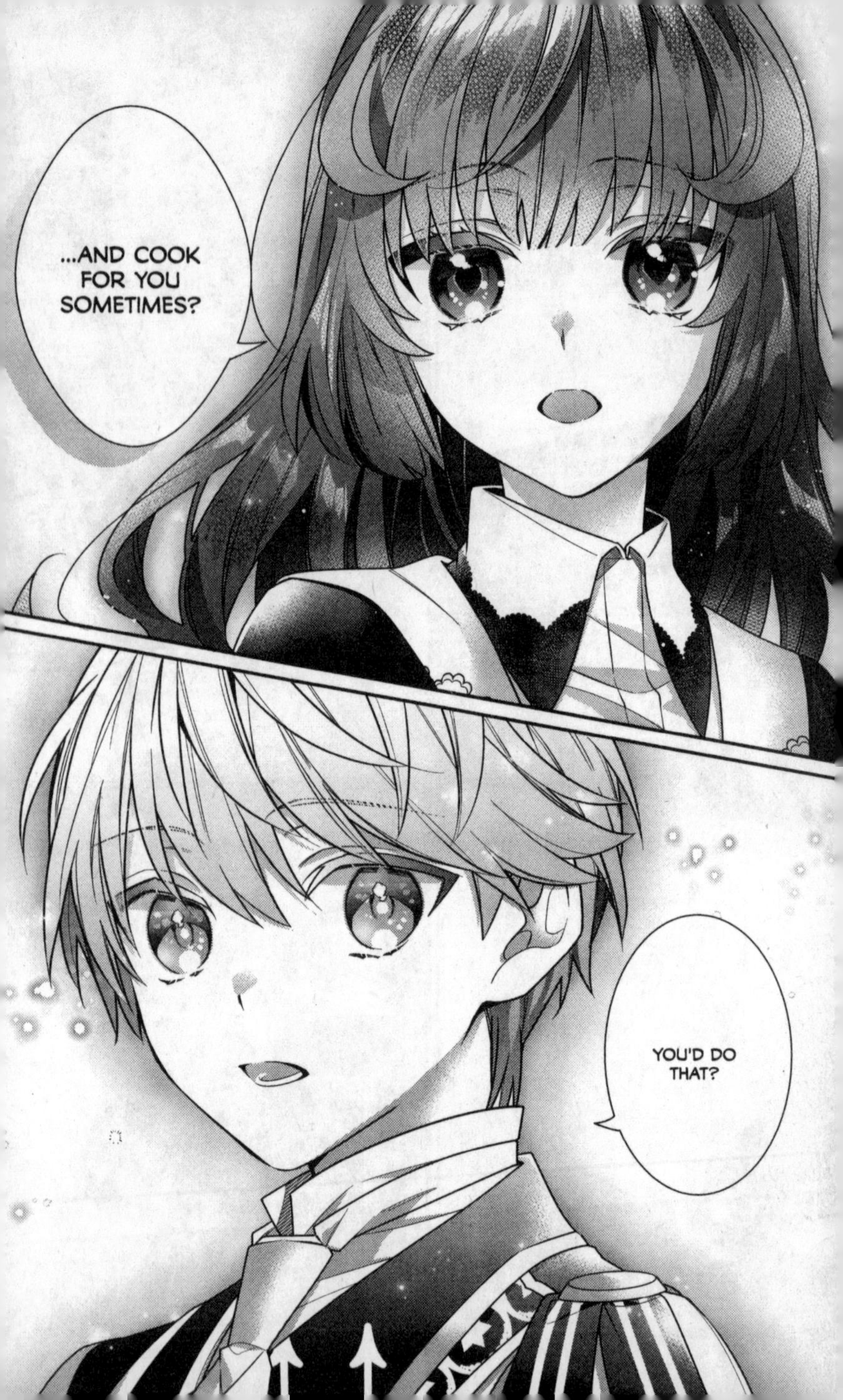
...AND COOK FOR YOU SOMETIMES?
YOU'D DO THAT?

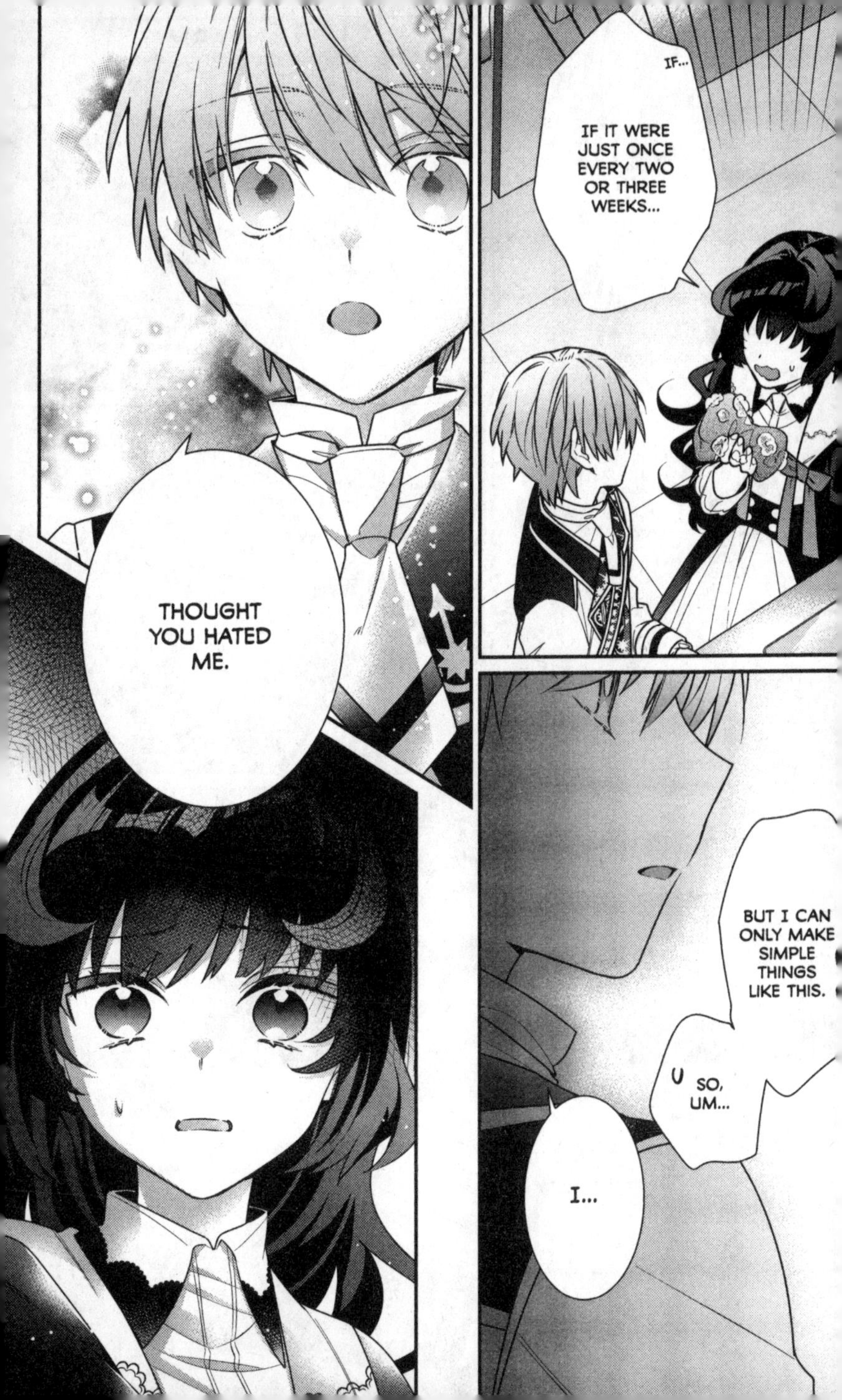

IF...
IF IT WERE JUST ONCE EVERY TWO OR THREE WEEKS...
BUT I CAN ONLY MAKE SIMPLE THINGS LIKE THIS.
SO, UM...
I...
THOUGHT YOU HATED ME.

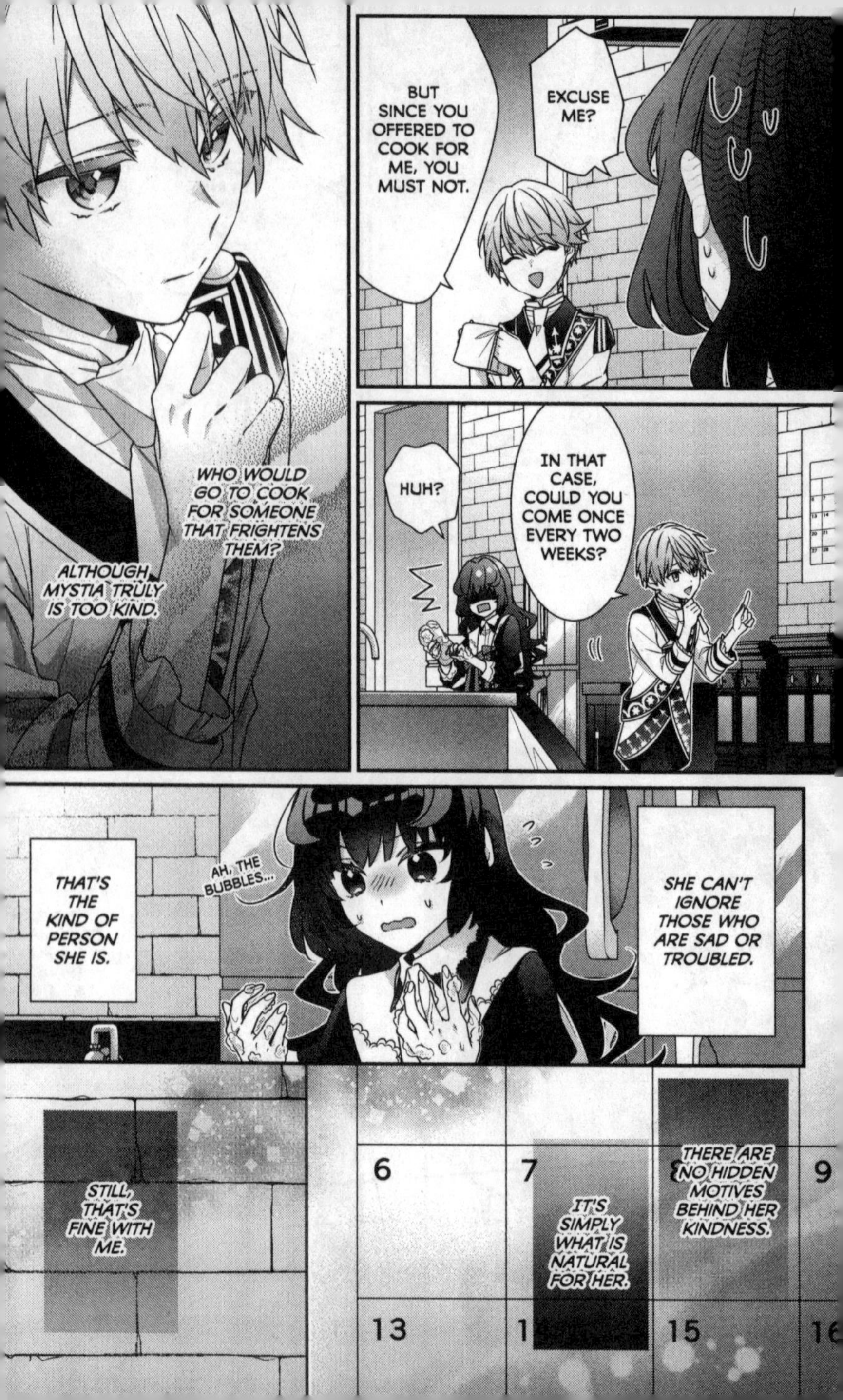
EXCUSE ME?
BUT SINCE YOU OFFERED TO COOK FOR ME, YOU MUST NOT.
IN THAT CASE, COULD YOU COME ONCE EVERY TWO WEEKS?
HUH?
WHO WOULD GO TO COOK FOR SOMEONE THAT FRIGHTENS THEM?
ALTHOUGH MYSTIA TRULY IS TOO KIND.
SHE CAN'T IGNORE THOSE WHO ARE SAD OR TROUBLED.
AH, THE BUBBLES...
THAT'S THE KIND OF PERSON SHE IS.
THERE ARE NO HIDDEN MOTIVES BEHIND HER KINDNESS.
IT'S SIMPLY WHAT IS NATURAL FOR HER.
STILL, THAT'S FINE WITH ME.

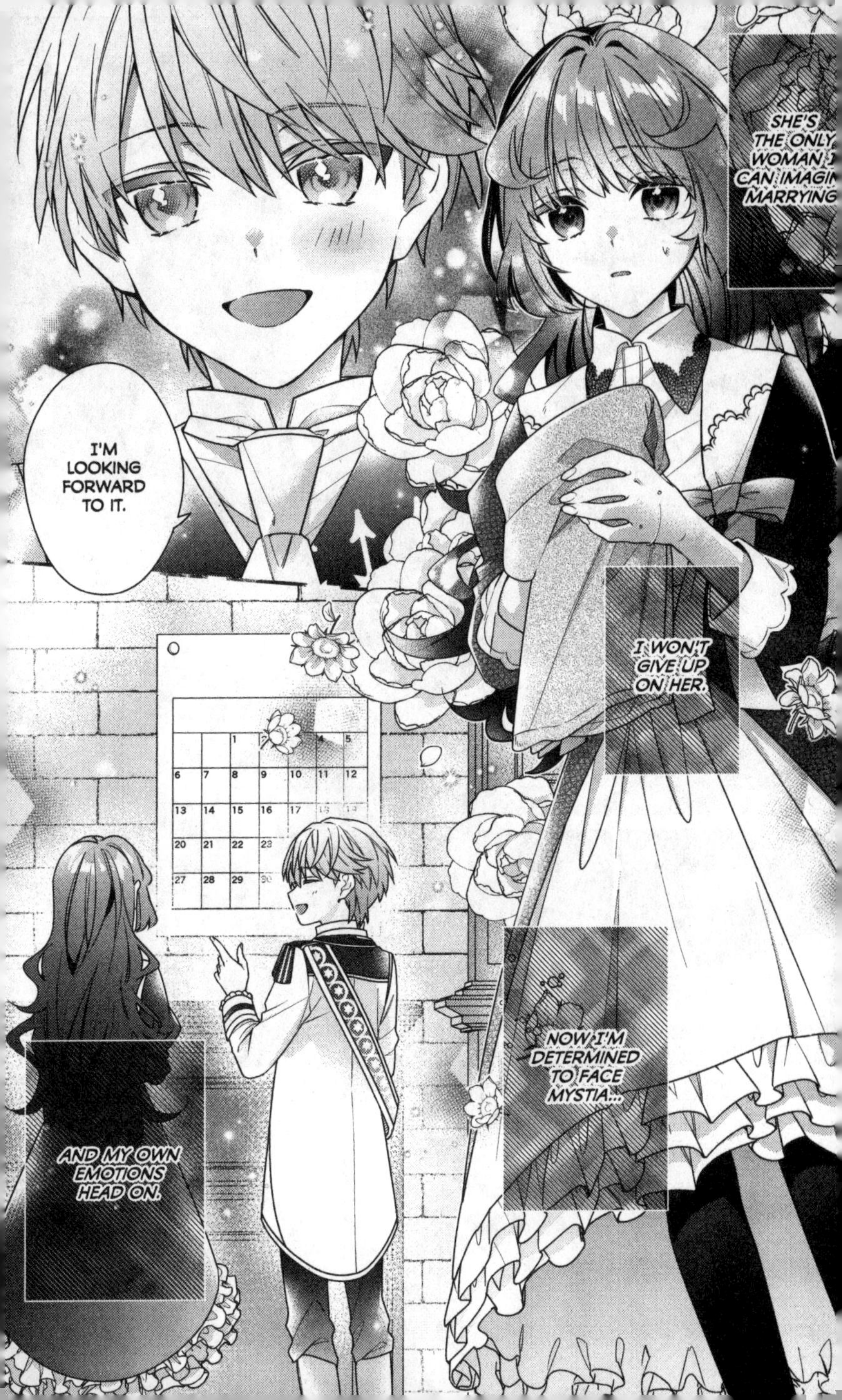
SHE'S THE ONLY WOMAN I CAN IMAGI MARRYING
I'M LOOKING FORWARD TO IT.
I WON'T GIVE UP ON HER.
NOW I'M DETERMINED TO FACE MYSTIA...
AND MY OWN EMOTIONS HEAD ON.

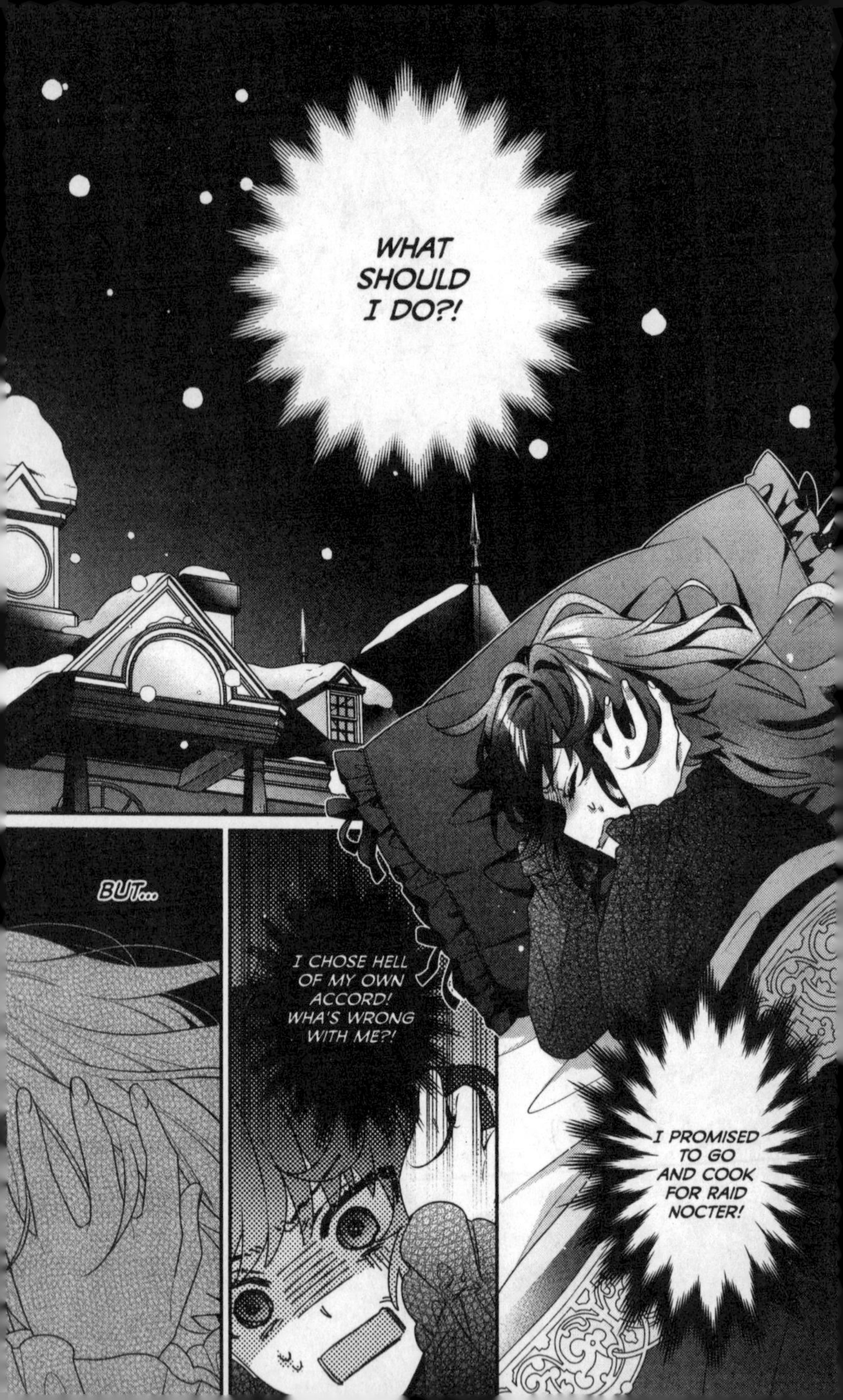
WHAT SHOULD I DO?!
I PROMISED TO GO AND COOK FOR RAID NOCTER!
I CHOSE HELL OF MY OWN ACCORD! WHA'S WRONG WITH ME?!
BUT...

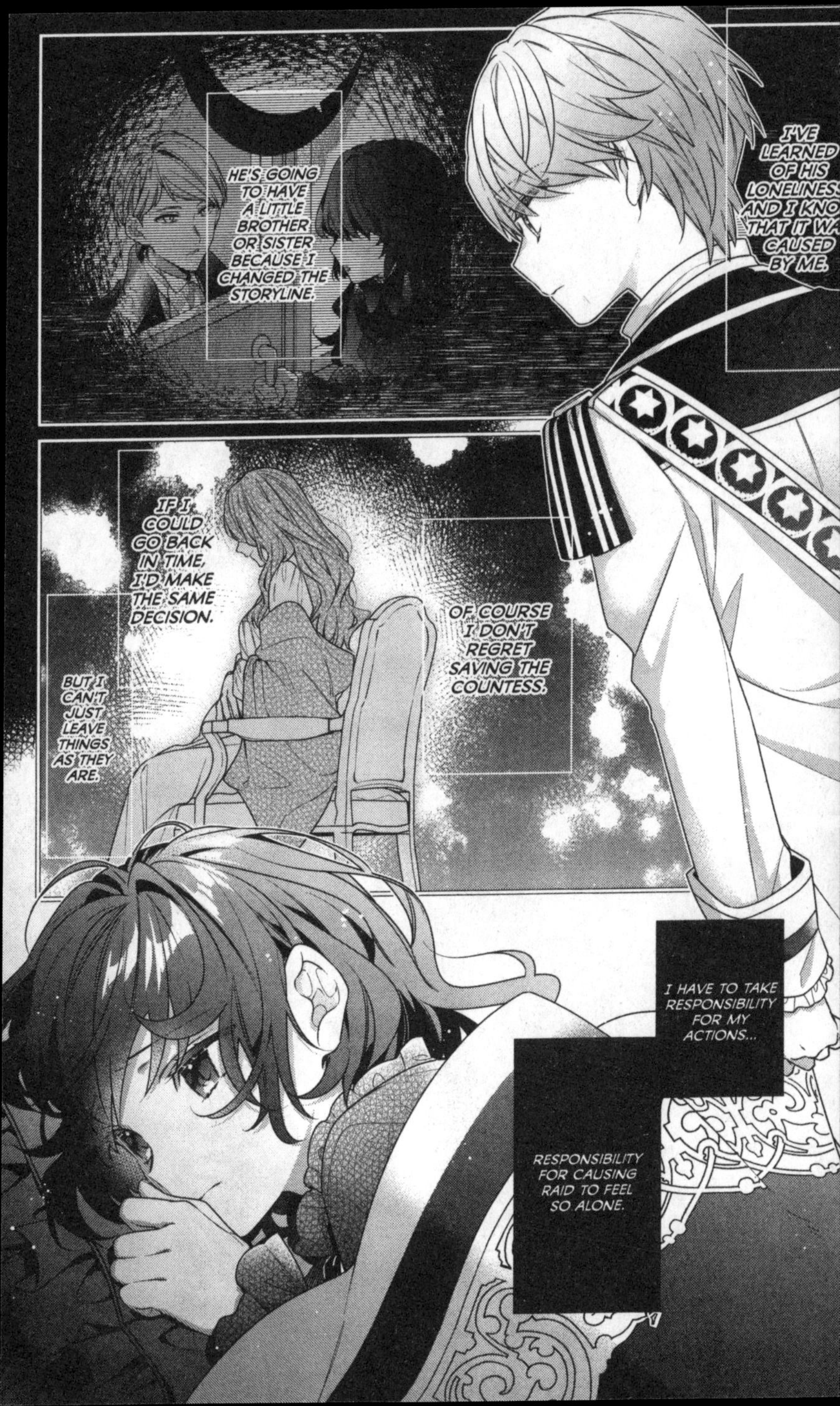
I'VE LEARNED OF HIS LONELINESS AND I KNO THAT IT WA CAUSED BY ME.
HE'S GOING TO HAVE A LITTLE BROTHER OR SISTER BECAUSE I CHANGED THE STORYLINE.
OF COURSE I DON'T REGRET SAVING THE COUNTESS.
IF I COULD GO BACK IN TIME, I'D MAKE THE SAME DECISION.
BUT I CAN'T JUST LEAVE THINGS AS THEY ARE.
I HAVE TO TAKE RESPONSIBILITY FOR MY ACTIONS...
RESPONSIBILITY FOR CAUSING RAID TO FEEL SO ALONE.

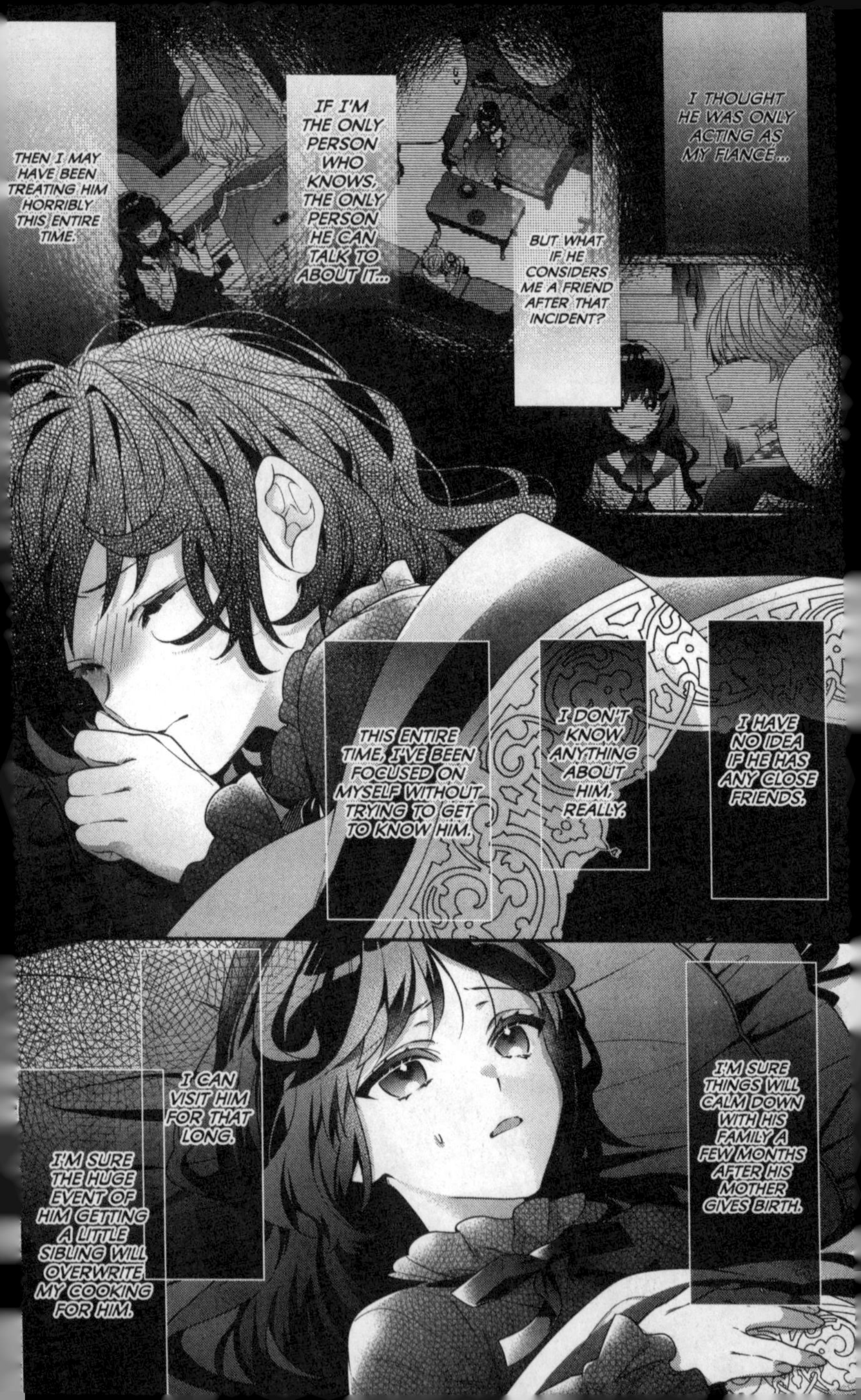
I THOUGHT HE WAS ONLY ACTING AS MY FIANCE...
BUT WHAT IF HE CONSIDERS ME A FRIEND AFTER THAT INCIDENT?
IF I'M THE ONLY PERSON WHO KNOWS, THE ONLY PERSON HE CAN TALK TO ABOUT IT...
THEN I MAY HAVE BEEN TREATING HIM HORRIBLY THIS ENTIRE TIME.
I HAVE NO IDEA IF HE HAS ANY CLOSE FRIENDS.
I DON'T KNOW ANYTHING ABOUT HIM, REALLY.
THIS ENTIRE TIME, I'VE BEEN FOCUSED ON MYSELF WITHOUT TRYING TO GET TO KNOW HIM.
I'M SURE THINGS WILL CALM DOWN WITH HIS FAMILY A FEW MONTHS AFTER HIS MOTHER GIVES BIRTH.
I CAN VISIT HIM FOR THAT LONG.
I'M SURE THE HUGE EVENT OF HIM GETTING A LITTLE SIBLING WILL OVERWRITE MY COOKING FOR HIM.

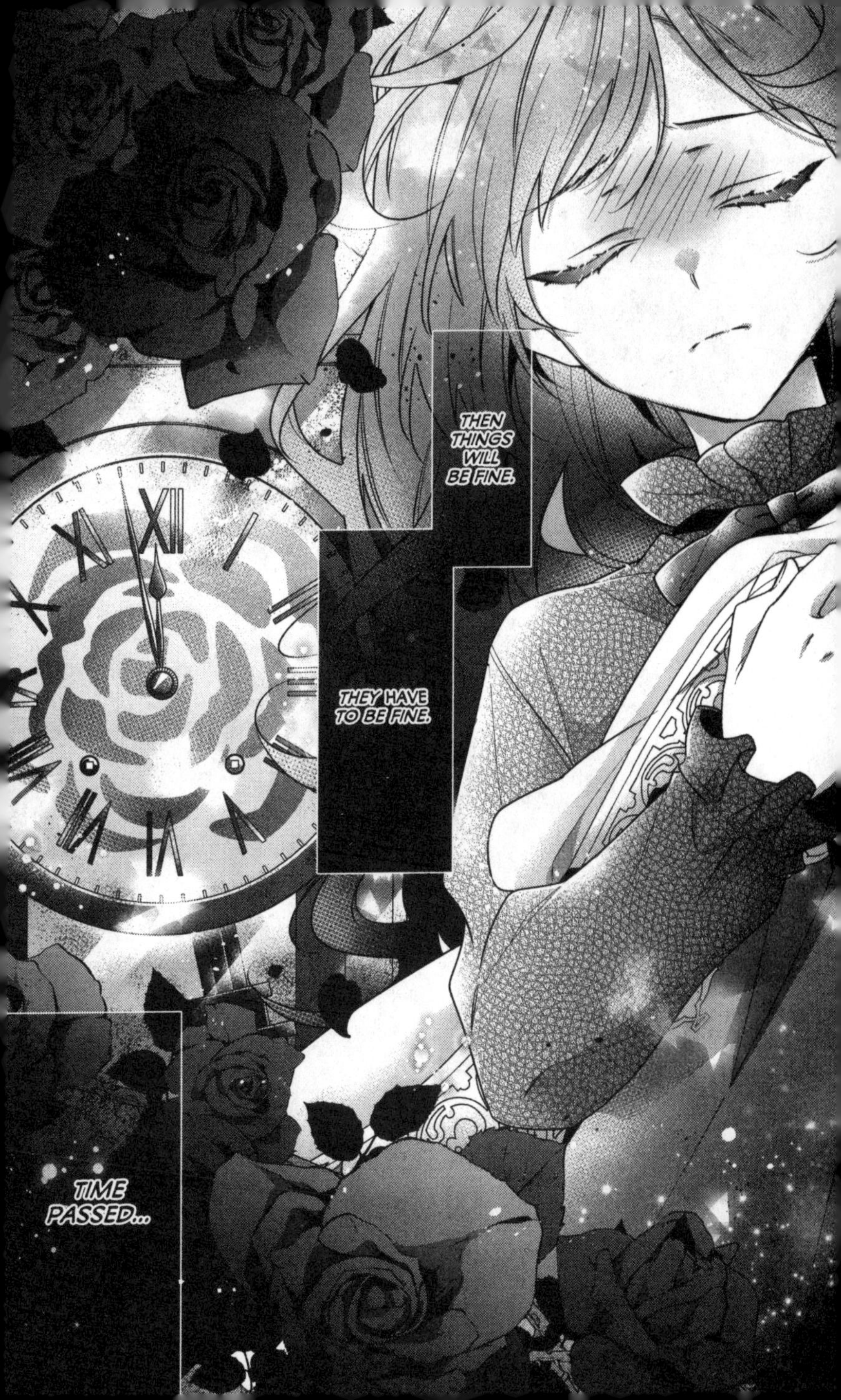
THEN THINGS WILL BE FINE.
THEY HAVE TO BE FINE.
TIME PASSED...

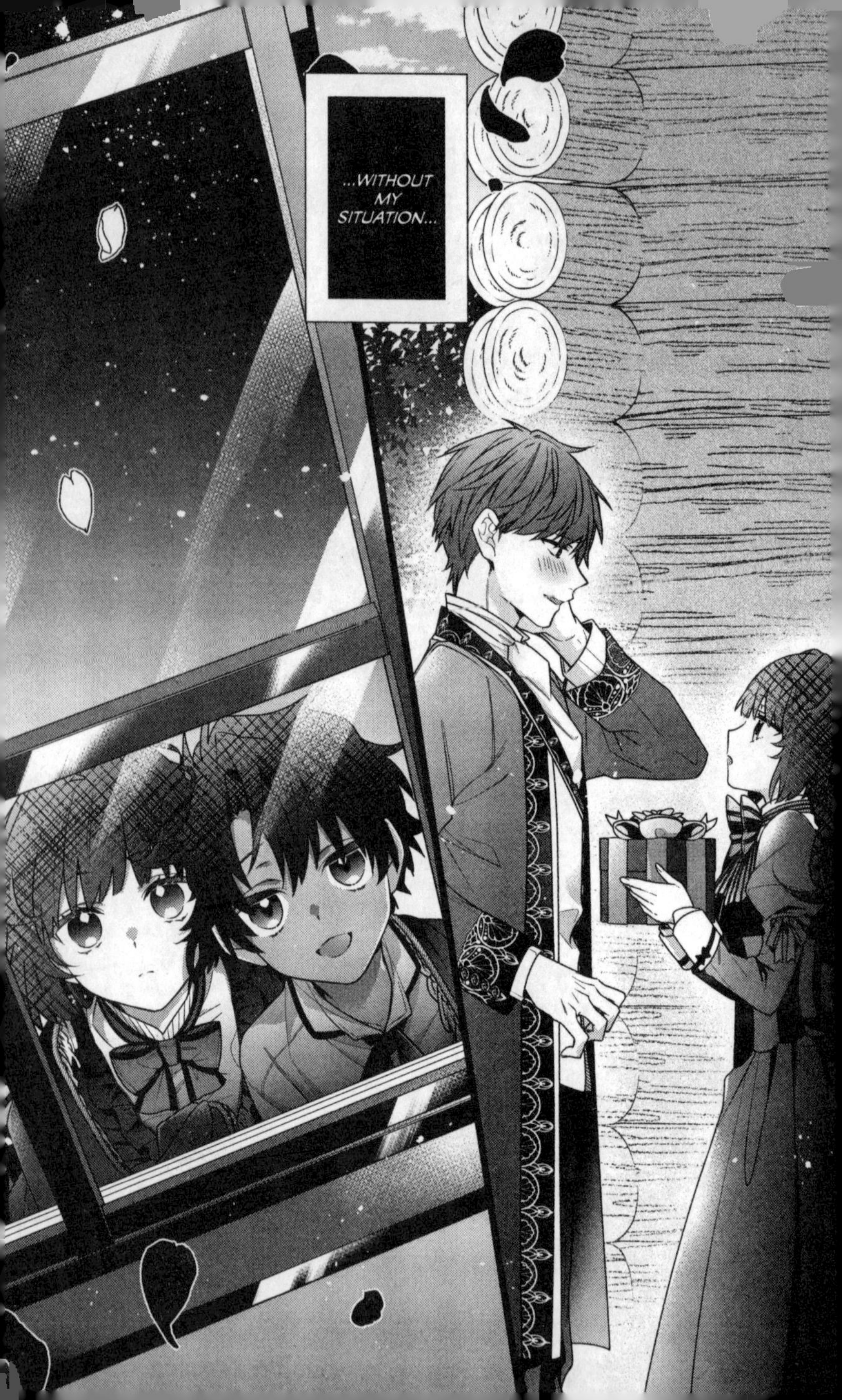
...WITHOUT MY SITUATION...

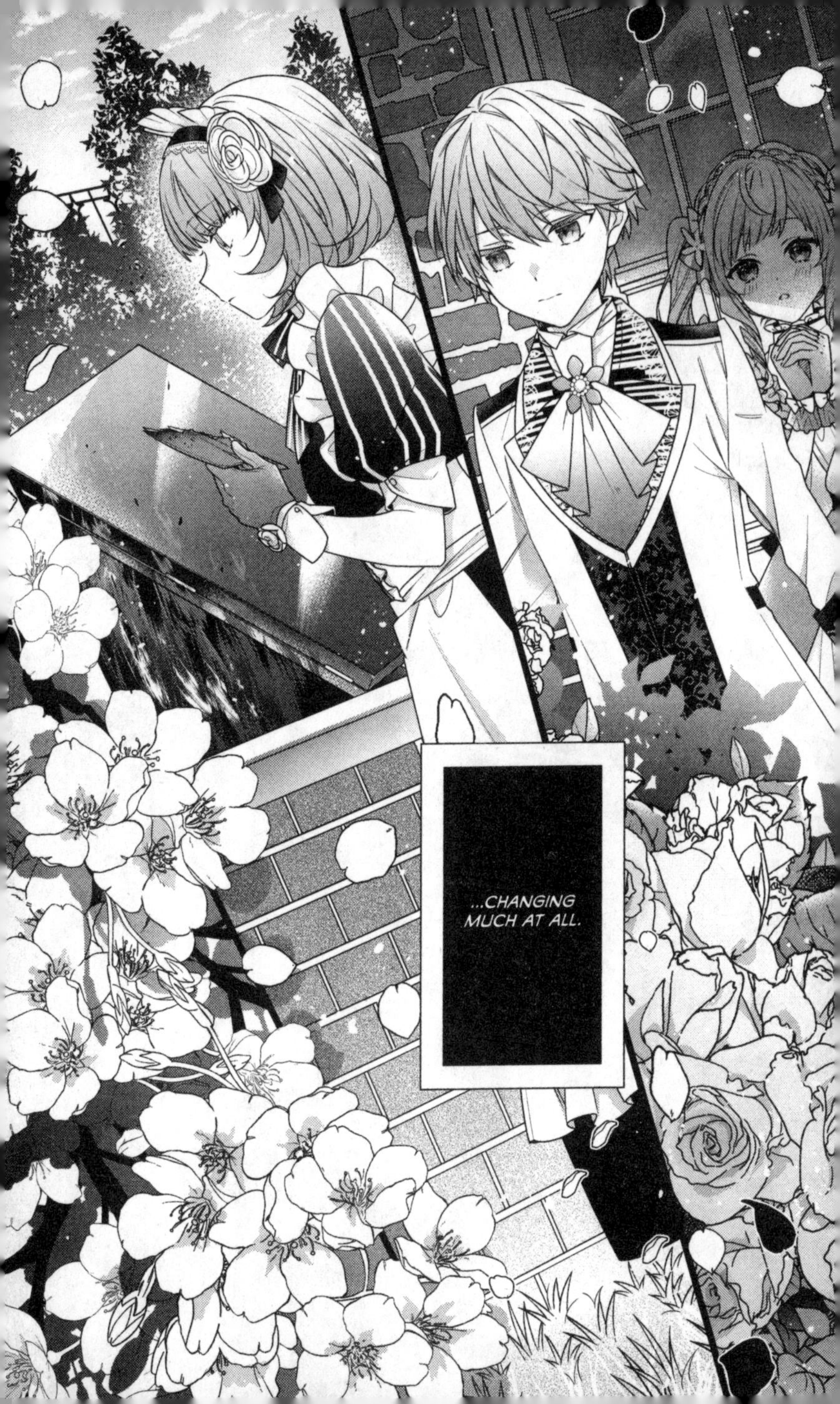
...CHANGING MUCH AT ALL.

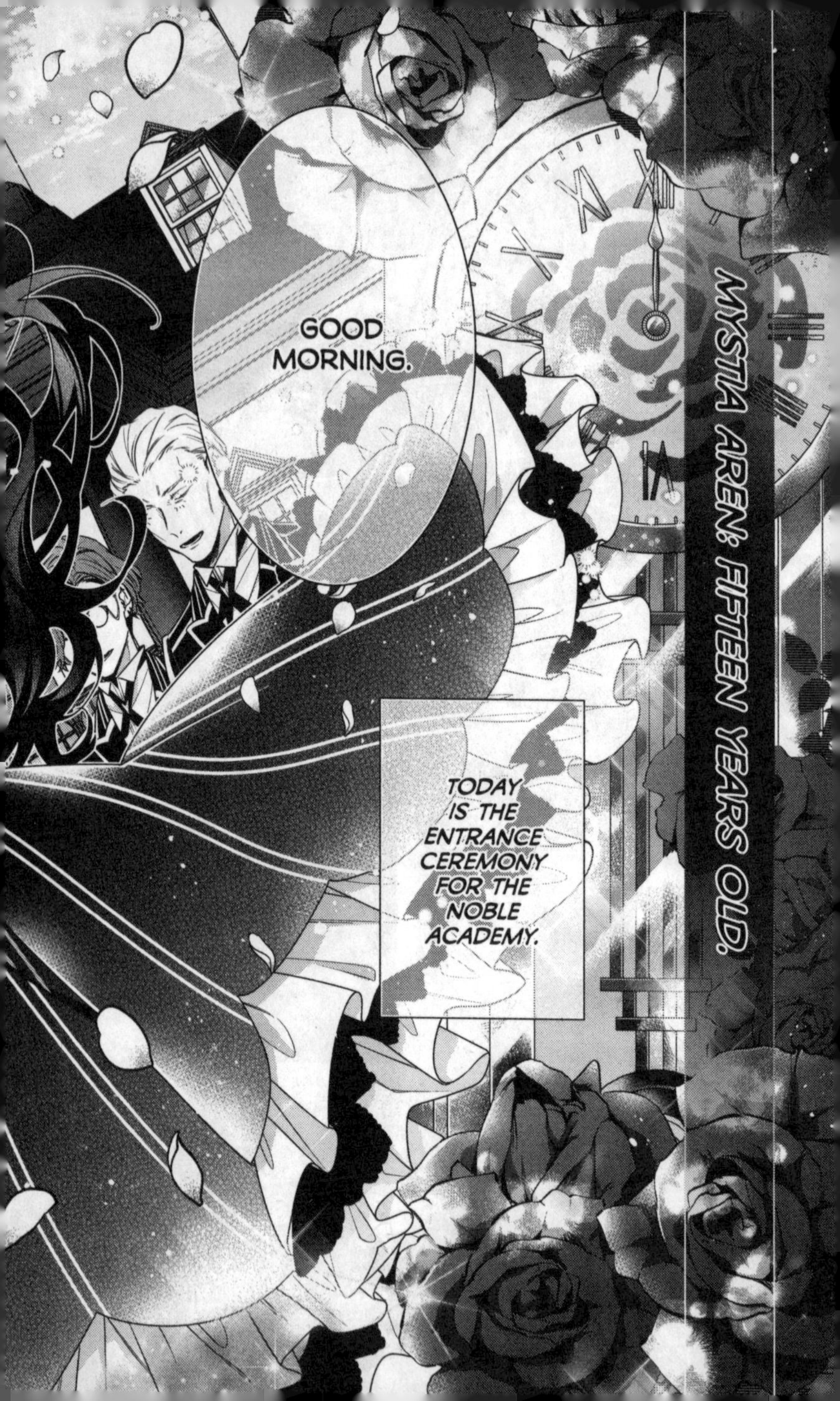
MYSTIA AREN: FIFTEEN YEARS OLD.
GOOD MORNING.
TODAY IS THE ENTRANCE CEREMONY FOR THE NOBLE ACADEMY.

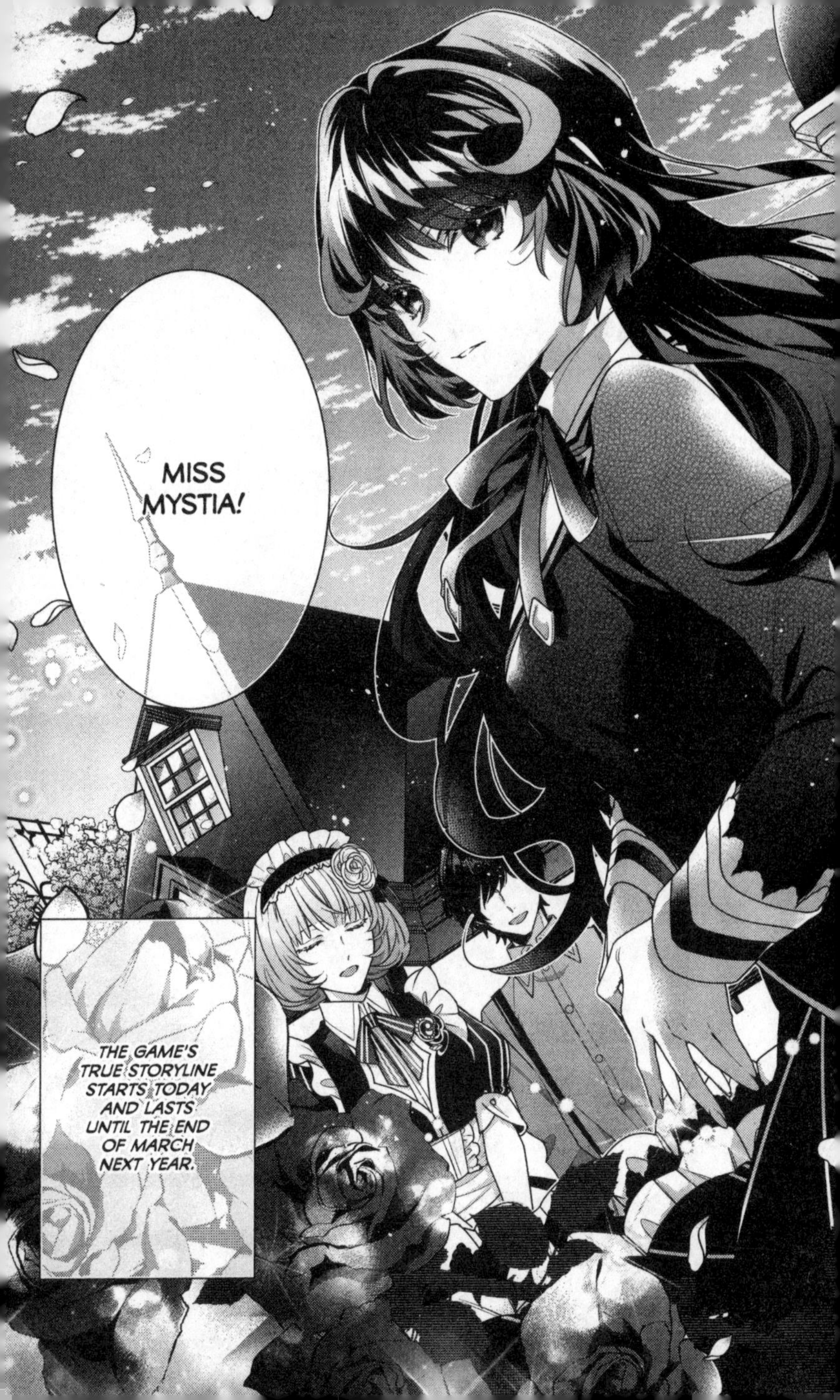
MISS MYSTIA!
THE GAME'S TRUE STORYLINE STARTS TODAY AND LASTS UNTIL THE END OF MARCH NEXT YEAR.

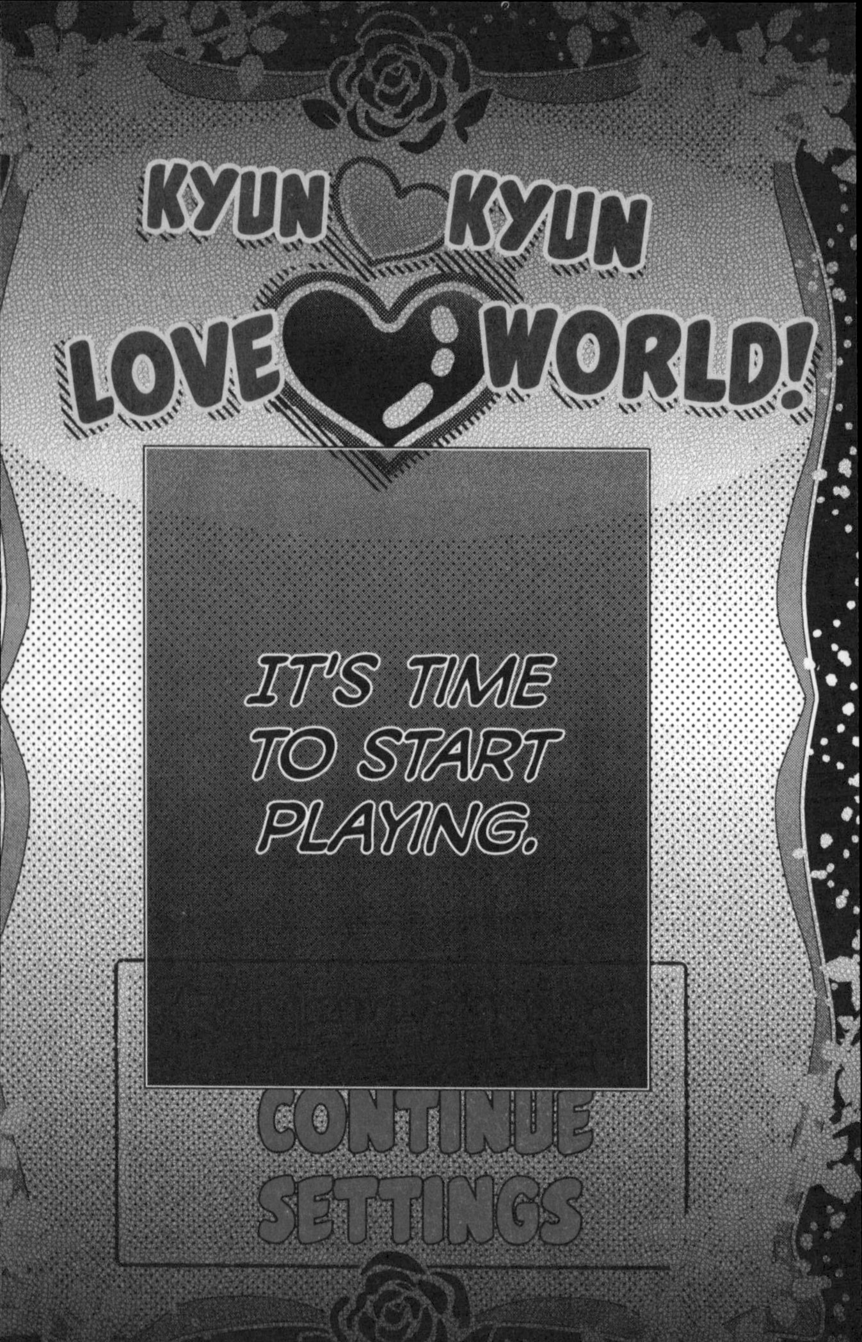
KYUN KYUN
LOVE WORLD!
IT'S TIME TO START PLAYING.
CONTINUE
SETTINGS

I was REINCARNATED as the
Villainess
in an OTOME GAME *but the boys love me anyway!*

I was REINCARNATED as the Villainess in an OTOME GAME but the boys love me anyway!

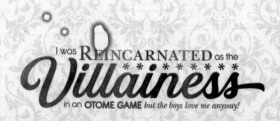

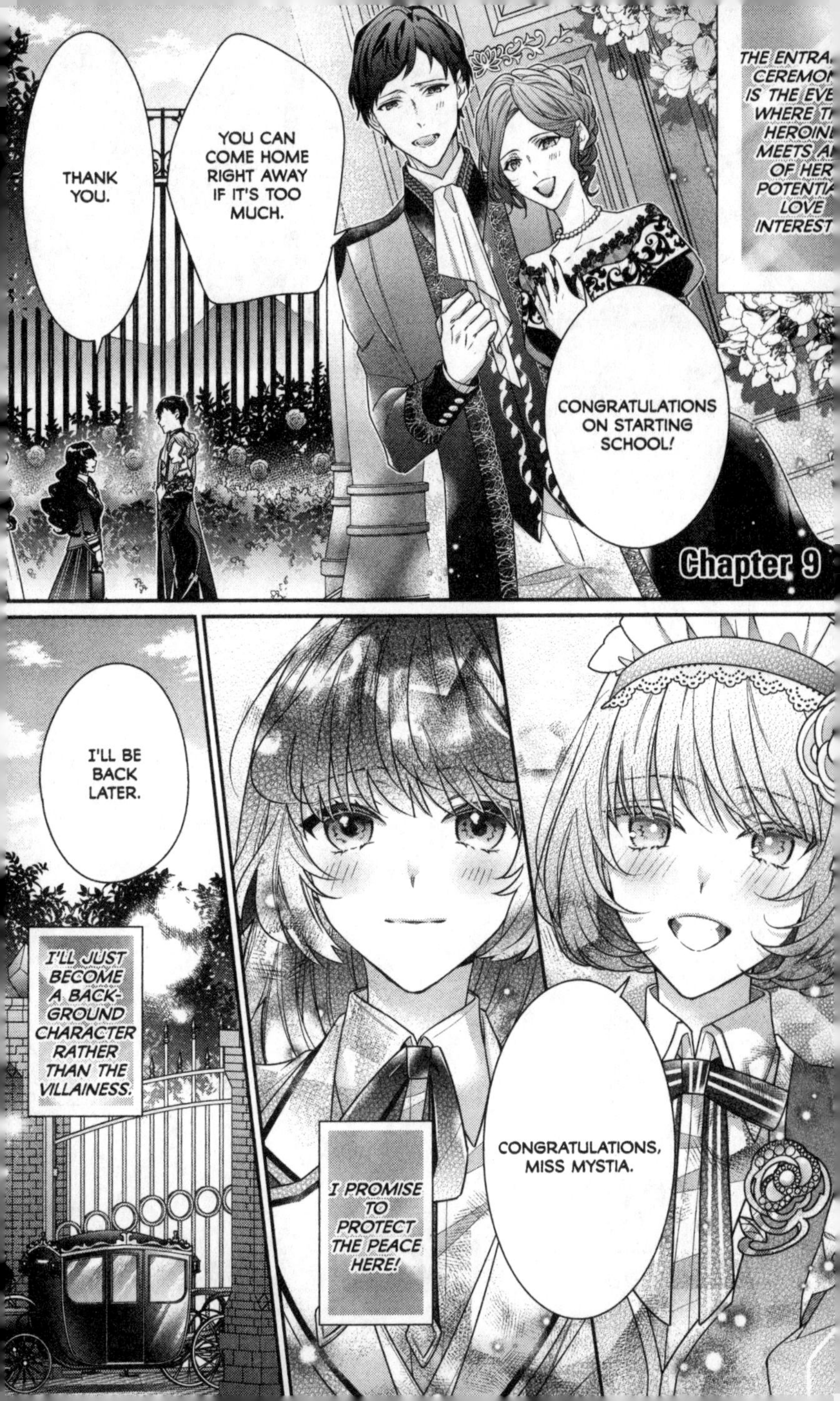
THE ENTRA CEREMON IS THE EVE WHERE T HEROIN MEETS A OF HER POTENTIA LOVE INTEREST
CONGRATULATIONS ON STARTING SCHOOL!
YOU CAN COME HOME RIGHT AWAY IF IT'S TOO MUCH.
THANK YOU.
Chapter 9
CONGRATULATIONS, MISS MYSTIA.
I PROMISE TO PROTECT THE PEACE HERE!
I'LL BE BACK LATER.
I'LL JUST BECOME A BACK-GROUND CHARACTER RATHER THAN THE VILLAINESS.

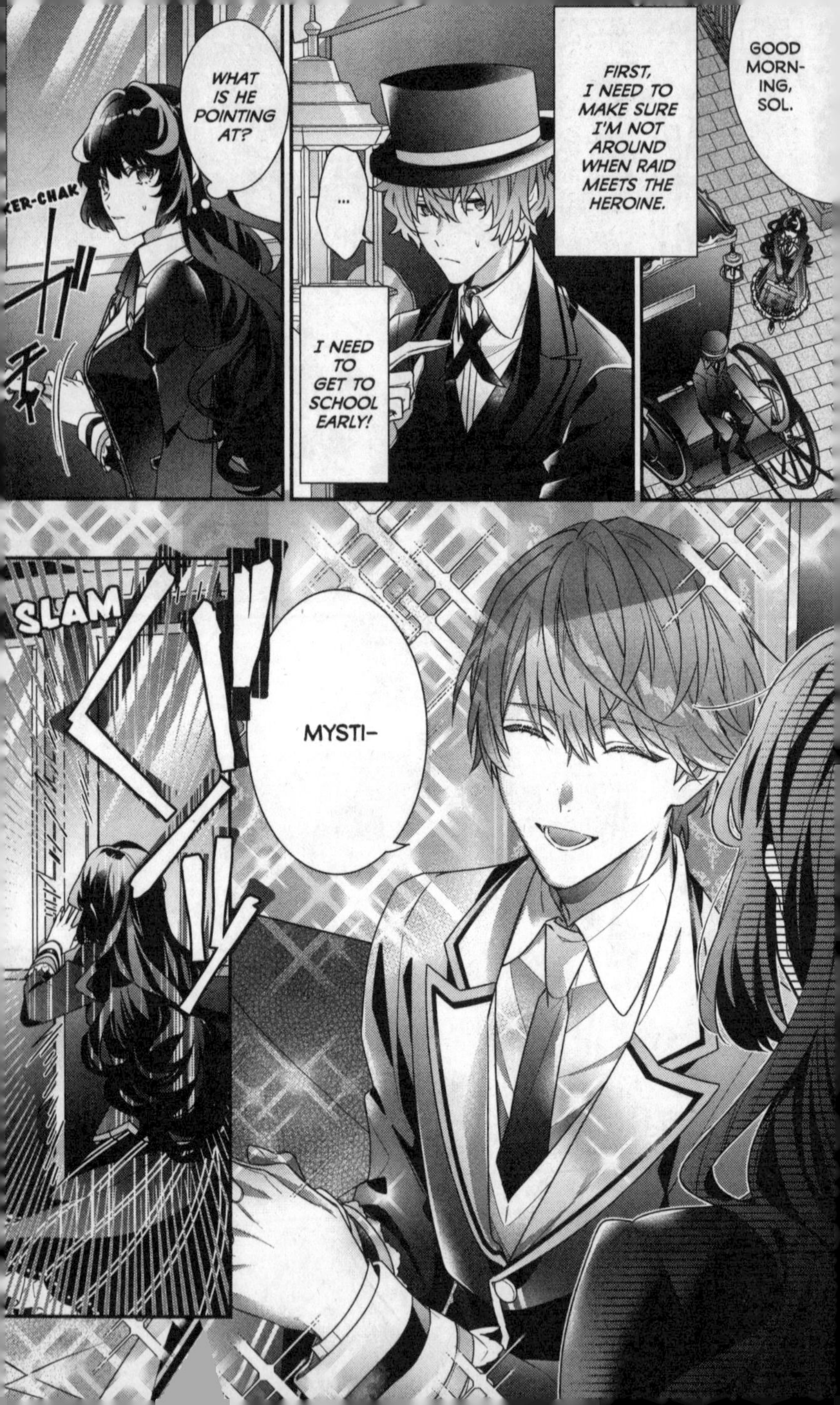
GOOD MORN-ING, SOL.
FIRST, I NEED TO MAKE SURE I'M NOT AROUND WHEN RAID MEETS THE HEROINE.
...
I NEED TO GET TO SCHOOL EARLY!
WHAT IS HE POINTING AT?
KER-CHAK
MYSTI–
SLAM

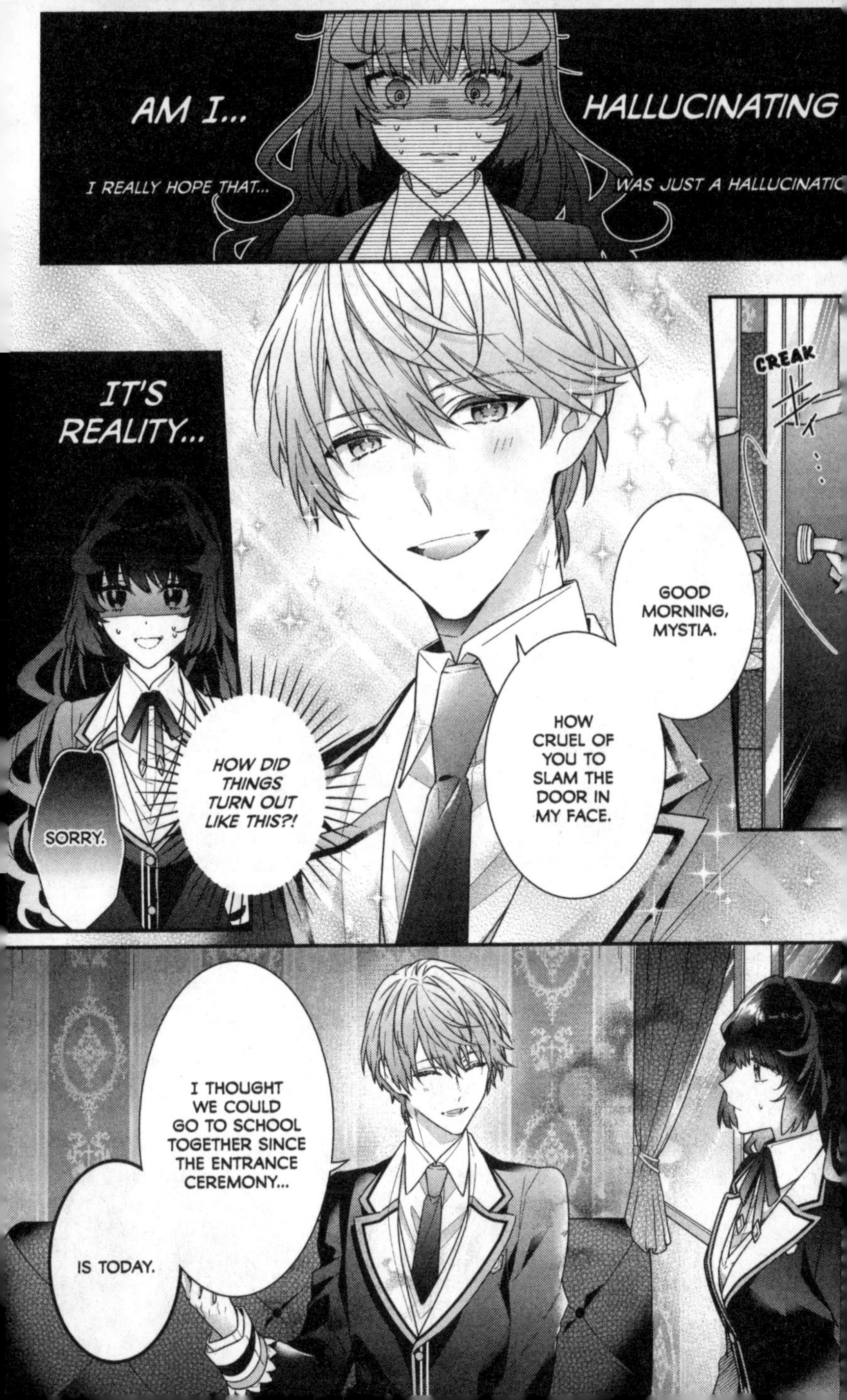
AM I...
HALLUCINATING
I REALLY HOPE THAT...
WAS JUST A HALLUCINATIO
CREAK
GOOD MORNING, MYSTIA.
HOW CRUEL OF YOU TO SLAM THE DOOR IN MY FACE.
IT'S REALITY...
HOW DID THINGS TURN OUT LIKE THIS?!
SORRY.
I THOUGHT WE COULD GO TO SCHOOL TOGETHER SINCE THE ENTRANCE CEREMONY...
IS TODAY.

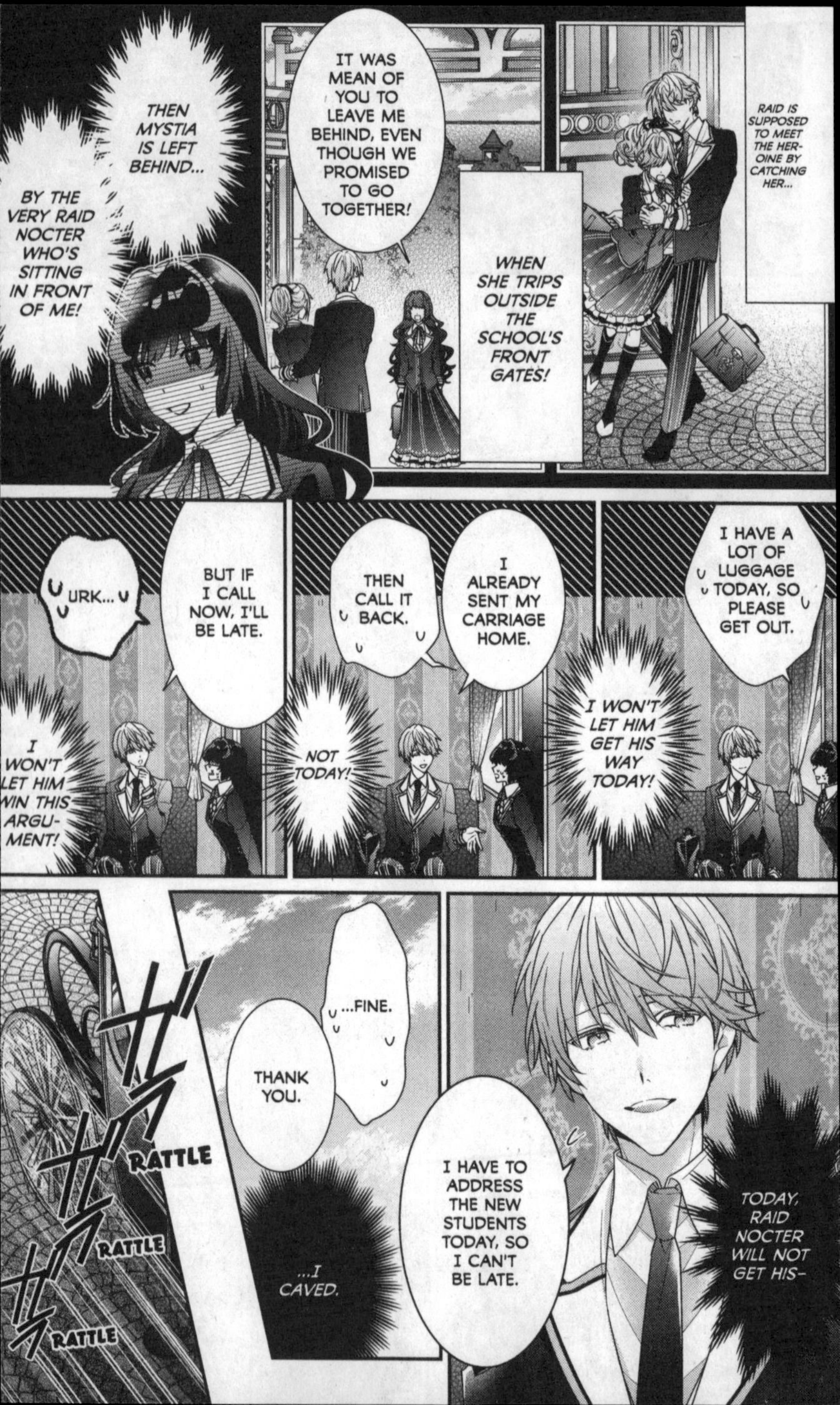
RAID IS SUPPOSED TO MEET THE HER-OINE BY CATCHING HER...
WHEN SHE TRIPS OUTSIDE THE SCHOOL'S FRONT GATES!
IT WAS MEAN OF YOU TO LEAVE ME BEHIND, EVEN THOUGH WE PROMISED TO GO TOGETHER!
THEN MYSTIA IS LEFT BEHIND...
BY THE VERY RAID NOCTER WHO'S SITTING IN FRONT OF ME!
I HAVE A LOT OF LUGGAGE TODAY, SO PLEASE GET OUT.
I WON'T LET HIM GET HIS WAY TODAY!
I ALREADY SENT MY CARRIAGE HOME.
THEN CALL IT BACK.
NOT TODAY!
BUT IF I CALL NOW, I'LL BE LATE.
URK...
I WON'T LET HIM WIN THIS ARGU-MENT!
I HAVE TO ADDRESS THE NEW STUDENTS TODAY, SO I CAN'T BE LATE.
TODAY, RAID NOCTER WILL NOT GET HIS-
...FINE.
THANK YOU.
...I CAVED.
RATTLE
RATTLE
RATTLE

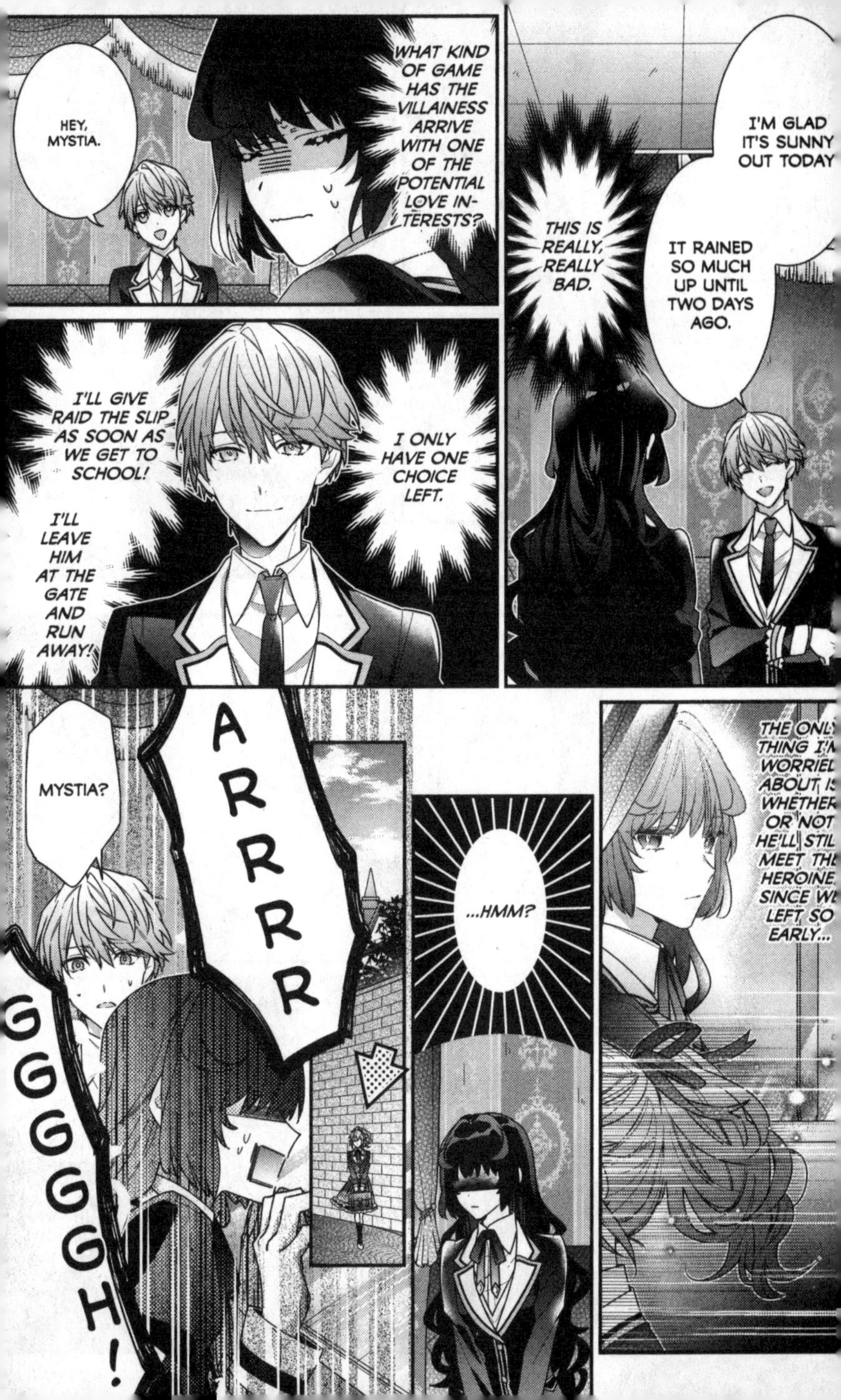
I'M GLAD IT'S SUNNY OUT TODAY
IT RAINED SO MUCH UP UNTIL TWO DAYS AGO.
THIS IS REALLY, REALLY BAD.
WHAT KIND OF GAME HAS THE VILLAINESS ARRIVE WITH ONE OF THE POTENTIAL LOVE IN-TERESTS?
HEY, MYSTIA.
I ONLY HAVE ONE CHOICE LEFT.
I'LL GIVE RAID THE SLIP AS SOON AS WE GET TO SCHOOL!
I'LL LEAVE HIM AT THE GATE AND RUN AWAY!
THE ONLY THING I'M WORRIED ABOUT IS WHETHER OR NOT HE'LL STILL MEET THE HEROINE SINCE WE LEFT SO EARLY...
...HMM?
MYSTIA?
ARRRRGGGGGH!

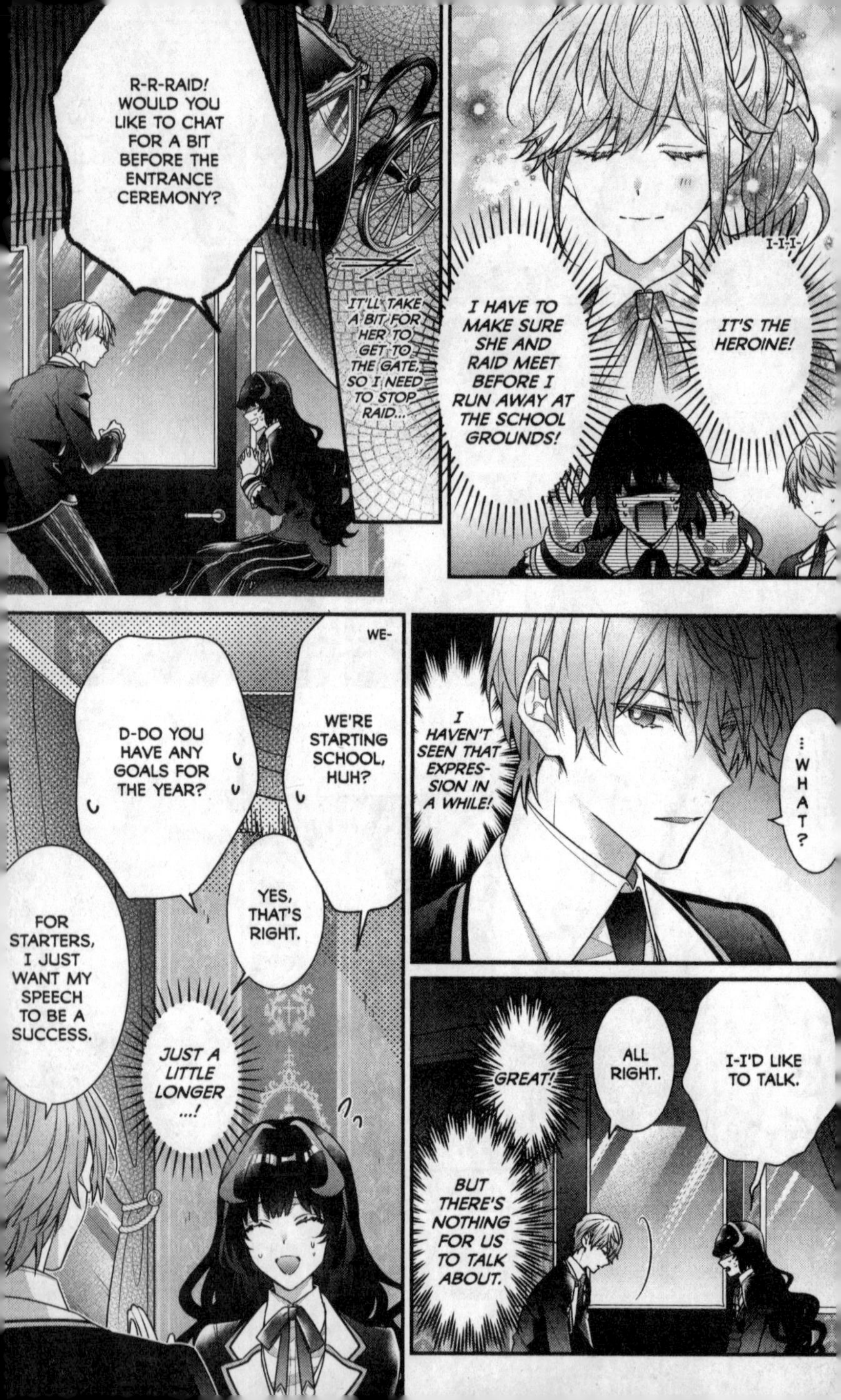
I-I-I-
IT'S THE HEROINE!
I HAVE TO MAKE SURE SHE AND RAID MEET BEFORE I RUN AWAY AT THE SCHOOL GROUNDS!
IT'LL TAKE A BIT FOR HER TO GET TO THE GATE, SO I NEED TO STOP RAID...
R-R-RAID! WOULD YOU LIKE TO CHAT FOR A BIT BEFORE THE ENTRANCE CEREMONY?
...WHAT?
I HAVEN'T SEEN THAT EXPRESSION IN A WHILE!
I-I'D LIKE TO TALK.
ALL RIGHT.
GREAT!
BUT THERE'S NOTHING FOR US TO TALK ABOUT.
WE-
WE'RE STARTING SCHOOL, HUH?
YES, THAT'S RIGHT.
D-DO YOU HAVE ANY GOALS FOR THE YEAR?
FOR STARTERS, I JUST WANT MY SPEECH TO BE A SUCCESS.
JUST A LITTLE LONGER ...!

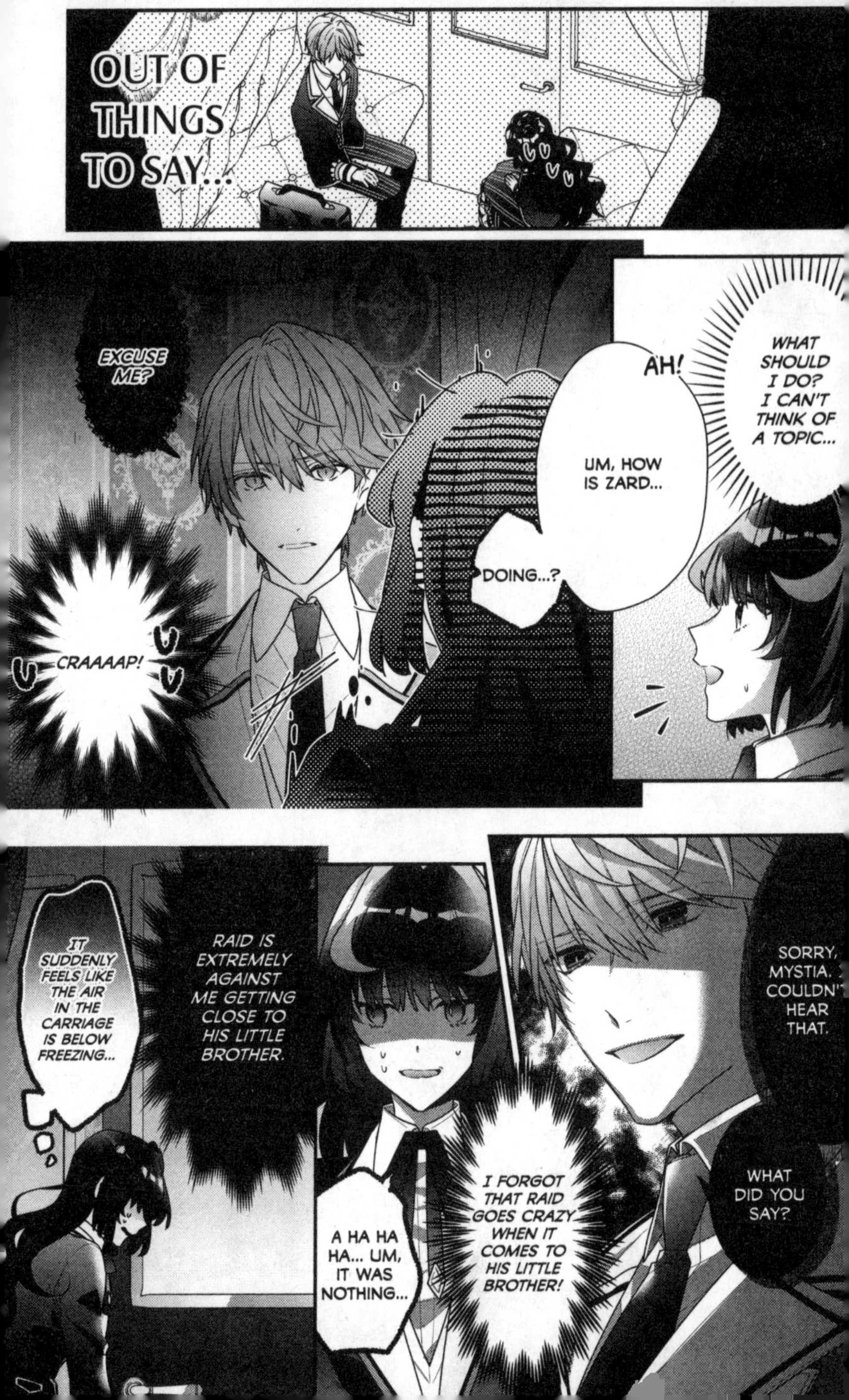
OUT OF THINGS TO SAY...
WHAT SHOULD I DO? I CAN'T THINK OF A TOPIC...
AH!
UM, HOW IS ZARD...
DOING...?
EXCUSE ME?
CRAAAAP!
SORRY, MYSTIA. COULDN' HEAR THAT.
WHAT DID YOU SAY?
I FORGOT THAT RAID GOES CRAZY WHEN IT COMES TO HIS LITTLE BROTHER!
A HA HA HA... UM, IT WAS NOTHING...
RAID IS EXTREMELY AGAINST ME GETTING CLOSE TO HIS LITTLE BROTHER.
IT SUDDENLY FEELS LIKE THE AIR IN THE CARRIAGE IS BELOW FREEZING...

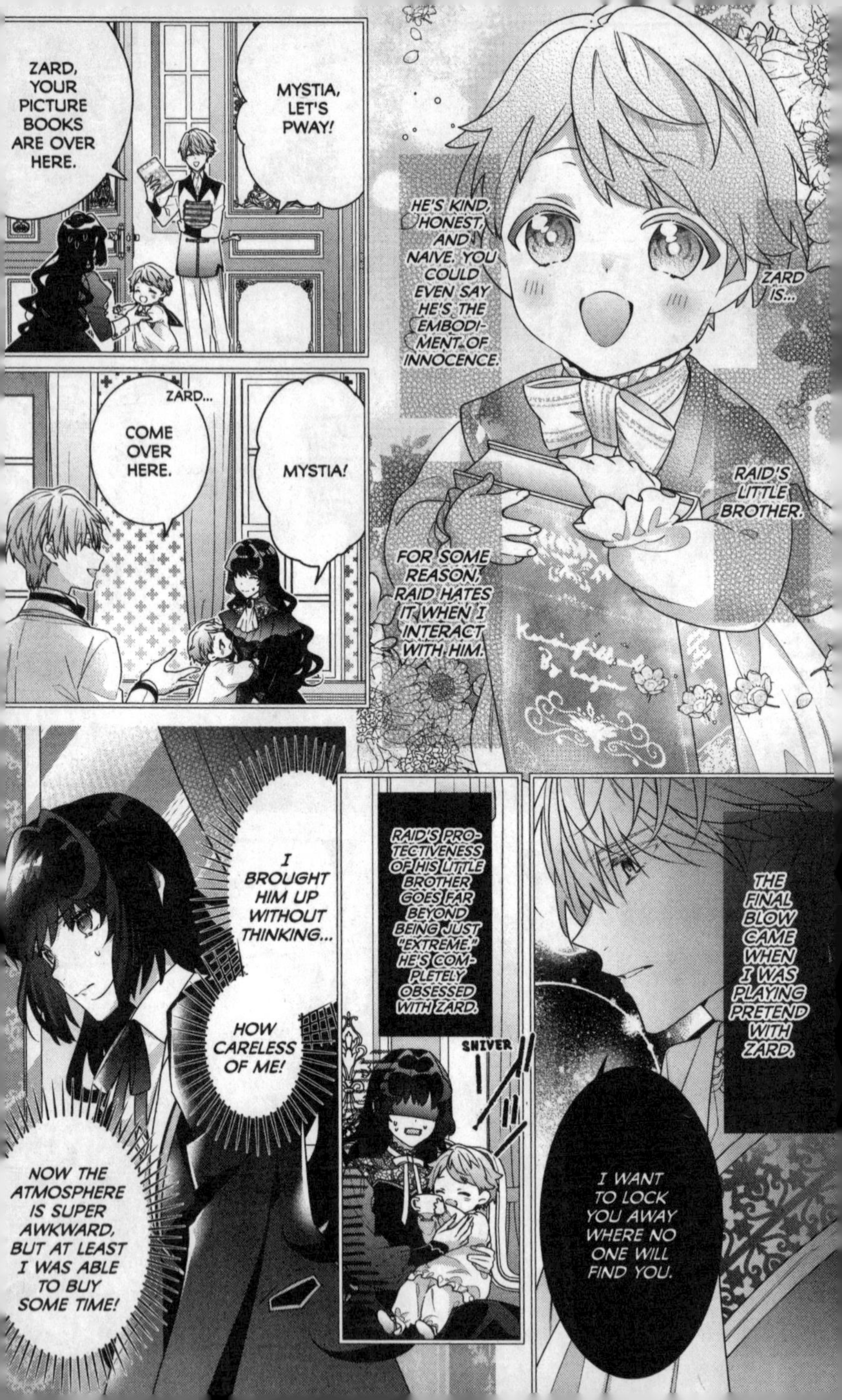
ZARD IS...
RAID'S LITTLE BROTHER.
HE'S KIND, HONEST, AND NAIVE. YOU COULD EVEN SAY HE'S THE EMBODIMENT OF INNOCENCE.
FOR SOME REASON, RAID HATES IT WHEN I INTERACT WITH HIM.
MYSTIA, LET'S PWAY!
ZARD, YOUR PICTURE BOOKS ARE OVER HERE.
MYSTIA!
ZARD... COME OVER HERE.
THE FINAL BLOW CAME WHEN I WAS PLAYING PRETEND WITH ZARD.
I WANT TO LOCK YOU AWAY WHERE NO ONE WILL FIND YOU.
RAID'S PROTECTIVENESS OF HIS LITTLE BROTHER GOES FAR BEYOND BEING JUST "EXTREME." HE'S COMPLETELY OBSESSED WITH ZARD.
SHIVER
I BROUGHT HIM UP WITHOUT THINKING...
HOW CARELESS OF ME!
NOW THE ATMOSPHERE IS SUPER AWKWARD, BUT AT LEAST I WAS ABLE TO BUY SOME TIME!

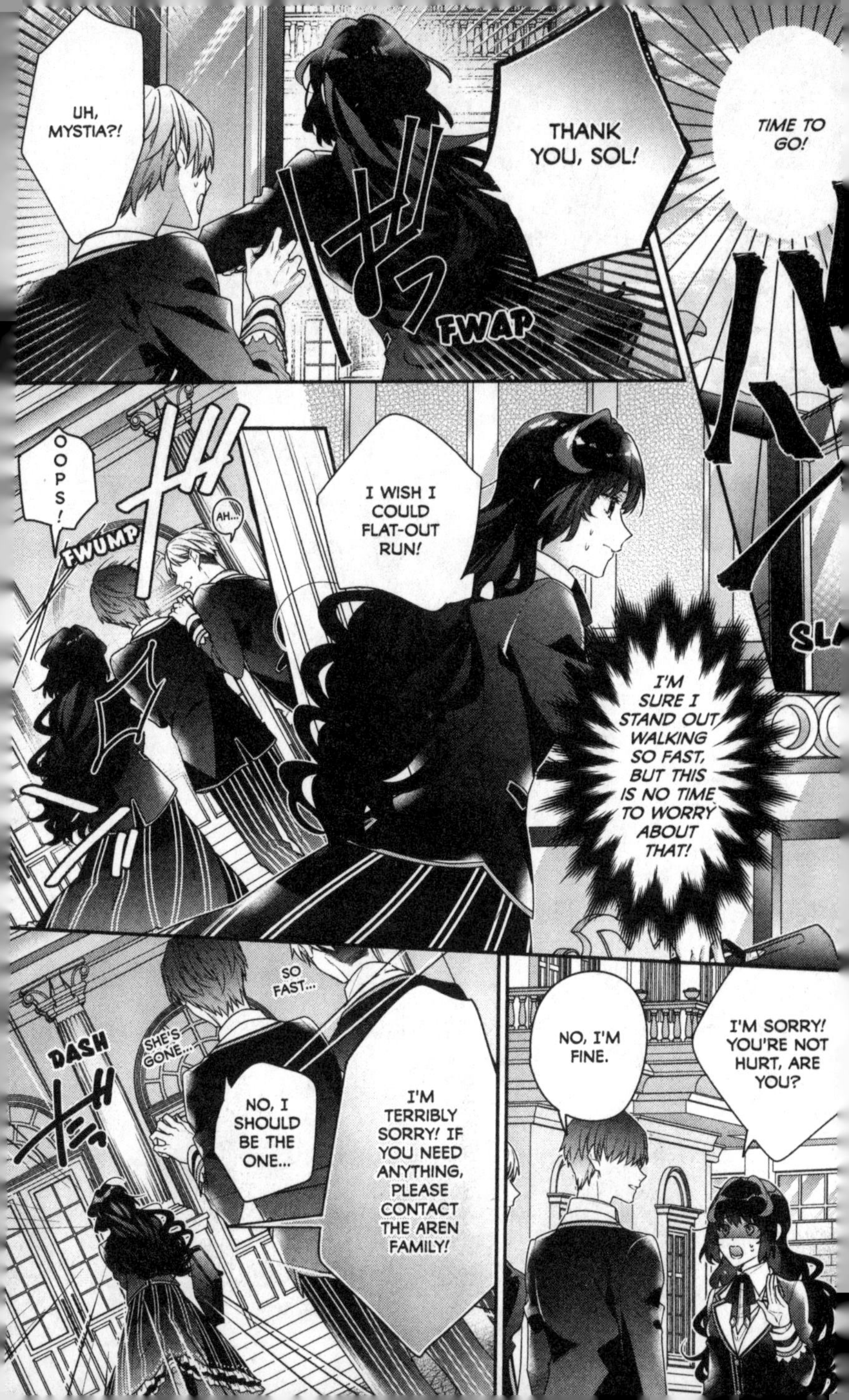
TIME TO GO!
THANK YOU, SOL!
FWAP
UH, MYSTIA?!
I WISH I COULD FLAT-OUT RUN!
I'M SURE I STAND OUT WALKING SO FAST, BUT THIS IS NO TIME TO WORRY ABOUT THAT!
AH...
OOPS!
FWUMP
I'M SORRY! YOU'RE NOT HURT, ARE YOU?
NO, I'M FINE.
I'M TERRIBLY SORRY! IF YOU NEED ANYTHING, PLEASE CONTACT THE AREN FAMILY!
NO, I SHOULD BE THE ONE...
SO FAST...
SHE'S GONE...
DASH

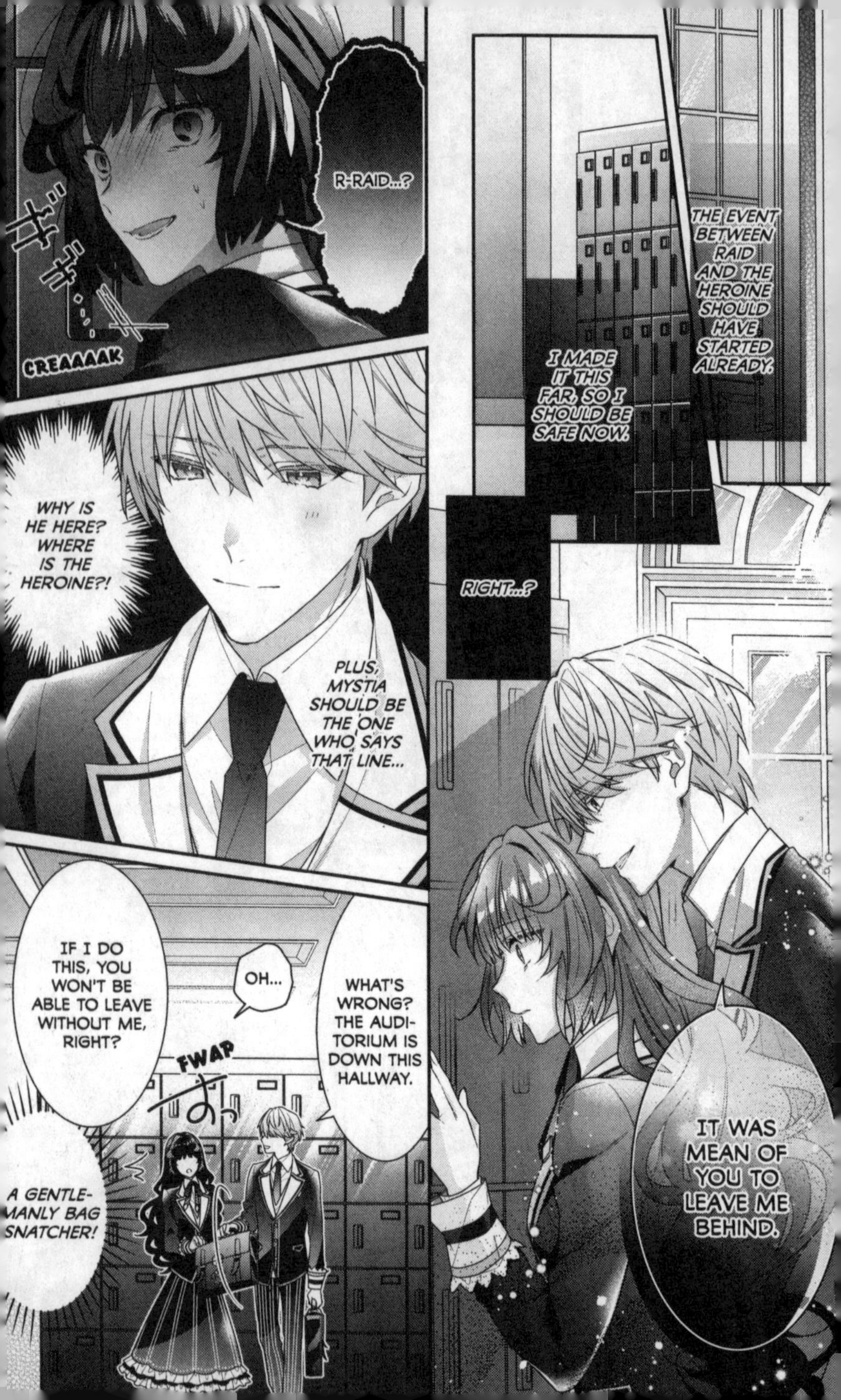
THE EVENT BETWEEN RAID AND THE HEROINE SHOULD HAVE STARTED ALREADY.
I MADE IT THIS FAR, SO I SHOULD BE SAFE NOW.
RIGHT...?
IT WAS MEAN OF YOU TO LEAVE ME BEHIND.
R-RAID...?
CREAAAAK
WHY IS HE HERE? WHERE IS THE HEROINE?!
PLUS, MYSTIA SHOULD BE THE ONE WHO SAYS THAT LINE...
WHAT'S WRONG? THE AUDITORIUM IS DOWN THIS HALLWAY.
OH...
IF I DO THIS, YOU WON'T BE ABLE TO LEAVE WITHOUT ME, RIGHT?
FWAP
おっ
A GENTLEMANLY BAG SNATCHER!

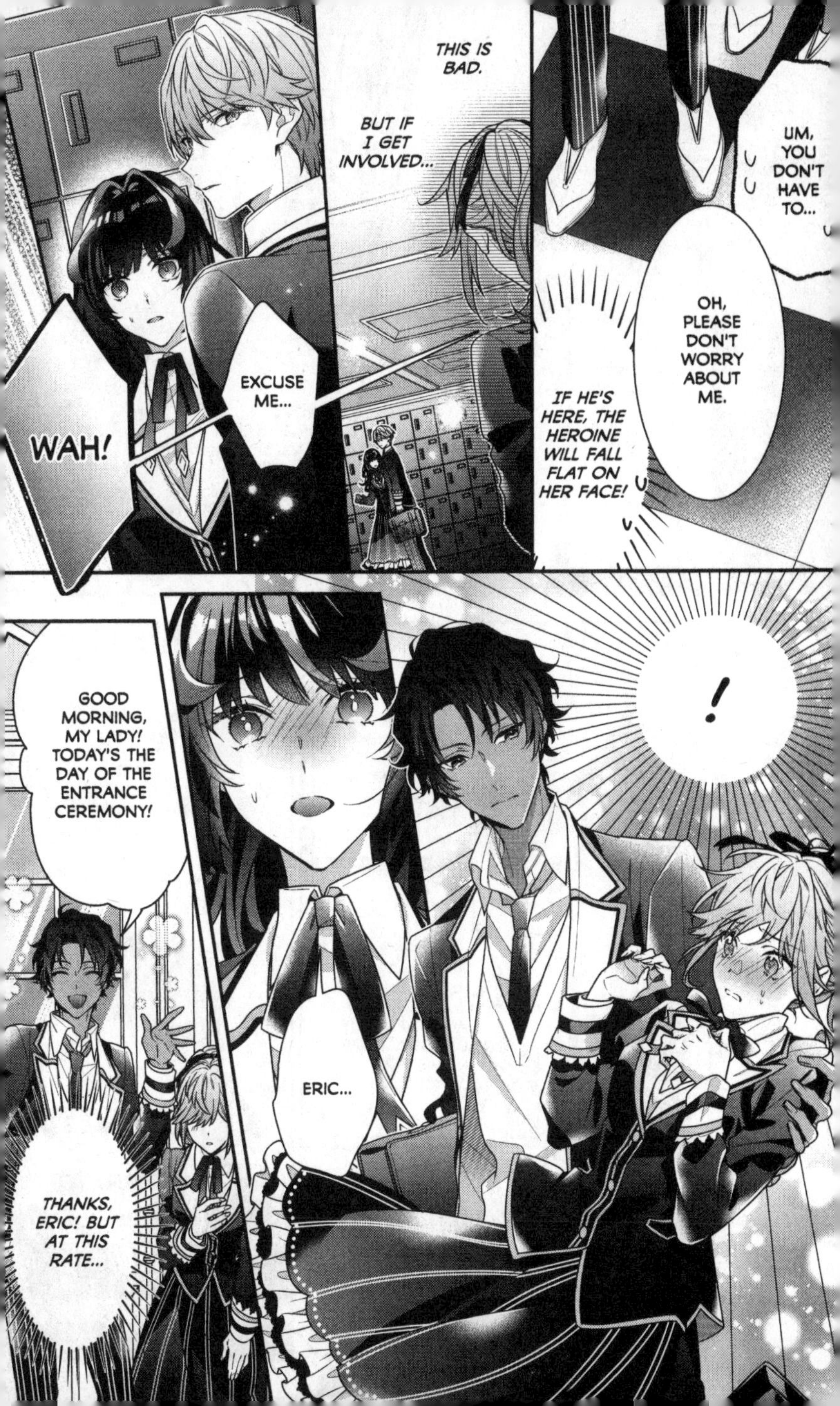
UM, YOU DON'T HAVE TO...
OH, PLEASE DON'T WORRY ABOUT ME.
IF HE'S HERE, THE HEROINE WILL FALL FLAT ON HER FACE!
THIS IS BAD.
BUT IF I GET INVOLVED...
EXCUSE ME...
WAH!
!
ERIC...
GOOD MORNING, MY LADY! TODAY'S THE DAY OF THE ENTRANCE CEREMONY!
THANKS, ERIC! BUT AT THIS RATE...

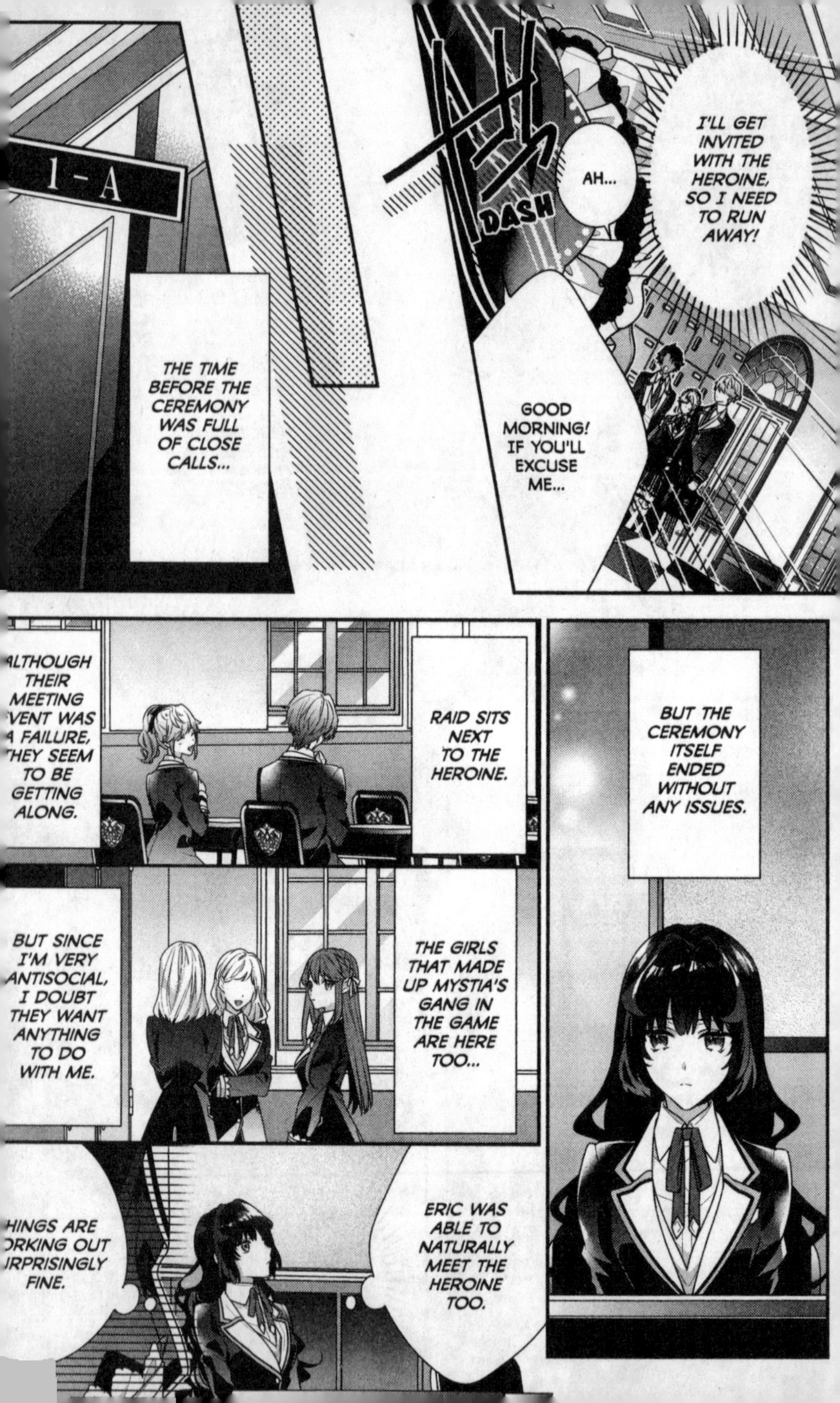
I'LL GET INVITED WITH THE HEROINE, SO I NEED TO RUN AWAY!
AH...
DASH
GOOD MORNING! IF YOU'LL EXCUSE ME...
1-A
THE TIME BEFORE THE CEREMONY WAS FULL OF CLOSE CALLS...
BUT THE CEREMONY ITSELF ENDED WITHOUT ANY ISSUES.
RAID SITS NEXT TO THE HEROINE.
LTHOUGH THEIR MEETING VENT WAS FAILURE, HEY SEEM TO BE GETTING ALONG.
THE GIRLS THAT MADE UP MYSTIA'S GANG IN THE GAME ARE HERE TOO...
BUT SINCE I'M VERY ANTISOCIAL, I DOUBT THEY WANT ANYTHING TO DO WITH ME.
ERIC WAS ABLE TO NATURALLY MEET THE HEROINE TOO.
HINGS ARE ORKING OUT IRPRISINGLY FINE.

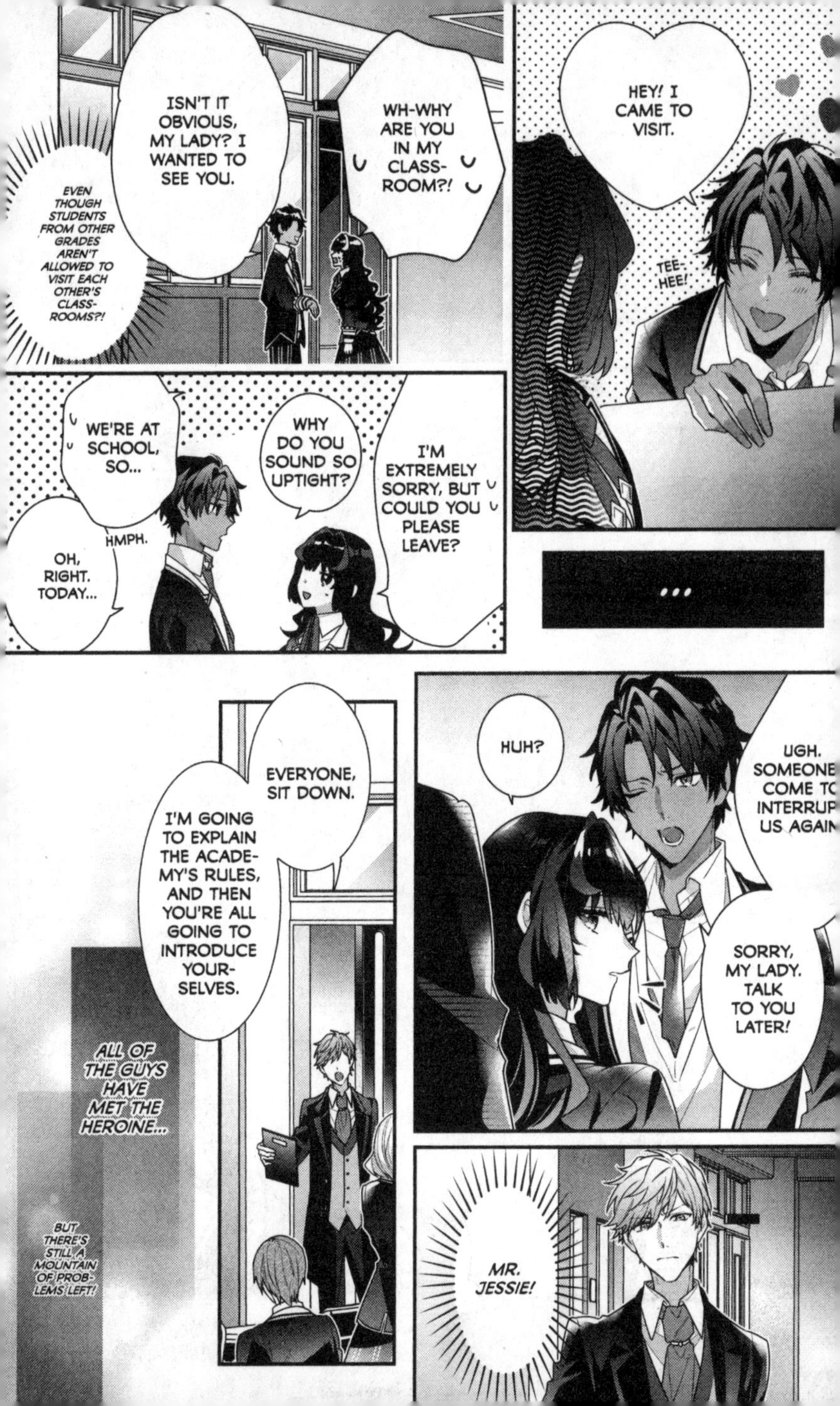
HEY! I CAME TO VISIT.
TEE-HEE!
WH-WHY ARE YOU IN MY CLASS-ROOM?!
ISN'T IT OBVIOUS, MY LADY? I WANTED TO SEE YOU.
EVEN THOUGH STUDENTS FROM OTHER GRADES AREN'T ALLOWED TO VISIT EACH OTHER'S CLASS-ROOMS?!
I'M EXTREMELY SORRY, BUT COULD YOU PLEASE LEAVE?
WHY DO YOU SOUND SO UPTIGHT?
WE'RE AT SCHOOL, SO...
HMPH.
OH, RIGHT. TODAY...
...
UGH. SOMEONE COME TO INTERRUP US AGAIN
HUH?
SORRY, MY LADY. TALK TO YOU LATER!
MR. JESSIE!
EVERYONE, SIT DOWN.
I'M GOING TO EXPLAIN THE ACADE-MY'S RULES, AND THEN YOU'RE ALL GOING TO INTRODUCE YOUR-SELVES.
ALL OF THE GUYS HAVE MET THE HEROINE...
BUT THERE'S STILL A MOUNTAIN OF PROB-LEMS LEFT!

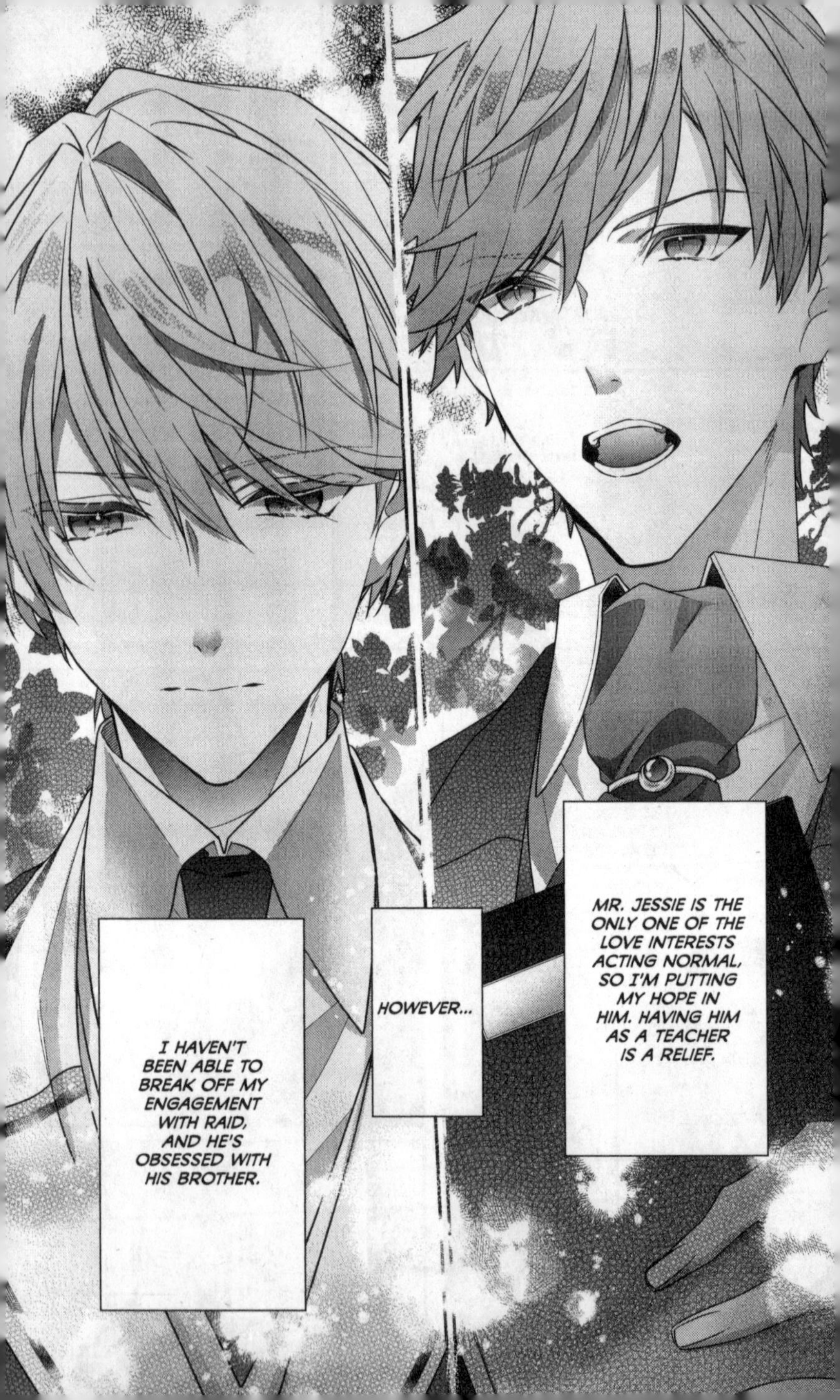
MR. JESSIE IS THE ONLY ONE OF THE LOVE INTERESTS ACTING NORMAL, SO I'M PUTTING MY HOPE IN HIM. HAVING HIM AS A TEACHER IS A RELIEF.
HOWEVER...
I HAVEN'T BEEN ABLE TO BREAK OFF MY ENGAGEMENT WITH RAID, AND HE'S OBSESSED WITH HIS BROTHER.

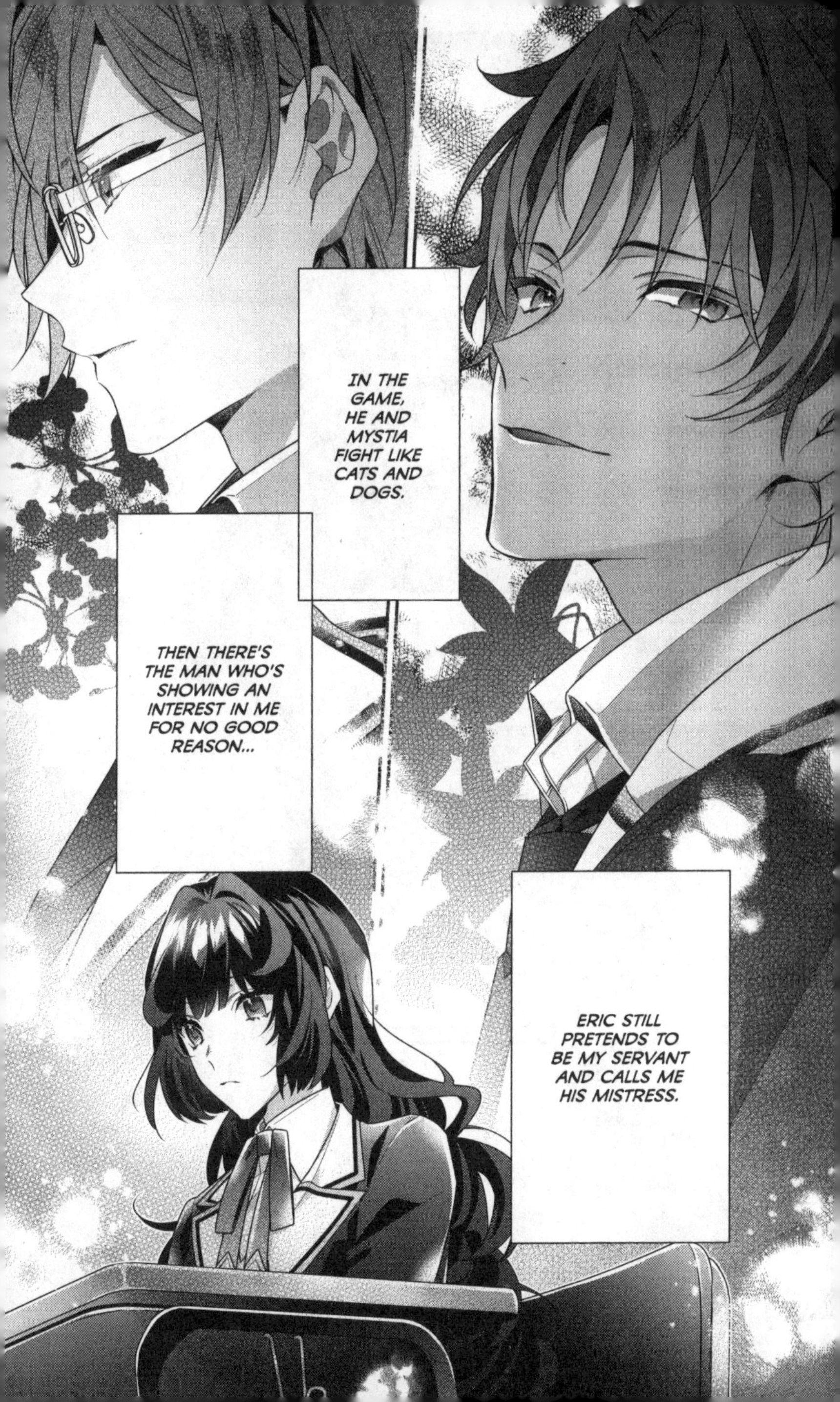
IN THE GAME, HE AND MYSTIA FIGHT LIKE CATS AND DOGS.
THEN THERE'S THE MAN WHO'S SHOWING AN INTEREST IN ME FOR NO GOOD REASON...
ERIC STILL PRETENDS TO BE MY SERVANT AND CALLS ME HIS MISTRESS.

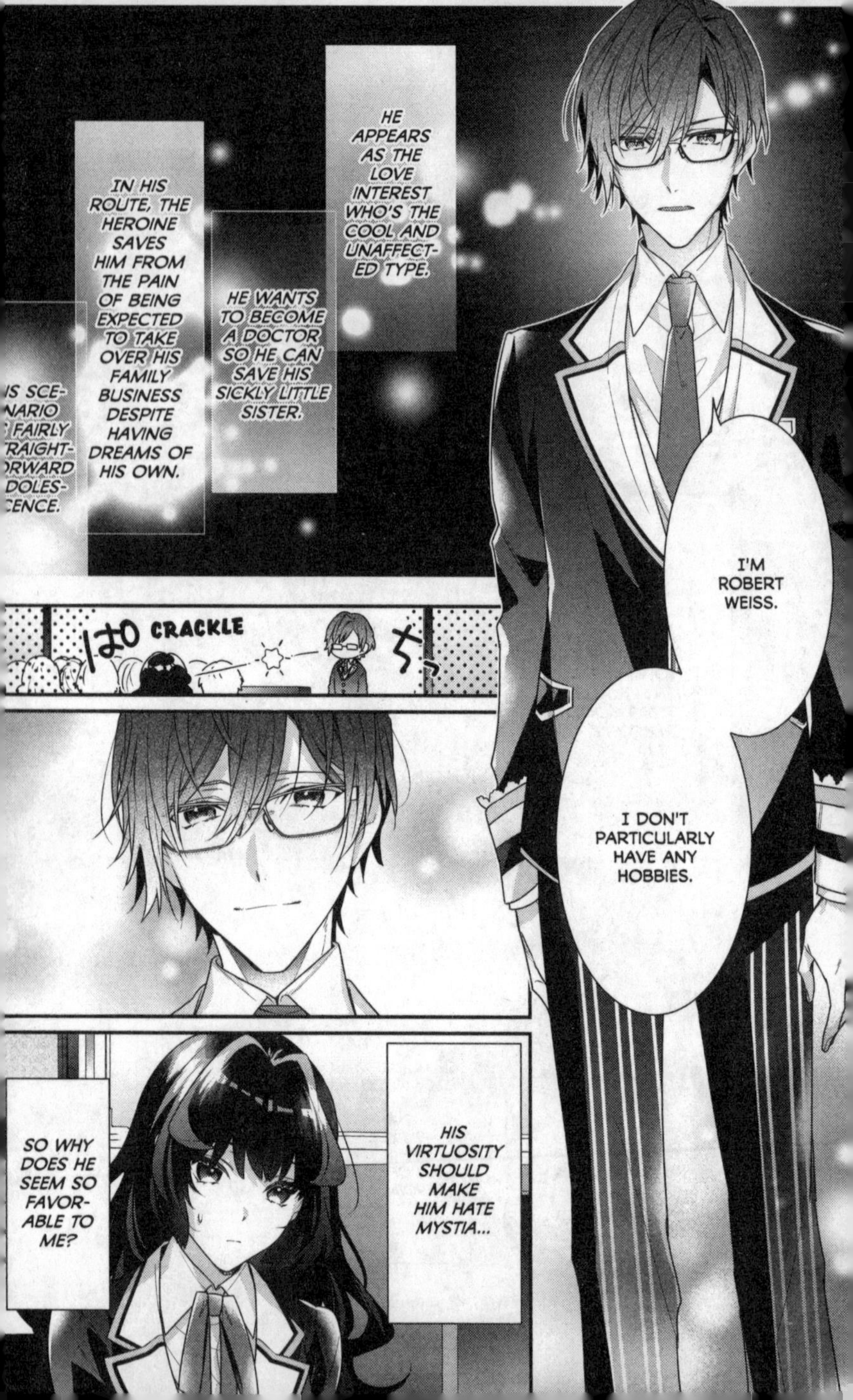
I'M ROBERT WEISS.
I DON'T PARTICULARLY HAVE ANY HOBBIES.
HE APPEARS AS THE LOVE INTEREST WHO'S THE COOL AND UNAFFECT-ED TYPE.
HE WANTS TO BECOME A DOCTOR SO HE CAN SAVE HIS SICKLY LITTLE SISTER.
IN HIS ROUTE, THE HEROINE SAVES HIM FROM THE PAIN OF BEING EXPECTED TO TAKE OVER HIS FAMILY BUSINESS DESPITE HAVING DREAMS OF HIS OWN.
IS SCE-NARIO FAIRLY
CRACKLE
HIS VIRTUOSITY SHOULD MAKE HIM HATE MYSTIA...
SO WHY DOES HE SEEM SO FAVOR-ABLE TO ME?

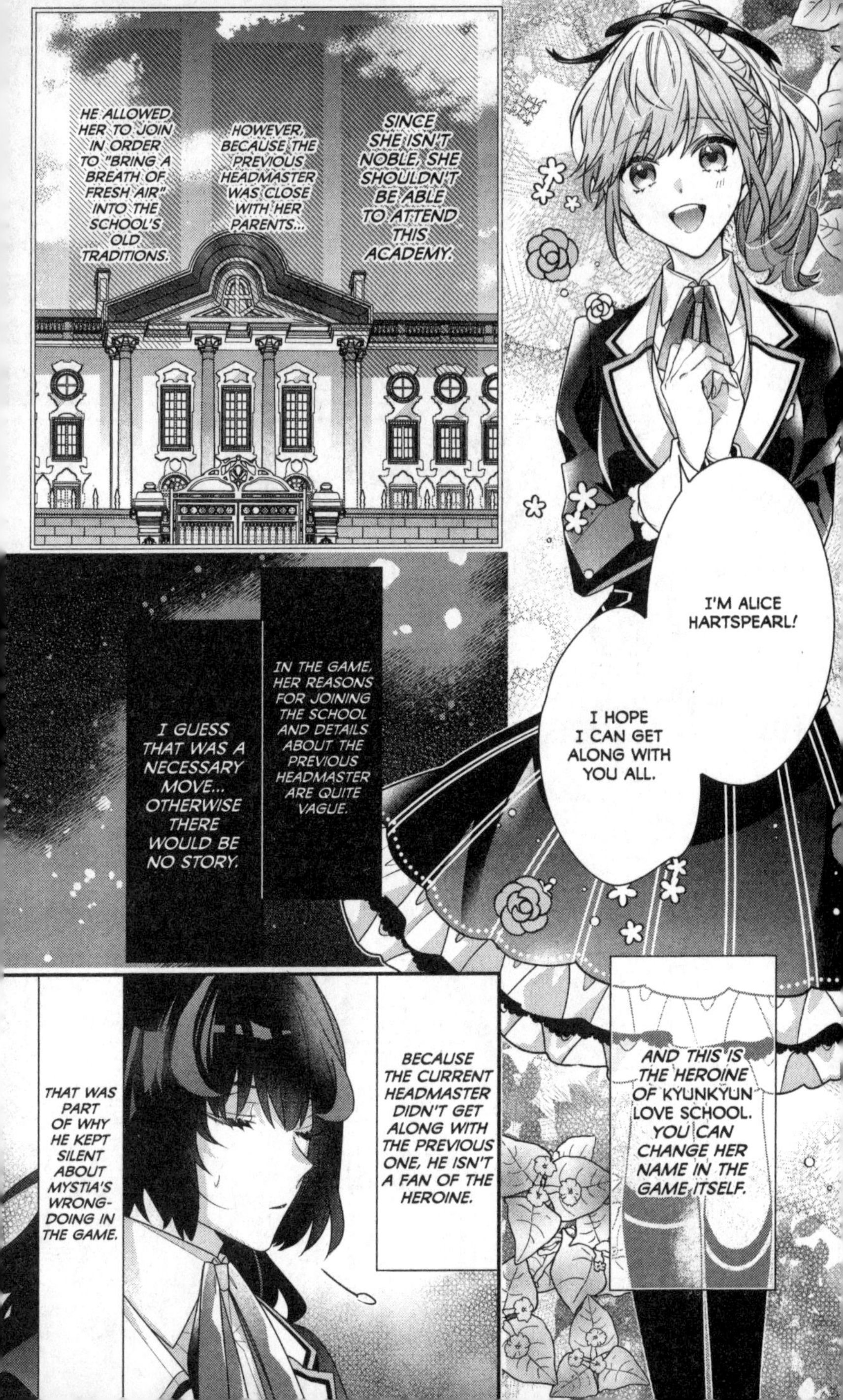
I'M ALICE HARTSPEARL!
I HOPE I CAN GET ALONG WITH YOU ALL.
AND THIS IS THE HEROINE OF KYUNKYUN LOVE SCHOOL. YOU CAN CHANGE HER NAME IN THE GAME ITSELF.
SINCE SHE ISN'T NOBLE, SHE SHOULDN'T BE ABLE TO ATTEND THIS ACADEMY.
HOWEVER, BECAUSE THE PREVIOUS HEADMASTER WAS CLOSE WITH HER PARENTS...
HE ALLOWED HER TO JOIN IN ORDER TO "BRING A BREATH OF FRESH AIR" INTO THE SCHOOL'S OLD TRADITIONS.
IN THE GAME, HER REASONS FOR JOINING THE SCHOOL AND DETAILS ABOUT THE PREVIOUS HEADMASTER ARE QUITE VAGUE.
I GUESS THAT WAS A NECESSARY MOVE... OTHERWISE THERE WOULD BE NO STORY.
BECAUSE THE CURRENT HEADMASTER DIDN'T GET ALONG WITH THE PREVIOUS ONE, HE ISN'T A FAN OF THE HEROINE.
THAT WAS PART OF WHY HE KEPT SILENT ABOUT MYSTIA'S WRONG-DOING IN THE GAME.

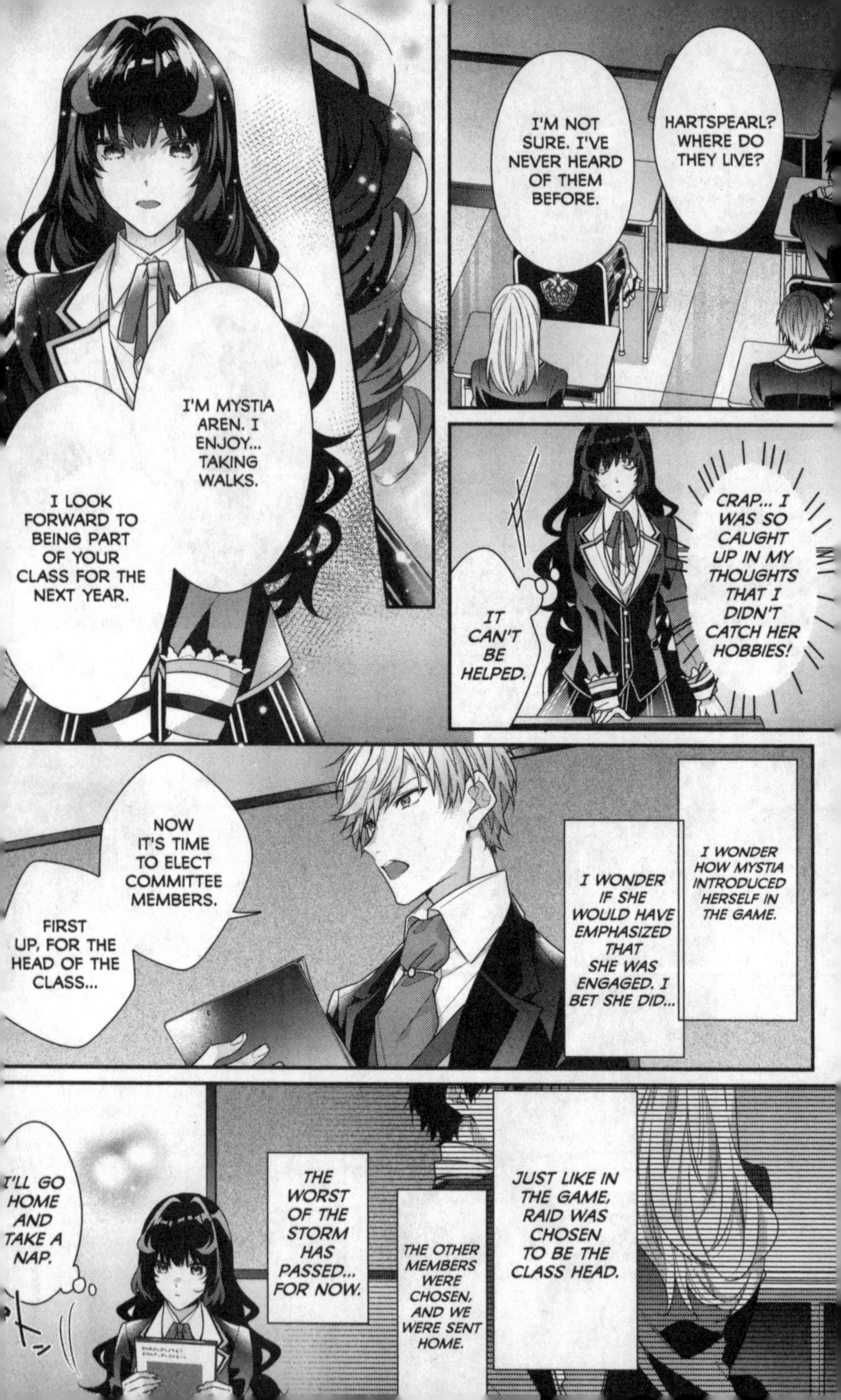
HARTSPEARL? WHERE DO THEY LIVE?
I'M NOT SURE. I'VE NEVER HEARD OF THEM BEFORE.
CRAP... I WAS SO CAUGHT UP IN MY THOUGHTS THAT I DIDN'T CATCH HER HOBBIES!
IT CAN'T BE HELPED.
I'M MYSTIA AREN. I ENJOY... TAKING WALKS.
I LOOK FORWARD TO BEING PART OF YOUR CLASS FOR THE NEXT YEAR.
I WONDER HOW MYSTIA INTRODUCED HERSELF IN THE GAME.
I WONDER IF SHE WOULD HAVE EMPHASIZED THAT SHE WAS ENGAGED. I BET SHE DID...
NOW IT'S TIME TO ELECT COMMITTEE MEMBERS.
FIRST UP, FOR THE HEAD OF THE CLASS...
JUST LIKE IN THE GAME, RAID WAS CHOSEN TO BE THE CLASS HEAD.
THE OTHER MEMBERS WERE CHOSEN, AND WE WERE SENT HOME.
THE WORST OF THE STORM HAS PASSED... FOR NOW.
I'LL GO HOME AND TAKE A NAP.

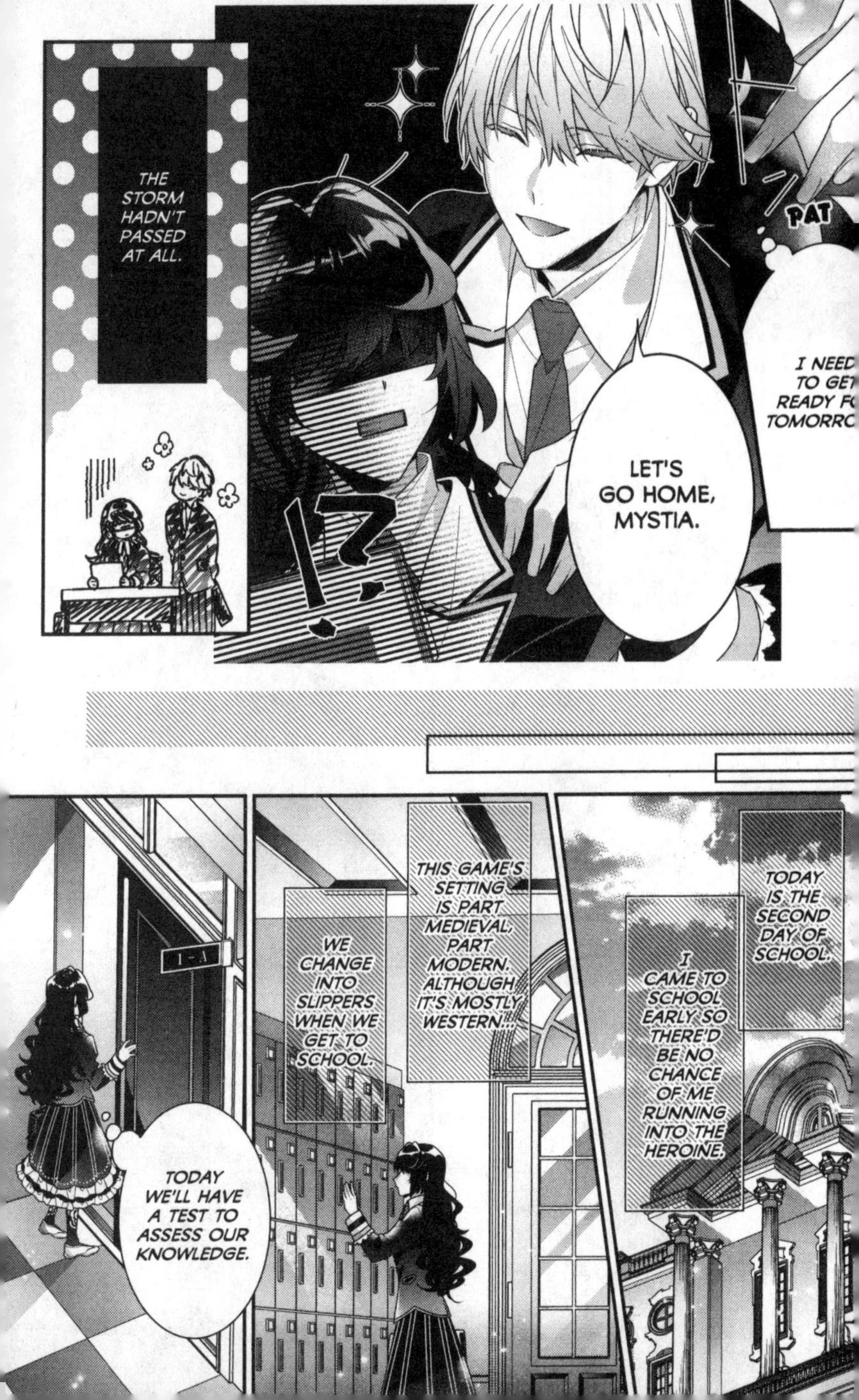
PAT
I NEED TO GET READY F TOMORRO
LET'S GO HOME, MYSTIA.
!?
THE STORM HADN'T PASSED AT ALL.
TODAY IS THE SECOND DAY OF SCHOOL.
I CAME TO SCHOOL EARLY SO THERE'D BE NO CHANCE OF ME RUNNING INTO THE HEROINE.
THIS GAME'S SETTING IS PART MEDIEVAL, PART MODERN. ALTHOUGH IT'S MOSTLY WESTERN...
WE CHANGE INTO SLIPPERS WHEN WE GET TO SCHOOL.
1-A
TODAY WE'LL HAVE A TEST TO ASSESS OUR KNOWLEDGE.

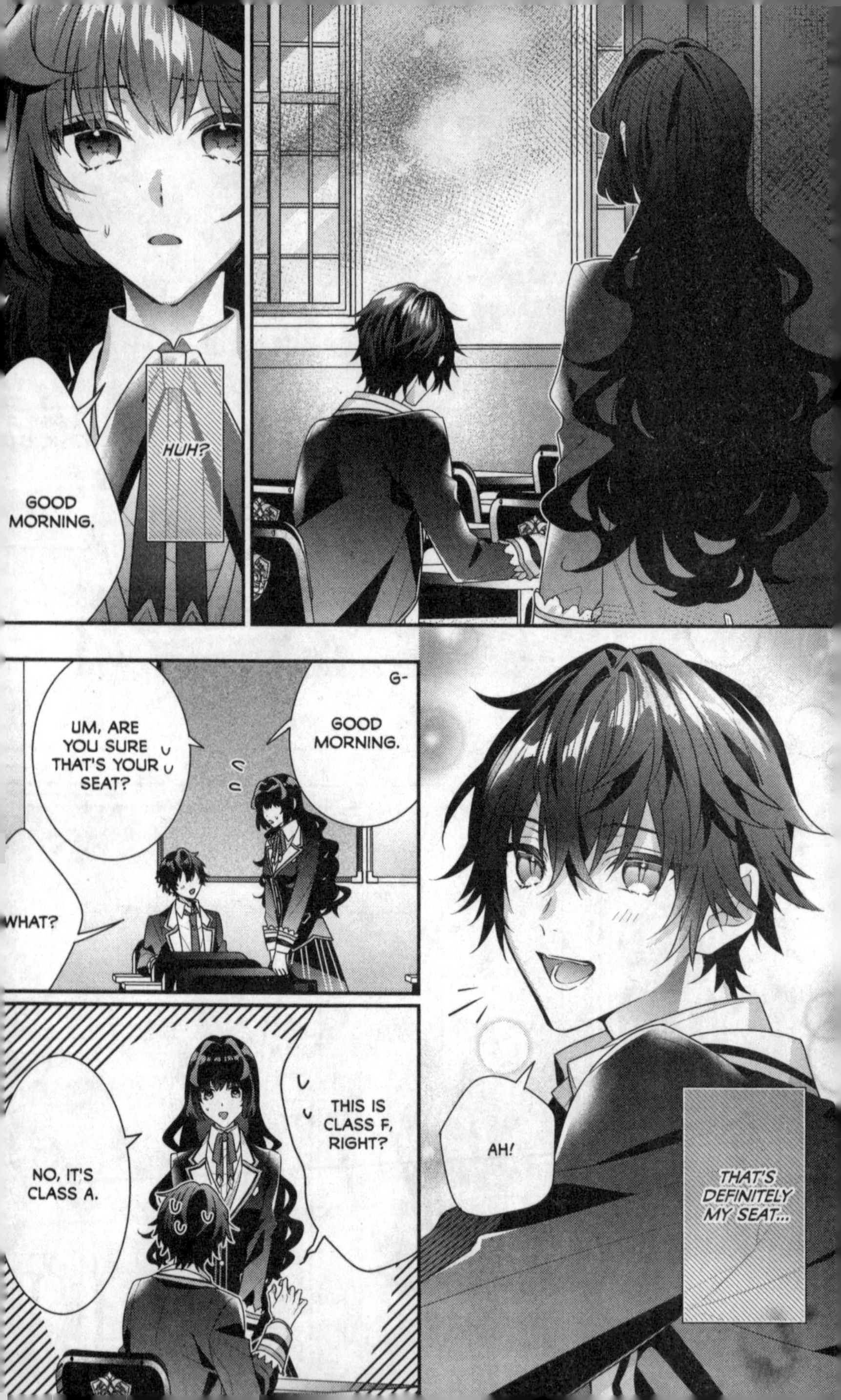
HUH?
GOOD MORNING.
AH!
THAT'S DEFINITELY MY SEAT...
G-
GOOD MORNING.
UM, ARE YOU SURE THAT'S YOUR SEAT?
WHAT?
THIS IS CLASS F, RIGHT?
NO, IT'S CLASS A.

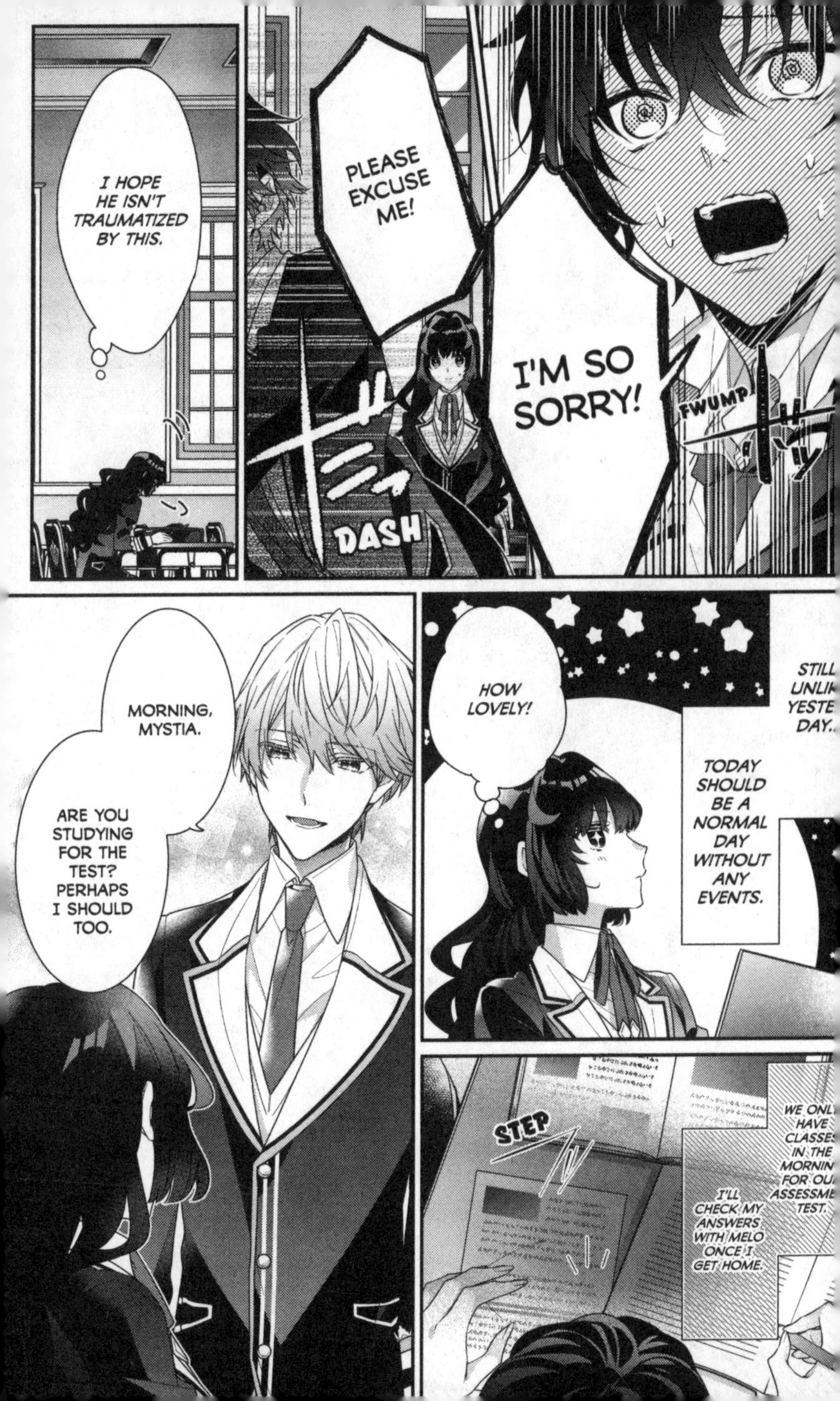
I'M SO SORRY!
FWUMP
PLEASE EXCUSE ME!
DASH
I HOPE HE ISN'T TRAUMATIZED BY THIS.
STILL UNLIK YESTE DAY..
TODAY SHOULD BE A NORMAL DAY WITHOUT ANY EVENTS.
HOW LOVELY!
WE ONL HAVE CLASSES IN THE MORNIN FOR OU ASSESSME TEST.
I'LL CHECK MY ANSWERS WITH MELO ONCE I GET HOME.
STEP
MORNING, MYSTIA.
ARE YOU STUDYING FOR THE TEST? PERHAPS I SHOULD TOO.

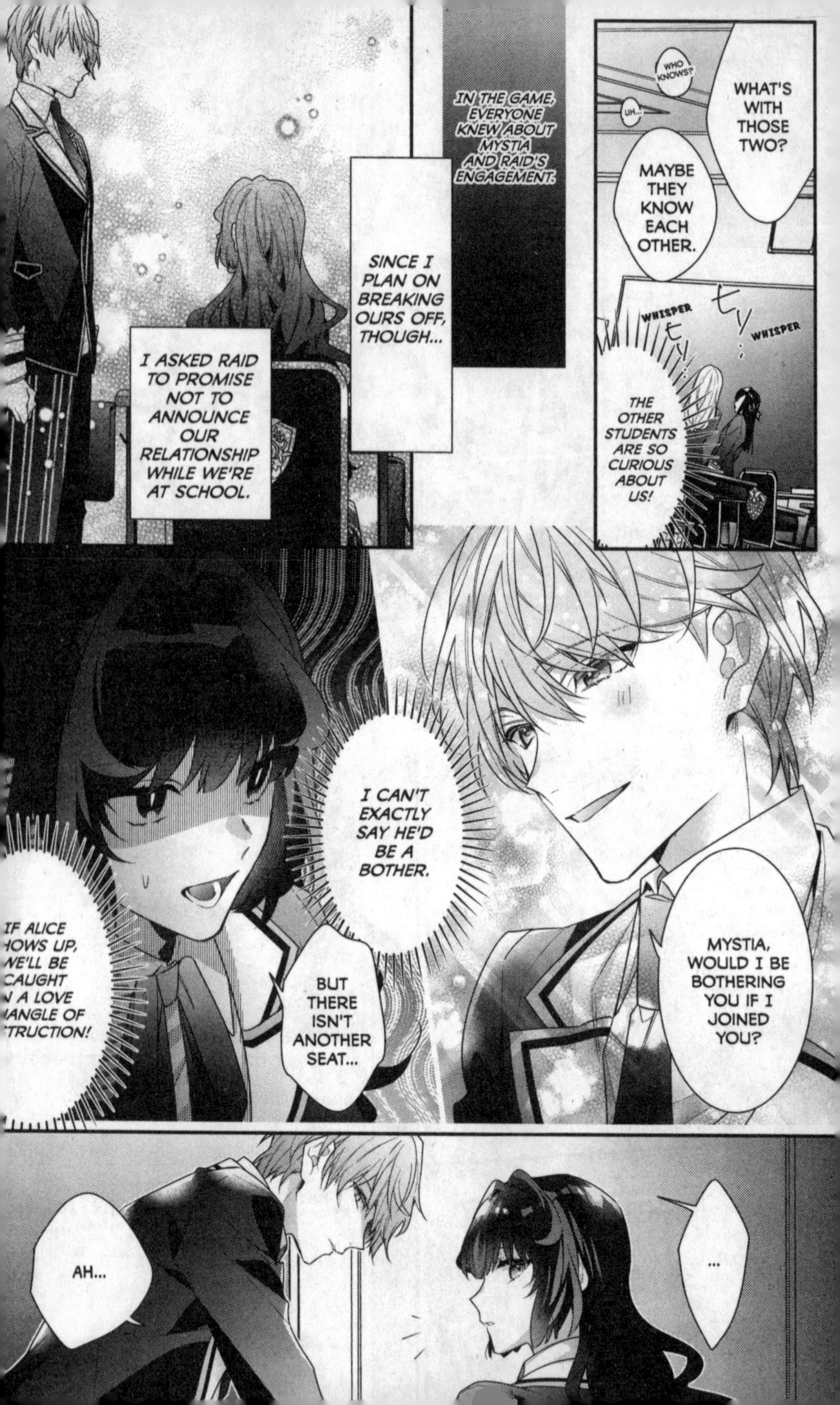
WHAT'S WITH THOSE TWO?
WHO KNOWS?
UH...
MAYBE THEY KNOW EACH OTHER.
WHISPER
WHISPER
THE OTHER STUDENTS ARE SO CURIOUS ABOUT US!
IN THE GAME, EVERYONE KNEW ABOUT MYSTIA AND RAID'S ENGAGEMENT.
SINCE I PLAN ON BREAKING OURS OFF, THOUGH...
I ASKED RAID TO PROMISE NOT TO ANNOUNCE OUR RELATIONSHIP WHILE WE'RE AT SCHOOL.
MYSTIA, WOULD I BE BOTHERING YOU IF I JOINED YOU?
I CAN'T EXACTLY SAY HE'D BE A BOTHER.
BUT THERE ISN'T ANOTHER SEAT...
IF ALICE HOWS UP, WE'LL BE CAUGHT N A LOVE ANGLE OF TRUCTION!
...
AH...

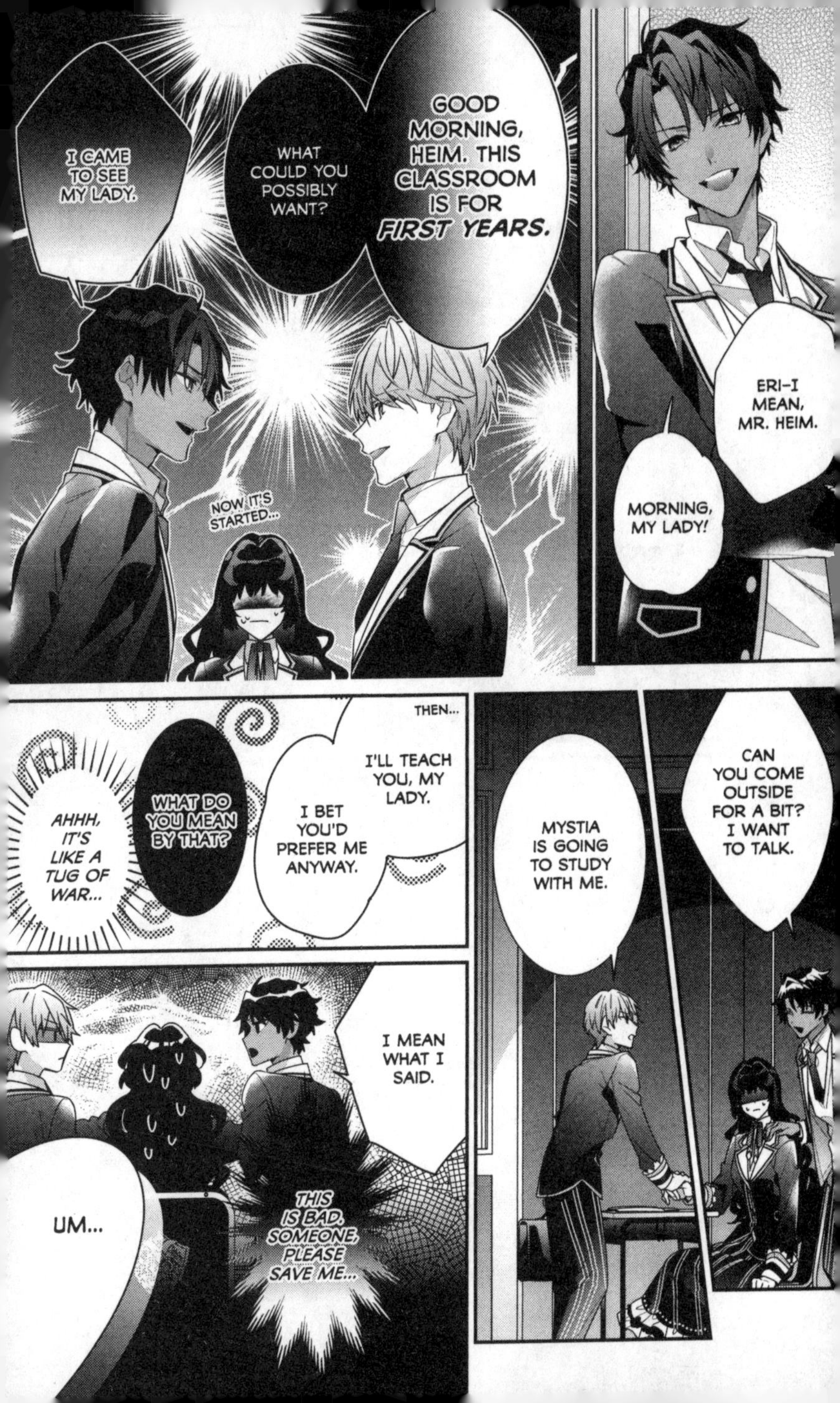
ERI–I MEAN, MR. HEIM.
MORNING, MY LADY!
GOOD MORNING, HEIM. THIS CLASSROOM IS FOR FIRST YEARS.
WHAT COULD YOU POSSIBLY WANT?
I CAME TO SEE MY LADY.
NOW IT'S STARTED...
CAN YOU COME OUTSIDE FOR A BIT? I WANT TO TALK.
MYSTIA IS GOING TO STUDY WITH ME.
THEN...
I'LL TEACH YOU, MY LADY.
I BET YOU'D PREFER ME ANYWAY.
WHAT DO YOU MEAN BY THAT?
AHHH, IT'S LIKE A TUG OF WAR...
I MEAN WHAT I SAID.
THIS IS BAD. SOMEONE, PLEASE SAVE ME...
UM...

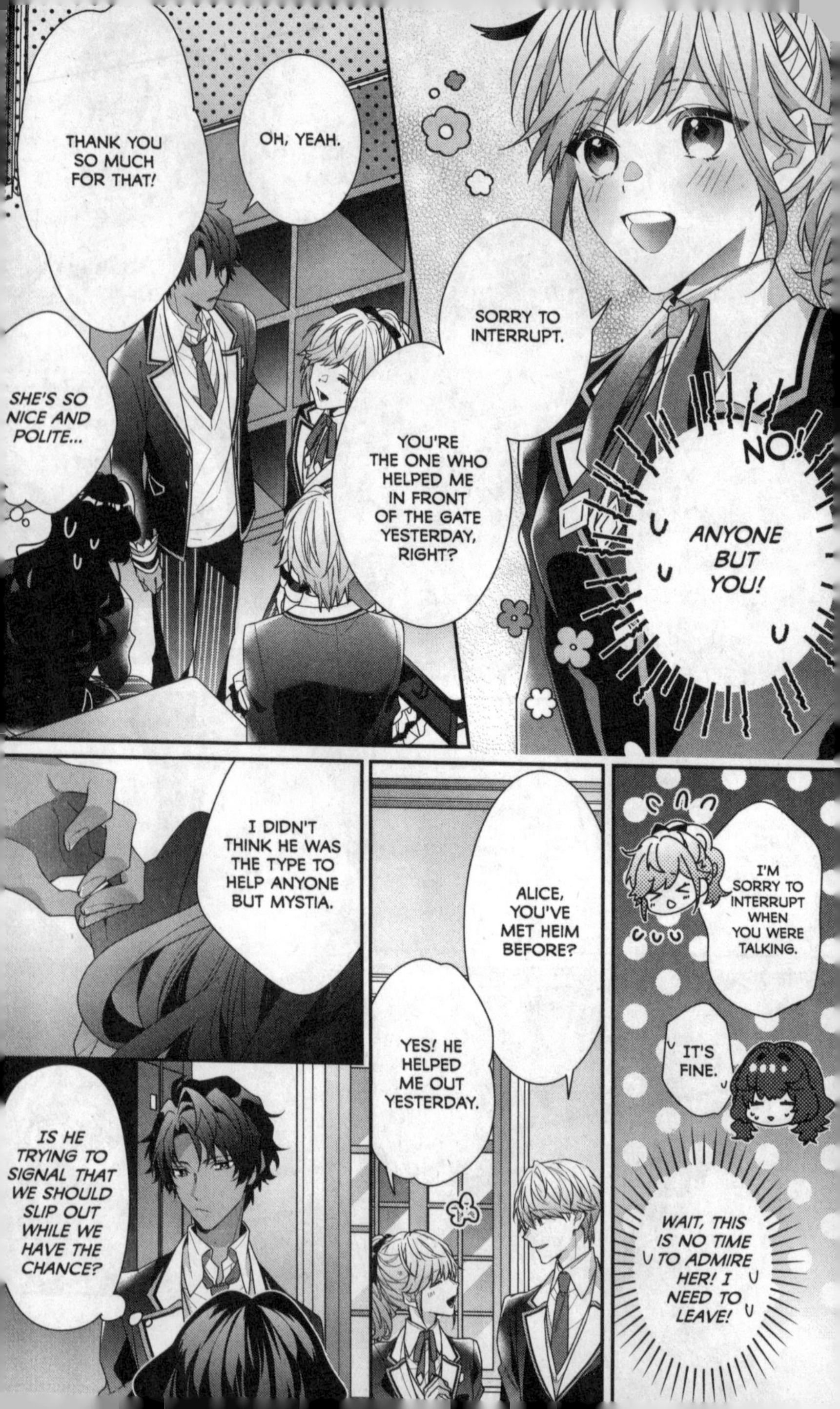
SORRY TO INTERRUPT.
YOU'RE THE ONE WHO HELPED ME IN FRONT OF THE GATE YESTERDAY, RIGHT?
NO! ANYONE BUT YOU!
OH, YEAH.
THANK YOU SO MUCH FOR THAT!
SHE'S SO NICE AND POLITE...
I'M SORRY TO INTERRUPT WHEN YOU WERE TALKING.
IT'S FINE.
WAIT, THIS IS NO TIME TO ADMIRE HER! I NEED TO LEAVE!
ALICE, YOU'VE MET HEIM BEFORE?
YES! HE HELPED ME OUT YESTERDAY.
I DIDN'T THINK HE WAS THE TYPE TO HELP ANYONE BUT MYSTIA.
IS HE TRYING TO SIGNAL THAT WE SHOULD SLIP OUT WHILE WE HAVE THE CHANCE?

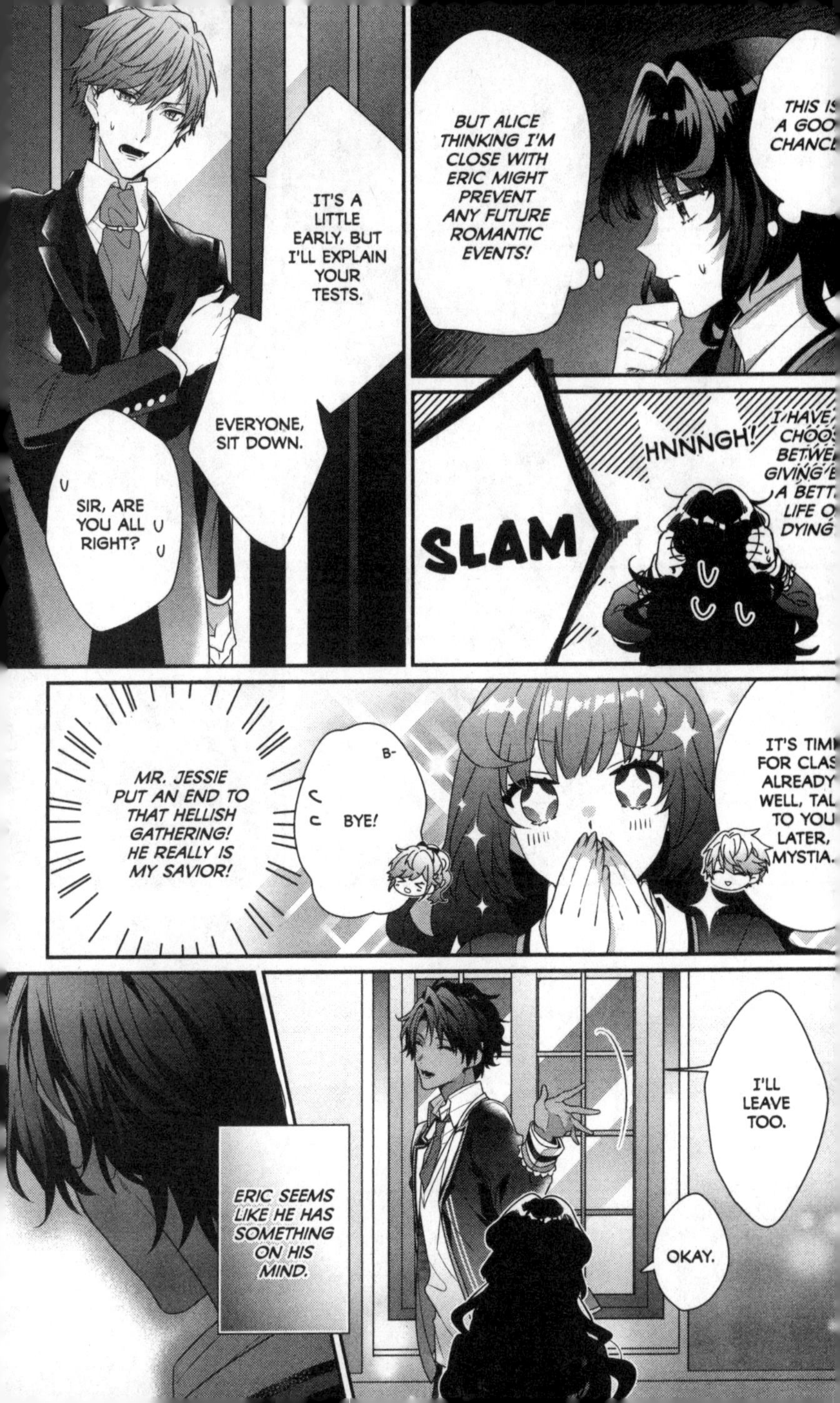
THIS IS A GOO CHANC
BUT ALICE THINKING I'M CLOSE WITH ERIC MIGHT PREVENT ANY FUTURE ROMANTIC EVENTS!
I HAVE CHOOS BETWE GIVING A BETT LIFE O DYING
HNNNGH!
SLAM
IT'S A LITTLE EARLY, BUT I'LL EXPLAIN YOUR TESTS.
EVERYONE, SIT DOWN.
SIR, ARE YOU ALL RIGHT?
IT'S TIM FOR CLAS ALREADY WELL, TAL TO YOU LATER, MYSTIA.
B- BYE!
MR. JESSIE PUT AN END TO THAT HELLISH GATHERING! HE REALLY IS MY SAVIOR!
I'LL LEAVE TOO.
OKAY.
ERIC SEEMS LIKE HE HAS SOMETHING ON HIS MIND.

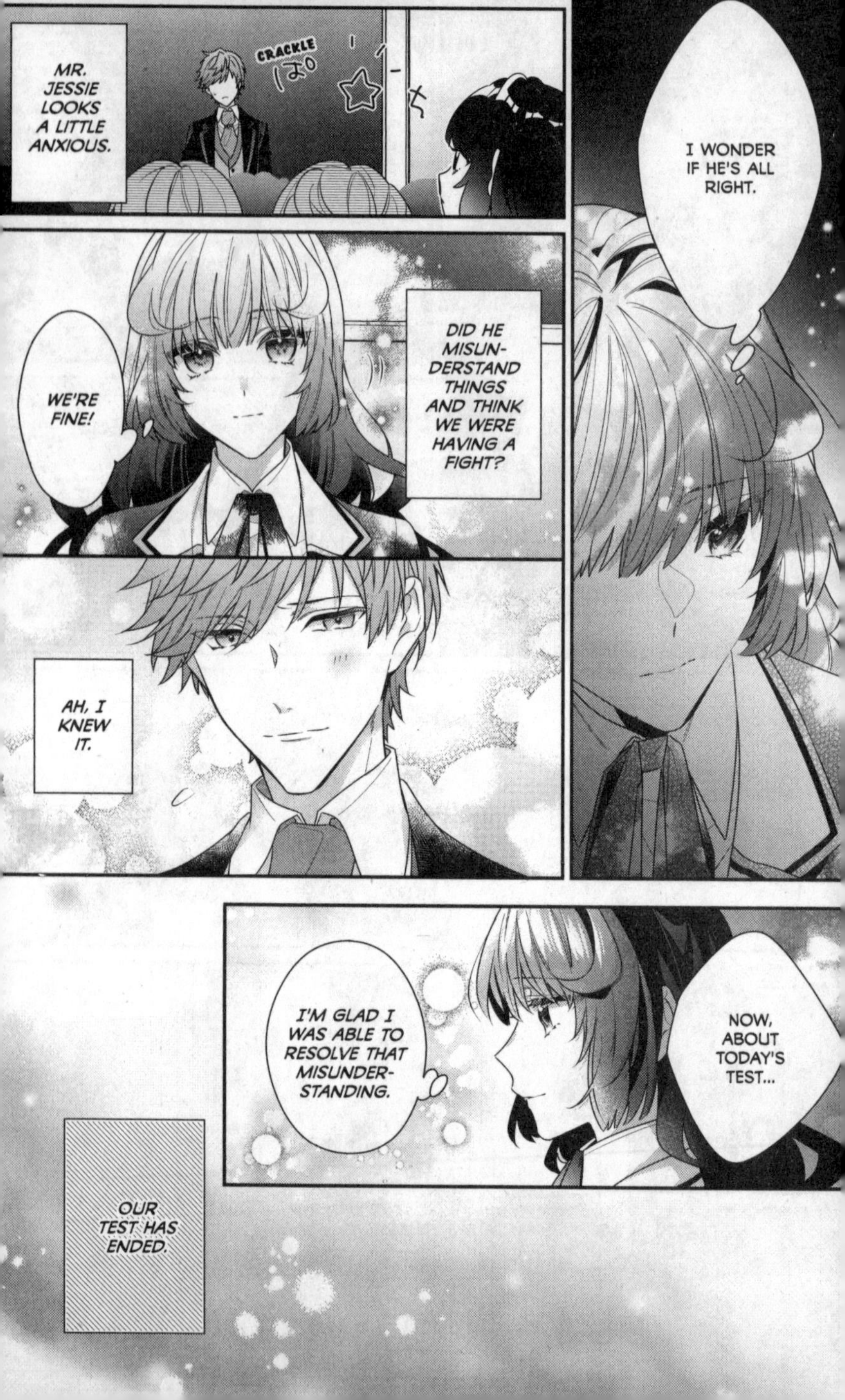
I WONDER IF HE'S ALL RIGHT.
MR. JESSIE LOOKS A LITTLE ANXIOUS.
CRACKLE
DID HE MISUNDERSTAND THINGS AND THINK WE WERE HAVING A FIGHT?
WE'RE FINE!
AH, I KNEW IT.
NOW, ABOUT TODAY'S TEST...
I'M GLAD I WAS ABLE TO RESOLVE THAT MISUNDERSTANDING.
OUR TEST HAS ENDED.

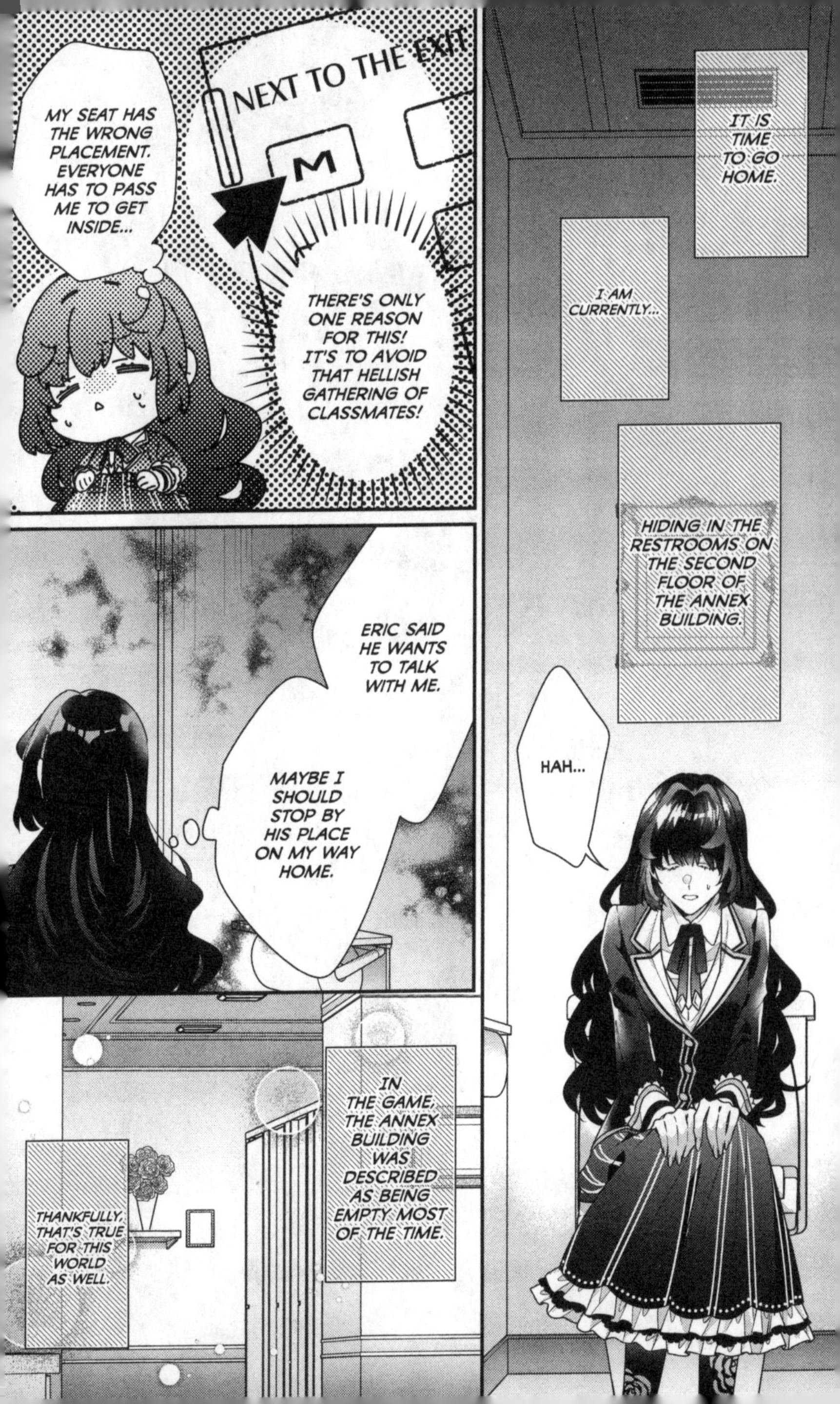
IT IS TIME TO GO HOME.
I AM CURRENTLY...
HIDING IN THE RESTROOMS ON THE SECOND FLOOR OF THE ANNEX BUILDING.
HAH...
NEXT TO THE EXIT
M
MY SEAT HAS THE WRONG PLACEMENT. EVERYONE HAS TO PASS ME TO GET INSIDE...
THERE'S ONLY ONE REASON FOR THIS! IT'S TO AVOID THAT HELLISH GATHERING OF CLASSMATES!
ERIC SAID HE WANTS TO TALK WITH ME.
MAYBE I SHOULD STOP BY HIS PLACE ON MY WAY HOME.
IN THE GAME, THE ANNEX BUILDING WAS DESCRIBED AS BEING EMPTY MOST OF THE TIME.
THANKFULLY, THAT'S TRUE FOR THIS WORLD AS WELL.

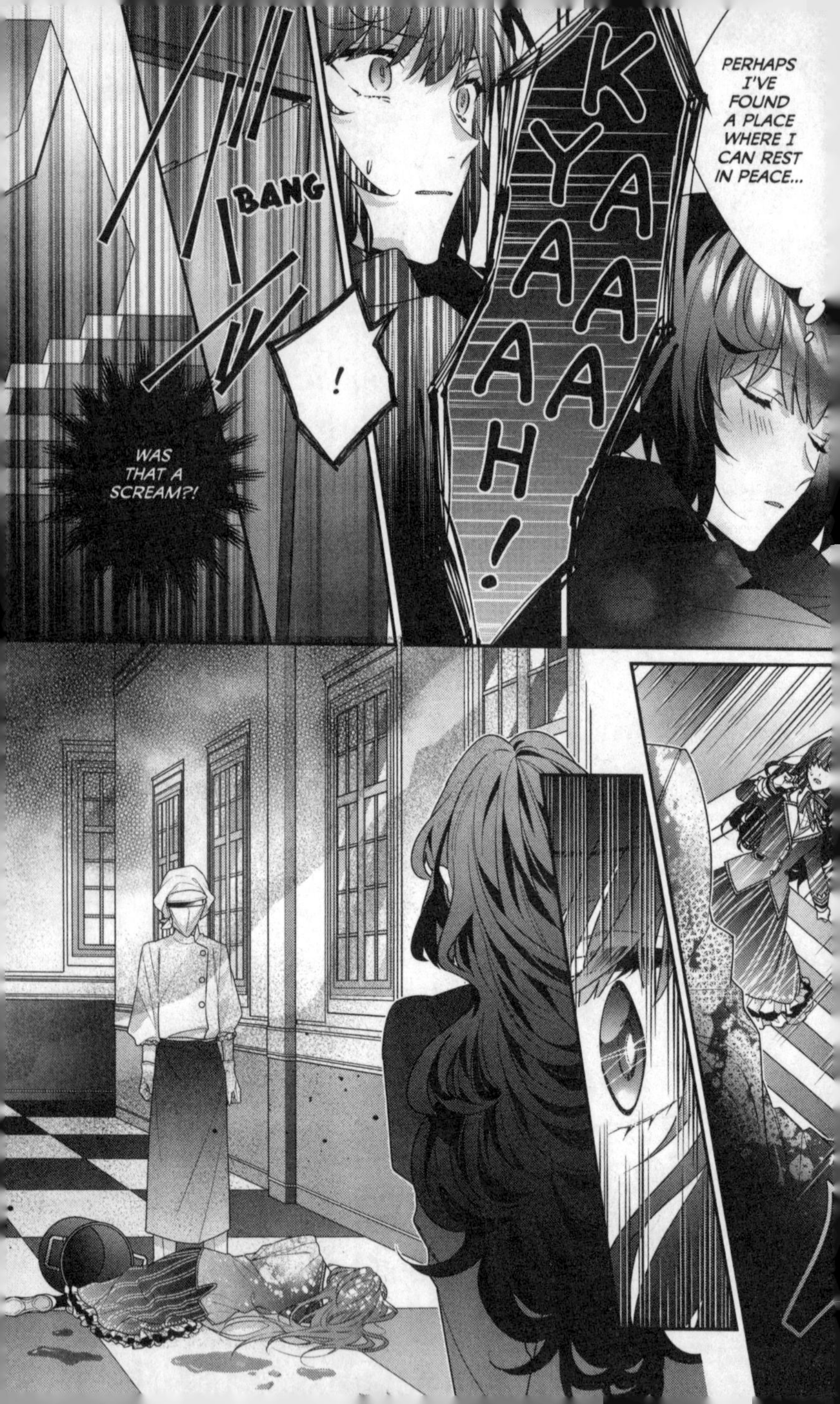
PERHAPS I'VE FOUND A PLACE WHERE I CAN REST IN PEACE...
KYAAAAAH!
!
BANG
WAS THAT A SCREAM?!

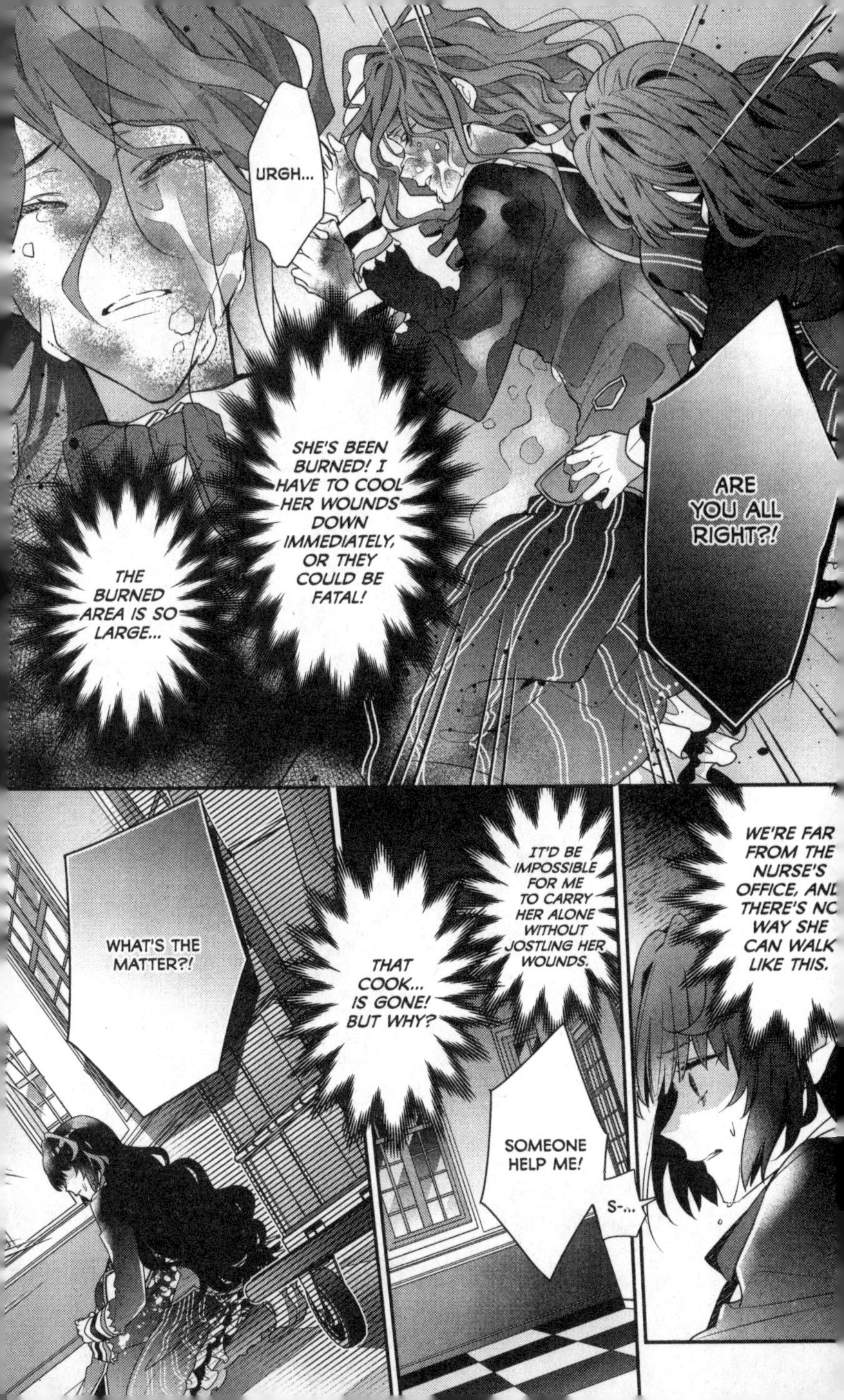
ARE YOU ALL RIGHT?!
URGH...
SHE'S BEEN BURNED! I HAVE TO COOL HER WOUNDS DOWN IMMEDIATELY, OR THEY COULD BE FATAL!
THE BURNED AREA IS SO LARGE...
WE'RE FAR FROM THE NURSE'S OFFICE, AND THERE'S NO WAY SHE CAN WALK LIKE THIS.
IT'D BE IMPOSSIBLE FOR ME TO CARRY HER ALONE WITHOUT JOSTLING HER WOUNDS.
S-...
SOMEONE HELP ME!
THAT COOK... IS GONE! BUT WHY?
WHAT'S THE MATTER?!

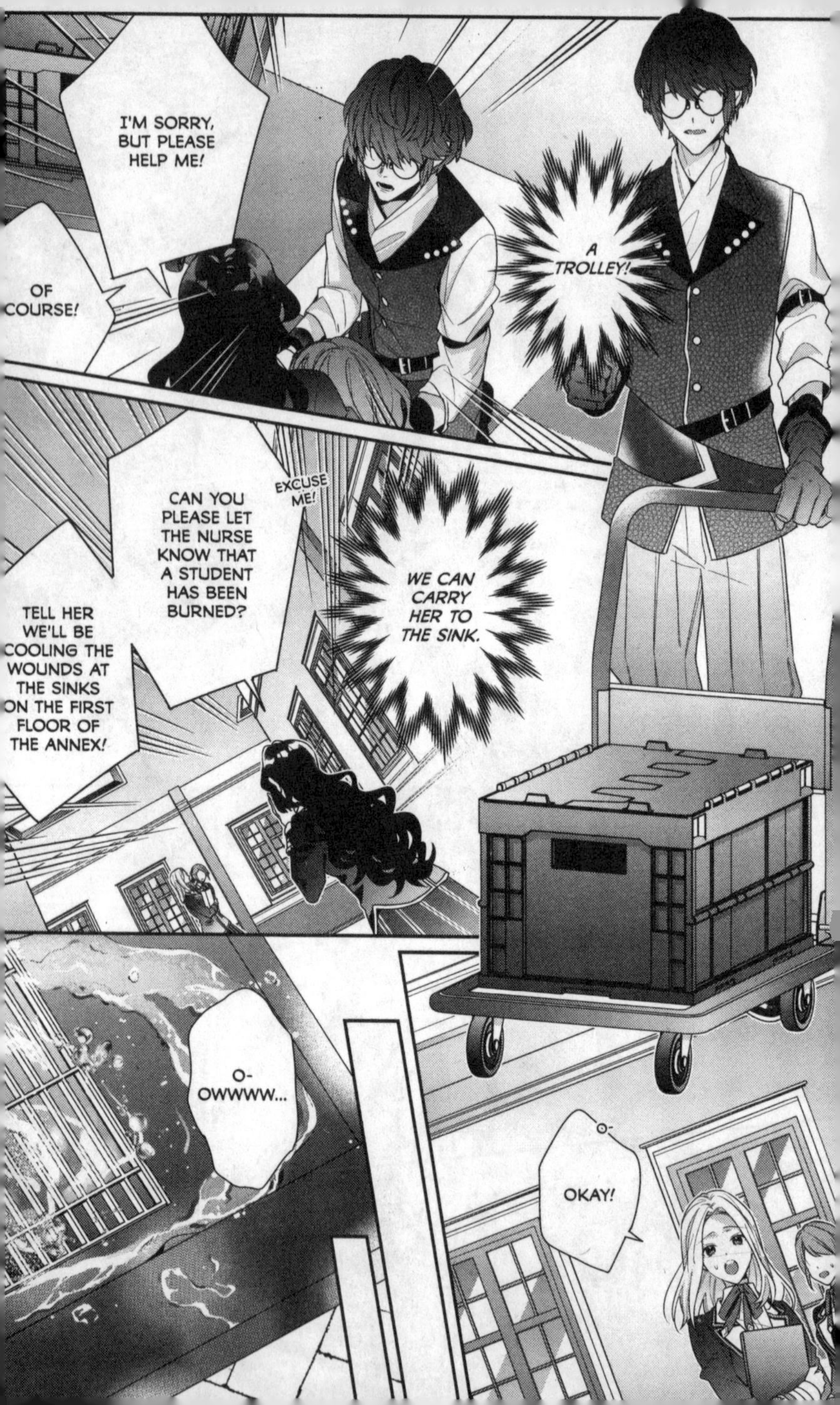

I'M SORRY, BUT PLEASE HELP ME!
OF COURSE!
A TROLLEY!
WE CAN CARRY HER TO THE SINK.
EXCUSE ME!
CAN YOU PLEASE LET THE NURSE KNOW THAT A STUDENT HAS BEEN BURNED?
TELL HER WE'LL BE COOLING THE WOUNDS AT THE SINKS ON THE FIRST FLOOR OF THE ANNEX!
O- OKAY!
O- OWWWW...

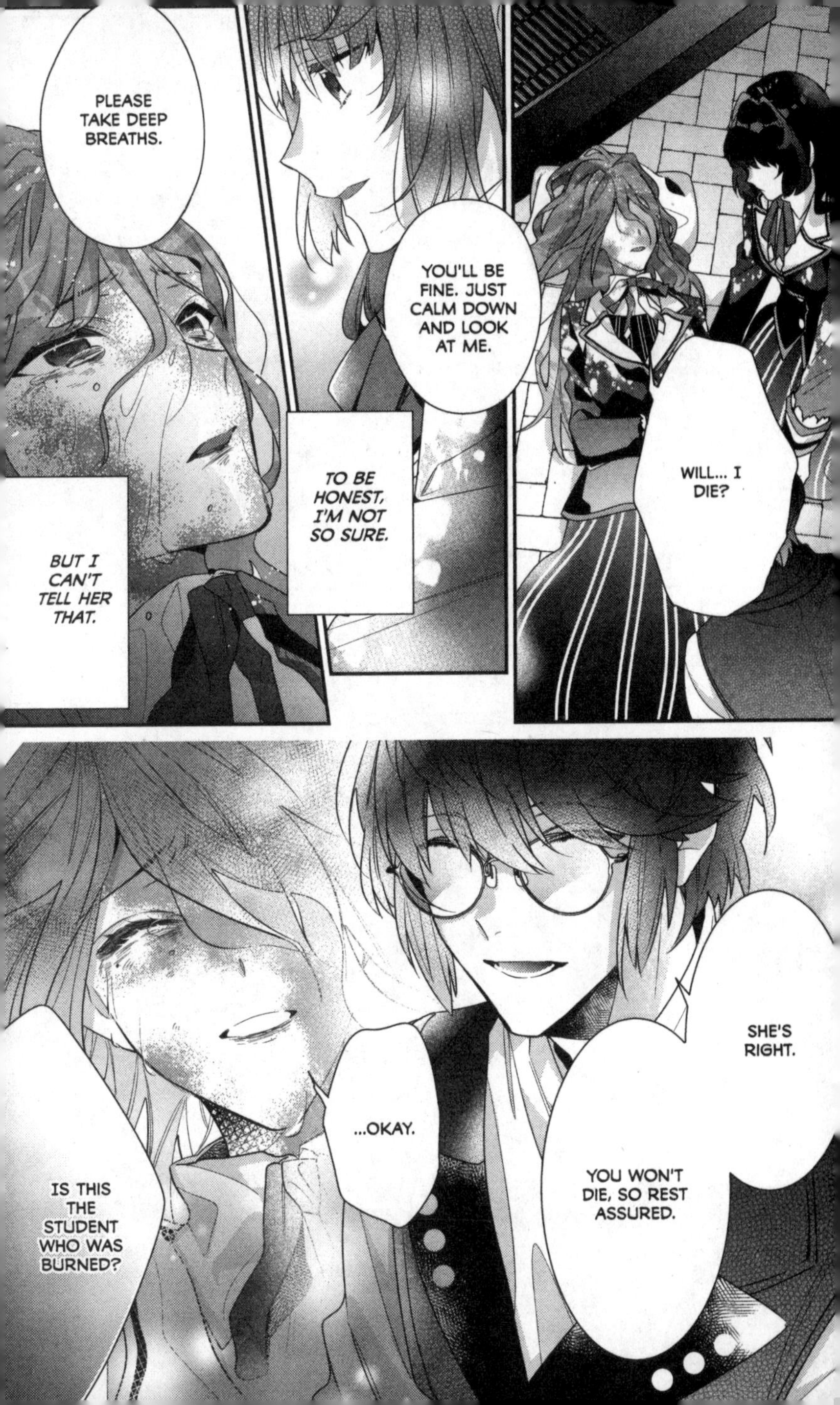
WILL... I DIE?
YOU'LL BE FINE. JUST CALM DOWN AND LOOK AT ME.
TO BE HONEST, I'M NOT SO SURE.
PLEASE TAKE DEEP BREATHS.
BUT I CAN'T TELL HER THAT.
SHE'S RIGHT.
YOU WON'T DIE, SO REST ASSURED.
...OKAY.
IS THIS THE STUDENT WHO WAS BURNED?

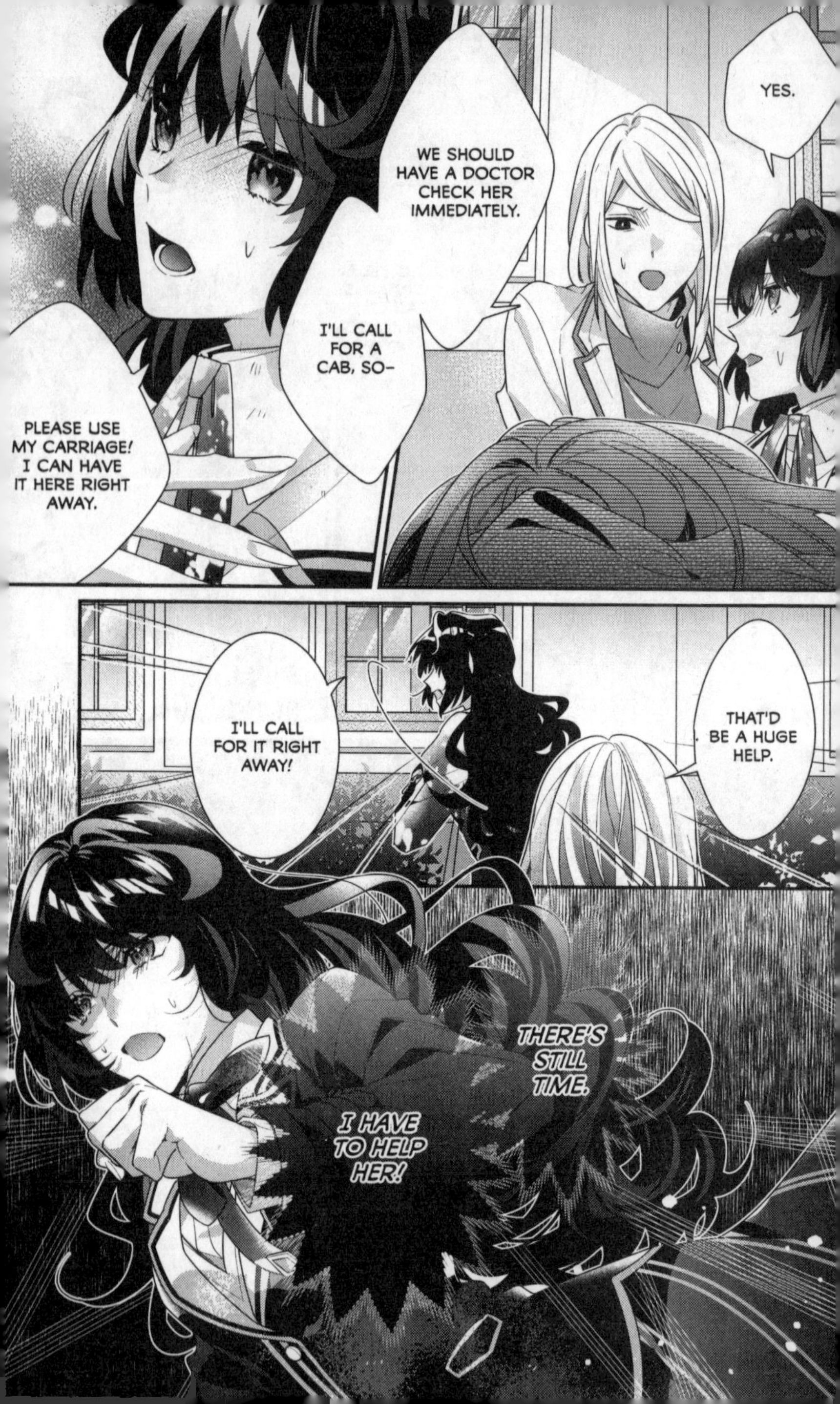
WE SHOULD HAVE A DOCTOR CHECK HER IMMEDIATELY.
YES.
I'LL CALL FOR A CAB, SO-
PLEASE USE MY CARRIAGE! I CAN HAVE IT HERE RIGHT AWAY.
THAT'D BE A HUGE HELP.
I'LL CALL FOR IT RIGHT AWAY!
THERE'S STILL TIME.
I HAVE TO HELP HER!

I was REINCARNATED as the *Villainess* in an **OTOME GAME** *but the boys love me anyway!*

I was REINCARNATED as the
Villainess
in an OTOME GAME but the boys love me anyway!

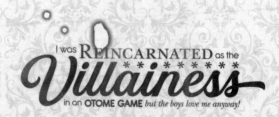

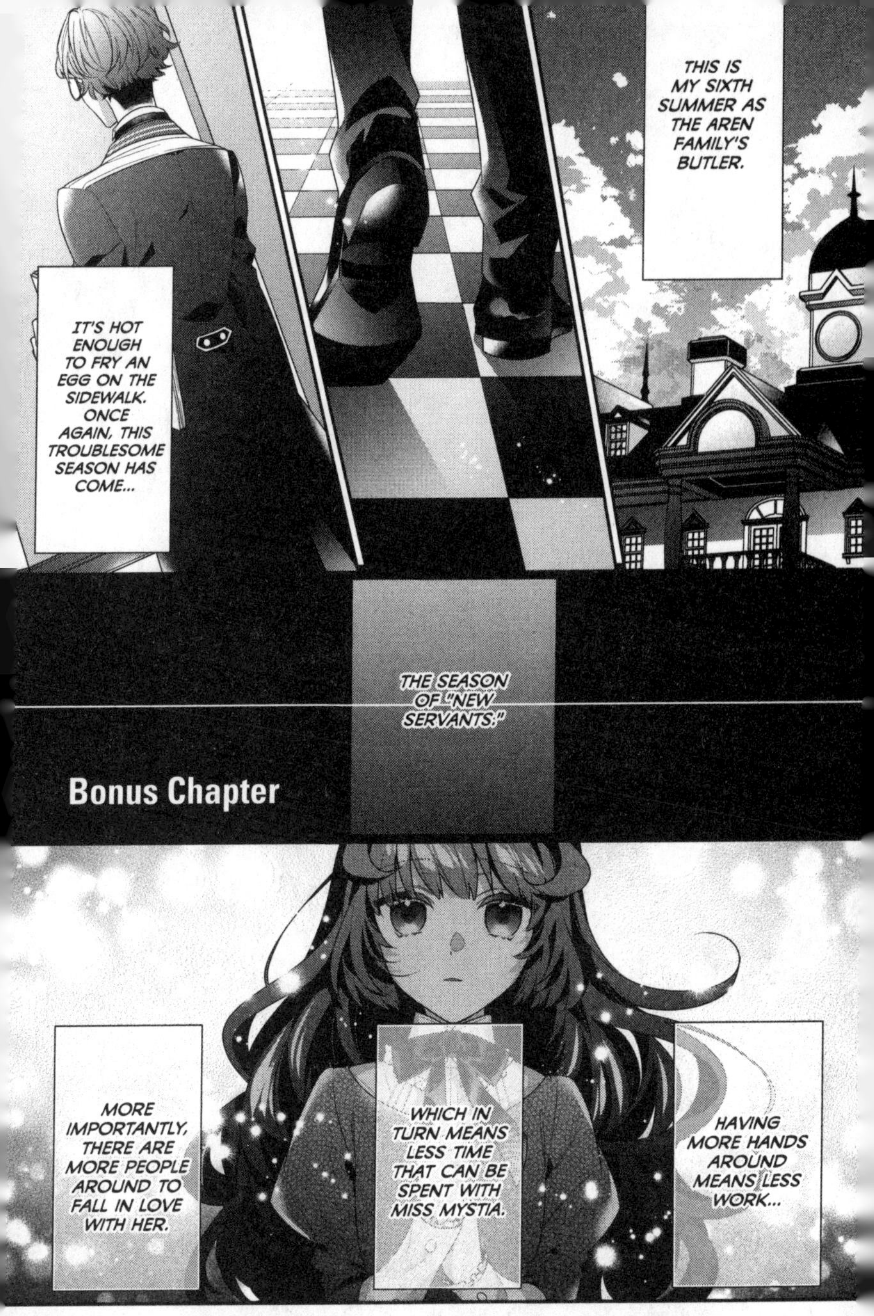
THIS IS MY SIXTH SUMMER AS THE AREN FAMILY'S BUTLER.
IT'S HOT ENOUGH TO FRY AN EGG ON THE SIDEWALK. ONCE AGAIN, THIS TROUBLESOME SEASON HAS COME...
THE SEASON OF "NEW SERVANTS."
Bonus Chapter
HAVING MORE HANDS AROUND MEANS LESS WORK...
WHICH IN TURN MEANS LESS TIME THAT CAN BE SPENT WITH MISS MYSTIA.
MORE IMPORTANTLY, THERE ARE MORE PEOPLE AROUND TO FALL IN LOVE WITH HER.

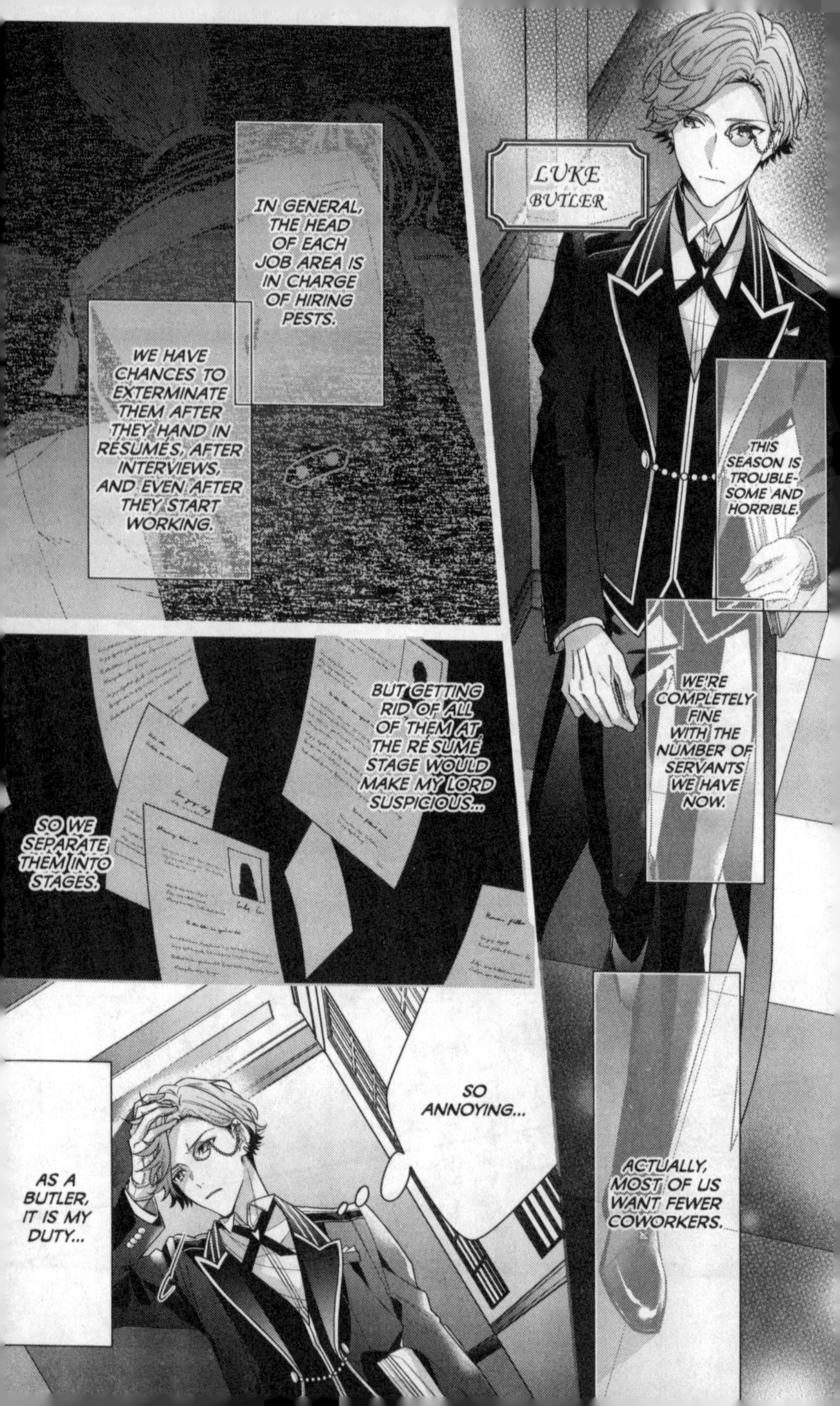
LUKE
BUTLER
THIS SEASON IS TROUBLE-SOME AND HORRIBLE.
WE'RE COMPLETELY FINE WITH THE NUMBER OF SERVANTS WE HAVE NOW.
ACTUALLY, MOST OF US WANT FEWER COWORKERS.
IN GENERAL, THE HEAD OF EACH JOB AREA IS IN CHARGE OF HIRING PESTS.
WE HAVE CHANCES TO EXTERMINATE THEM AFTER THEY HAND IN RESUMES, AFTER INTERVIEWS, AND EVEN AFTER THEY START WORKING.
BUT GETTING RID OF ALL OF THEM AT THE RÉSUMÉ STAGE WOULD MAKE MY LORD SUSPICIOUS...
SO WE SEPARATE THEM INTO STAGES.
SO ANNOYING...
AS A BUTLER, IT IS MY DUTY...

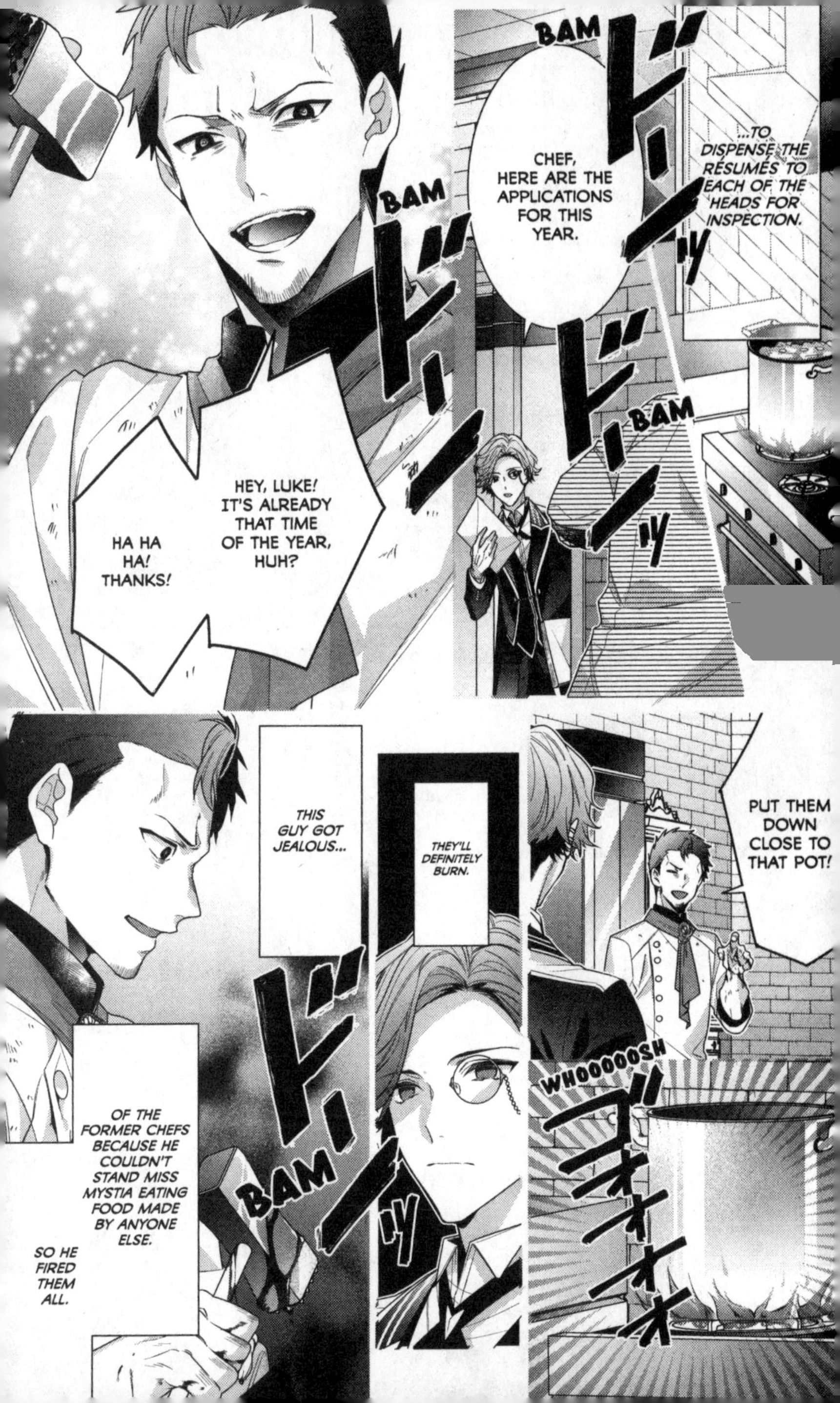
...TO DISPENSE THE RÉSUMÉS TO EACH OF THE HEADS FOR INSPECTION.
BAM
CHEF, HERE ARE THE APPLICATIONS FOR THIS YEAR.
BAM
BAM
HEY, LUKE! IT'S ALREADY THAT TIME OF THE YEAR, HUH?
HA HA HA! THANKS!
PUT THEM DOWN CLOSE TO THAT POT!
WHOOOOOSH
THEY'LL DEFINITELY BURN.
BAM
THIS GUY GOT JEALOUS...
OF THE FORMER CHEFS BECAUSE HE COULDN'T STAND MISS MYSTIA EATING FOOD MADE BY ANYONE ELSE.
SO HE FIRED THEM ALL.

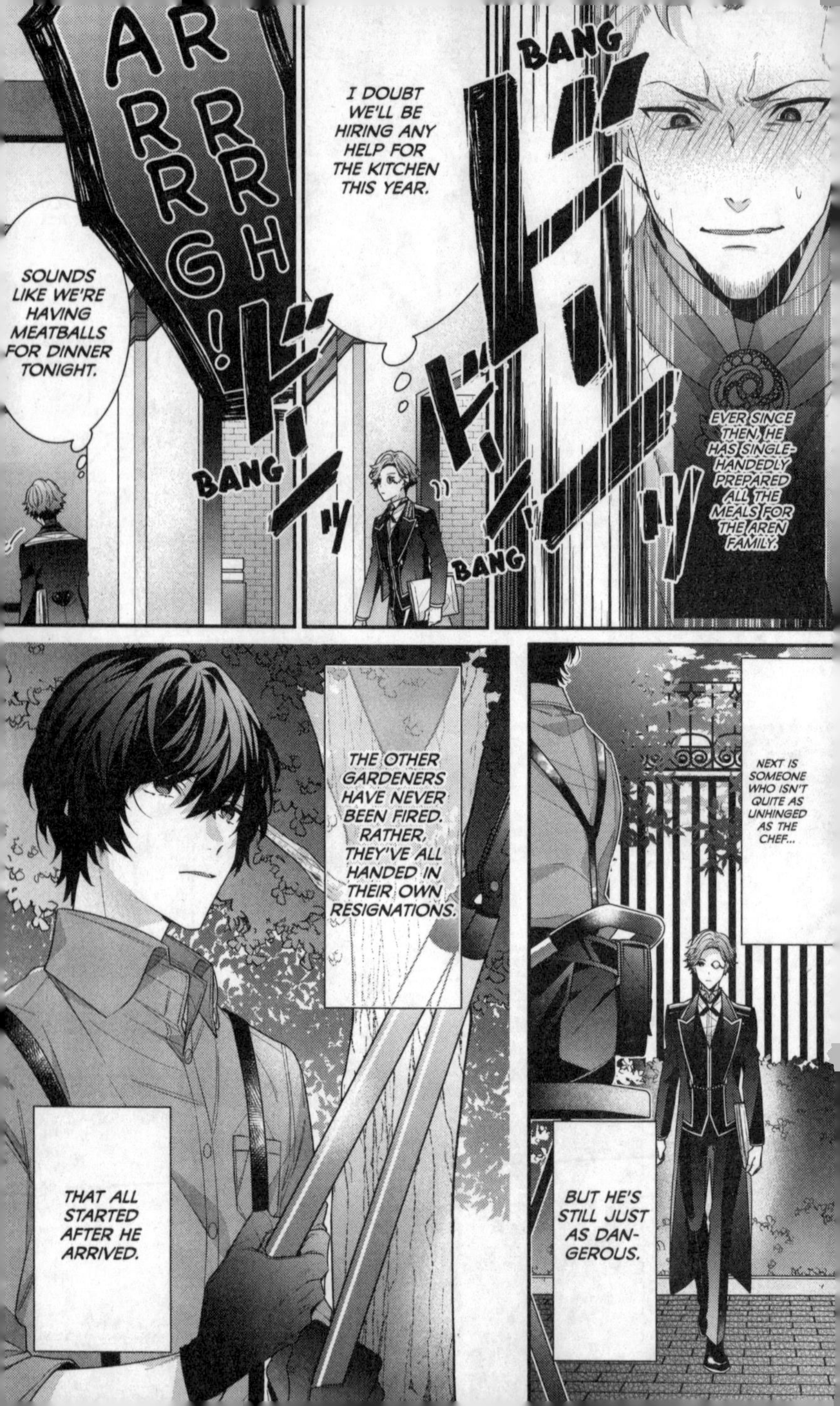
BANG
EVER SINCE THEN, HE HAS SINGLE-HANDEDLY PREPARED ALL THE MEALS FOR THE AREN FAMILY.
BANG
I DOUBT WE'LL BE HIRING ANY HELP FOR THE KITCHEN THIS YEAR.
BANG
ARRRRGH!
SOUNDS LIKE WE'RE HAVING MEATBALLS FOR DINNER TONIGHT.
NEXT IS SOMEONE WHO ISN'T QUITE AS UNHINGED AS THE CHEF...
BUT HE'S STILL JUST AS DAN-GEROUS.
THE OTHER GARDENERS HAVE NEVER BEEN FIRED. RATHER, THEY'VE ALL HANDED IN THEIR OWN RESIGNATIONS.
THAT ALL STARTED AFTER HE ARRIVED.

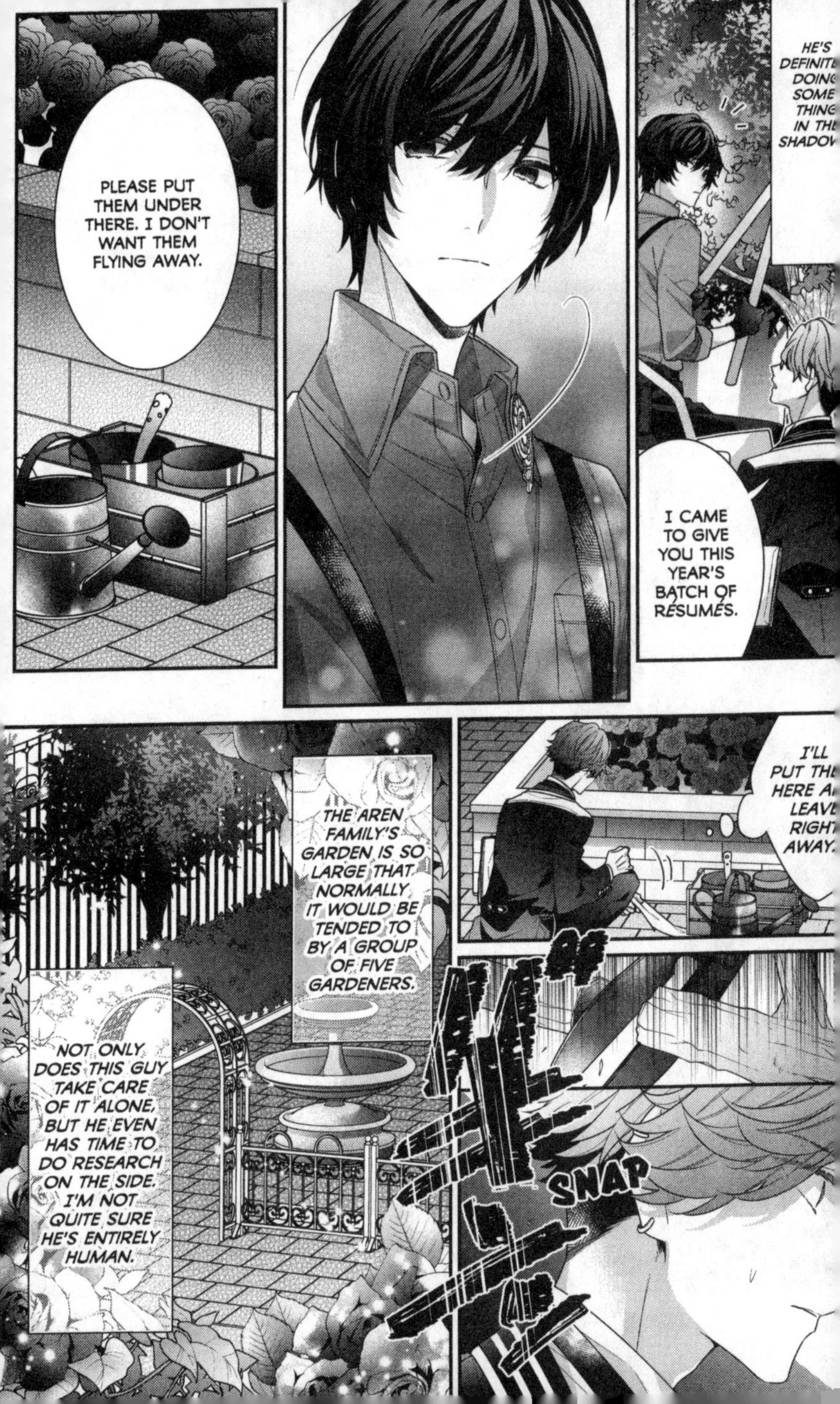
HE'S DEFINIT DOING SOME THING IN THE SHADOW
I CAME TO GIVE YOU THIS YEAR'S BATCH OF RÉSUMÉS.
PLEASE PUT THEM UNDER THERE. I DON'T WANT THEM FLYING AWAY.
I'LL PUT THE HERE A LEAVE RIGHT AWAY.
SNAP
THE AREN FAMILY'S GARDEN IS SO LARGE THAT NORMALLY IT WOULD BE TENDED TO BY A GROUP OF FIVE GARDENERS.
NOT ONLY DOES THIS GUY TAKE CARE OF IT ALONE, BUT HE EVEN HAS TIME TO DO RESEARCH ON THE SIDE. I'M NOT QUITE SURE HE'S ENTIRELY HUMAN.

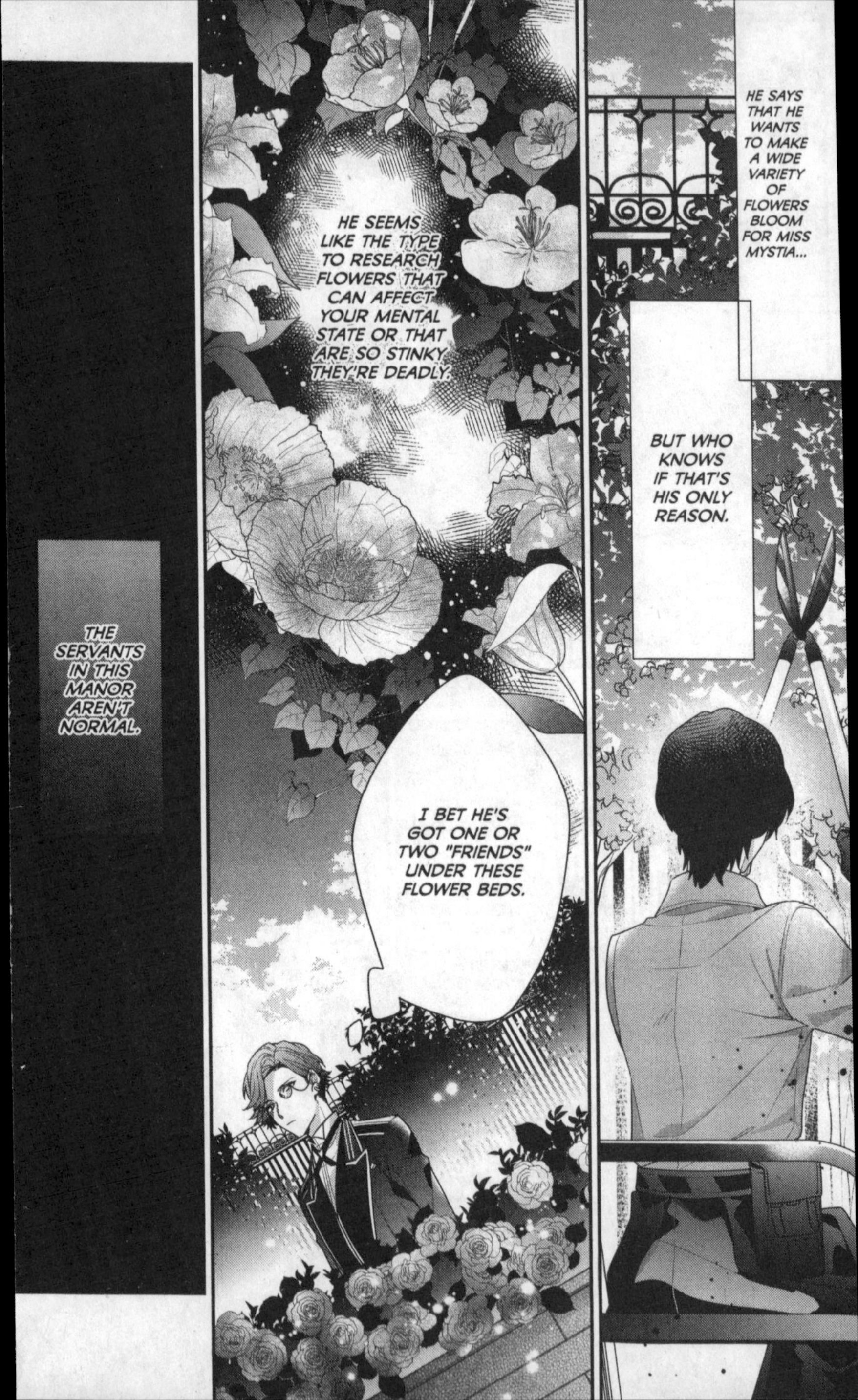
HE SAYS THAT HE WANTS TO MAKE A WIDE VARIETY OF FLOWERS BLOOM FOR MISS MYSTIA...
BUT WHO KNOWS IF THAT'S HIS ONLY REASON.
HE SEEMS LIKE THE TYPE TO RESEARCH FLOWERS THAT CAN AFFECT YOUR MENTAL STATE OR THAT ARE SO STINKY THEY'RE DEADLY.
I BET HE'S GOT ONE OR TWO "FRIENDS" UNDER THESE FLOWER BEDS.
THE SERVANTS IN THIS MANOR AREN'T NORMAL.

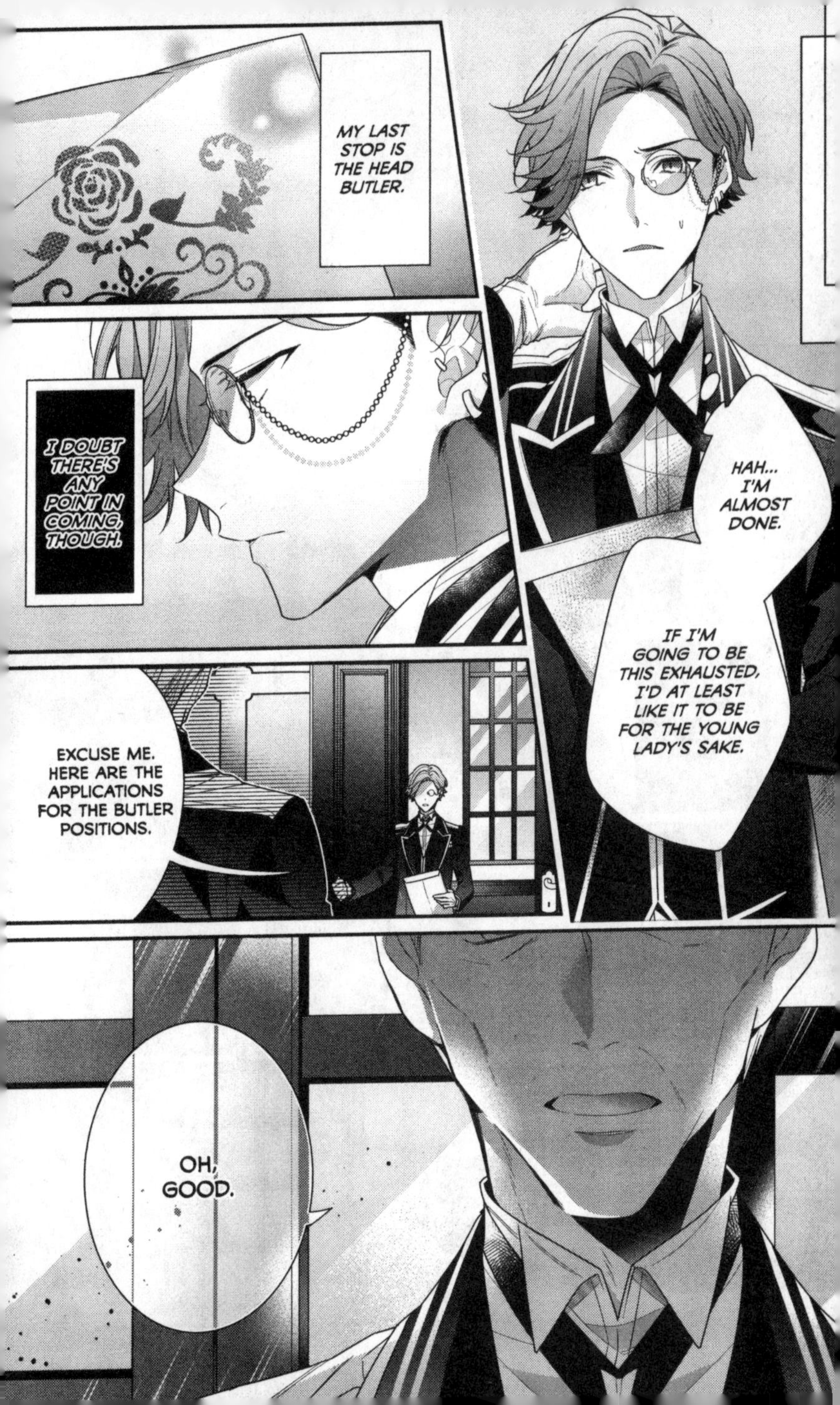
HAH... I'M ALMOST DONE.
IF I'M GOING TO BE THIS EXHAUSTED, I'D AT LEAST LIKE IT TO BE FOR THE YOUNG LADY'S SAKE.
MY LAST STOP IS THE HEAD BUTLER.
I DOUBT THERE'S ANY POINT IN COMING, THOUGH.
EXCUSE ME. HERE ARE THE APPLICATIONS FOR THE BUTLER POSITIONS.
OH, GOOD.

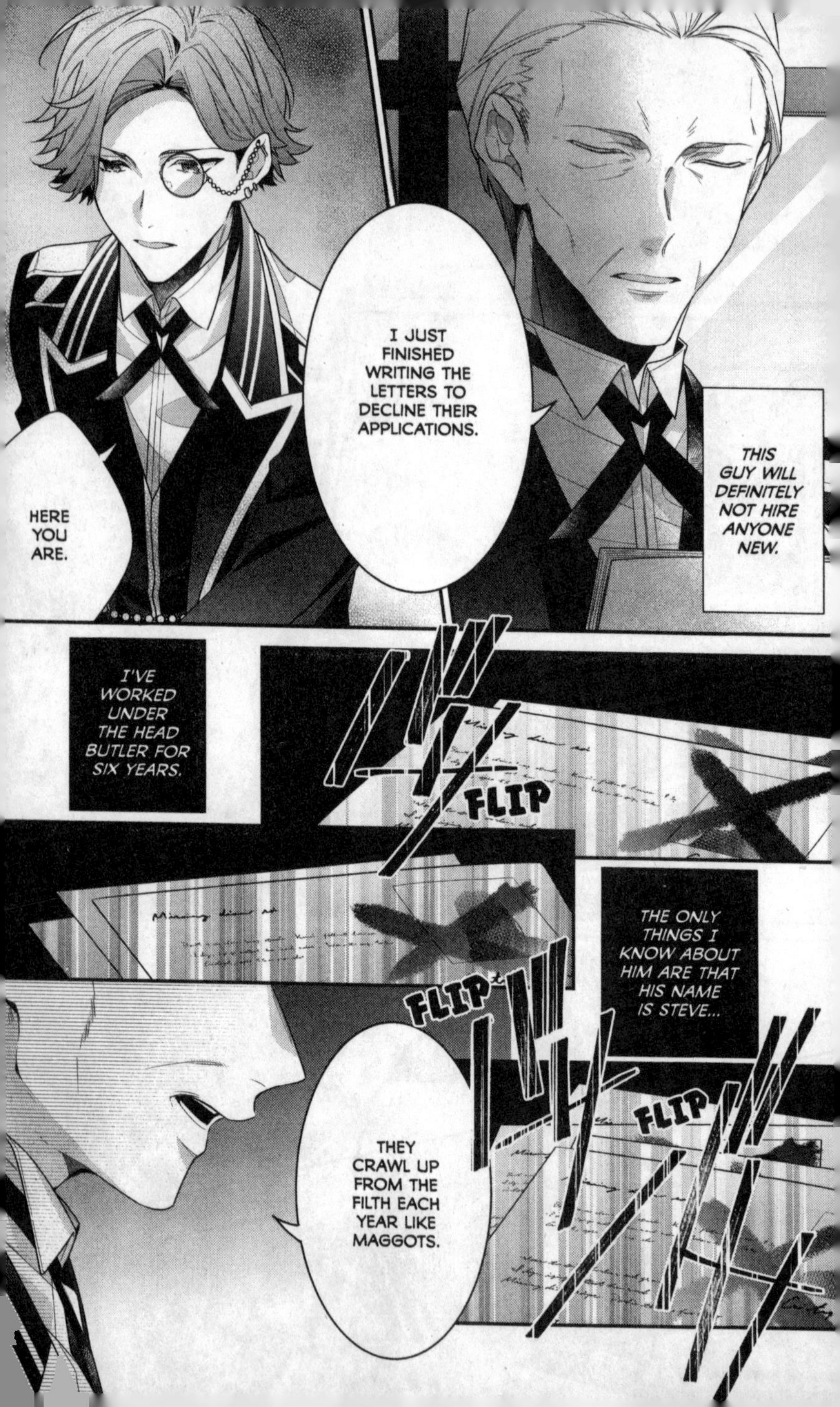

I JUST FINISHED WRITING THE LETTERS TO DECLINE THEIR APPLICATIONS.
THIS GUY WILL DEFINITELY NOT HIRE ANYONE NEW.
HERE YOU ARE.
FLIP
I'VE WORKED UNDER THE HEAD BUTLER FOR SIX YEARS.
THE ONLY THINGS I KNOW ABOUT HIM ARE THAT HIS NAME IS STEVE...
FLIP
FLIP
THEY CRAWL UP FROM THE FILTH EACH YEAR LIKE MAGGOTS.

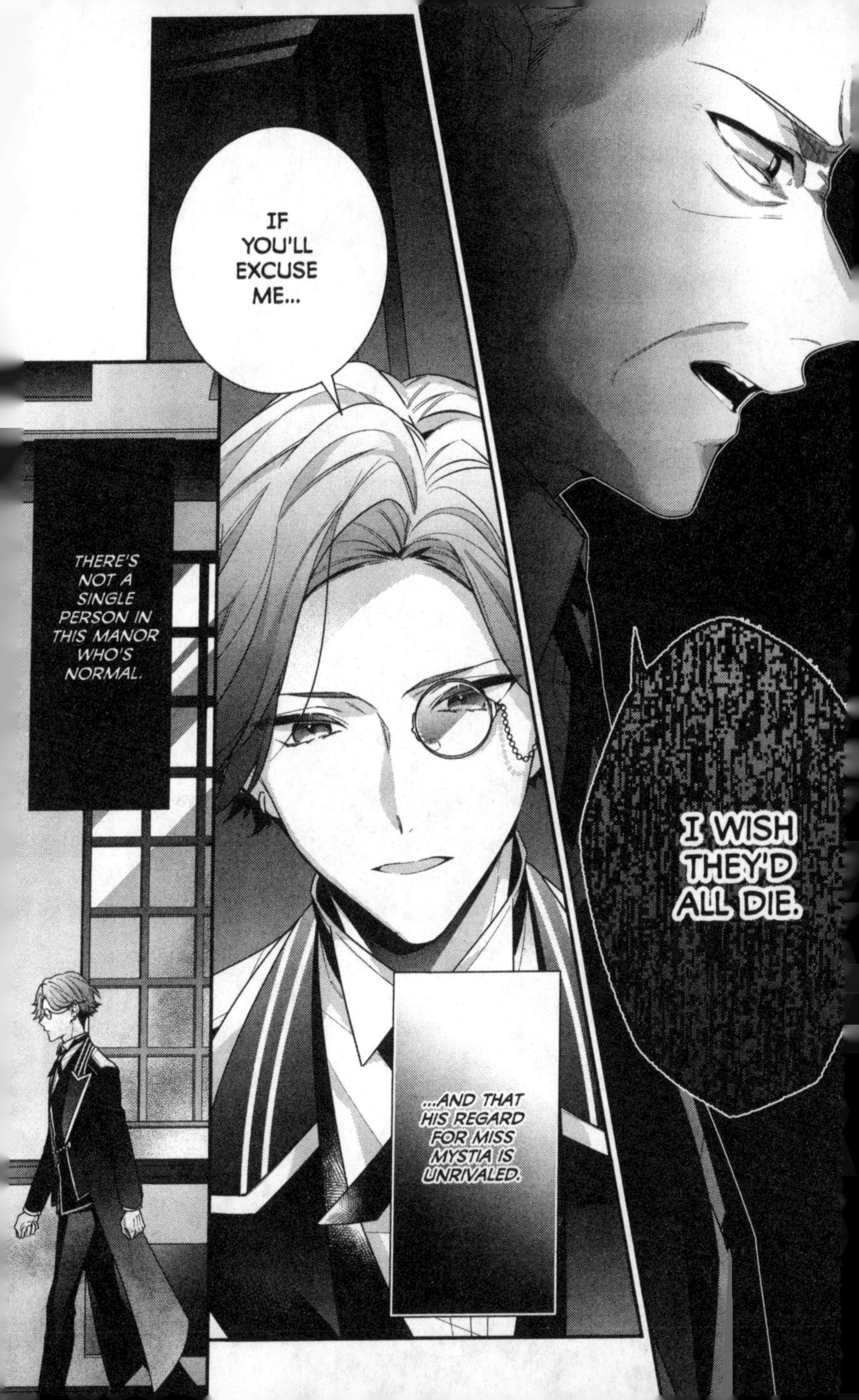
I WISH THEY'D ALL DIE.
IF YOU'LL EXCUSE ME...
...AND THAT HIS REGARD FOR MISS MYSTIA IS UNRIVALED.
THERE'S NOT A SINGLE PERSON IN THIS MANOR WHO'S NORMAL.

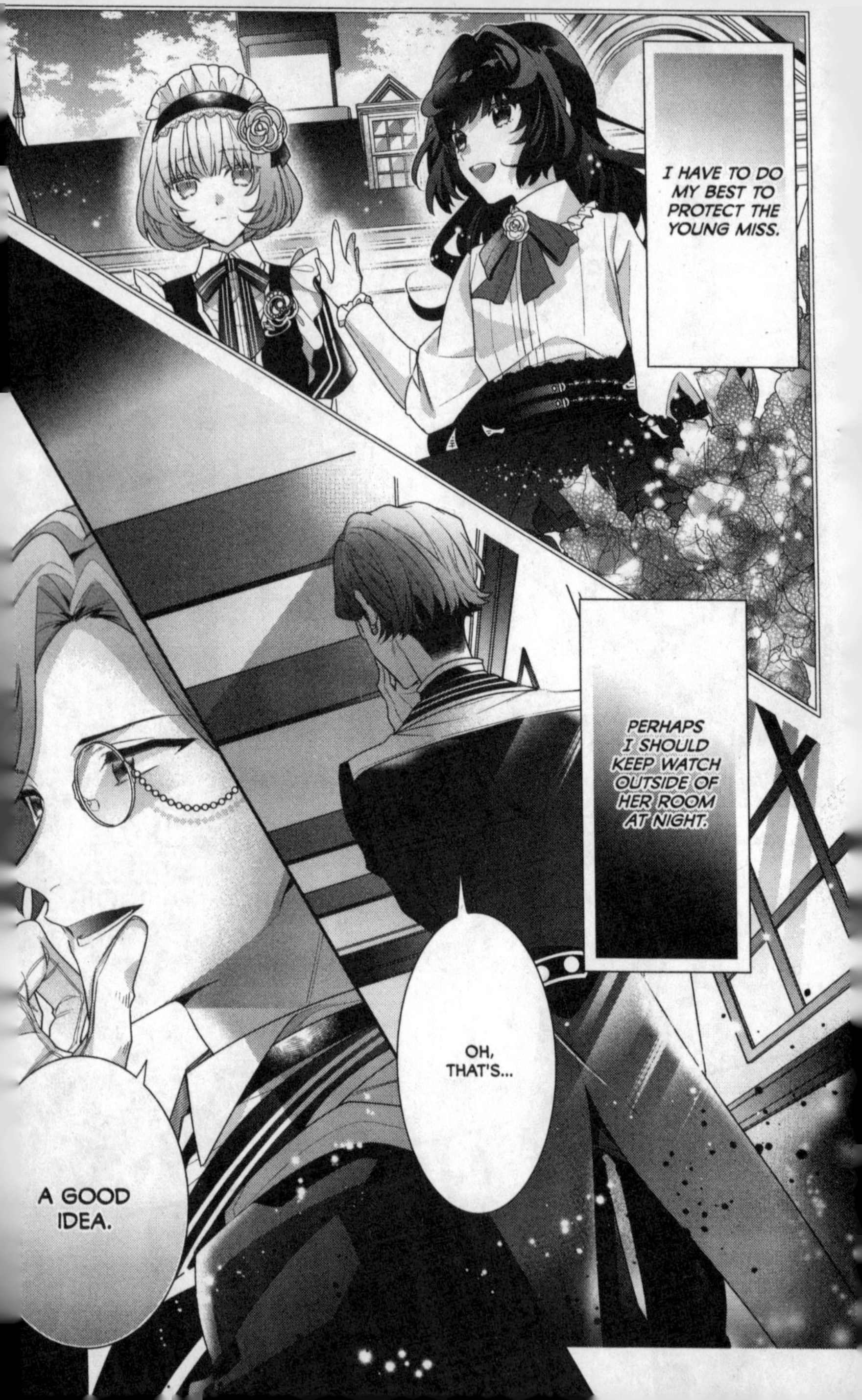
I HAVE TO DO MY BEST TO PROTECT THE YOUNG MISS.
PERHAPS I SHOULD KEEP WATCH OUTSIDE OF HER ROOM AT NIGHT.
OH, THAT'S...
A GOOD IDEA.

I was REINCARNATED as the
****
Villainess
in an **OTOME GAME** *but the boys love me anyway!*

VOLUME 2 - *END*

I was REINCARNATED as the ********* Villainess in an OTOME GAME but the boys love me anyway!

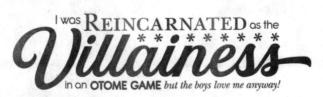

Bonus 4-Panel Comics

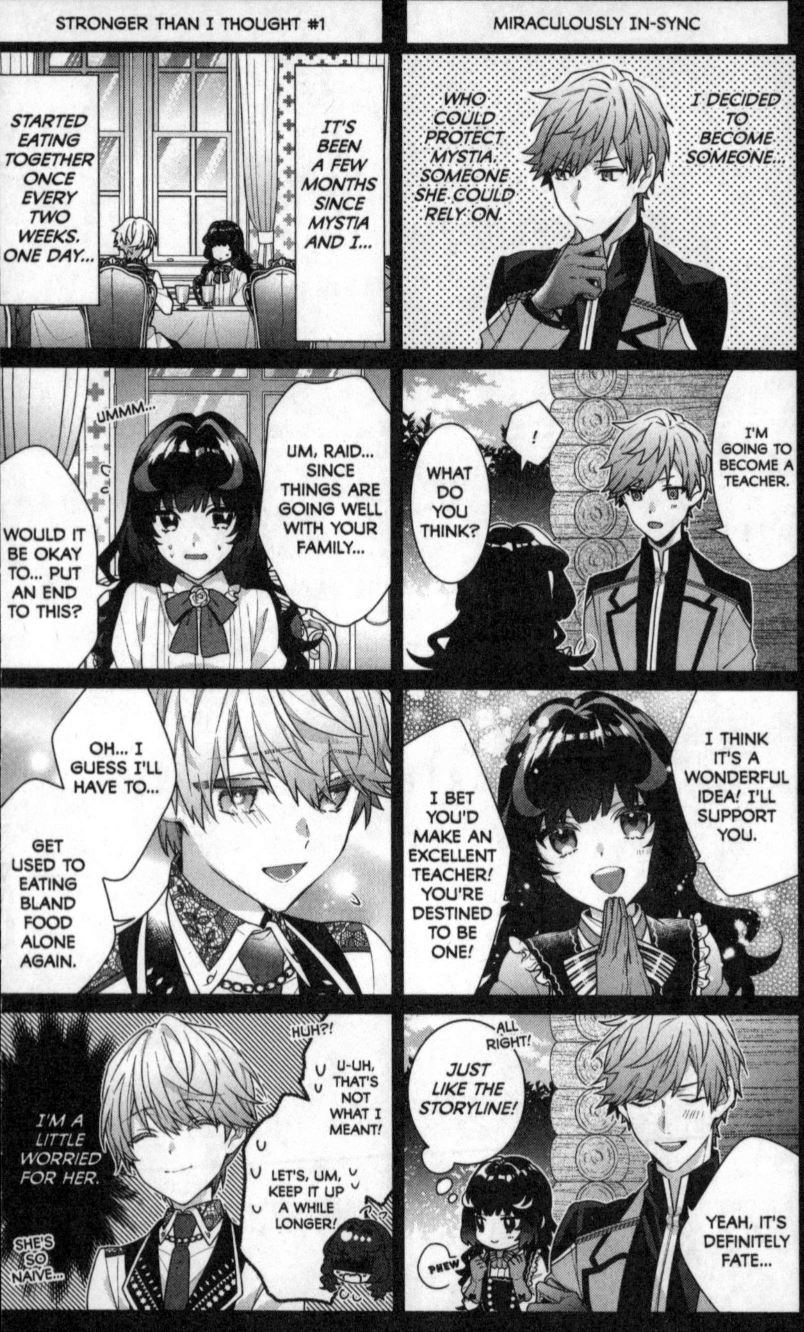
MIRACULOUSLY IN-SYNC
I DECIDED TO BECOME SOMEONE...
WHO COULD PROTECT MYSTIA. SOMEONE SHE COULD RELY ON.
I'M GOING TO BECOME A TEACHER.
!
WHAT DO YOU THINK?
I THINK IT'S A WONDERFUL IDEA! I'LL SUPPORT YOU.
I BET YOU'D MAKE AN EXCELLENT TEACHER! YOU'RE DESTINED TO BE ONE!
ALL RIGHT!
JUST LIKE THE STORYLINE!
YEAH, IT'S DEFINITELY FATE...
PHEW
STRONGER THAN I THOUGHT #1
IT'S BEEN A FEW MONTHS SINCE MYSTIA AND I...
STARTED EATING TOGETHER ONCE EVERY TWO WEEKS. ONE DAY...
UM, RAID... SINCE THINGS ARE GOING WELL WITH YOUR FAMILY...
UMMM...
WOULD IT BE OKAY TO... PUT AN END TO THIS?
OH... I GUESS I'LL HAVE TO...
GET USED TO EATING BLAND FOOD ALONE AGAIN.
HUH?!
U-UH, THAT'S NOT WHAT I MEANT!
LET'S, UM, KEEP IT UP A WHILE LONGER!
I'M A LITTLE WORRIED FOR HER.
SHE'S SO NAIVE...

THE TRUTH ONLY THE SERVANTS KNOW

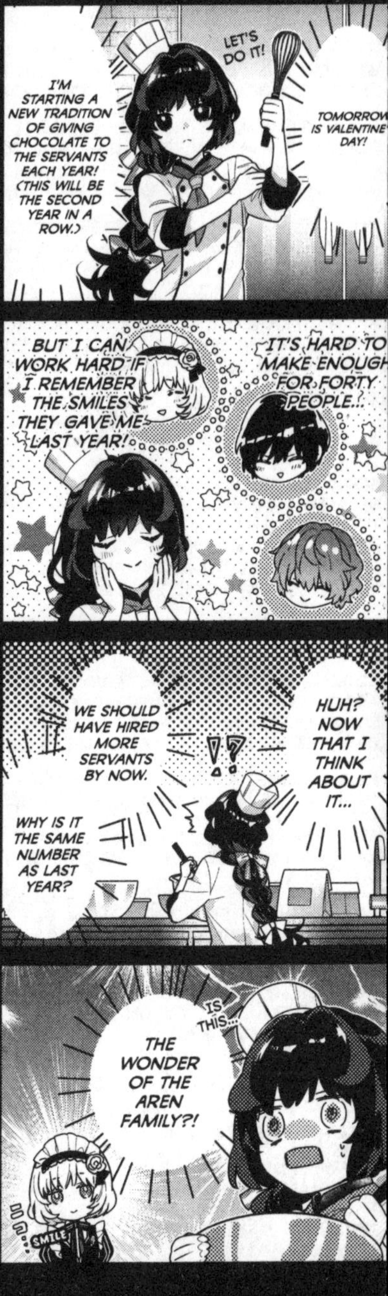
TOMORROW IS VALENTINE DAY!
LET'S DO IT!
I'M STARTING A NEW TRADITION OF GIVING CHOCOLATE TO THE SERVANTS EACH YEAR! (THIS WILL BE THE SECOND YEAR IN A ROW.)
IT'S HARD TO MAKE ENOUGH FOR FORTY PEOPLE...
BUT I CAN WORK HARD IF I REMEMBER THE SMILES THEY GAVE ME LAST YEAR!
HUH? NOW THAT I THINK ABOUT IT...
!?
WE SHOULD HAVE HIRED MORE SERVANTS BY NOW.
WHY IS IT THE SAME NUMBER AS LAST YEAR?
IS THIS...
THE WONDER OF THE AREN FAMILY?!
SMILE

STRONGER THAN I THOUGHT #2

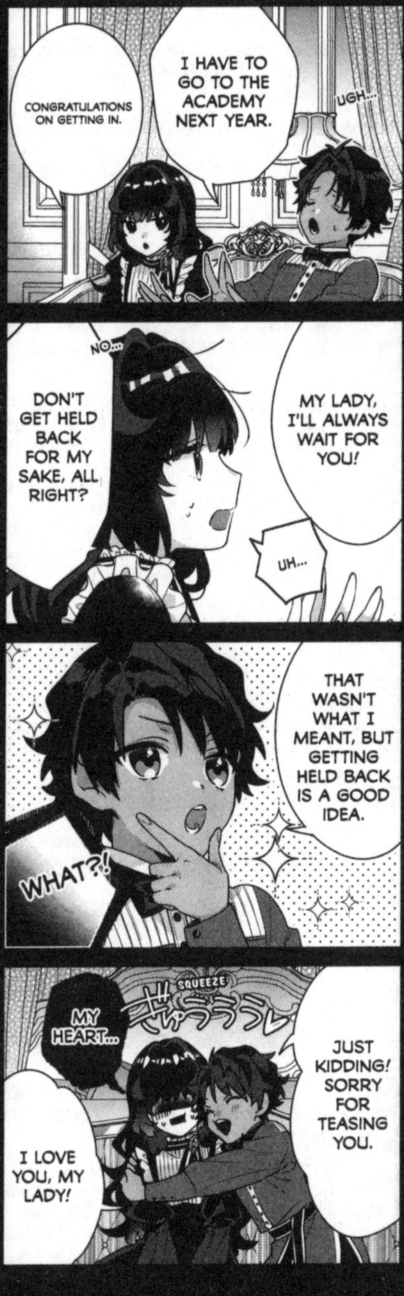
UGH...
I HAVE TO GO TO THE ACADEMY NEXT YEAR.
CONGRATULATIONS ON GETTING IN.
MY LADY, I'LL ALWAYS WAIT FOR YOU!
UH...
NO...
DON'T GET HELD BACK FOR MY SAKE, ALL RIGHT?
THAT WASN'T WHAT I MEANT, BUT GETTING HELD BACK IS A GOOD IDEA.
WHAT?!
JUST KIDDING! SORRY FOR TEASING YOU.
SQUEEZE
MY HEART...
I LOVE YOU, MY LADY!

AFTERWORD

LONG TIME NO CHAT! I'M SOU INAIDA, THE AUTHOR OF *I WAS REINCARNATED AS THE VILLAINESS IN AN OTOME GAME, BUT THE BOYS LOVE ME ANYWAY!* THANK YOU SO MUCH FOR PICKING UP THE SECOND VOLUME OF THE SERIES.

THE FIRST VOLUME PERFORMED QUITE WELL WHEN IT WENT ON SALE IN FEBRUARY, SO MY EDITOR GAVE THE APPROVAL TO SERIALIZE IT. I CAN'T THANK ATAKA-SENSEI, HACHIPISU WAN-SENSEI FOR THE CHARACTER DESIGNS, AND ALL OF THE READERS WHO PURCHASED THE FIRST VOLUME ENOUGH.

THE FIRST VOLUME HAD CHAPTERS REVOLVING AROUND RAID, MELO, AND ERIC, BUT THIS VOLUME FOCUSES ON JEY AND MYSTIA, AS WELL AS THE OTHER LOVE INTERESTS, AS THEY PREPARE TO JOIN THE ACADEMY.

AS A READER, MY FAVORITE SCENE IS THE ONE WHERE JEY FLIES INTO A FIT OF RAGE AT THE THOUGHT OF MYSTIA GETTING HURT. HE'S AS CRAZY AS YOU CAN IMAGINE, BUT HE'LL EXPERIENCE MANY THINGS AND GROW AS A SCHOOLTEACHER, SO PLEASE LOOK FORWARD TO SEEING HIM IN THE FUTURE.

ANOTHER GREAT PART OF THIS VOLUME IS GETTING TO SEE RAID FIGHT WITH ERIC. I'M SURE FANS OF BOTH ERIC AND RAID ARE HAPPY ABOUT THAT. RATHER THAN MAKING FUN OF THE OTHER MAN, THEY TRY TO ONE-UP EACH OTHER. THEIR FIGHTS SEEM LIKE THEY COULD GET UGLY AT ANY MOMENT BUT ARE DRAWN IN SUCH A WAY THAT THEY SEEM ALMOST PLEASANT. THAT MADE ME REALLY HAPPY, THOUGH I MIGHT SOUND LIKE AN ELEMENTARY SCHOOLER SAYING THAT. I STILL DON'T GET WHAT "YANDERE" MEANS. WHAT PARTS OF THE THINGS I LIKE ARE "YANDERE"? NO MATTER HOW MUCH I THINK ABOUT IT, I CAN'T DEFINE IT CLEARLY. I WAS REALLY TOUCHED TO SEE THAT THE SCENES ARE WRITTEN WITH A REFRESHING MARGIN FOR OBSESSION WITHOUT STRAYING INTO HORROR OR ANYTHING TOO DARK.

NOW THAT I'VE TAKEN UP A TON OF SPACE IN THE AFTERWORD BY WRITING MY OPINION AS A READER, IT'S TIME FOR ANNOUNCEMENTS!

ACTUALLY, *I WAS REINCARNATED AS THE VILLAINESS* IS GETTING A THEATRICAL ADAPTATION! PLEASE CHECK THE OFFICIAL SITE FOR FURTHER INFORMATION. AS THE SERIES CREATOR, I'VE ALREADY RECEIVED SOME INFORMATION, BUT SOME THINGS JUST CAN'T BE ANNOUNCED YET... I'M SORRY, BUT PLEASE CHECK THE WEBSITE FOR DETAILS!

ATAKA-SENSEI POSTED A CELEBRATORY ILLUSTRATION ON TWITTER, SO PLEASE CHECK THAT OUT AS WELL AS I'D LOVE FOR YOU ALL TO SEE IT.

ALSO, THE THEATRE'S PAMPHLETS WILL FEATURE ILLUSTRATIONS FROM ATAKA-SENSEI AND HACHIPISU WAN-SENSEI! IT WILL BE SO NICE TO HAVE SOMETHING ON PAPER TO KEEP AND TREASURE.

FINALLY, THIS IS SELF-PROMOTION, BUT THE FOURTH NOVEL IS OUT IN JAPAN NOW, SO I'D BE THRILLED IF YOU TOOK A LOOK AT IT AS WELL.

BY THE WAY, AN ILLUSTRATION BY HACHIPISU WAN-SENSEI WAS USED TO CREATE A COASTER THAT COMES WITH AN ACRYLIC STAND. YOU CAN PURCHASE IT FROM TO BOOKS'S ONLINE STORE (IN JAPAN ONLY). I PERSONALLY WOULD LIKE A FULL LINEUP OF MERCH FROM ATAKA-SENSEI AND HACHIPISU WAN-SENSEI. SOMETHING ACRYLIC THAT I CAN CARRY AROUND...

WHOOPS, SOMEHOW THE TOPIC CIRCLES BACK TO ME. THANK YOU TO EVERYONE WHO SENT FAN LETTERS. I LIVE CUT OFF FROM THE REST OF THE WORLD, SO IT MAKES ME TRULY HAPPY. THANK YOU SO, SO MUCH.

FINALLY, I'D LIKE TO AGAIN THANK ATAKA-SENSEI FOR THE COMICALIZATION, HACHIPISU WAN-SENSEI FOR THE CHARACTER DESIGN, TO BOOKS, MY PROOFREADER, MY DESIGNER, AND EVERYONE WHO SUPPORTS AND ENCOURAGES MY WORK. PLEASE CONTINUE TO READ *I WAS REINCARNATED AS THE VILLAINESS IN AN OTOME GAME, BUT THE BOYS LOVE ME ANYWAY!*

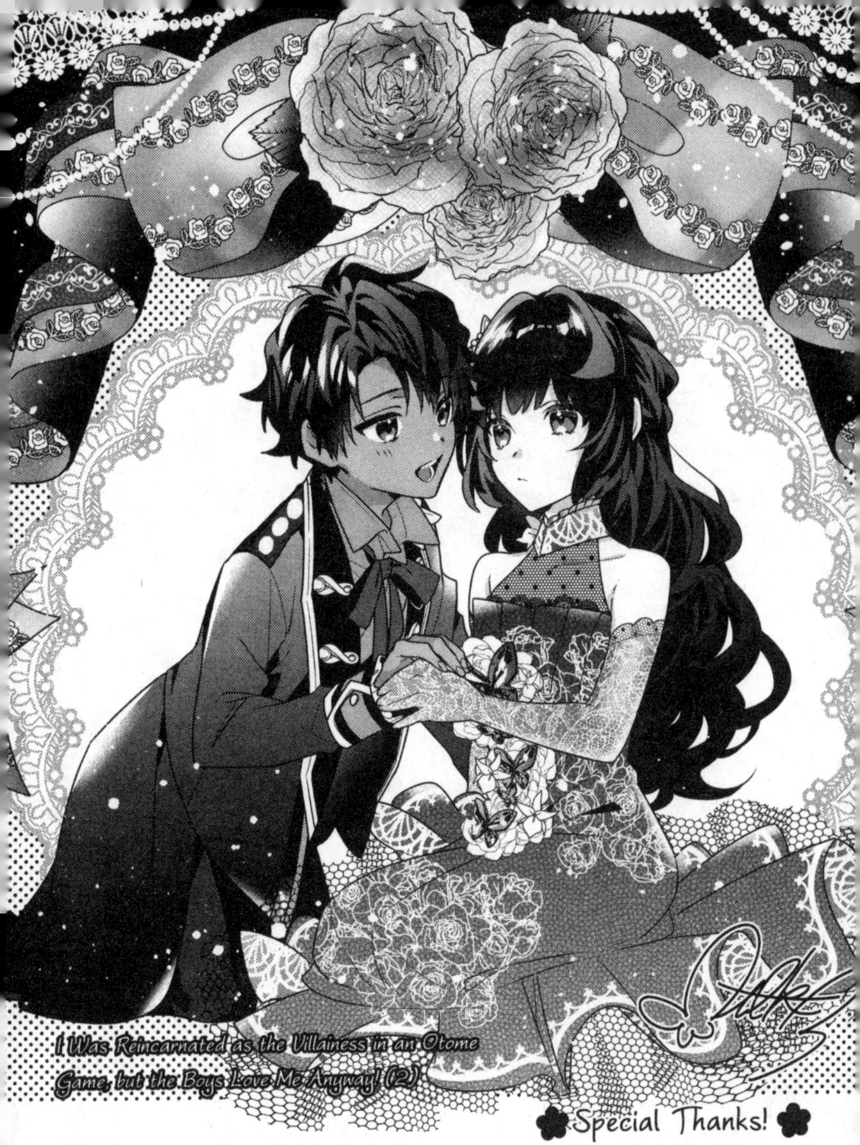
I Was Reincarnated as the Villainess in an Otome Game, but the Boys Love Me Anyway! (2)

Thank you for purchasing the second volume!
We're finally starting to get into the main storyline.
I love the design for the school uniform.
Please look forward to the next volume as well.
(And congrats on getting a theatrical adaptation!
I'm looking forward to it!)

Special Thanks!

Original Story: Sou Inaida
Character Design: Hachipisu Wan
My editor/everyone in the Editorial Dept.

Yuu Kaeki
Gomakuro
Eku Hachida
Shiki Sakuraya
Madachi
Kuromi

♀LOVE-x-LOVE♂

Check out *LOVExLOVE.info* for all kinds of romance!

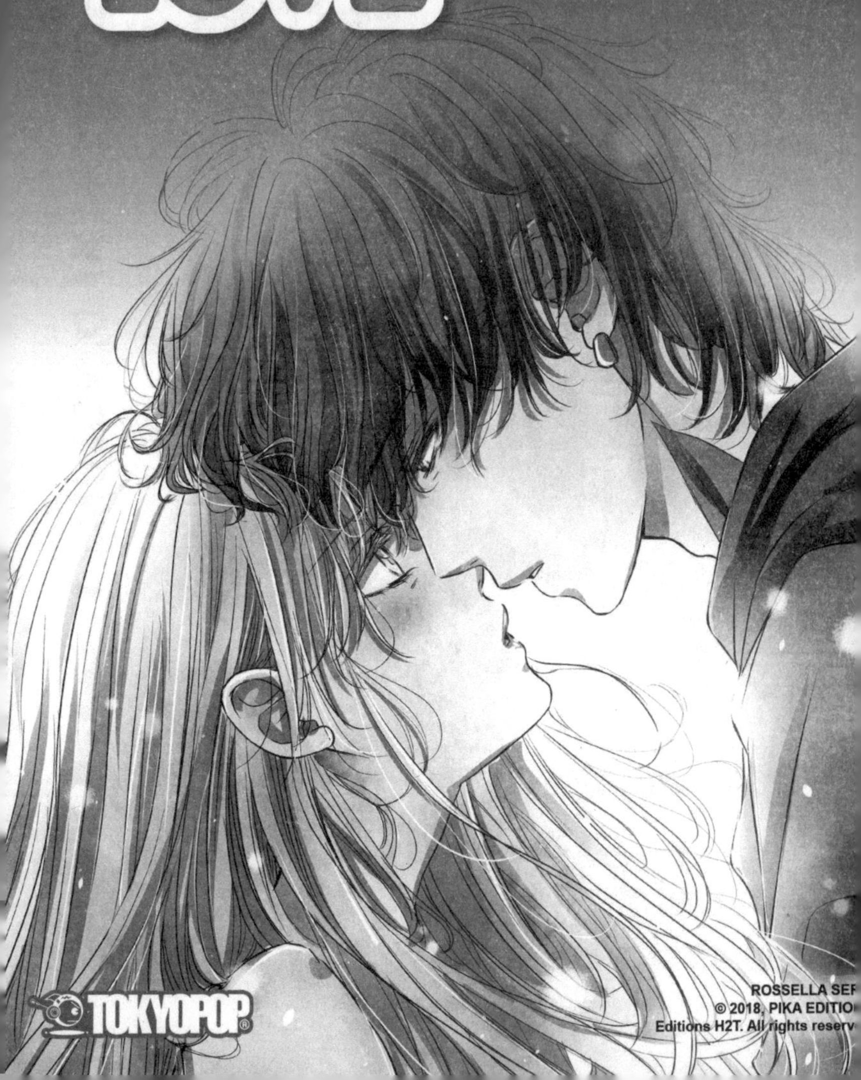

ALICE IN BISHOUNEN-LAND, VOLUME 1

Yushi Kawata, Yukito

COMEDY

Alice Kagami is an ordinary high school girl who doesn't really get her friend Tamami's obsession with idol games. There's more to life than handsome digital boys, dating sims, and mini-games, right? But then, Tamami is "chosen" as one of the top idol fangirls in the country and gets drawn into the game — and hapless Alice gets pulled in too!

Between dealing with the mismatched members of her idol group to intense pressure to spend real money on gachas, how is a total idol game newbie supposed to take them to the top?

HER ROYAL HIGHNESS SEEMS TO BE ANGRY, VOLUME 1

Neko Yotsuba, Kou Yatsuhashi

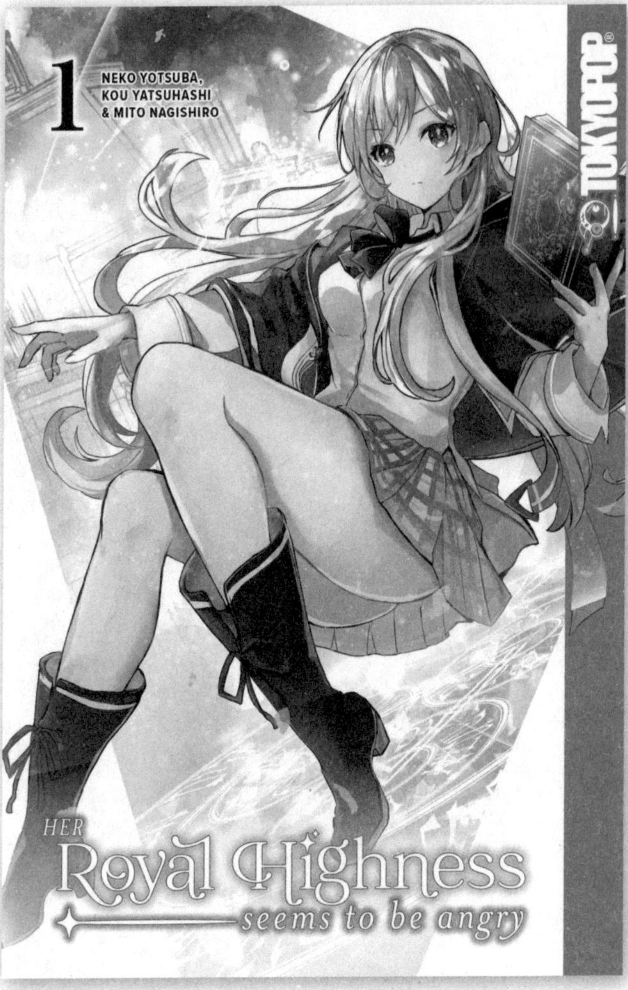
1
NEKO YOTSUBA,
KOU YATSUHASHI
& MITO NAGISHIRO
TOKYOPOP
HER
Royal Highness
seems to be angry

LOVE x LOVE

In a remote kingdom, there lived a princess, adored by her subjects and wielding powerful magic. But as her land was ravaged by an endless war, she lost everything: her people, her family, her loved ones, and eventually, her own life. Until she opened her eyes and awoke in a place she'd never seen before! A thousand years have passed, and she finds herself reincarnated into someone else's body. Realizing the person she's now living as is despised by her own family and even her fiancé, the former princess struggles to understand this new world and the events that have transpired since her death. There's a lot to be upset about, but first on the list: how in the world did future magic turn out so lame?

TOKYOPOP

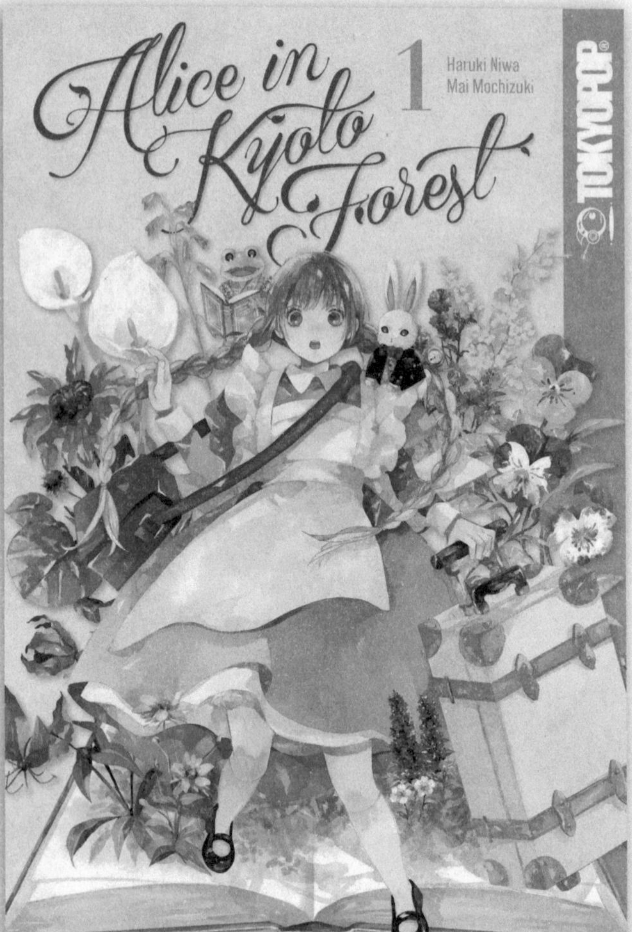

Alice in Kyoto Forest
1
Haruki Niwa
Mai Mochizuki
TOKYOPOP

ALICE IN KYOTO FOREST, VOLUME 1

Mai Mochizuki, Haruki Niwa

FANTASY

After being orphaned when she was very young, Alice has lived with her aunt for most of her childhood, but her uncle clearly doesn't want her around. At fifteen years old, Alice decides to return home to Kyoto and train as a maiko, an apprentice with the hopes of eventually becoming a full-fledged geisha.

But when she arrives back to the city where she was born, she finds that Kyoto has changed quite a bit in the years since she left it. Almost as if it's a completely different world...

TOKYOPOP

MAME COORDINATE, VOLUME 1

Sachi Miyabe

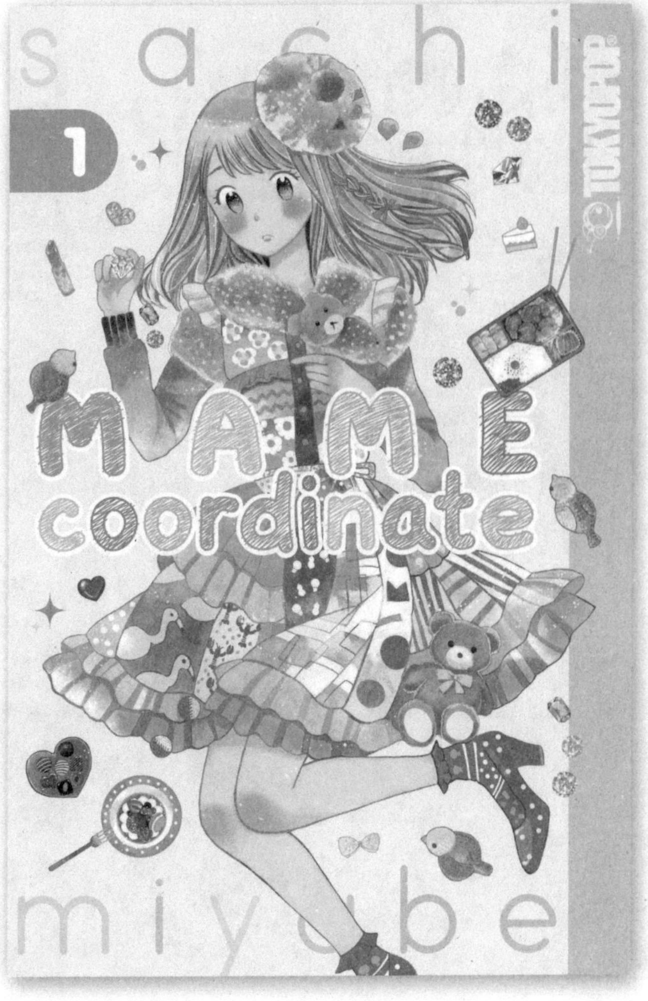
sachi
1
MAME
coordinate
TOKYOPOP
miyabe

SLICE OF LIFE & FASHION

She loves meat and fried foods, and eats only karaage bento. Wearing exclusively clothes with weird characters printed on them, her fashion sense is practically non-existent. No confidence in her own looks. Extreme social anxiety. She speaks with a country drawl, and even her name is unusual. But then Mame (born in Tottori prefecture) was discovered by an intimidating, bespectacled rookie manager, and now begins the arduous task of getting her ready for auditions! The road to Top Model looks awfully steep from here.

TOKYOPOP®

No Vampire, No Happy Ending

2

SHINYA SHINYA

Shinya Shinya

NO VAMPIRE, NO HAPPY ENDING, VOLUME 2

♀LOVE-x-LOVE♂

When die-hard vampire enthusiast Arika comes across a mysterious young man named Divo, it seems she struck the jackpot-- she's found a drop-dead gorgeous vampire of her own! Unfortunately, she quickly finds out the disappointing truth: Divo is all beauty, no brains, and no vampire instincts whatsoever. What's a vampire-loving girl to do? Teach him, of course! The grand finale of the laugh-out-loud supernatural love comedy featuring a vampire in beta and the vampire fangirl determined to make him worth her time!

SCARLET SOUL, VOLUME 2

Kira Yukishiro

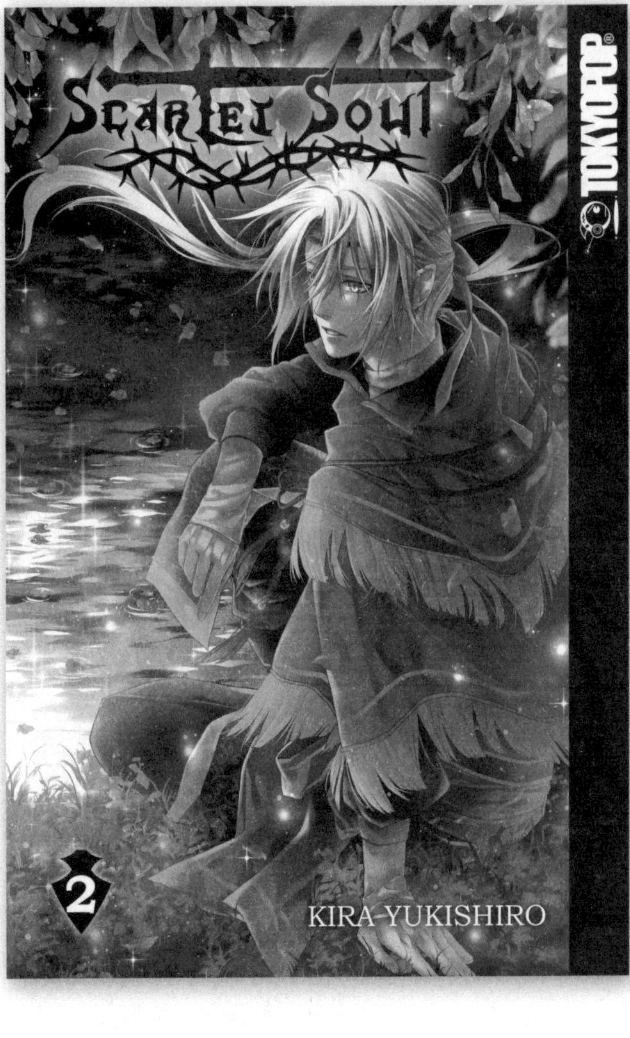
Scarlet Soul
TOKYOPOP
2
KIRA YUKISHIRO

LOVE-x-LOVE

After their search for the missing Great Priestess Lys leads Rin and Aghyr into trouble and an unexpected battle at the Water Sanctuary, they take some time to regroup among their friends of the Kaishin Clan. There, they meet up with the Fire Oracles Kara and Koru, who have prophesied the arrival of the Scarlet Soul— none other than Rin Shirano herself. With the Fire Oracles' help, Rin reclaims her sister's sword Hitaken, which has chosen her as its wielder. Whether she feels ready to take on the responsibility or not, she is the only one who can carry the ancient exorcist blade now. With demon activity increasing throughout the land, it's more important than ever that the Great Priestess is found as quickly as possible... even as forces gather that will stop at nothing to make sure Rin can never see her sister again!

TOKYOPOP

I Was Reincarnated as the Villainess in an Otome Game but the Boys Love Me Anyway!, Volume 2

Manga by Ataka
Original Story by Sou Inaida
Charachter Design by Hachipisu Wan

Editor	Lena Atanassova
Translator	Katie Kimura
Copy Editor	Becca Grace
Quality Check	Daichi Nemoto
Proofreader	Massiel Gutierrez
Marketing Associate	Kae Winters
Graphic Designer	Sol DeLeo
Editorial Associate	Janae Young
Retouching and Lettering	Vibrraant Publishing Studio
Licensing Specialist	Arika Yanaka
Editor-in-Chief & Publisher	Stu Levy

A TOKYOPOP® Manga

TOKYOPOP Inc.
4136 Del Rey Ave., Suite 502
Marina del Rey, CA 90292-5604

E-mail: info@TOKYOPOP.com
Come visit us online at www.TOKYOPOP.com

www.facebook.com/TOKYOPOP
www.twitter.com/TOKYOPOP
www.instagram.com/TOKYOPOP

First published in 2020 by TO BOOKS, Inc.

ISBN: 978-1-4278-6881-7

First TOKYOPOP Printing: March 2022

Printed in CANADA

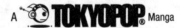

STOP

THIS IS THE BACK OF THE BOOK!

How do you read manga-style? It's simple! Let's practice -- just start in the top right panel and follow the numbers below!

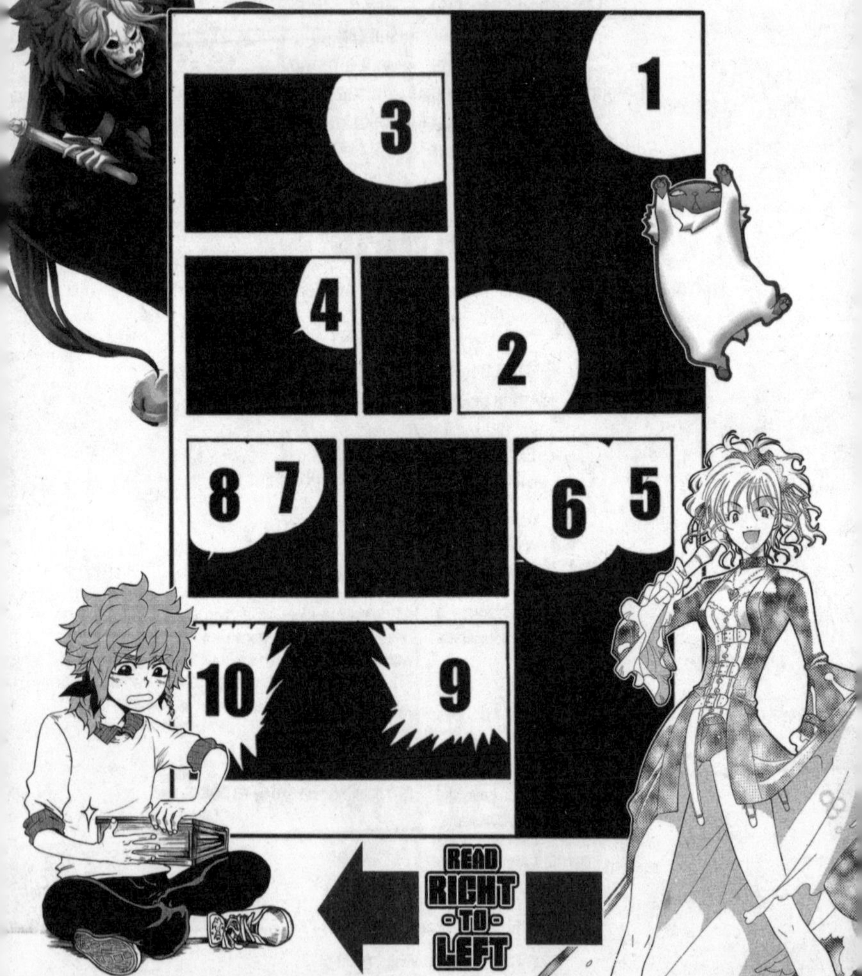
1
2
3
4
5
6
7
8
9
10
READ
RIGHT
-TO-
LEFT

Crimson from ***Kamo*** / Fairy Cat from ***Grimms Manga Tales***
Morrey from ***Goldfisch*** / Princess Ai from ***Princess Ai***